GIFTED TONGUES

PRINCETON STUDIES IN CULTURAL SOCIOLOGY

EDITORS

PAUL DIMAGGIO

MICHÈLE LAMONT

ROBERT WUTHNOW

VIVIANA ZELIZER

Origins of Democratic Culture: Printing, Petitions, and the Public Sphere in Early-Modern England by David Zaret

Bearing Witness: Readers, Writers, and the Novel in Nigeria by Wendy Griswold

Gifted Tongues: High School Debate and Adolescent Culture by Gary Alan Fine

GIFTED TONGUES

HIGH SCHOOL DEBATE AND
ADOLESCENT CULTURE

Gary Alan Fine

PRINCETON UNIVERSITY PRESS   PRINCETON AND OXFORD

Published by Princeton University Press, 41 William Street,
Princeton, New Jersey 08540
In the United Kingdom: Princeton University Press, 3 Market Place,
Woodstock, Oxfordshire OX20 1SY

Library of Congress Cataloging-in-Publication Data

Fine, Gary Alan.
Gifted tongues : high school debate and adolescent culture /
Gary Alan Fine.
    p.   cm.—(Princeton studies in cultural sociology)
Includes bibliographical references and index.
ISBN 0-691-07449-6 — ISBN 0-691-07450-X (pbk.)
1. Debates and debating. I. Title. II. Series.
PN4181.F53   2001
809.53—dc21   00-048319

This book has been composed in Sabon

The paper used in this publication meets
the minimum requirements of
ANSI/NISO Z39.48-1992 (R 1997)
(*Permanence of Paper*)

www.pup.princeton.edu

Printed in the United States of America

10   9   8   7   6   5   4   3   2   1

10   9   8   7   6   5   4   3   2   1
(Pbk.)

For Todd David Fine

Contents

Preface

ALTHOUGH I do not recall it, my parents told me that, as a preschooler, I had a severe speech impediment. My words were slurred and indistinct. After much therapy, my enunciation improved to the point that past difficulties were not noticeable. When elected president of my high school debating club, my parents were justifiably proud, recalling my past struggles and their fears.

Perhaps therapy should be blamed, but talking proved easy. Conversation is good fun. I must confess, however, that I was not an outstanding debater. I do not recall having a winning record. My partners and I were bright, but lacked the verbal facility, piles of evidence, and training of the more successful teams in our New York City circuit.

Some friends and I decided as juniors, under the guidance of a well-liked speech teacher, to organize a debate team. The Horace Mann School had not previously participated in competitive debate, but such an enterprise seemed appropriate for boys at an elite private school. So, the debate club was born. That speech teacher left the following year, but we persuaded the school librarian to be our official coach and hired a college student to serve as our *de facto* mentor. Within a year after graduation, the club disbanded. During my years of debate (1966–1967, 1967–1968) we debated criminal justice reform and foreign aid—with great vigor, if not with impressive success. For twenty years after high school, I paid high school debate no notice.

In 1988 I happened upon a short article by Michael McGough, published in *The New Republic*, that described how high school debate had changed over the decades. This article, critical of new styles of debate, objected to some of the logical overreaching and rapid, incomprehensible speech that the author felt had come to characterize high school debate.

The article piqued my interest, particularly in light of the increased attention given to discourse and rhetorical analysis in the social sciences. If we are to address the role of discourse, we should observe and analyze those for whom talk is central to their identity. Further, if we can understand how people learn to talk in particular ways and learn to deploy evidence to persuade others, we might take a small, but essential, step in placing the rhetorical turn in the social sciences on a solid empirical basis. Thus, investigating adolescent talkers seemed more than of passing interest. As a social psychologist and sociologist of culture, learning how groups of adolescents acquired the skills of debate and the use of evidence seemed significant, as did the connection of this activity to teenage identity. This research built upon my previous studies on youthful leisure, specifically Little League baseball and fantasy role play gaming. High school debate was a topic of personal appeal, theoretical importance, and descriptive significance.

When my schedule cleared, I decided to spend a year observing high school debate, and relived a part of my high school experience—only this time in two coeducational, suburban, public high schools with experienced debate coaches and talented students. Spending a year in a pair of public high schools expanded my understanding of the daily lives of teens, clarifying the nature of that "stage" we label adolescence.

As always, there are many people to thank. In the academy I thank Patricia Adler, Peter Adler, Joel Best, Grant Blank, Norman Denzin, Brian Donovan, Susan Herbst, Thomas Hood, Phillip Howard, Jay Mechling, Scott Nobles, Robert Scott, Patrick Schmidt, Ira Silver, Teresa Sullivan, and David Zarefsky for sharing their ideas and experiences. Like all ethnographers I am grateful to the multitudes of supportive individuals whom, for reasons of confidentiality, I cannot name, except by pseudonyms in the text. However, the debate teachers and coaches in Minnesota, and their fine students, have my permanent gratitude for helping me to learn what I should have learned in high school. Some of these students are now becoming academics themselves, and may wish to speak for themselves about the issues that I raise. I am also grateful to James Copeland, Executive Director of the National Forensic League during this research, for spending a day with me at NFL headquarters in Ripon, Wisconsin, and showing me great courtesy at the 1990 Nationals at San Jose State University, as well as providing very helpful comments on the manuscript. The Spencer Foundation provided me with a valuable and timely grant that aided in the transcription of tape-recorded interviews. I thank Lisa Mapp for her aid in organizing the data in this analysis, and to Lori Holyfield and M. K. Park for their skills as research assistants. The writing of this volume began when I was a fellow at the Center for Advanced Study in the Behavioral Sciences in Stanford, California. I am grateful for the time to prepare this work, and for National Science Foundation grant #SBR-9022192. The surveys of debates and coaches, conducted in collaboration with Patrick Schmidt, were supported with a grant from the University of Minnesota's Undergraduate Research Opportunities Program. I also thank my friends at Princeton University Press, including Ian Malcolm, my editor, Joan Hunter, my copyeditor, and Michèle Lamont and Robert Wuthnow, of Princeton University, editors of the series in which this book appears.

In 1990 my eldest son, Todd, then nine years old, viewed a videotape of the final round at the National Forensic League tournament and decided as a third-grader that he wanted to become a debater. He had a career of great distinction, first at Woodward Academy in College Park, Georgia, under the guidance of two gifted and nationally respected debate coaches, Paula Nettles and Frank Seaver, and then at Glenbrook South High School in Glenview, Illinois, under an equally gifted and respected coach, Matthew Whipple. During Todd's two years in Illinois, he and his partners won the Tournament of Champions, a tournament I describe in this volume, and the Barkley Forum at Emory University. I have incorporated parts of his experience at points in the text, along with the experiences of his teammates. He, too, may wish to speak directly about his experiences in ways that may contradict my claims, as he often does, sometimes with justice.

Parts of chapters 2 and 3 were previously published as "Games and Truth." *Sociological Quarterly* 41, no. 1 (2000): 103–23.

GIFTED TONGUES

Introduction _____

STUDENTS of social life routinely speak of their subjects as *actors*: an image derived, in part, from the dramaturgical approach pioneered by sociologist Erving Goffman,[1] and before him from the various approaches labeled behaviorism, including the social behaviorism of the pragmatist philosopher George Herbert Mead. What people *do* is judged to be central for human understanding. Yet, if we are honest, we recognize that on many occasions we are less actors than *talkers*, realizing, of course, that talk is a class of behavior. Talk constitutes much of the meaningful behavior that defines humanity.[2] As sociologist Florian Znaniecki has noted, verbal claims can be more consequential than the behaviors that the claims represent.[3]

I became interested in this project—the analysis of high school debate—from the increasing interest by humanists and social scientists in narrative and discourse. I wished to examine how a community explicitly and self-consciously immersed in issues of talk developed verbal skills. Some argue, passionately, that rhetorical skills have atrophied in American culture, leading us to become an "inarticulate society."[4] Recognizing the centrality of talk to the organization of human society, I address issues surrounding the production of talk. In particular, I am concerned with how talk is *spoken of*.

Although talk is my focus, I do not intend, as a practical matter, to produce a microscopic analysis of discourse, focusing on each half-drawn breath, sibilant *S*, or parapraxis. In contrast, I examine a talking world as a social space: an arena of deeds *and* diction, of action *and* words. My goal is to investigate how adolescents learn to talk: to talk in a distinctive way, a style easily caricatured and derided for its distance from "natural speech." Yet, it is precisely that speech and its content as a topic of attention that makes this community of particular interest.

Anyone who has listened to an American high school policy debate would not confuse that form of discourse with other speech domains. Contemporary high school debate has been vigorously criticized as downplaying rhetorical skills. The goal in debate is not to persuade a listener, but to demonstrate to a trained judge that one has "beaten" the arguments of one's opponents—and may contribute to an "argument culture," as described by sociolinguist Deborah Tannen.[5] An outsider will immediately notice that speech in debate is extremely rapid—sometimes incomprehensibly so—and evidence is used in ways that differ from the way that evidence is treated elsewhere. High school debate is a highly formalized and competitive world of talk, whose value must be established: much as the somewhat obscure skills of a decathlon victor must be defined to support the claim that this person is the greatest athlete in the world. Some critics suggest that high school debate no longer matters; it has no future. Yet, it is precisely this formalization, this socially structured, competitive, and judged component, that provokes sociological interest.[6] Debate is a talking world defined by age, institution, and class.

Debate as an Adolescent World

Before examining the issues involved in learning to speak, collecting evidence, and presenting arguments, I argue that high school debate needs to be understood in light of its social placement as an activity that is engaged in by adolescents.[7] Just as this book is about talk, it is about teens. This does not mean that high school students are not affected by their collegiate role models or adult mentors, but that the domain I examine is fundamentally an adolescent social world. High school debate allows not only for the understanding of talk but also of adolescent development. I address broader issues of teenage behavior in light of the expansion of behavioral options at this age.

Debate is an arena in which one can observe the cultural and social dynamics of adolescent life. High school debaters are not a random sample of adolescents; yet, the participants are still adolescents, and their moral and emotional development parallels that of their peers. Observing a debate team permits one to learn about a teen community, status system, and cultural world.

With their prodigious knowledge and abilities, sometimes these "children" seem much like adults. Surely they know more about the debate topic than do most adults, and they are more skilled at research and public speech than most "grown-ups." Yet, on other occasions (and sometimes on the same occasions), they seem to be children. How can this apparent paradox of childishness and maturity be understood, and how does it relate to other "mixed-role" adolescents: drug dealers, tennis stars, teen mothers, computer nerds, poets, political activists, and mass murderers. I argue that adolescence should not be thought of as a stage of development, but rather as a period in which one can select from behaviors characteristic of both children and adults: from the "toolkits"[8] to which boys and girls have access in creating appropriate adolescent activities. This theme—that adolescence is not primarily a stage, but a toolkit—appears throughout my analysis.

Debate as an Educational World

Debate is justified as a learning tool, not merely as a means by which adolescents enjoy themselves. In a society concerned about the perceived failures of its educational institutions, high school debate is a voluntary activity in which some students—a small and highly select group—choose to engage in research, practice socially valued skills, and demonstrate these abilities in public settings. Anecdotal evidence suggests that students who participate in intermural debate do extremely well in their schoolwork and then (and as a consequence) are successful in college and in graduate or professional school, achieving occupational success. Since debate does not appeal to a random sample of the student body, causality is hard to establish, but the claim that debate is beneficial is surely plausible. Debate is one program through which an often shaky institution encourages adolescents to acquire culturally valued skills. While debate is not the only activity in which the adolescent attachment to competition is mixed with the acquisition of socially valued skills—Model UN, academic bowls, math teams, chess clubs, and mock trials also have these attributes—it provides an exemplary case in its organization, its longevity, and its intensity. High school debate potentially could produce curricular reform based on "teaching the conflicts"[9]: learning how to discuss contentious social issues can permit students to engage and confront moral ideals.

Today many find America's school systems in disarray, attempting, often ineffectively, to solve seemingly insoluble social problems. If we cannot educate the masses effectively, some suggest that at least we should properly educate our "best and brightest." Gifted education is a concern for both educators and parents. High school debate teams are highly selective—sometimes self-selected, but often with the assistance of coaches, teachers, and principals who recruit their most energetic, brightest, and most articulate students. Debate helps to reproduce the class system. Most debaters—although not all—are high achievers. In general, debaters are young men and women from affluent homes in which education is valued and in which ideas are discussed. Many of these students have succeeded in school and have established, prior to their immersion in the world of debate, a record of achievement. High school debate magnifies these successes, providing an enriched atmosphere in which students expand their educational horizons. The competitiveness of debate motivates this achievement drive, particularly among those students who have already succeeded in academic competitions.

Within the social world of high school, status systems develop. Debate is an activity in which individuals are stereotyped by others. High schools contain distinct status systems, and individual schools differ in the prestige accorded different activities.[10] In some schools debate is central to the status system—a high-status pursuit—whereas at other high schools, debate is a low-status, stigmatized activity, left to social outsiders.

In addition to earning school status, debaters belong to a team, with a group culture and local status system. The team generates intense loyalty, but simultaneously creates tensions that must be managed if it is to survive and prosper. This team culture and structure is set within a larger—national, regional, and local—subculture of debate, in which individuals know each other and develop meaningful social ties over months and miles. "National circuit" teams travel to tournaments across the country on weekends, with the season lasting from the start of the school year to its close at the National Forensic League tournament in June. The months of July and August may be spent at debate camps ("institutes"), typically held at college campuses. The season of less-extensive programs typically lasts from October to January.

Debate as a World of Talk

Justifying this research in light of education, training for gifted and talented youth, and adolescent culture specifies the social and institutional locus of debate, a crucial feature of any social world. Yet, specifying the location of this research should not downplay the behavior itself. Debate involves not only the acquisition of knowledge, but a set of verbal and research skills that all persons, not only debaters, use: techniques of persuasion and reasoning. To be competent, one must acquire information-processing skills: the ability to gather, organize, and present information. To induce another to ratify one's claims demands facility with words and with evidence. Those who acquire professional skills learn to put forth a line of discourse, and to counter alternate arguments. Learning how to talk—to argue, to counter, and to persuade—is such a critical skill that an explicit focus on how this skill is acquired seems valuable but, surprisingly, has been largely ignored. I examine the process of argumentation. In this, my argument is congruent with a group of cognitive psychologists who are interested in how people argue in practice, such as Michael Billig, Charles Antaki, Adrian Furnham, and Deanna Kuhn.[11] An argument is not something that happens in isolation, but that happens in a social and strategic context. Humans situate themselves in social life through argumentation, creating allegiances and divisions. As these writers note, argumentation is as social as it is cognitive, a linkage of the mind to systems of interaction. My goal is to produce a social psychology that takes rhetoric seriously. As high school debate makes clear, it is people, not minds, that make arguments. Unlike this group of cognitive social psychologists,

I do not attempt to understand the nature of thought, but to treat argument as a form of behavior.

Of course, the value of an activity, even as seemingly worthy as debate, should not be taken for granted. Some worry about the effects of a brutal and disputatious culture of argument in which discourse becomes a game, and question the notion that the conflict between ideas is necessarily a social good. Certainly this activity favors those with the cultural capital to engage in claims making. Further, such activity privileges competitive models over cooperative ones; individualism over communalism; empiricism and efficacy over faith and morality. Competitive high school debate is an activity that is largely limited to the United States, and reflects American values, as linked to the American system of politics and law with their emphasis on game-like conflict and winning at all costs, even if this means that the larger community is harmed. The American oppositional system in which two sides fight with whatever weapons are at hand is found in debate, as well as in legislatures and courtrooms. This leads some to suggest—somewhat harshly—that even with the presence of women and minorities, high school debate models the value system of white male hegemony. Recognizing this counterperspective (part of the debate about debate), little doubt exists that given our current social structure, the ability to present one's perspective effectively serves one well. While I discuss the political implications of debate in the conclusion, I argue that it fits easily into American culture.

In understanding how these adolescents acquire information-processing skills, I focus upon four aspects of their training. First, I address how adolescents learn to "talk"—orality is a social challenge. Second, I examine the means by which students create arguments that they perceive as persuasive, given a logical structure. Third, I examine the evidence on which adolescents draw to develop meaningful arguments. Finally, I recognize that debate is a competitive activity, in which two-person teams rapidly construct strategic discourse to persuade a judge, given a set of rules.

I begin by examining the activity itself, as well as the ways that the world of high school debate models the use of persuasion. Debate involves oral presentation, and this orality, while highly stylized, is central to the doing of the debate. Adolescents must learn—again—how to talk. Yet, as noted, this talk has different standards from those that make effective oral communication. In preparation for debate tournaments, instructors teach students skills of oral presentation, although in the debate itself these rules are transformed in the guise of presenting as much information as possible.

However, talk does not fully constitute debate. Ultimately, the justification for debate is that adolescents learn how to create arguments with underlying logical presuppositions. While the rules in practice are both similar to and different from formal rules of argumentation as presented by rhetoricians and logicians, the rules of arguments as ideal types legitimate the practical doing of argumentation. Further, debate is argumentative talk that uses evidence to persuade. But what constitutes effective, persuasive, good evidence must be determined.

Within a policy debate round there are eight turns at talk, plus three-minute cross-examinations that occur after the first four speeches. The debates that I observed in 1989–1990, before rebuttals were lengthened to five minutes, were structured:

- First Affirmative Constructive (8 minutes)
- Cross-Examination of the First Affirmative by the Second Negative (3 minutes)
- First Negative Constructive (8 minutes)
- Cross-Examination of the First Negative by the First Affirmative (3 minutes)
- Second Affirmative Constructive (8 minutes)
- Cross-Examination of the Second Affirmative by the First Negative (3 minutes)
- Second Negative Constructive (8 minutes)
- Cross-Examination of the Second Negative by the Second Affirmative (3 minutes)
- First Negative Rebuttal (4 minutes)
- First Affirmative Rebuttal (4 minutes)
- Second Negative Rebuttal (4 minutes)
- Second Affirmative Rebuttal (4 minutes)

A debate reflects an hour of talk. However, a critical difference exists between the first speech in a debate round (the first affirmative) and those that come later. The first affirmative is a "canned" address, which some speakers memorize. The later turns of talk are locally constructed, reacting to what has been said previously. While debaters often use fully or partially canned responses to particular issues (what they label briefs, following legal jargon), the whole of the discourse constitutes a "spontaneous" response.

In a given round a team of two debaters is assigned either to the affirmative or the negative side of a topic. The affirmative team has the responsibility of making a positive argument: a case. They must present a plan that achieves the end for which the debate resolution calls. During the year in which I observed, the topic involved reducing prison overcrowding, and so every affirmative team had to present a scheme to achieve this end, and then defend this plan. Of course, they had an advantage—the benefit of surprise—in that the negative team was unaware at the outset of the round of the details of the case that the affirmative would make. This ability to create an affirmative plan and then back it up contributes to instrumental attitude change. While our legal system finds a negative argument sufficient in the establishment of a *reasonable doubt*, in most domains action depends on a plan.

Debaters lug heavy boxes (called "oxes" or "tubs") that are filled with evidence, but how is this evidence used, and what does it mean to the debaters? Throughout the year this material is created and processed, much as we process fact and opinion, but what does this processing mean to participants? Evidence reflects a truth claim: the allegation that there is a direct and transparent relationship between what is said and the world out there. The evidence must be seen as relevant, rhetorically resonant, recent, and reliable. Further, the evidence must have a warrant, connected to some moral model of what ought to be. Some truth claims carry more weight than others, and the novice debater must learn the rules for truth, as defined by debaters, coaches, and judges.

Debate is ultimately competition, dependent upon a situated performance. The activity is known not only by the preparation of adolescents, but by their activity within the round. Two teams compete in real time, under enormous temporal pressures. During the round, four young men and women make arguments, and respond to the arguments of others. They speak and prepare to speak. To understand high school debate requires that one understand the strategies that permit debaters to persuade a judge that they have presented a better and more complete set of arguments than their opponents—strategies that are both substantive and presentational. Debate is organized so as to produce a definitive outcome, given a set of criteria.

Ethnographic Ears

This research is based on participant observation and in-depth interviews that I conducted for an academic year with two high school debate squads in the suburbs of St. Paul, Minnesota. The location is not a trivial matter, as high school debate is organized on a state level (in Minnesota by the Minnesota Debate Teachers Association). States differ widely in the vigor of high school debate and in the type of debate permitted. Although I shall have more to say about the regional peculiarities of Minnesota debate in the appendix, debate in Minnesota was still popular among public high schools (although the number of teams had significantly diminished over the previous twenty years), and debate was more "conservative" in what arguments were considered permissible than many other states with strong debate competition, such as Texas, Illinois, or Georgia. These factors affected the specific observations of my research. Although I consider my observations generalizable in their sociological analysis, the particular analysis of debate styles is tied to my research sites in Minnesota.

I name my two research sites Randall Park High School and Greenhaven High School—pseudonyms, as is true for the names of Minnesota coaches and students. Randall Park serves an upper-middle-class first-tier suburb; Greenhaven serves an outer-ring middle-class suburb, which, during the course of research, was undergoing a transformation from farmland to development.

During my observation, both schools had strong debate teams; each won local tournaments. I began the year by planning to focus on a single debate squad, that of Randall Park, but during the year I came to know the debaters at Greenhaven quite well, and when the debaters at Randall Park did not win the preliminary tournament that would permit them to attend the National Forensic League Championship, I followed the Greenhaven debaters as they prepared, and I later attended that tournament with them. I attended debate class at Randall Park, and the after-school activity that followed the class, on most days from September to February. I also traveled with the team to tournaments on most weekends from September until February, including one tournament in South Dakota. In February, I began attending practices with Greenhaven High School, typically two afternoons a week. I also traveled with the team to the Tournament of Champions at the University of Kentucky and to the National Forensic League Championship at San Jose State University in California.

My ethnographic field notes were bolstered by interviews with fourteen members (all but one) of the Randall Park team, and with fourteen Minnesota high school debate coaches.[12] I also read the publications of the National Forensic League during this research project. Subsequently, with the aid of a student at the University of Minnesota, Patrick Schmidt, a former Minnesota debater and assistant debate coach, two questionnaires were sent to a random sample of schools. One questionnaire was completed by high school coaches. We also sent questionnaires for student debaters, and requested that coaches distribute these questionnaires to their student debaters. For several years I also read all the messages on an on-going e-mail discussion list for debaters and coaches. While these messages by no means represented the views of the typical debate participant, they provided an insight into some of the divisions in the activity.

At both Randall Park and Greenhaven, the debate team was coached by an English teacher (Mrs. Annette Miller at Randall Park and Ms. Janice Nyberg at Greenhaven); each had coached debate for many years. Both women were well liked by students, respected by peers, and had successful records as coaches. At each school, debate was cocurricular, organized as both an academic class and an extracurricular activity. In each school, approximately fifteen students debated, with about eight regularly attending weekend tournaments. Both schools had two varsity debate teams, and several junior varsity and freshman teams.

During my research, two types of debate were practiced in Minnesota: policy (two-person) debate and Lincoln-Douglas (LD) debate. The latter, also known as values debate, is a newer form, in which individual debaters face each other, arguing a topic that changes every two months. In LD debate, evidence is not of primary importance; moral argumentation is more central. For my research, I observed policy debate. As noted, policy debaters work in teams of two and have a single topic assigned for the entire year. During the 1989–1990 academic year the topic was: Resolved: That the federal government should adopt a nationwide policy to decrease overcrowding in prisons and jails in the United States.

In the typical tournament, lasting five preliminary ("prelim") rounds, the teams switched sides, debating both affirmative and negative. Each tournament has a set of "break rounds" (quarterfinals, semifinals, finals) for the teams with the best records in the prelims. In a round, debaters attempt to persuade the judge that their argument is stronger than their opponents', but this evaluation is made in the context of the standards of the activity. The winner is not the team that presents the "best" argument—in the sense of the argument that the judge most agrees with—but rather the team that presents the strongest argument given the rules of the game. What constitutes the rules of this game can be a matter of contention.

The History of Debate

If debate refers to a structured oral contestation between several participants on a limited topic, then the history of debate surely recedes into the mists of time. The Socratic dialogues presented by Plato from ancient Greece are, in effect, debates—although admittedly one-sided in Plato's self-interested account. Monks in Middle Age monasteries indulged in interminable discussions and arguments, and rabbinical debates about the meaning of the Torah and the Talmud are widely known and treasured. In the nineteenth century, the debating societies, literary societies, and lyceums that flourished throughout America (including the Chataqua movement) serve as models for high school debate as it later developed.[13]

Both legislative activity and legal engagement can properly be thought of as debates—rivalrous, competitive, with structured outcomes. These events, capturing the cut and thrust of opposing sides, involve debate, and provide models for the history of debate, as did the Lincoln-Douglas debates of the Illinois Senatorial Campaign of 1858. Indeed, today when many people think of "debates," they frequently refer to presidential debates—a style that debate purists often consider to be little more than joint press conferences, with participants talking past each other.[14]

Competitive speech events pitting teams of students against each other are more recent. According to one source, the first recorded intercollegiate debate occurred between Harvard and Yale in 1892;[15] however, my colleague David Zarefsky informs me that in 1872 Northwestern University debated the old Chicago University. The Harvard-Yale match serves as a nice origin myth, legitimating the activity, except, of course, here in Evanston. Within a few years, intercollegiate debate had spread across the country, to large universities, smaller colleges, and eventually to high schools.[16] The National Forensic League, the organization regulating high school debate, was founded at Ripon College in Wisconsin and began its national tournament in 1931. Rhetorical skills were valued and were considered, in the early decades of this century, central to an adequate education. While high school debate has waxed and waned during the twentieth century, it has played a major role in preparing elites for positions in the professions and in politics. At one point the majority of members of Congress had been high school or college debaters.[17] While this proportion has fallen, in part a function of the increasing diversity of our representatives and in part because of the decline of debate, many politicians received their rhetorical training through this activity.

Who Debates?

Before turning to the plan of the book, additional background issues need to be addressed to set the activity in its proper context. Who are the children who come to the world of debate? How did they come to find this corner of the social world? What are the characteristics of high school debaters, and how are they recruited?

Characteristics of Debaters

In the spring of 1990, I surveyed a sample of debaters to determine their demographic and social characteristics.[18] With the assistance of Patrick Schmidt, I mailed brief (four-page) survey questionnaires to two sets of coaches: all those schools that sent policy debate teams to the 1989 National Forensic League tournament (approximately 150 schools) and another 150 randomly sampled schools with NFL charters, but which had not qualified for the national tournament. Each coach received six questionnaires for his or her debaters to fill out (the results of the survey of coaches are discussed in chapter 7). A total of over 400 students completed surveys.[19]

Of the debaters who responded, 64 percent were male. Eighty-three percent of the students were Caucasian, and approximately 10 percent were Asian; the latter is a significant overrepresentation. African-Americans represented just 2 percent of the total, although there are now attempts to establish debate programs in inner-city schools. In general, families of debaters are financially comfortable: upper middle class. The majority came from families that earned over $45,000 per year, indicating that debaters do not represent a cross section of American youth.

Debaters are not representative in another way. Just as they are children of privilege, they have used that privilege well. If debaters are not always the best and brightest, they do surpass many of their fellow students. On average, those who responded to our questionnaire ranked in the top tenth percentile of their high school class. While this may in part be a function of the nature of the sampling (coaches may have distributed the six questionnaires to their brightest or most responsible students), it accords with my observation. These debaters also perform well on standardized tests. The average SAT score[20] was 1270 (math 650, verbal 620), and their ACT scores averaged 29. These numbers are well above the national average. Over 99 percent said that they expected to enroll in college. Only three claimed to be undecided. Of those who had selected a career, a plurality (40 percent), planned to become lawyers. In contrast, only 5 percent indicated a desire to become teachers, suggesting difficulty in replenishing the ranks of debate coaches.

Politically, high school debaters are difficult to define. Of those who link themselves to a political party, more classify themselves as Republicans than Democrats (52 percent to 26 percent), yet their attitudes are more liberal than the general public, at least on issues of criminal justice (the debate topic that year), as measured by Gallup Surveys. Whether this is a result of discussing prison overcrowding for a year or because of previous background is uncertain. Of the general public, 16 percent oppose capital punishment; for debaters, the figure is 34 percent. Among the public, 83 percent feel the courts are not harsh enough in dealing with criminals; only 47 percent of debaters feel the same way.

Several striking findings differentiate successful from less successful programs. Students in the two sets of schools were not significantly different in their gender, race, academic performance, and career goals. There was no intellectual gap between the two groups. Not surprisingly, competitive teams participate in many more tournaments that require overnight stays, their school budgets are significantly higher, and they have coaches with more experience. Members of competitive teams seem more dedicated to debate. Students on competitive teams were more than twice as likely to have attended a summer institute than their counterparts. Beyond this, more competitive schools are those in communities that have higher incomes. Of the competitive schools, 57 percent were in communities where, according to the coaches, the average household income was over $35,000. The comparable figure for the less competitive schools was 30 percent. Apparently, community wealth facilitates conditions that encourage successful participation in debate.

Recruitment to Debate

Given that high school debate does not, in most circles, have high visibility, how do adolescents come to judge this as an activity in which they would enjoy participating? Americans do not read debate results in the newspaper, debate is not broadcast on ESPN, and pep rallies are rarely held to encourage debaters. Somehow, debaters must overcome public apathy and lack of publicity to decide that this is an activity in which they might thrive. Indeed, according to accounts of many debaters, they were unaware of what they were becoming involved in when they joined the team. From my observation, the drop-out rate is high—far greater than would be found in such culturally validated activities as football, basketball, band, or even chess. Of the eighteen students signed up for debate at Randall Park, only eleven were actively involved in the activity by the middle of the season. Many debaters told me that they joined with a group of friends, and that by the end of the season they alone remained involved as others discovered that debate was not for them. Not only do most students not know what is involved, but often they are unaware of the large time commitment that active and successful participation requires. One championship debater explained why he joined:

> I wasn't doing much. I was doing theater-related activities at the time, and I enjoyed that. I really had no idea what debate was going to be. People were suggesting it to me. It looked alright. I don't think I knew anybody that were debaters at the time, and I don't remember really an intent to do it. (Interview)

Despite lack of publicity about this world, recruitment routes are similar to those that we find in other leisure worlds and social movements. Some individuals join because of a perceived strategic interest (it will be instrumental for their future goals), others join because the activity seems pleasurable (it meets their expressive needs), but most join because of personal networks (friends, teachers, or family members).[21]

STRATEGIC INVOLVEMENT

To the extent that debate is known to the outside world, it is often linked to the worlds of politics and law. Several students indicated that their desires to follow those career paths made debate a "logical choice." For some, the goal was simply to add a line to their résumé that would look impressive on college recommendations or law school applications. One coach noted that these students debate "for all the wrong reasons," even if their strategies often result in considerable occupational success.[22]

For others, the connection is more substantive and idealistic:

I suppose at that point in my life [ninth grade] I had aspirations of being a lawyer, so I thought this was the thing to do—be a debater. (interview)

I kind of wanted to be a politician. . . . My eighth grade social studies teacher did a big thing on JFK and I really admired how JFK was a speaker, and I read that he was a big debater, and I thought that maybe I'll take debate. I'll be able to learn some really good speaking skills. (interview)

Indeed, many politicians and attorneys had their start in high school debate, and so this argument, grounded in the value of anticipatory socialization to one's future occupation, has some surface validity, even if we cannot be entirely certain as to whether debate produces better lawyers or politicians or whether, simply, those with such orientations select debate.

LOOKING FOR FUN

The number of students who join because "I always liked to argue" is considerable. Perhaps debate is an effective way to push adolescents away from their soapbox at the dining room table. Parents have been known to suggest debate for just this reason. Obviously, if the clash of ideas were unappealing, this would not be an activity one would pursue. One former debater notes of the first round he watched:

I remember I liked the clash of arguments. . . . I can see these guys very clearly still debating and they were very witty, and I liked the clash of ideas. . . . I think they impressed me intellectually; they impressed me with the argumentation, and they just seemed cool or something. (interview)

Of course, debate is not free-form arguing, but a stylized clash of ideas with rules for evidence and standards of claims. When potential debaters learn that the activity is not merely expressing one's opinion, many leave.[23]

NETWORK RECRUITMENT

Most debaters had contact with others who teach, participate, or once participated in the activity. These other individuals indicated that the activity is both worthwhile and enjoyable (instrumental and expressive) and, further, that the recruit is likely to find participation personally satisfying.

Friends are particularly effective recruiters in that they know the talents and tastes of the potential recruit:

> Some friends of mine when I was coming from junior high to high school just said that we should join. They were in it, and they were having fun, and we said okay. . . . For the first few weeks, you know, our friends were there so it was some place to go after school where your friends were at. . . . Within the first week or so that we joined up, we were all debating and we . . . got a blue ribbon, and from that point on I was hooked. (interview)

Siblings and parents who had previously been involved in debate also serve as potent motivators. One Randall Park student joined because his mother had been a debater at the same school two decades before. Another had a father who was a successful debater and told him "good stories about debate." A third explained that his sister had been a debater and felt he would be successful. A fourth had a brother who was a successful debater; he came to respect those analytical skills that his brother claimed he learned from the activity.

Others relied on a recommendation from admired teachers who felt that the recruit had the requisite interests and talents. A dramatic example comes from an esteemed coach:

> When I was younger I had a stammering problem, very severely, [I was] very shy, and I had a junior high counselor who enrolled me in a debate course in high school . . . without my even knowing it. (He laughs.) And I ended up in the debate class, and I think a lot of it had to do with self-confidence, and I ended up enjoying debate so much I overcame the stammering, and was able to communicate more effectively. (interview)

To aid in recruitment, coaches often ask other teachers which students are likely prospects. Some coaches mail letters or stage demonstration debates at the junior high school to inspire recruits. These letters and demonstrations were sufficient for some students to take the class or attend club meetings. Then they decide to stick with the activity.[24] The rest, as they say, is history.

The Skeleton of the Text

In this analysis I begin with an examination of the activity itself—talk—eventually analyzing those skills, such as the use of evidence and the creation of cases, and the way in which young men and women become socialized to this activity: how they learn to speak, use arguments, and rely on evidence. Through this, I examine how debate is simultaneously a game and a serious activity. From there, I examine debate as an adolescent social world, and then as an institutional world, an activity situated within educational institutions. As a result, I work from the essential activity to those domains that surround it, beginning with debate as an experienced, embodied activity, to a consideration of the world of debate as interactional domain, to a consideration of debate within the institutional order.

Within the eight substantive chapters and an appendix, I discuss (1) the acquisition and display of verbal skills, (2) learning the rules of argumentation within the context of debate, (3) skills involving the effective use of evidence and the marshaling of that evidence to create affirmative cases, (4) the nature of interaction and the immediate creation of practical reason within the context of the round, (5) the culture and structure of teams as social units, (6) the debate culture as an adolescent social world, (7) the role of adults—teachers and coaches—within the social world, and the way in which institutional pressures from the school system influence the organization of debate, and (8) the role of gifted education, and the justifications of high school debate in an educational system, exploring the reasons for the decline of the activity over the past several decades. I conclude by suggesting ways in which debate might be expanded and redefined to make it more central to the educational process and more inclusive of a more diverse range of American students. Finally in an appendix, I discuss the different cultures and styles of debate.

Central to the book is the recognition that the participants in the activity are adolescents. A central concern is explaining the reality that these people can seem simultaneously like both sophisticated adults and immature children, and in this, despite the particularities of their activities, they mirror other teens. I hope that this ethnography will permit a more nuanced view of adolescent development, and implicitly provide a challenge to those who wish to see adolescence as a distinct stage with its own unique patterns of activity. In contrast, I argue that adolescents have gained a wider set of options that they use in ways that adults may praise or condemn. Adolescents have expanded their cultural toolkit. The skills of both adulthood and childhood work for them at this social moment.

Despite its peculiarities and political ambiguities, high school debate is a valuable training ground for adolescents. Our educational system would be more successful in its goal of producing competent citizens if all, or many, students had the opportunity to participate in this activity. High school debate is a voluntary leisure and competitive sport, but it also captures the skills of competent expression, self-confidence in public activities, the use of logic, the gathering of evidence, and the presentation of policy options that we expect of all citizens. That debate can provide the grounds for the establishment of a meaningful social community is an additional nontrivial benefit for these adolescents, who otherwise face a sometimes alienating high school environment.

I consider the claims of those who suggest that the hypercompetitiveness of the activity creates a culture based on seeing differences in value orientation as a mere game, leading to cynicism, and that debate skills serve further to stratify the social order, favoring the privileged. Ultimately, I disagree with these claims, even though they are not wholly without merit. The benefits of high school debate to individuals and to the community outweigh its troubles, and a further expansion of the activity to groups that are now excluded will serve us better than a contraction. High school debate is not a panacea for all of the ills that beset our educational system, but it is, I believe, a tool by which a school system can do well by doing good.

One

Learning to Talk

BY EARLY afternoon Friday, vans begin to pull into the parking lot at Harrison High School—a modern, well-landscaped campus in the suburban outskirts of St. Paul, Minnesota. Soon the parking lot and entryway of Harrison High fill with well-dressed adolescent boys and girls, most carrying or rolling large plastic containers ("oxes" or "tubs") plastered with bumper stickers or other markers referring to their home schools or the tournaments that they have attended. This is the early November weekend of Harrison High's annual debate tournament, part of a debate "season" that begins in early October and continues until February. As in years past, the school expects about sixty varsity teams, another thirty-five competing on the junior varsity level, and about forty more on the novice level. A few schools have driven to the tournament from Iowa and Wisconsin, and a smattering from North and South Dakota. Occasionally a school will travel from Florida, Massachusetts, or Texas, but none has made the trek this year. The large majority of schools are, like Harrison, from the suburbs of the Twin Cities, although a few are from private schools and others are from small towns throughout the state.

Squads vary in size, but most schools have brought six to eight students, accompanied by a coach or an assistant coach. Most of the latter are former debaters, now in college or recently graduated. While many tournaments have sections for Lincoln-Douglas debate, also known as values debate, in which students debate each other one-on-one on a topic selected every two months, Harrison's tournament is only policy debate, in which teams of two persons each compete.

Shortly after three o'clock on Friday afternoon, the coaches and debaters gather in the theater where the school's debate teacher welcomes them and briefly explains the rules of the tournament, the policies of the school (a total prohibition on smoking, for instance), introduces the organizers, and points out the important locations: the rooms in which rounds will be held, the cafeteria, the tab room (where ballots are to be handed in and tabulated, and pairings for the following rounds set), the coaches' lounge, and the restrooms. Although hundreds of adolescents and adults have descended on the school, the principal is not present; the debate tournament is not considered that significant. Throughout the welcome, the rustling of paper and nervous whisperings are heard, but the students accept the routine with grace and humor. Finally, organizers inform the debaters that the first round pairings are available. Students rush to reach those pages that reveal the location of one's round, one's opponent, and the name of the judge. While some tournaments mask the name of the opposing school, attempting to prevent the better networked schools from gaining an advantage by means of the files that they had compiled, this is not done at Harrison, and is becoming increasingly uncommon.

The three Randall Park teams have mixed reactions to their pairings. The top varsity team is on the affirmative side against the top team from one of their rivals. In some tournaments this would never happen, as "A" teams debate "B" teams in the first round, but apparently the Harrison tournament is using fully random pairing for the first two rounds, after which teams with identical records at the tournament will be competing against each other ("power pairings"). The second varsity team is fortunate by comparison; they are scheduled to be negative against a team from a school that set up a debate program only this year, and whose teams are laughably weak; it should be an easy victory for them. The novice team, one of the strongest in the state, is affirmative against an unknown novice team from a rural high school, probably an easy victory, but novice rounds are often unpredictable. Mrs. Miller, an experienced coach, will work in the tab room, determining, with the aid of a computer program, which teams will face each other in future rounds, while Don Davis, a former varsity debater at the school, now a freshman at the University of Minnesota, is scheduled to judge a junior varsity round.

The debaters quickly huddle with Davis, a font of knowledge, most of it valuable. Don rapidly explains what he knows about their opponents and suggests strategies. While he continues to talk to the varsity teams, Mrs. Miller walks the novices to their room. The halls are clogged with students anxiously talking with their teammates, coaches, and occasionally friends from other schools. Although the season has been under way for almost two months, tension is still palpable, as it always is before the first round of tournaments. Eventually, the students march off to their respective classrooms, two teams and a judge per room, and the halls fall silent. In the rooms quick introductions are made, the teams organize their files, the judge fills out information on the ballot, and the round begins. In about an hour, the debate concludes, students shake hands, reorder their files, and the halls clog again as teams begin filtering to the cafeteria, waiting for the second-round pairings. Judges remain in the classrooms, attempting to provide helpful, if sometimes caustic, feedback, while completing the ballot quickly so as not to delay the tournament or anger the coaches in the tab room.

The first round appears to be a triumph for the Randall Park team. While the "official" decision of the judge is not supposed to be announced after the round, most judges provide "oral critiques" of the two teams, which typically provide a strong indication of which team did the better debating. While the judge for the "A" team was not as explicit as the team wished, both debaters—Brian James and Doree Tennant—were confident that their "Women's Prison" case had prevailed. The second varsity team easily triumphed. Their relatively inexperienced opponents ran a "squirrel case" involving sending prisoners into outer-space to reduce overcrowding, which Phil Carstain and Diane Chen effectively destroyed. The novice team also easily triumphed over their less able opponents.

Between rounds, debaters plan strategy with their teammates and meet friends from other schools. Some trade evidence with those on other teams, although certain coaches object to this practice. Two other rounds are held that evening, which pass uneventfully for the Randall Park, although the "B" team learns that they have lost the second round, and the "A" team is surprised by the weakness of the team that they meet in the power-matched third round.

With the conclusion of the third round at about ten in the evening (Harrison, like most debate tournaments, ran late), debaters from the area, such as those from Randall Park, head to their vans for the trip home. Those from out of town find their motels, where they spend half the night talking and laughing. Tubs and suitcases packed with evidence remain at the locked school—although there are horror stories about evidence being "lost" at tournaments.

The next morning broke crisp and fine as the Randall Park debaters met for the van ride to Harrison. Two more rounds were scheduled that morning, and then the top teams broke to quarterfinals: the top eight teams would debate in three "break" rounds until a winner was determined. Some larger tournaments break to octofinals (the top sixteen teams) or even "double octos" (the top thirty-two teams), but Harrison wanted to end its tournament early, so that students could begin the trip home before dark.

After the fifth round, the debaters gather again in the school auditorium, speaker awards are handed out, the tournament organizers are thanked, and the packet of ballots are distributed to coaches. This permits those teams that did not break to leave at their convenience. When the results are announced, the teams react with a mixture of joy and sadness. The novice team is still undefeated, while the "B" team has gone 2 and 3, a disappointing performance. The "A" team does break, but it turns out that they had lost their first round despite their confident assumptions, had wound up with a record of 3–2, and had been placed in the break rounds only because they had received more speaker points than any other 3–2 team. While they were satisfied to have made it to the quarterfinals, they were frustrated by a record that they judged as mediocre. For a team that had hoped to win the tournament, they were hanging on, scheduled to debate the top-ranked team.

The quarterfinals proved successful for both Randall Park squads. The novices, Barry Globus and Ram Rao, continued to win easily: the combination of fast though clear speech, coupled with a case backed by considerable evidence, proved overwhelming. The varsity team also, surprisingly, won their quarterfinal round against Lakes Academy, one of the Twin Cities's most prominent private schools, a school with perennially strong debate teams. Lakes ran a drug legalization case, which if passed, they claimed, would significantly reduce prison overcrowding. Randall Park argued as negative that the plan would not solve the problem, but would only increase crime, and eventually prison crowding. Further, they suggested that the plan, if adopted, should occur on the state level, claiming that there were major disadvantages to ignoring the federal system; and finally they claimed that this would lead to increased drug use, negatively affecting the balance of foreign payments of the United States, and weakening our economy. The three judges were persuaded by these arguments, and Randall Park won unanimously. These break rounds are always more intense, and Brian admitted to feeling queasy before the round. Afterward, once they discovered the outcome, the elation was palpable, although the Lakes team seemed to melt into their chairs as the judges gave their oral critiques.

The semifinal round started out well for the Randall Park varsity, debating the affirmative. They claimed that placing female offenders in halfway houses where they could be with their children would reduce prison overcrowding, and simultaneously would decrease the likelihood that their children would break the law, decreasing overcrowding in the future. Maternal bonding could also prevent a set of severe social ills. Their opponents from Greenhaven, another suburban school, ran a similar affirmative case, and so were familiar with the arguments pro and con. Greenhaven argued that the case could cause men to be resentful, and that the special treatment based on gender might cause social dislocations. Further, some female prisoners might commit crimes while at the halfway house. Finally, prisons would immediately be filled up with others, widening the net of social control. The round was hard fought, but in the end Greenhaven received the votes of two of the three judges. The Greenhaven debaters hugged each other, while Diane and Brian looked at the floor, and slowly packed up their tubs of evidence. For them, there would be next week. Exiting the round, they discovered that Barry and Ram had won once again by a unanimous decision. They would be in the finals.

By now, entering into Saturday evening, the school seemed deserted; few debaters remained. Those still present chose between sitting in the rear of the varsity, junior varsity, or novice final round. Because of Barry and Ram's reputation, many selected their round. This time on the negative, they faced a "Seniors Case" that proposed that adult men be released from jail if they were 55 years of age or older and if they had served at least half of their sentences. Emphasizing the dangers of these "violent seniors," and claiming that this could lead to crime among those who were middle-aged, they eventually prevailed, although by a 2–1 margin. They received a huge plastic trophy for their efforts, while their varsity teammates, who placed fourth, received a smaller, though respectable, trophy. All four won speaker awards.

As the team rode in the van back to Randall Park, they felt satisfied, although because of the competition of debate, the varsity "A" team regretted those arguments that they had not made in their semifinal round, and in the failure—in their view—of the judges. So ended another weekend: part of a season that would conclude on a balmy June evening in California.

To be a debater is to be a talker—and a listener. As any parent knows, adolescents love to talk—although not always to their parents. While those with severe speech impediments can succeed in many domains, debate is not among them. Yet, this might lead to the belief that either one is born a debater with a golden, gifted tongue, or not. Like Demosthenes, the Athenian orator, with great effort most can improve their oratorical skills (although perhaps not while speaking with pebbles in their mouth or declaiming as they run uphill). However, in debate, mouthing words is not sufficient. The challenge is to acquire the verbal facility to string words together, so as to convince others that one's arguments are superior: at least within the rules of this somewhat artificial and brittle persuasive world.

With the exception of the first affirmative speech, previously composed, the other speeches are spontaneous creations, although often cobbled together based on previous arguments, composed of written briefs. With little preparation time, speakers must prepare an argument within a set time period that meets the criteria by which judges evaluate debate.

To understand how debaters speak, one must recognize the mechanisms of speech, the emotional resonance of the speech act, and the constraints that the temporal organization of debate imposes. Separate from the content of what is said (described in chapters 2, 3, and 4), these elements constitute how arguments will be spoken.

Most adolescents join a debate team with few and uncertain speaking skills. In schools and colleges, both writing and "thinking" are given greater weight than speech, which in most educational venues is now seen as secondary.[1] Speech depends on a willingness to put one's physical body forward as an object of attention: a visual and aural focus. In speech, one's errors become markers of one's self, and if they are not as permanent as errors in writing, they are immediately noticeable and potentially discrediting.

The debater rises before opponents who are seeking fault in the talk; a judge, whose responsibility is to evaluate presented talk critically; and on occasion an audience of peers or strangers who learn about the ability of the speaker by what is said and how it is spoken.

The novice enters this world with a sense of how persuasive talkers—politicians, actors, salespersons—communicate. For many novices there is an ideal of speech. One of the first challenges for a coach is to indicate that this model of persuasive *oratory* is not fully adequate to the activities at hand, and may even be counterproductive. The most oratorical speeches are not always the most prized, as one debater was criticized for having an introduction that was "too glossy" (i.e., too literary or rhetorical). Those with highly modulated voices, modeling themselves on television announcers, are told that their voices sound "phony." One junior-varsity debater explained that he was disparaged because "I like to be the Jimmy Swaggart kind of [debater]" (interview). His oratorical preference, involving speaking directly to the judge, is denigrated by coaches as not sufficiently "businesslike" and as contributing to his marginal position on the team. Such teens are scorned as "bullshitting" their way through the round or as being "snake-oil salesmen." What is acceptable in oratory is not necessarily desirable in debate. High school policy debate, as practiced, is grounded on argumentation, not persuasion per se. The most persuasive speakers are not the best debaters. The difference might seen of minor consequence, but in reality is central. For many outside of the world of debate, the key virtue of speech might seem to be a smooth and easy clarity, an aesthetic glibness. If one does not enjoy hearing a speaker's words, it is hard to be persuaded that the speaker has a valid argument. Yet, in high school debate such a view needs to be modified. Because the goal is to present as many arguments and as much information as rapidly as possible within a limited amount of time, clarity can be lost in the face of content.

Novices learn in their rounds that, in the words of one of them, "We will just stumble and fall." A coach, trying to persuade her novices to attend a small tournament, exhorts them: "We're not here for winning and losing. You'll be surprised how much you improve in two rounds" (field notes). But improve how? It is the act of public speaking—putting oneself on the line—that is the heart of darkness for the novice. Novices wonder how they can fill up all that time in their speeches, and to make the task seem less daunting some tournaments or jurisdictions limit the cases that affirmatives can run (providing "case limits") or have teams debate only affirmative or negative. Not only are novices intensely nervous about what to say during their speeches (and occasionally only use two or three minutes of their eight-minute speeches), but the very act of speaking terrorizes them, with the possibility of making them look foolish. As one junior varsity debater noted about a friend:

> Danny was up against me in debate institute. We had a round and I ran my women's case, and he got up there and he said, "If I was a man, I would be mad." And it was like we were all laughing because he was thinking so fast; he was like, you know, "If I was a man, I would be mad at this case." And it was, like, aren't you? [Laughs] (interview)

Even this explanation of another's verbal embarrassment, stated calmly in an interview, reveals how imperfectly grammatical speech can be.[2] A literate observer of this activity is impressed simultaneously by how much these teens know and do not know. For instance, New York City mayor Rudolph Giuliani's name was routinely mispronounced by these well-meaning Minnesotans.

Coupled with speech errors—a marching army of mistakes that Sigmund Freud labels "parapraxes"—is the thicket of jargon that is indigenous to debate. Debaters must master technical terms, learning not just their meaning but how to use them in active speech. Adolescents learn "topicality," "inherency," "solvency," "generic arguments," "kritiks," "brink cards," "off-case," and many others. Added to these are acronyms and abbreviations that refer to these technical terms: PMA (Plan Meets Advantage), DA (disadvantage), D-rule (decision rule), T (topicality), or CBA (cost benefit analysis). Further, within each topic area (such as penology and criminology) there is terminology that must be mastered. When my son debated China policy, MFN (most-favored nation) policy was never far from his lips; during the prison-overcrowding topic year, debaters referred to ISP (intensive supervised probation). Added to these content-laden terms, there are the informal forms of folk speech. Some are widely known in the debate community: squirrel cases (bizarre, silly, excessively narrow plans), "run and gun" (rapid speech), "up (or down) them" (give a team a victory or loss). Others are likely to be more local: a slug (a short point in rebuttal), a hondo (a person consumed by debate), "day at the circus" (a case with too many parts), or a "meatball" (a large generic argument). I return to jargon later, in discussing debate subculture; here, I note that in order to speak properly novices must master this novel, awkward terminology, so that they can present it credibly and without thinking to critical evaluators. These terms must enter their natural speech.

Speed Bumps

One of the most dramatic elements of high school debate is how rapidly participants talk; outsiders confront a blur of words: sometimes as many as 400 words per minute.[3] Since much of the evaluation of debate in practice is based on how many arguments one presents (particularly those unanswered by opponents), speed can contribute to effective debate. By "spreading" their arguments by presenting a large number of points with a rapid delivery, these teens give their opponents more to answer and perhaps less to understand. Even though some teams use strategic slowness to appeal to judges, contrast themselves with other teams, or appear thoughtful and serious, rapid speech is the norm, and, over the past quarter-century has become part of a somewhat arbitrary fashion[4] of debate, serving, along with other fashions of argumentation, to differentiate the "Old Guard" from the "Young Turks." The debate world's status system has increasingly enshrined speed as proper.

Speed is more than simply an instrumental goal, it also has status-enhancing expressive qualities. In much competitive high school debate, those who can speak fastest are accorded the greatest peer esteem, and so adolescents time each other in speech rushes, and speed-speaking contests are held at summer institutes.[5] Speaking fast, whatever its value in the round itself, is a subcultural marker. It is an esoteric skill that many adolescent talkers admire. As one commented admiringly about a fast round: "I've never seen a mouth at Mach 2 before" (field notes). A novice explained wistfully and admiringly early in the season after listening to a particularly fast round: "I only wish for a gifted tongue that I could speak that fast" (field notes). Soon he could.

In fact, a battle has been waged between those who choose to speak fast and those who object to that method. In 1979, after receiving complaints from a representative of their corporate sponsor, Phillips Petroleum, the Executive Council of the National Forensic League created what is called "Lincoln-Douglas Debate," or "Values Debate," in which single debaters argue value-based topics—topics that changed every two months (see appendix). This format was designed to be more persuasive and oratorical; but over time, debaters have sped up, hoping to cram as many arguments as possible into their speeches. An ongoing discussion continues as to whether the NFL should create a special division for those schools that wish to "go slow," reminding us that speed is not inevitably desirable. However, as long as speaking fast is advantageous in including more arguments,[6] and as long as it is seen as a self-enhancing skill, rapid speech will be part of debate. Fast-speaking teams were given high status, while teams that were smart and slower did not receive the same esteem, and even surprised others on those frequent occasions in which they reached the final rounds.

Some insist that rapid speech is beneficial. If debate should emphasize information processing, the more information processed, the better. The more arguments there are, the more ideas that debaters have presented and evaluated. Some evidence suggests that speed increases memory and comprehension.[7] Ostensibly, rapid speech trains participants to think quickly on their feet: a self-evident virtue. While some, such as social psychologist Michael Billig,[8] argue that people do not process information in these formal and precise ways, the image is a powerful one. One prominent coach notes:

> The working world will increasingly value people who can plow through vast loads of information, distill it, make arguments out of it, try to find the truth from it; who can think very broadly and longitudinally about big problems. The strength of debating in front of blank slate judges who can follow fast rounds is that the round can encompass quite a lot more complexity . . . AND that the blank slate mindset, while it's never perfect, means that arguments which sound improbable by current, common person standards can get a hearing.[9]

With the development of previously prepared briefs summarizing an argument, some spontaneous talk is lost, particularly in the constructive speeches, but linking threads need to be spoken.

Others doubt the value of rapid speech in debate. In careful transcripts of collegiate final rounds, passages are often marked unintelligible,[10] surely disturbing when the speakers are supposed to address an audience.[11] Perhaps the extreme argument is the "speed kills" critique that claims that rapid speech can lead to hypertension, among other ailments.[12] Here is a case—potentially—of "blood on the flow." The fact that debaters have not seen those bodies—that the ailments are silent, if they do exist—weakens the potency of the argument.

For critics, rapid speech leads to poor arguments, and in the extreme threatens the moral stature of the activity. The famous (or notorious) 1988 critique of high school debate in *The New Republic* by Michael McGough, a former debater, singled out speed as a cause of concern. The goal of rapid speech is to present as many arguments as possible to which one's opponents must respond, creating a "time suck" or "spread." Yet, part of the value of analysis is in understanding claims globally, metaphorically, and with subtlety, largely lost under this model. Surely we discover powerful responses when we let arguments marinate; yet, contemporary debate prevents thoughtful deliberation. Slower teams needing to respond to every argument find themselves in a bind, particularly when facing judges who decide the round on dropped arguments. Speed limits argumentation, creating thin debate. Critics of speed also point to the absence of emotional or rhetorical speech. They note, with justice, that the great speeches have been richly textured and deeply felt. Imagine the Reverend Martin Luther King's "I Have a Dream" speech at 400 words per minute, attempting to spread the segregationists. Lincoln's Gettysburg Address would have been completed in under a minute, leaving plenty of time to tour the battlefield. But perhaps this rhetorical argument is empty: debate is not about speaking well (other speech events have been created for that purpose, such as humorous interpretation or original oratory), but is about processing information and creating webs of logic, backed by evidence. Rapid debate involves addressing judges who are trained to evaluate talk in that context. One coach, sympathetic to debate as communication, told me; "Debate has become, with the number of arguments and everything else, an arena for experts in the field who have learned to listen at a rapid rate, who are generally concerned more with substance than they are with the oral" (interview). A young coach revealed that he would no more judge on speaking style, voice timbre, or persuasive ability than on whether the speaker was cute (interview). A collegiate debater elaborates:

> As opposed to audience debate, in which we present ideas with John Q. Public in middle America in mind (most of the time), Academic policy debate has tended towards the complex, the critical, and yes, the "quick." This is not something that happened absent the judging pool. We often forget than when judges listen and think as active critics, they are involved in the act of communicating. . . . With that in mind, we must realize that "speed" is communicating.[13]

This connects to the need for "judge adaptation" (see chapter 4), whereby debaters—at least the best debaters—can adjust to an audience. As a varsity debater notes:

> Nor do I think learning to debate "fast" is detrimental in the real world. It teaches efficient communication . . . precise elocution and enunciation (when done correctly) and teaches debaters to think quickly on their feet. In my experience, debaters can control how quickly they speak . . . and in fact that policy debaters have a great deal more control over their mode of speech, and are more aware of specifically what they are doing, than most of the population.[14]

Perhaps, said one, rapid speech does not help convince a company's board of directors, but "You can't pole vault over them either. Should we get rid of the track team?"[15] Rapid speech is a skill with its own benefits, not the benefits of oratory.

Different models (or paradigms) determine how one will value speech: emphasizing courtroom oratory or narrative is likely to be associated with a rhetorical focus. In contrast, those who emphasize that debate is a game are likely to be more sympathetic to argument processing. Given the dozens of paradigms, where one stands on the value of speed in debate is surely complex.

Talk in Practice

This theoretical discussion on rapid speech serves at the backdrop for understanding what individuals do within a round. On some level debaters, however fast they wish to speak, must be intelligible to judges. However, on those occasions in which I was asked to judge, instances occurred in which I simply could not understand the words being said before me, a feeling that other judges shared. One prominent coach explained that it took her two rounds to adjust to hearing the debaters, making early rounds problematic for judges and students. Another prominent coach, whose teams were known for their speed and who vigorously defended fast debate, admitted that some rapid speech had "no value whatsoever," adding, "I would not want debaters to become used-car salesmen" (field notes).

An unintelligible speaker will surely fail, even though, as is now more common, opponents and judges can request written cases, evidence, arguments, and briefs. Debaters are sufficiently realistic to recognize that speed coupled with clarity is the ideal. Some debaters, realizing their potential unintelligibility, hand briefs to the other team when they have finished so that their opponents can understand what is being argued, permitting a response to aurally incomprehensible material,[16] with the judge sometimes outside the loop. Although it is possible to recognize the gist of the argument, often from tag lines, spoken slightly more slowly than the evidence itself, the details of the evidence, including author, publication, and date, can easily be lost. Fast novice teams have a particular advantage. Brian, a Randall Park varsity debater, notes of Sean and Ram: "That's why they win with that case. The other [novice] team can't flow it [because Sean speaks so rapidly]." Brian later jokingly suggests that his partner Doree read the introduction of their case in French, speaking so rapidly that the judge and their opponents think they are mumbling (field notes).

Older coaches may attempt to restrain their charges. If rapid speech is status-enhancing for adolescents, many more traditional coaches feel that what they define as an excess emphasis on speed threatens the activity. One coach commented about a particularly rapid round: "I walked by a room and heard something that sounded like auctioneering" (field notes).

Another coach from a small program told me that, during one round, he actually stopped one debater, telling him that he could not understand him: he was "speaking a mile a minute, and said, 'therefore 96 equals 105'. . . . They felt that no matter whatever he said, it was my job to understand things" (field notes). More sophisticated coaches would have been less likely to inject themselves into the round, however sympathetic they might have been to this coach's plaint.

While effective coaches permit their debaters leeway, realizing they have little control of what happens within the round, they emphasize the importance of the communicative paradigm. Annette Miller felt that she was in a continual, if futile, battle with her students, insisting that if they chose to speak rapidly, they had to enunciate clearly. She explains in class:

> You know I nag you about not talking too fast. I know you think I'm some fuddy-duddy old lady who has her head in the ground, but I was troubled by what I heard at the tournament. If you're mumbling, you can't be understood. When you are speaking at a microphone [as in some final rounds], it makes it worse. You are absolutely obsessed with going fast, but what is the use of going fast if you can't be understood? Open your mouth wider, if you want to go fast. You're going to have to exaggerate every single letter. You're going to have to make every single syllable. A speed demon has no effect if no one could understand you. . . . Judges won't get it if you go so fast. College [student] judges sometimes think that it's cool, but even they won't understand most of what you are saying. . . . I'm very upset about this. We'll still win debates if we don't talk so fast. (field notes)

For her, as for other adult coaches, debating should be "a lifelong skill." She adds, "If you can't persuade people, it isn't going to do us any good, it doesn't do you any good, it isn't going to do anyone any good" (field notes). While regional variations, personal preferences, and different orientations to what is called national circuit debate exist (see appendix), the struggle is between students, whose role models are fashionable college debaters, and their coaches, most of whom see themselves as teaching communication skills.

Part of the problem with rapid speech is that speed becomes an end in itself; less effective debaters find themselves gulping for air, mumbling, speaking in a high, squeaky voice, using a robotic, inflectionless monotone, or talking in a singsong or harsh fashion. At first I was concerned for the health and safety of some fast debaters, although no one ever collapsed.[17] Some admitted, however, that if they spoke too rapidly, they found themselves "running out of gas"; they become exhausted. Vic Herman, one of the most respected debaters in Minnesota, finished a very fast rebuttal in a tournament final round with a flourish, concluding his woman's prison case by saying, "We speak for the mother, we speak for the children." On finishing, he pretended to collapse from having spoken so rapidly (field notes).

The best "national circuit" debaters were crystal clear though very fast. One coach asserted that "there is a big difference between spewing and communication" (field notes). A critical task for a coach is to teach effective rapid speech, a goal that Mrs. Miller takes seriously with variable success. She routinely has debaters practice in front of her, providing detailed critiques of their speaking style. Don Davis, Mrs. Miller's assistant coach, tells a novice that he has "slush mouth," and that he should practice speaking to gain clarity. To another, he suggests, "You're going too loud. There's too much air going through. If you go quiet, you can go much faster and clearer."

Debaters themselves recognize this problem—at times. Doree, a senior at Randall Park, tells me critically: "I realize that I have problems in articulation because I don't breathe. I try to say too much on one breath" (field notes). On another occasion, Doree tells Phillip that he speaks too fast and jokes that he should speak "one word per second," far slower than rapid speech at 400 words per minute or even natural speech. Others joke, following Demosthenes, about practicing with a mouthful of marbles, or, more seriously, in speaking in front of a mirror, taping one's practice, warming up before a round, or even avoiding dairy products, which are said to coat one's vocal cords, preventing speed and clarity.[18]

Part of the job of the coaches is to teach their students how to talk. Speed—or, for that matter, all effective speech—does not come naturally. Adolescents (and also adults) have problems with breathing, enunciation, pitch, stumbling, monotone, and volume—a range of difficulties that drills are designed to address. Various techniques have been developed to aid the acquisition of this technical skill. One handout from Glenbrook South High School suggested nine drills: (1) read a text aloud naturally ("The Generic Speaking Drill"); (2) read a text "over-pronouncing" each syllable, forcing debaters to open their mouths widely ("The Over-Enunciation Drill"); (3) read a text beginning softly, steadily increasing the volume, and then decreasing one's volume ("The Vocal Volume Drill"); (4) read a text stressing particular words, as if one were telling a story ("The Vocal Emphasis Drill"); (5) read a text with a pencil as far back in one's mouth as possible (near one's molars), speaking as clearly as possible; this allows for better articulation but produces spit ("The Spit on your Shirt Drill"); (6) read a text placing an "a" between each word ("Taking the "A" Train Drill"); (7) read a text backwards, producing better eye-mouth skill ("The Backward Reading Drill"); (8) read a text after having placed the text on a chair which one will lift while speaking, forcing one to speak from the diaphragm, increasing speaking power ("Carry the Chair Drill"); and (9) read tongue twisters quickly and clearly ("There Once Was a Boy from Nantucket Drill").[19]

Not all advice comes with specific drills, but with the assumption that the debater can fix the problem. On one occasion, Mrs. Miller explained to a varsity debater after listening to her read her first affirmative: "Try to read it without being so singsongy. . . . It's all streaking together. Exaggerate, but get your articulation clear. Move your mouth. . . . The background you can read fast, but when you get to the evidence, you need to make the points you want. The judge won't pick up what is important" (field notes). On another occasion, Mrs. Miller warns her: "That's way too fast. There was no variability in your voice. We need to cut [the length of the first affirmative speech], so that you can sound like an orator, not a speed demon." A debater is warned to start slowly, so she can build up later in the speech, as the judge gets used to the timbre of her voice. Mrs. Miller later tells this same student that she must slow down when reading her introduction, a quotation from *Les Miserables*, noting, "If you want a first affirmative that has a dramatic opening, which is fun and people like, you have to read it dramatically" (field notes). Her comment emphasizes that although we think of speed as something that is present or absent, in fact it is something that is strategically situated in particular parts of the talk. One emphasizes tags and introduction, while rushing through the background and the citations. Speech is treated differently if it is the "canned" first affirmative speech, presenting the plan, which needs to be fast and clear (rapid but oratorical), which some top debaters memorize so they can look directly at the judge;[20] the reading of short texts (previously written briefs and evidence cards), which have been prepared, but which are read without planning prior to the round, the leading source of unintelligible rapid speech; extemporaneous speech, often filled with errors, but often not as fast because it is newly minted; or questions and responses in cross-examination, which typically are spoken in a normal vocal register. Debate speech is not all of one speed, but is locally constructed. Speed is a function of its production: not given, but chosen, taught, learned, and manipulated—a skill, rather than a talent.

Listening to Oneself

With the exception of the first affirmative speech, the other turns at talk are black holes: time slots that must be fitted with words. From the opening moments of the first affirmative, the negative team begins to plan the arguments with which to respond. The second affirmative speaker does the same, with both sides using their preparation time—typically five or ten minutes—to cull through the evidence and select arguments. Most teams have "briefs," arguments that have been composed on frequent topics that serve as the backbone of talk in the constructive speeches and that are briefly recapitulated in the rebuttals. Still, these arguments must be linked by webs of talk: talk that is unscripted in its details, even while its outlines have been determined. One successful debater revealed that although he composes a general outline, he mentally attempts to boil his speech down to a key point, feeling that this subliminally permits him to refer continually to the central argument in his speech. The challenge for him and for all debaters is to incorporate thoughtful deliberation into talk.

Due to the speed of their discourse, debaters must find ways to think on their feet: no easy task. The demands for including information are such that little time is left for reflective consideration. Much planning for what one will say in response to other speakers occurs during those other speakers' talk and during preparation. Yet, this time is insufficient, and debaters have to adjust their thoughts and words while talking. They must speak fluently, while being self-monitoring, so they can change course if necessary. Debaters advise:

> If I'm stumbling, or even when I am smooth, I listen to what I'm saying, and [ask] is this logical? Should I be presenting this? And even when I'm reading through evidence, I'll think it through in my head, and I think does this apply here? Does this actually belong here? And if it doesn't—I've done this a couple of times—I'll just stop reading it and go on to the next point. (interview)

> If I've gone through everything . . . I'll start to do a quick summary at the end, and during the summary I sort of put my mouth on auto and say, OK, go over what's done, and then I'll think, have I missed anything. I'll interrupt what I'm doing and put this out real quick. . . . I've found myself going through the straight structure, then the quick summary, then I'll put another DA [disadvantage] on at the end real quick. (interview)

Structure, based on the flow, coupled with adjustments, based on self-reflection, produces effective debate for those who have learned speaking skills that permit them to be flexible.

As a result of the pressures of spontaneous speech, debaters are always on the edge of error, humorous to an observer who long ago proved that he could do no better himself. Because of the push toward speed, debaters do not have the luxury of considering what they mean to say. While we all make errors as we talk, debaters are especially likely to flub. Given the pressure, it is a challenge to think and talk simultaneously. For instance, one speaker routinely said "mythology" instead of "methodology." Another, "indignant," when he meant "indigent." Others say "exasperate" instead of "exacerbate" or "premeable" for "permeable." These bright adolescents know these words perfectly well, but these are words that required a moment's thought to be said correctly: time that was not available. One novice literally read the stage direction passed by his partner: "Read the following passage." This hapless, though talented, youngster did not have time to examine the words before he read them. Errors are a continuing source of embarrassment. Often debaters respond by repeating what they have just said, hoping to find a way to escape from the trap. Some break frame, apologizing to judges for being unable to read their own handwriting (and implicitly for having no idea of what they mean to be saying). I have heard debaters remark, "Oops, read the wrong evidence," or, "Whoa, poor handwriting," simply throwing up their hands, muttering "Aw, screw it," or perhaps, most honestly, flooding out, "I don't understand what I'm saying at all. . . . I don't know what I'm saying" [breaking down in laughter] (field notes).[21]

Related to these errors are instances in extemporaneous speech in which "informal discourse" is spoken. A debater may be making a point, but finds that the appropriate technical term does not come to mind, and, because of the pressures of time, relies on slang or words from different social worlds. One debater refers to the fact that in her presentation she will discuss "topicality, significance, and stuff." That "stuff" comes from a different verbal realm that does topicality and significance, yet it is a realm which has a border that is uncomfortably close to "normal" speech for the speaker searching desperately for the exact phrase. As radio announcers recognize, saying something is better than having dead air.

Another way that debaters speak is to repeat phrases or to insert unnecessary words. While this gives them moments to think and collect themselves, it also takes time, and with training should be eliminated. Debaters, although they know they should not, repeat themselves, if only to gain breathing room. Indeed, this repetition, coupled with the use of informalities, such as "uhh," "ummm," or "you know," is the target of coaches who wish to provide their charges with the maximum amount of speaking time: every millisecond counts. If one could eliminate all unnecessary words, a debater would gain significant seconds. For instance, Don tells Sean, a novice, that he needs to learn not to use "really," which he inserts often, noting that it is "really" very weak and that he "really" can gain time. Don works with Sean in shortening his words, becoming more efficient and precise: every syllable matters. To Frank, another novice, Don emphasizes that he should pare down his tag phrases, replacing "You know it's not quantified" with the simple "not quantified." Don even suggests that Frank should replace the word "never" with "no," shaving a fraction of a second. Later he asks Frank to cut "you know," "we will," and "we are." Frank tries—and over time does improve—but it is difficult to eliminate all of his unconsidered speech patterns.

Another technique widely known by singers of epic poetry[22] and other spontaneous talkers is to rely on ritual talk or formulaic phrases, which provide momentary opportunities to think during recitations. Coaches recognize the utility of this technique, even while seeing them as time-consuming:

> We teach people not to use verbal pauses, no ahs, no ums, no mmms, uh, no silence, and so it's a substitute for that. And I think it's inherent in thinking on your feet because you can't proofread what you've said . . . and yeah, you use certain words over and over again . . . and repeat yourself to buy time. (interview)

> The reason [repetition of words and phrases occurs], and my speech coach explained this to me very well. I called them think words, think phrases. Your mind is trying to catch up and so to do it you say words like therefore, this, um, or whatever words you hear so your mind can catch up. I used to do that in [extemporaneous speaking] all the time. I'd say, "Therefore, we can see," you know. That's like three seconds where my brain is thinking about what can we see." (interview)

All debaters repeat words or phrases throughout the round to bolster their arguments rhetorically, allowing for a smoother presentation, even if the phrases are empty in content. These phrases differ for each debater, and include such "verbal tics" as "and that's very important" (after each point), "That's going to be key," "I'm going to say," "That is very clear," "You know that . . . ," or "This is very crucial." It is not that the phrases are inappropriate, but they are emptied of meaning by their continued usage. They replace the less appropriate "uhs" and "you knows," but have much the same role in talk. In one four-minute rebuttal, a debater used "look" twenty-nine times [as in "Look, the first point is . . ."]. Another speaker used "I'll say" [as in "I'll say the first point is . . ."] thirty-five times in eight minutes. Both of these speakers were fine varsity debaters, and their repetitions helped the flow of their delivery, but to an audience their repetitions could be annoying, more so because sympathetic audience members knew how hard those patterns were to break. These phrases are excluded from planned talk, but mark spontaneous speech.

Even though coaches recognize how frequent and "natural" this ritual talk is, it remains something to be overcome. In trying to "cure" Doree of her tendency to say "that is" on [the first point], the assistant coach would call out "dumb shit," when she used this term, and later joked that he would spank her or slap her face. Despite Doree's position on the top varsity team, she found the habit hard to break; she spoke too rapidly to consider carefully what she had to eliminate (field notes). Even more dramatic was the attempt of one coach to break the bad habit of one of his debaters:

> I really, really hate the "and my second point is going to be, and my third point . . ." I watched one of my girls once and I counted 43 times she said "and my second point is going to be." And as an exercise I stood up in front of class, and I said, "OK, I'm gonna do what one of you did, and I'm not gonna tell you who did it," but everybody knew, and it was kind of funny at the end, but . . . the girl got real embarrassed. I went through, and I said, "and my first point's going to be, and my second . . ." and I said it 43 times, and it took a surprising amount of seconds. I told the kids that that stuff's all garbage. I mean that you talk a certain percentage of your speech and throw it out the window when you do that. I think you can still think fast enough that you don't need to say that type of thing. (interview)

The very fact that these patterns of speech are so taken for granted means that cutting them in rapid speech is particularly challenging.[23] One can no longer be on automatic pilot, but if one is not, how can one be flexible in the creation of talk in situ. It often seems that deep thought in debate can be found everywhere but in the midst of speeches.

Speech Games

While these bright adolescent have been talking steadily for some fifteen years when they enter the realm of debate, they must reconsider the skills of talking. Talk becomes problematic and a source of pain and anxiety: not a window to the self, but the self itself. With the exception of cross-examination questioning, conversational skills are not of much direct use in rounds, and even the oratorical expressions of gifted speakers might not serve particularly well. Status adheres to other forms of talk.

Most dramatically evident to any casual observer of this social world is the speed with which words are used. Debate, for good or ill, is less concerned with rhetorical persuasion than with information processing. The processing of arguments and evidence becomes crucial, processes that I examine in detail in the next two chapters. Rapid speech must be learned, and the demand for speed places a set of constraints on adolescents, forcing them to deal with the inevitable errors that temporal pressures produce and demanding that they develop skills that permit them, for a moment at least, during their talk to create mental niches in which their arguments can be adjusted.

Yet, to see rapid talk as only a technical matter is to miss the point. Debate is a social world, and talking rapidly is one means by which social standing is distributed. Spewing is not only an issue of technique, but a form of impression management. This is a world in which one is known and judged by how one speaks, not only by what one says. If this is also true within other social domains, the form that this evaluation takes is distinctly different in policy debate, reminding us that talk is not only a channel for information transfer but is itself a social construction on which reputations depend.

Two

Rites of Arguments

IT WILL BE no surprise to parents that adolescents enjoy arguing. Even if these offspring are not, by parental standards, fully persuasive, they often vigorously and tenaciously defend their positions. This contrarian impulse does not begin in the teen years, as studies of childhood arguments demonstrate. As early as preschool, children argue with passion and fire.[1] By preadolescence, argumentation skills are well developed, and some disputatious conversations are lengthy, socially sophisticated, and intellectually complex.[2] Arguments do not only involve cognition, but occur in social worlds, and must be understood as practical achievements, even if this suggests that they are less logical and more rhetorical than cognitive theory suggests.[3]

Policy debate represents a special case of argumentation. As in the law, and, similarly, as in much of American politics, the activity is based on an oppositional structure. Two competing sides are established, and outcomes depend on the facility of adversaries to persuade others. As is well established in the theory of argumentation, people may disagree about empirical truth claims (statements about the nature of the world or "what is") and how a well-functioning social system should operate (statements of value or "what ought to be"). In the analysis of arguments, these are referred to as claims and warrants. Of course, adolescents, prior to their immersion in the world of debate, do not see their arguments in theoretical terms.

Behind arguments as they occur in natural discourse is a central assumption: that the speaker believes the claims and warrants presented. Whether the arguments are legitimate, parties to the dispute assume that they are tightly held. If not, why bother? This may not always be true, but such an assertion (arguing for its own sake) undercuts the moral standing of the speaker. The allegation that a speaker is taking a position only because he or she "likes to argue," "wants to be contrary," or, significantly, "is just a debater" is a call to reject the legitimacy of the claim by rejecting the speaker's motivation. In natural conversation, arguments should be something other than games utilized for personal satisfaction. They should, in some sense, be "real."

Through our rhetorical strategies, we attempt to align audiences with our view of the world. We attempt to foster identification,[4] promoting acceptance of our arguments. One way we accomplish this is through truth claims—asserting that something is truly an instance of something else (e.g., that today is Thursday; that the sky is a beautiful blue; that Bill Clinton is a lying womanizer). However, such claims are only partially effective. When the claims are unproblematic, or when our interests are in accord with those of others, or when our relationships are powerful, such claims serve well. If our audiences are predisposed to accept our claims because the claims accord with their own views, because they wish to gain our favor or avoid our wrath, or because they admire our discourse and what lies beneath it, then the claims are likely to be accepted. But acceptance of a depiction of the world is not automatic. The goal in debate, and elsewhere, is to make truth claims stick in the face of opposition through the use of of persuasion.

Social scientists have long been intrigued with the metaphor of social life as a "game," suggesting that many actions are strategic. Philosopher George Herbert Mead memorably employed the game metaphor to understand how children take the roles of others.[5] Perhaps the most explicit metaphor of social life as a game is Norton Long's "Community as an Ecology of Games." Long argues that community life can be seen as a set of intersecting social worlds. In each social world, participants struggle for strategic and tactical advantage. As in more artificial games, success is measurable, as players are able to tell the score.[6] Memorably, sociologist Erving Goffman argued that social life could be understood as a form of "strategic interaction." Goffman's dramaturgical analysis, although grounded in the metaphor of the theater, suggests that in practice social life is a game, in that human activity, for Goffman, is strategic, contingent upon the responses of others, and is unscripted.[7]

The game metaphor assumes that individuals develop strategies for dealing with others and for maximizing their own advantages. This view depends on two core social psychological concepts: those of relations and of interests. Both relations and interests are advanced through claims about the nature of the world in which the parties to the interaction belong. If one can persuade others that one's image of reality should be taken as a primary framework for action, one gains power to define situations and to direct action.[8]

The game metaphor is not only an academic tool, but connects to the structure of American institutions. Many institutions assume the provisional nature of truth. Both our legal and our political systems are structured as an ecology of games, based on an adversarial, rather than a cooperative, model of truth, a model some reject as overly contentious and warlike.[9] We assume that truth emerges most effectively from the clash of opponents, pursuing their own strategies, judged by a set of noninterested third parties (e.g., juries or electorates). These institutions assume competing versions of truth. In these institutional arenas it is not necessary to accept that the speaker truly believes the line she or he is putting forth. The ability to put forth a line, rather than the absolute merit of that line, makes our legal and political systems flourish. As a result, the question "What is truth?" becomes both a plaint and a challenge to those who doubt the existence of a single social reality—the postmodern dilemma. The assumption is that no eternal truths exist, only local, provisional truths, a perspective that often seems endemic to American society.

In the realm of policy, opposing sides debate issues and each party has its own self-interest, despite claims of altruism and justice. Those who support increasing welfare payments or drug rehabilitation may benefit from heightened funding. While this could be (and sometimes is) taken as cynical, it is also legitimate because those opposing the policy change have their own economic or social interests. The audience is expected to weigh the analysis, logic, and evidence, and then reach a conclusion.

Trials, too, are organized as a competition between opposing sides. The goal is not for the two opponents to arrive at a consensus, but rather for each to attempt to win, given legal rules. As a result, "trial lawyers are essentially salesmen . . . smooth-talking strangers."[10] In the court, judges, like referees, assure that the rules are being followed, and judges and juries assess the outcome. At the end of the trial, the prosecution (or plaintiff) and defendant are not expected to agree, unless they voluntarily step outside the game and settle out of court or accept a plea bargain. Ethical lawyers fight hard with whatever strategies they can get away with. That this model is not inevitable is clear from the stance of the "truth school" approach to legal theory. This minority approach claims, in the words of Yale legal scholar Akhil Reed Amar, "Criminal trials shouldn't be a sport or a game where judges just try to even the odds between the two sides."[11]

In a similar vein, American politics is structured as a partisan battle between two sides in eternal dispute. Unlike some fragmentary and shifting political systems, American's commitment to having two opposing parties has been remarkably consistent throughout the nation's history, even if occasionally those parties changed or their policies shifted. While policy concerns and bipartisanship are never wholly absent, partisan rivalry is more apparent, even if this requires policy shifts to ensure the continuation of the rivalry.

High-school policy debate reflects this institutional model, and simultaneously provides a training ground for practitioners of these institutional arenas.[12] Many former debaters eventually become lawyers and politicians. In this chapter, I examine how young people are socialized into this game metaphor, as reflected in their arguments. Through debate, adolescents learn, contrary to middle stages of moral development[13] in which absolute morality holds sway, that morality is not given, but is contingent, depending on one's interest. Truth can legitimately be argued from several perspectives. This seeming radical relativism, endemic to debate, perhaps encourages a cynical polity—a problem of our public sphere—but it simultaneously helps adolescents to learn that ability to argue persuasively both sides of an issue does not prevent them from persuading themselves that one position is right. The challenge for adolescents is to recognize that while truth is contingent for a community, any given individual can hold a belief tenaciously.

High school debate is ambiguously situated as both a game and a process of systematic analysis. The empirical validity of a particular set of arguments is not judged; what is crucial is the skill and logical force with which the arguments are made. This makes high school debate an odd intellectual world in which the ostensible purpose of persuasion in practice—that of presenting empirically plausible arguments—is transformed to a formal exercise in which "bad" arguments can triumph if not countered effectively.

The Game of Persuasion

High school debate, as currently practiced, has been conceptualized as a game in which strategic choices and rules for argumentation dominate.[14] Tension exists as to whether debate constitutes a pure game, without concern as to the probative truth of arguments, or whether truth is one component of an effectively made argument. In practice, debate constitutes a "communication game,"[15] in which making claims that one does not personally hold is necessary.

Debate as Game

For many, a game model per se has value. A former college coach bluntly suggests that "Debate is a game like football or chess" (field notes). One prominent coach whose teams are successful at national tournaments embraced this model, explaining, "So what if it becomes something of a game. Winning is good. Learning to lose is good" (field notes). Others are more explicit in their justification of the value of playing:

> All sorts of strategic things that you're going to decide how to deal with, and that a person can be brilliant in terms of argumentation, but if they don't understand the game aspects, I don't know how successful they're going to be. Theatrical things that you might do during a debate round are all part of the game aspect. (interview)

> Debate is a game, a sport. It is a sport of the mind, the voice, and the argument. It is a game of strategy, argumentation, and battle. . . . Take Johnnie Cochran. He used more B.S. debate tactics in his closing arguments than many of us do in 3 or 4 rounds. He used just about every debate tactic in the book. Guess

what, being an attorney is almost the same thing as being a debater. . . . Debate is three things, a sport, a game, and an invaluable experience.[16]

The model of debate as a game (or sport) challenges and motivates adolescents for whom the spice of competition enlivens the presentation of arguments. Competition is endemic to the fiber of human life, and can even be justified as part of our humanity.[17]

Making arguments that do not apply in "the real world" is a means by which one plays with ideas, increasing critical thinking skills. For many students and coaches debate is an educational game, but a game nonetheless.[18] Thus, debaters argue that *any* plan, if successful and popular, has the potential to give the government more power and money, thus increasing the possibility of war. Any program that increases individual rights leads to overpopulation and thus a Malthusian scenario of mass starvation and death. It is asserted with published quotations that increasing the rights of citizens increases the birth rate. Other evidence suggests that overpopulation is the greatest threat to humanity. Thus, it follows logically, if implausibly, that we need tyranny to protect the human race. Judges on the national circuit expect opponents to counter these and other disadvantages. As Don informed me, judges expect speakers to "tell [them] why it's dumb; don't just say that it is." If not countered, these claims can triumph. As one debater put it, "a great number of cases are a lot of crap. . . . They are OK in debate, but one knows that the REAL policy implications for them are bad."[19] These arguments must be analyzed and answered, or the team can lose for having "dropped" the argument, no matter its silliness.

The specifics of these arguments can strike some as eccentric or bizarre. One assistant coach recalled hearing some college debaters discussing whether the United States should change sides on a border dispute between Kenya and Uganda, "They claimed [that it would lead to nuclear war]. I couldn't believe it." A student added, "It's just a game isn't it?" (field notes). One coach put it: "I think you never find truth in a debate round [he laughs]" (interview). These arguments do not mirror "the real world."

The Real World

Does it matter the extent to which arguments are relevant to what is described as the "real world"? Of course, the "real world" is a rhetorical and social construction. The term putatively refers to that set of arguments, claims, and evidences that listeners see as legitimate within their "primary frameworks" of knowledge.[20]

In practice, it is common for participants to distinguish between what is argued and what makes sense in "the real world." One coach emphasized that in his view, "Debate is not real world. It's a chess game" (field notes). A student explained, "I think [debate is] in every way truly reality until the minute you start debating. Because you get sources from the real world, and it is the real world until the 1AC [first speaker] starts up there and makes their first word" (interview).

This is seen in the leeway to present cases that are defined as topical under the resolution. While the resolution seems straightforward, and the possible solutions limited, in fact debaters can narrow, broaden, or alter the topic considerably—discussing repatriating undocumented immigrants, contracting with foreign nations to provide prison spaces, building military stockades, expanding the death penalty, or sending prisoners to outer space. While some do argue topicality, the presumption is that most cases are included under the resolution. Other argumentative practices such as fiat (the assumption that a plan or counterplan will be implemented, despite constitutional or structural obstacles)[21] are legitimate, reminding debaters that "debate is not a real world activity. They don't have fiat in the real world" (field notes).

Don, the assistant coach at Randall Park, suggested that one should distinguish between the "real world," "the debate world," and the "real debate world." It is in this third world that values such as freedom or equality do not matter; all that matters is the argument: what is labeled "death on the flow." It was in this world that one could argue that prison overcrowding might lead to nuclear war or to the destruction of the ozone layer. For most, though not all judges, coaches, and students, debate is not a "real-world" exercise in which the most plausible policies win, but an exercise in which the team that presents the best logical structure triumphs.

The reality that arguments can be judged outside "real world" discourse emphasizes that persuasion typically depends upon a set of shared understandings. The willingness to present arguments that stand outside public plausibility challenges taken-for-granted understandings, demonstrating how much depends upon what is said.

Debate as Truth

While some abjure the "real-world," pragmatic treatment of problems, others believe that the balance has swung too far from considering the empirical grounding of arguments. One participant claimed strongly that the content of arguments should be considered:

> Just because debate is a competitive game doesn't mean that it ought to be. . . .
> It can be nice to bask in the glory when your name is announced at the awards
> ceremony. Just remember, it means nothing, there is always someone better

somewhere, no one will know who you are in a few years, so why not lose rounds in the name of integrity and truth? Why not call the debate community on one of the largest fallacies that exists at its very heart.[22]

In the immediate aftermath of the assassination of Israeli Prime Minister Yitzhak Rabin, debaters argued whether it was appropriate to use "impacts" from that event in their arguments—and whether they had spent enough time mourning. One claimed, "I for one will refuse to benefit from the tragedy and encourage others to do the same. Morals have a place in debate."[23] While others argued that attempting to understand the effects on the peace process paid tribute to the Israeli leader and was excruciatingly "real world," the eagerness to create arguments from the tragedy struck some as unseemly. For critics, the goal of victory seemed to transcend grief. The winning-at-all-cost attitude may undermine the activity's benefits: the ends corrupt the means.

A distinction is often made between the arguments within the round and those that bracket it—in class and while preparing for rounds. Prior to rounds, debaters are more likely to see ideas as consequential, even if they argue anything in the round itself. One veteran coach suggested:

> If you actually want to talk about walking into a room and having a debate, I think it is more a sport. It is more a game. . . . The object is clear. It is to win when you walk in the room, and that's the goal of both teams, and so educational concerns are really secondary at that point in time. Outside of that room I think it is more educational or at least . . . the benefits that you get from a debate would tend to line up more on an educational line than on a sports line. (interview)

While preparing, Mrs. Miller asks Doree, a varsity debater, about how her team will determine if their plan is effective. Doree answers, "Continual evaluation of the system"—a response with little meaning in practice. Mrs. Miller responds: "That's a nice pat answer, but tell me really." There is a difference between providing nice answers and "telling really" (field notes). This "really" constitutes substantive learning. When asked a question outside of the round students may respond, "Do you want me to think as a real person or do you want me to try to win a debate?" In this context one claims: "I made a resolution not to win debates, but to present good arguments. I want to have fun. Next year I want to cream my opponents" (field notes). This adolescent articulates his assumption that debating issues will be more fun, but that while he presents good arguments, he is not likely to win as often as he might otherwise.

The desire to present good arguments is particularly common in establishing an affirmative case that a team may present for much of the season, and with which often they become identified.[24] An established coach suggested, "Bottom line for me, education is what it is all about. I'd rather run a case that is really real world"—even if they lose (field notes). This claim suggests that students *as citizens* learn from embracing a plausible position.

The Tension between Games and Truth

A distinction exists between these two models—a tension revealed at critical junctures. As two prominent coaches reflect:

> I don't think there's anything wrong with the word manipulation when you're talking about persuasion. As long as the strategy or manipulation is used from an ethical standard. To develop a Sophist approach I think is reprehensible, but at the same time if anybody is to be persuasive in our society they certainly have to learn to use strategy, they have to learn how to use manipulative techniques . . . within a responsible framework. (interview)

> More traditional debaters and coaches are more likely to place a high value on what they consider to be "true" arguments, and to see the round as an attempt to search for truth and education. Obviously there is tension between that goal and the competitive framework. . . . I don't think anybody wants to think that debate is *just* a game—neither teacher nor coach can easily justify it as that, not to mention parents or school board. But it *is* a game. We deal with the tension between that and the educational goal (and our resultant guilt, perhaps) in different ways. . . . My major point is that strategy and tactics, even games playing, ought not to be seen as dirty words.[25]

As these extracts suggest, the tension between truth and games is evident when discussing the strategies used in a round. As one varsity debater notes:

> Ethics and strategy do not necessarily go together very well. I would say it would be very unethical for you to do something purposely [to] the other team for them to screw up. I think that's really unethical, because you're not winning by anyone's standards except for your own, unless you're a games person, which I'm not. (interview)

Debaters believe that even when an affirmative case is empirically well grounded, it can still be beaten by a smart negative, even if this victory is sleazy. Affirmative cases may be excessively vague or slimy—structured to prevent attack, through eliding the controversial aspects (as, for instance, in a case to establish a national commission to decrease prison overcrowding that might or might not reduce overcrowding). Don explains to his students what to do if they are challenged on the feasibility of their drug legalization case: "When you're stuck in this situation, the best way is to find a way to win"; meaning that they should not attempt to best the argument empirically, but to try to get more points from the judge who is constrained not to evaluate the plausibility of the argument, but to decide whether the other team has responded effectively.

Once, several debaters were discussing a plan that would release female offenders from jail and might lead to revolution (through male anger). Mrs. Miller asks one: "Do you really believe this?" He responds: "Does anyone believe any DAs [disadvantages]?" (field notes). In the debate it does not matter whether one really believes an argument, but whether one can win:

> A lot of it is . . . being forced to stand for things that you just kind of know don't make sense, and being able to actually support that and not let everyone know you don't support it. (interview)

The tension between the game and truth models may be an issue of how to respond to questions that could harm one's team's chances. This edges close to lying about one's case—an event that in its extreme form is rare, though not unknown. The dilemma is evident in quasi-humorous remarks. For instance, when one debater was caught not having a mandate or plank in his plan that would require lowering prison overcrowding—the goal of the debate—he responded, honestly, that the plan lacked this mandate, but then joked: "Damn it. I hate telling the truth sometimes" (field notes). Likewise, in a practice round between two members of the Randall Park squad, one tells the other about some evidence that will undercut his own case, and then jokes: "I'll just have to cover that up. I should just shut up" (field notes). As powerful as the drive to win is, ethical standards constrain the kinds of truth claims that debaters present, and while they cut corners, the rule against outright fabrication is a powerful constraint.

Both Sides Now

A key reality of policy debate is that participants must, in later rounds, take positions that oppose claims they had previously made. In the first round, a team may be affirmative; in the second round, as the negative team, they may have to argue against a case similar to the one that minutes before they had vigorously defended.

To understand the structure of argumentation, one must recognize the implications of defending both sides of an issue. For those who wish debaters to be fundamentally *sincere*, such a view is problematic; yet, because debating both sides of an issue is so integral to the activity, it is a position that is rarely explicitly put forth. One wonders if every topic deserves two sides—or should be limited to only two sides.[26] I suggest that the fact that the structure of debate forces students to take positions that they don't believe also legitimizes their making an array of arguments that they (or any rational citizen) would reject. Debating both sides of an issue constitutes both a strength of the activity and a potential underside.

During 1996, an e-mail message posted on the high school debate list raised a troubling possibility:

> I am student teaching through a class offered at my school and discovered something very troubling from the speech teacher with whom I teach. Her husband recently received a flyer from Ralph Reed . . . from the Christian Coalition. In the flyer it stated that high school debate is a dangerous activity because it forces our kids to see both sides of every issue and forces us to question our moral framework.[27]

The student had not seen the flyer, and the Christian Coalition denied having any such position (and were surprised that anyone should believe that they had). Still, the belief that debating both sides of an issue could weaken one's moral position is not outrageous. In fact, Minnesota and other states used to have four-person teams, in which two debaters took the affirmative in each round, and two took the negative. It was assumed that it would be unethical for teams to debate both sides of an issue; indeed, at one time the Minnesota state championship was based on these four-person teams, a structure that was eventually ended because of the difficulty that some schools had in fielding teams of this size.[28]

Sophists use whatever arguments are available in advancing their positions. Debaters who at one moment argue *passionately* in favor of drug legalization and the next hour argue equally intensely that it is dangerous could be seen as sharing that cynicism. Do they take from this exercise the postmodern belief that nothing is inherently right or wrong? Holding to one's position has value, as a novice noted:

> I can debate both sides, but I don't like to. If I have a point that I'm arguing, I like to keep that point, because that's my personal opinion. If you have a point of view, you should stick with it. (interview)

Another suggested that one's beliefs can be eliminated by taking all positions, and that one can be defined as the kind of person whose statements are not to be believed:

> I think the one problem that debaters suffer from is that since we have to do both sides, we sort of eliminate our own personal beliefs. It helps when we

believe in something. You can tell [what one's belief is] because the debater is even more effective. . . . I have no problem going from affirmative to negative. It just sort of happens. You just sort of do it. You get used to it. Now, of course, sometimes that carries over into real life. People will sometimes see you as some sort of person who doesn't necessarily have a firm conviction one way or the other. (interview)

One potential topic for the 1997–1998 debate year was that the federal government should institute a program to decrease discrimination. The topic was not selected (the topic eventually chosen was on increasing the use of renewable energy), possibly because such a topic could have led to negative arguments (backed with published "evidence") that suggested that racism and gender bias are valuable and legitimate. For minority students to argue against increased protection from discrimination would have been too personal. Perhaps the possibility of those arguments triumphing ("KKK good"; "Hitler solves"; "PMS leads to nuke war") may have filled with horror those who had the responsibility of choosing the topic. A coach of a city school noted that he had students who quit when the topic was poverty because "it was too close to them. . . . They were the ones getting food stamps. . . . Some of the arguments that these poor people deserve what they're getting, you know, [they] didn't want to hear that." For minority students from an impoverished community to argue against fighting discrimination or poverty is self-negating. Perhaps some arguments do not belong in a round.

Despite these concerns, most individuals with whom I discussed the issue felt that debating both sides of an issue was valuable, perhaps the greatest benefit of the activity, teaching the value of respect for differing opinions, multiple perspectives, and the dangers of absolutism. For some the ability to argue both sides of an issue is profoundly moral:

I have seen some people become cynical as a result. I would hope with students I teach that they learn some ethical responsibilities. But I think what debate does is allow students to seriously consider important questions from both sides of the issue and see other perspectives before they become committed themselves to a position. I have students who will say, "Well, I can't argue against this, because I really believe it." But after they've done some research they are not so certain of their convictions. They at least can see the other side. I think they become more humane as a result of looking at both sides. (interview)

The ability to see both points of view has the potential in this view to make one more humane and less self-righteous. Others suggest that not only does debating both sides of a position not weaken one's position, but it strengthens it, perhaps by inoculating one to opposing arguments. Many debaters have strong political positions, which the activity seems to do nothing to diminish:

> I think what happens is that you learn that there are two sides to every issue. I think most debaters come down on one side or the other in their mind, but they are able to argue both sides. And I think that is an important thing to be able to do. I mean because it makes what you believe in, it makes that belief even more justified, because you do know both sides. (interview)

The ability to take a position that is contrary to one's own beliefs has several benefits: making one appreciate the perspective of one's foes, making one's own thoughts more complex, and helping one become aware of counterarguments. Perhaps this stance does suggest that "positions" are gamelike, but it is a game that corresponds to the way that much political decision making operates in the real world.

The Logic of the Round

In their haste to read briefs and cards, debaters sometimes neglect one of their prime assets: their brain. Fundamentally, debate is not about amounts of evidence or types of arguments, but about analysis and logic. Judges want debaters to weigh evidence and arguments, so that they, as judges, will not be forced to "intervene" to make a decision. This weighing typically involves a claim that one position is most reasonable and should determine the decision.

Despite the prominence of perfect cards and generic arguments, logical analysis is the hidden weapon in most debate rounds, even if it often gets little respect. Perhaps because logic mirrors how we believe that we make decisions, and seems so close to how we think naturally, it does not gain the prestige of more subcultural claims. Of course, in practice, the illogical or irrational (the emotionally compelling) argument may triumph—often in the name of common sense—but we comfort ourselves by asserting that our decisions are built on logical arguments, even when they embrace claims that philosophers would assert are fallacies.

Despite the rhetorical attachment to logic, in the rounds themselves logic often seems at some remove. Perhaps adolescents, recently introduced to adult discourse, are uncertain of their ability to make connections on their feet, without the support of previously written briefs or collected evidence. Indeed, to adult ears, some of the analysis seems naive and far-fetched, such as the debater who argued, lacking evidence, "The public won't want far-out liberal things like community service and whipping. You have to be realistic. This is the twentieth century. It's in the Constitution. We're not in medieval Greece" (field notes).

The secondary position of logic in debate is not from lack of trying by coaches, who argue vociferously that logic should be central. They exhort students to analyze critically what they hear, on the assumption that unlikely disadvantages can easily fall with a logical push:

> Mrs. Miller tells the Randall Park team that they can defeat arguments that they have never heard before simply by thinking about them: "You need to take a second. I know when you get in the pressure of rounds, you don't really think. . . . One of the things you have to do is develop the why. . . . It's your intelligence that gets you going. What doesn't seem right? What won't work?" (field notes)

> I think that [logic] is at the heart of the activity. I mean you have to make logical sense. . . . Logic is more important than evidence, because you can have a card which supposedly is evidence, but without logic it isn't evidence. And if you have a card that's really, you know, radical, or something, you can disprove it easily with logic. You can win a round with logic but without evidence, but I don't think just with evidence. If you could read evidence and provide no logic . . . you wouldn't win. (interview)

In an extreme case, an assistant coach took all the negative evidence cards away from his team before a tournament, forcing them to think about the affirmative cases, rather than simply repeat evidence. These exhortations sometimes persuade debaters that "logic is your friend," particularly those without reams of evidence and briefs, who by their wits stand some chance of defeating better prepared opponents:

> [The final round] at DeSoto I thought was really enjoyable. I thought if they're gonna run a stupid case [about sending prisoners to the Soviet Union] and still expect to win the round, we'd have to show that we could adapt, that we could point out the logical flaws in the round or in the case, and I really enjoyed debating that because we didn't really have to put out any evidence at all. There wasn't any evidence to put out. It was just a battle of analysis and logic. . . . If there wasn't any logic in debate, there probably wouldn't be any debate. . . . Basically, the cause/effect relationship is just invaluable. I mean that's what debate's all about. (interview)

Debate ultimately rests on the ability of adolescents to see strengths, weaknesses, and links in arguments. In this, debate is perhaps closer to natural reasoning than many of its practitioners—particularly the younger ones—recognize.

Blood and Numbers

How does one make an argument stick? The crucial thing is to claim that one's position is highly significant; what one says *matters*. This is the heart of the tactic of those moral entrepreneurs who wish us to attend to social problems; the problem counts for something, either through its extent or through the intensity of its consequences. While different topics give different weight to the importance of extent and personal impacts, both are fundamental tools that social problems entrepreneurs can deploy to fashion a need for action.

Numbers

One traditional way in which we argue that an issue is significant is to demonstrate that it affects many individuals. It has scope. A key tactic in the arsenal of the moral entrepreneur is to inflate statistics as best one can.[29] It is not that those who care about social problems lie (although sometimes they may), but it is more likely that they will find estimates that support their beliefs. Precise claims as to the number of missing children, HIV-infected individuals, or torture victims in war are instances that demonstrate how statistics can be massaged. If statistics do not lie, many do not care how ignorant those statistics may be.

Quantification has a central place in rounds; debaters analyze social problems though harms and significance. Statistics cannot be dismissed as merely anecdotal; they must be countered. Numbers appear scientific, and at least in debates over *decreasing* prison overcrowding, discussion of numbers occurred in nearly every round.[30] Negative teams argue—not unreasonably—that if the affirmative team cannot demonstrate the existence of prison overcrowding and the amount of the decrease under their plan, they cannot win: "If they don't give us a *number*, you cannot give them an affirmative ballot" (field notes). Some teams emphasize this repeatedly: "They must show a quantifiable harm. . . . There is no definite quantitative harm. . . . When it comes down to the end, they must quantify harms. You must show significant harms in order to change. . . . Quantification is our main position in the round" (field notes). Of course, for some affirmative cases and teams, this demand for a ritual number is "abusive" when it is clear that records are not kept or that the harms are psychological. A number adds security and precision to a general claim, indicating that the danger is real and the benefit outweighs the cost.

Blood

Numbers are not the only way we evaluate the significance of a social problem. We also evaluate through dramatic accounts. A problem that causes annoyance to many can be trumped by a problem that causes death to some. As a result, social problems entrepreneurs become adept at placing before the public dramatic and compelling instances: accounts that, even if they represent extreme instances, are used to characterize the whole of the problem. The heart-wrenching, searing accounts of child abuse and wife battering characterize problems in which the more "typical" instances are less dramatic, no matter how sad they are. Most children are not burned by cigarettes; most women are not hit with crowbars. Few in either category are killed; yet, it is these rare, compelling instances that are used in argumentation.

In debate, the attempt to find the most dramatic instances is labeled "blood on the flow," or "death on the flow."[31] In these cases, opponents cannot merely dismiss the affirmative plan as outweighed by disadvantages. If "everyone's dead [without the plan], that's a comparative advantage" (field notes).

Along with the emotional resonance of dramatic cases, is the fact that in our culture, like many others, life is a taken-for-granted advantage. We rarely argue about why we should wish to preserve life, although in societies in which communal survival is crucial or in which an afterlife is a palpable reality, life would not have the power that it does in ours—even if life always has a value of *some* magnitude. Thus, if prison overcrowding only causes insomnia, any significant disadvantage of changing the status quo, say, leading to a slightly greater likelihood of murder, might be sufficient to outweigh the plan. Death is not as easily dismissed as sleeplessness. Debaters strive to convince judges that without the use of their plan, death would result:

> One debater noted in his first affirmative: "The status quo promotes the cycle of death. . . . This extends the bloody cycle of death to the society at large. The bloodshed born in the prisons is spread outside the barbed wire walls of the prison . . . . Riots cause death. Do you consider death fine? . . . They can't deny the cycle of death." (field notes)

"Death on the flow" was also used by negative teams who were arguing against cases that proposed the legalization of drugs:

> The Carroll Falls debaters argued against Randall Park's drug legalization case: "When we legalize drugs, it will cause death. Since we're winning the war, why do something that will increase death," and "I'd like to read another card on

death. Legalization of drugs will kill. If we do legalize drugs, there will be more death." In another round, the negative team notes: "Urban genocide with the legalization of drugs . . . Drugs will only transform our tragedy from murder to suicide." (field notes)

This does not mean that there are no effective counterarguments; drug legalization cases did well (drive-by drug shootings also put death on the flow), but blood grabs the attention of an audience and suggests that the claims are significant.

Blood and numbers together provide a prima facie case that something needs to be done, whether in the debate world or in the world of policy discourse. Without either, demonstrating a need for the status quo to change becomes difficult.

The Status of Arguments

One aspect of policy debate that is surprising to the naive outsider is the existence of a thriving area of academic discussion labeled "debate theory." Debaters do not *just* argue; scholarly rationales stand behind what they do. Debate theory seems to be in a continual state of ferment, as intellectual and social fashions affect the status of particular arguments. The ideas that were current in 1990 (even among the more au courant national circuit teams and their collegiate friends) are not the issues of the year 2000. Issues such as topical counterplans, kritiks, plan/plan debates now stand beside or have supplanted issues such as should/would arguments, hypothesis testing, permutations, flips, and frontlines. The discussion of what arguments to run and how to structure those arguments— along with the substance of the annual topic—constitutes the core of debate education.

The rules of what arguments can be made in a round are in a state of dynamic tension. In part, this is a function of the fact that different resolutions lead to the prevalence and prominence of different types of arguments. A relatively narrow topic such as reducing prison overcrowding is likely to produce different types of argumentation than a broader one calling for changes in policy toward Russia. Over time, as well, expectations change: a trickle-down effect operates from college debate, to national circuit high school debate, to local debate communities. In 1990, counterplans were only hesitantly being accepted in Minnesota; a negative team that proposed a counterplan that fell under the resolution (i.e., a plan that was topical) would have conceded the round to the affirmative, since at the end of the round both teams would be affirming the resolution. Today, a team can win a round in Minnesota by presenting the same counterplan. In contrast, hypotesting (seeing the affirmative as testing the resolution as a hypothesis), popular during my research, is considered passé and out of fashion.[32]

I claim no expertise on the nuances of debate theory, and I do not attempt to assess the validity or acceptability of any argument. In contrast, my concern is with how arguments serve not only as cognitive achievements but also as social markers. In the world of debate, all arguments are not created equal. One is known by the arguments one runs and the briefs [pages of written arguments] one has prepared.

The more esoteric and collegiate arguments that one can run, the more social status one gains among peers, if not always with more conservative coaches. Coaches note:

> Most kids are attracted to [esoteric arguments]. . . . [They ask:] "Paradigm shifts and counterplans and counterwarrants, what is all that?" [Debaters] get a real kick out of it, and often times I just say, OK . . . you can't do this [in a round] unless you ask me. You know, because [when] we run counterplans, we must make sure we have [a judge] back there who will listen to them. (interview)

In practice, debaters see arguments as having varying status:

> Danny says that he is looking forward to running a counterplan and other "strange" arguments at the Macalester College tournament (judged largely by college debaters). The counterplan, which he traded for with friends on another team, has something to do with anger control, sugar reduction, and visits from the Prophets of God. Danny notes: "I won't stick to conventional rules. When I think of it, I do it. I hate case-side arguments [arguments directly aimed at the issues raised by the affirmative case: typically significance, inherency, and solvency]." Sean notes: "2N [the second negative speaker] gets fun. They get to throw in PMAs [Plan Meets Advantages] and DAs [Disadvantages]. 1N [the first negative speaker] does the same thing again and again. It gets boring." (field notes)

> Darrin wants to run "an Emory switch," a style of argumentation in which the 1N presents 2N arguments and the reverse. He says to Mrs. Miller, "Let me do an Emory. It's so slimy. It's so much fun." She responds, "I'm not into slimy." (field notes)

Debaters just want to have fun. Playing with esoteric, strategic, subculture arguments is fun. In the process debaters attempt to avoid those arguments that they define as "boring": "stock issues" such as solvency, inherency, or harms. Perhaps even the shorthand, jargony labels for these desirable arguments—T, Ks, PMAs, DAs, and CBA—indicate that to know and run them is a mark of community membership. The fact that these are often arguments learned from college debaters enhances their status among high school students.[33] Thus, in one final round in which a team that used "radical" generic disadvantages was defeated by a traditional team, a young assistant coach told me that he felt the outcome was unfortunate: "I'm disappointed because of the message it will send out. It will discourage some of the more radical arguments" (field notes). He did not need to worry. Indeed, radical arguments are so status-enhancing that at times debaters will run arguments that they think judges will not accept or that they do not fully understand:

> At the Covina tournament I was running things I didn't know existed. I was running extra-topicality. I didn't know what that was. I was running problem area topicality. I didn't even know what the problem area was. I mean I know what it was, but I didn't know what that kind of topicality was. (interview)

On occasion, a judge may even buy into the role of argument as status symbol, accepting any esoteric argumentation, even if poorly run, so as not to be thought of as a "dinosaur" or an "old stone." One well-known coach suggests this explains why kritiks[34] (Ks or meta-arguments about the consequences of presenting particular debate arguments) have become so popular:

> To my knowledge my teams were the first to run Kritiks in high school (after hearing a fine Texas team at the Baylor tournament). I say this not to brag, but to explain that I am NOT against Kritiking but think that they have received an elevated status in debate. Debaters overclaim their importance, and judges don't really know how to evaluate them. In fact, too much credibility is given to them by certain judges for fear of being perceived as unprogressive.[35]

It is striking that the author distances himself from his school's priority in running kritiks; otherwise, this comment could be read as a transparent attempt to brag.

During my research, no form of argumentation was as controversial as counterplans. Although counterplans had been well established elsewhere and are now accepted in Minnesota, they were not fully accepted in 1990. Some teams (and their coaches) were profoundly "afraid" of them:

> In a novice round, Ian mistakenly claims that Penny had raised a counterplan. Penny denies it, and says that she is arguing for the status quo, and that she doesn't even know what a counterplan is. After the round, she asks the judge if she had run a counterplan, and he tells her that it wasn't really a counterplan, but that Ian had misunderstood her. Penny's partner says to her: "I didn't mean

to run a counterplan." Penny responds: "I think he confused it," and the judge adds: "It wasn't really a counterplan. It could have been a minor repair," and then describes counterplans. Penny explains that their coach doesn't let them run counterplans. (field notes)

Mrs. Miller tells her team: "We don't run counterplans, not all those crazy things." Brian responds: "Not usually." Mrs. Miller says, half joking: "Not when I know of it." Jay, a novice debater, comments: "We were thinking of running a counterplan, but we didn't have one." Mrs. Miller laughs, saying: "Thank God!" (field notes)

Debaters can and do run counterplans and other "crazy" arguments in rounds, where their coaches have no control and are unaware that their debaters are using these strategies unless notation is made on the judges' ballot. This was particularly true at Randall Park, where Mrs. Miller was adamantly opposed to these arguments, and the desire to sneak in counterplans became part of the team culture. Darrin explained that the previous year, as a novice, he had run a counterplan, and that "for three months after that everyone knew me as the counterplan kid." He added that when Mrs. Miller found out what he had done, he got chewed out (field notes). Prior to a tournament, Carl jokes, "Danny says we'll grant them inherency and harms, but we're going to run a counterplan" (field notes). On another occasion, Carl jokes with me of his round with Danny: "I hate to admit this, but we won on a counterplan" (field notes). The point, of course, is not whether counterplans have any place in debate or whether they are *by nature* either good or evil. In fact, often when we are presented with a plan for action, we will, in natural conversation, come back with an alternative—a counterplan. The issue is how the argument is judged. Counterplans have not become more logical or better arguments; rather, their social standing has changed. At one time, counterplans only could stand outside the resolution; today, increasingly, any plan that the affirmative has not advocated can be advocated by the negative. This change is not a moral one, but it is social, dependent on the attitudes of participants.

Some arguments get no respect. During my research—at least in Randall Park—this was true of the argument known as Hasty G (Hasty Generalization), a seemingly straightforward claim that suggests that the speaker's examples or assertions with regard to the resolution are not representative, do not prove a general rule, or represent only a minute portion of the resolution.[36] Yet, the argument was not well accepted on the team, being seen as illegitimate:

I think [Hasty G] is stupid. It's just not a legitimate argument. It's just saying that this idea was generalized. . . . Just because it's a sort of a generalization of

everything doesn't necessarily mean it's bad. I've never run Hasty G. I've mis-
named an argument Hasty Generalization, when it should have been a solvency
argument. (interview)

Danny, a junior varsity debater, tells Sean, a novice: "Don't run Hasty G. I'm
not kidding. . . . It's not real. It's sleazy and it's slimy. It's based on the resolution, not on solvency." Brian, a varsity debater, describes Hasty G as "a scary
argument." (field notes)

Arguments are linked to the social and moral order, and are seen as having value in and of themselves.

The Boundaries of Argument

Not only do arguments have moral meanings, tied to status, but they also
rub off on the self of a debater. Listening to adolescents analyze policy
issues can simultaneously be inspiring and profoundly unsettling. Because of the rush of talk, debaters often say whatever pops into their
minds, guided by phrases written during a few minutes of preparation
(and by whatever briefs are available). Because of the demand for talk, the
round generates parapraxes, gaffes, half-baked stereotypes, and hasty
generalizations. Further, as bright as these young men and women are,
they are still teenagers and their lack of training and exposure limits them.
They draw from both childhood beliefs and adult knowledge.

Certain arguments can only be described as "incredible," despite our
admiration for those teens who attempt to use them. Descriptions of some
rounds are decidedly odd:

My team went into Semis. And we had completely briefed this case. We had
everything under control. However, then the team ran a paradigm shift saying
all speeches had to be in a foreign language, then proceeded to run a new aff
[affirmative] case all in Spanish. My partner is fluent in Spanish so he survived
that and went up there and actually debated in English and then translated into
Spanish. However, then the next debater got up and changed the language to
French. That was OK, 'cause I can understand French. But then they added
something new to their paradigm, a new language must be used every time. So,
since I can't speak any other language, I got up and spoke in Ebonics. I first
explained to the judge that it was horrible that they added this new criteria. I
explained that the only language I would feel comfortable in was Ebonics. This
judge voted me down, because I failed to meet the first criteria of a foreign
language.[37]

Satire? Perhaps. Yet, if it is satire (and it is hard to imagine that a team
would not challenge the paradigm shift), it is the kind of story that *could*

be told as true—joyously indicating that anything is possible. In more mundane rounds, bizarre remarks are common:

> A debater says in reference to a community service case: "My parents certainly would like it if a criminal would mow my lawn. They don't want to mow my lawn." (field notes)

> A debater claims that shocks and whippings have beneficial effects, adding, "It's very humane." (field notes)

The list of whoppers could be extended indefinitely, and few rounds lack some claims that are childishly incredible on their face, although typically these are ignored by opponents and judges, and are considered part of the natural detritus of talk.

While some judges claim to be willing to listen to or vote on anything, "anything" has its limits. Absolute tolerance is precisely the sort of absolute that breaks down. Adolescents are effective in demonstrating that total tolerance leads to the tolerance of unacceptable values. On occasion, claims in a round can be offensive, including racial and gender slurs aimed at other participants or the subjects of debate. This became a significant issue during a 1997 tournament, in which a team from Highland High School ran a Theater of Cruelty/Marquis de Sade/sadism argument against a Caddo High School affirmative case that wanted to reduce child abuse. Rather than attempting to defeat this peculiar argument, suggesting, in part, that debate was analogous to anal intercourse, the Caddo team walked out, forfeiting the round. For the Caddo team, the arguments were repugnant and outside the boundary of legitimate discourse, leading other teams to joke that they would meet a Theater of Cruelty argument with physical violence.[38]

These occasions lead coaches to worry about the arguments that their charges run. Should teens be permitted to read briefs about ideas of which they have only a hazy understanding? One coach noted:

> I, as a high school educator, do not believe kids are sophisticated enough to really have the logic behind a lot of those arguments. That's where I become cynical. . . . What all too often happens is these kids have got set responses and it's not just a canned [prewritten] first negative speech; it's a canned second affirmative speech. And to me as an educator, what we're trying to do is to get those kids to think. . . . I don't necessarily disagree with the idea of having these arguments set up. What it is, is it takes the place of critical thinking. . . . I think that kids have to understand the basics of argumentation, logic, and structure of reason. And if they understand that and they want to play those games, fine, but I don't know too many high school kids that in a couple of years of debating and studying logic are going to master those things. . . . What I hate as a judge is when students don't understand what they are arguing. They will support a point, read evidence for a point,

and not understand that everything they're supporting is totally specious. (interview)

The complexity and speed of rounds is such that at one point a debater got the pages of a first affirmative out of order, and for several minutes the audience was not aware that there was a problem. One judge told me, "I thought I wasn't listening well. I wasn't going to blame the kid. I blamed myself" (field notes).

Coaches worry whether they should let their debaters run particular analyses (in one case, a cost benefit analysis observation and in another, effects topicality) that could be effective if used properly, or whether they should demand that the debaters stick with what they understand. To be sure, this training is precisely what constitutes debate education, but, as in any subject matter, a little knowledge can be dangerous. Debate arguments are seductive, and perhaps we should be grateful that these adolescents are old enough to be seduced, even if they do not have the experience to understand the siren songs that they are hearing.

Justifying Generics

An effective negative strategy is to compile a set of briefs that potentially apply to a range of affirmative cases: arguments that have come to be known as "Generic Disadvantages." As Minnesota debate is less "progressive" than that found in National Circuit debate, these arguments— federalism, feminism, nuclear war, Japanese rearmament, authoritarianism, environmental degradation—were only beginning to be accepted during my research. These arguments postulate enormous harms that might possibly occur as the result of an affirmative plan, which often is structured through a series of connections or "links," each one less plausible than the last. In a sense this is arguing from ignorance, suggesting that the potential risk is so great that action is essential, even if all the evidence is not consistent, analyzed, or plausible.[39] For instance, a plan, such as building more prisons, that would increase a U.S. President's popularity, might lead to more bold actions in foreign policy, leading to war, leading to global nuclear destruction. The argument that building prisons could cause nuclear war seems implausible, although arguments exist for each of the links. In risk analysis, even small risks may be unacceptable (for instance, consider additives that cause a small number of cases of cancer in rats). These arguments focus on unanticipated consequences: Rube Goldberg policies. One writer humorously suggested that sliced bread leads to communism:

Sliced bread led inevitably to the sandwich.
The sandwich led to the portable meal.

The portable meal led to the meal away from home.

Meals away from home have led to the breakdown of the family.

The breakdown of the family has led to crime in the street.

Crime in the street led to large numbers of police.

Large numbers of police led to police abuse.

Police abuse led to distrust of the police.

Distrust of the police led to the acquittal of O. J. Simpson.

The acquittal of O. J. Simpson will lead to "white rioting."

Whites riot by voting Republican and cutting social programs.

Cutting social programs will lead to a greater gap between classes.

A large gap between classes leads to class warfare.

Class warfare leads to the resurgence of communist ideology.

Therefore, we should outlaw sliced bread because it leads to communism.[40]

Despite this humor, some believe that the prevalence of generic arguments has led to the demise of policy debate in America, pushing it outside "the real world":

> None of the cases or disads being run are in the least bit believable, none of it has any impact in the real world. When people are actually making policies, they don't discuss three or four possible scenarios for nuclear war that people seem to be able to get out in a debate round. The problem is that too many kids have been raised being able to get away with junk like that and win. . . . Who can seriously with a straight face name one way that immigration, for example, could cause nuclear war. . . . Has anyone out there actually tried to explain a case to a real person who doesn't debate? . . . Debate has gone way off course.[41]

> In my opinion, the search for "apocalyptic impacts" to DAs is a sign of the decadence of contemporary policy debate. There are many in the activity who have decided that it simply isn't "fun" to debate unless one is able to claim that one's opponent will be responsible for the death of the universe or similar silliness. . . . As a coach I find it progressively more difficult to justify the time commitment required in debate to my students when they see silly, nonsensical arguments prevailing.[42]

In Minnesota, most coaches felt that the debate should revolve around the case and plan raised by the affirmative team: the affirmative team should set the terms of the round, and coaches should contend that specific, detailed links to the affirmative case are necessary, emphasizing the agenda setting role of the affirmative team. Minnesotans, during my research, were adjusting to the increased legitimacy of generic arguments by suggesting that they were acceptable when they were not "really" generic but could be specifically linked to the case. "Look at the links" was a ritual refrain of Minnesota coaches. Generic arguments were acceptable only when one lacked evidence and logic, and the alternative was only silence or babbling. If they lacked specific links or creative and meaningful logical connections, these "meatballs" (generic arguments) were unacceptable and represented the pollution of pure Minnesota debate by outsiders. Some people could be quite vehement about this, warning against overclaiming arguments, even giving up a strategic advantage:

> We would never use [generic disadvantages] on a case that we have evidence on. We would never use them as a substitute for direct attacks. We will use them [when] we're left without direct attacks on planside. . . . We don't try to overclaim the disadvantage. We don't say the world's going to end because of it. (interview)

At least as far as generic arguments are concerned, Minnesotans emphasize the real world, and are not merely playing at talk. While some argue that the best way to defeat generic disadvantages is to find evidence against them, critics suggest that in the absence of unlimited time, some research is more worthy than other kinds.

The popularity of these arguments suggests that there are vigorous supporters of this style of debate. Playing with wild ideas is fun. As one debater put it: "How [much] fun do you think a round would be if the only advantage was increased juvenile crime? Arguing nuke war, genocide, and economic collapse is 'fun,' and makes rounds more interesting."[43] In another sense, these arguments can be justified because they shift the ground of a round toward the negative, providing a break against an affirmative team that has specialized in collecting evidence supporting its plan.

However, support for generic arguments goes beyond the idea of leveling the field for teams that cannot research every case. For proponents, generic arguments are not meatballs, but risk analysis. There are all kinds of risks—more or less likely—and it is the responsibility of the policymaker to consider them, even those that seem, at first glance, to be implausible. How likely did the rise of Nazism, the spread of the AIDS virus, the fall of the Soviet Union, or the rise of the Pacific Rim seem before they occurred? Each event has reverberations that are difficult to predict: debaters should make these predictions, even if the predictions are hazy. Indeed, some of these far-fetched arguments are central to military strategic planning.

Some suggest that arguing generic disadvantages through risk analysis, weighing how much low risk should be tolerated, can be educational and intellectually liberating:

> Fast national circuit debate may, in a systematic way, give too much credence to the avant-garde, the futurist, the on-face implausible. Stock issues debate is/was systematically rigged in favor of Things As They Are. Sometimes Things As They Are turns into The Real World for purposes of discussion. . . . One of the great things about debate is that we can argue about what is in fact "real"

in the world. I don't mean that in any abstruse philosophical sense; just that we can argue about what's true.[44]

> The reason that I coach this activity and support it to the level I do is because it challenges our beliefs and preconceptions. It allows a young person to expand their mind and take the greatest kind of risk, that of developing a position and trying to defend it. . . . Our strength is our openness.[45]

These critics believe that all arguments can potentially expand adolescent insight. Implausible arguments *may* turn out to be true, but even when they are not, they still expand the mind.

The ultimate question is, given limited time, effort, and money, in what arguments do we choose to invest our resources? We can make a cost-benefit analysis of types of arguments, such as, Are nuclear war impacts worth fighting over? Clearly, since their presence or absence affects the direction and control of the world of debate, they are. Oversimplifying, the issue becomes whether high school teachers control the activity or collegiate debaters do. While university professors and their students would not endorse many of these far-fetched arguments directly, they are more likely to argue for a laissez-faire free play of ideas for which some high school educators feel their students are not ready. The battle in the world of debate, as it is with so many adolescent worlds, is between control and free choice.

Arguments are not socially neutral, but are situated within communities in which the use of arguments have moral meanings. To make an argument is to put oneself on the line—not necessarily claiming that one believes it, but claiming that the argument is fit to make.

Mess and Clash

At its best, a debate round is an aesthetic event. Although most debaters, even those in relatively traditional Minnesota, no longer see debate as primarily an oratorical occasion filled with flowery language, the battle of arguments—and wits—can still be profoundly satisfying. When two sides engage each other in sustained argumentation, everyone—winner, loser, and judge—can emerge satisfied. Debaters have a sense of what constitutes good and poor rounds, and these evaluations do not depend only on whether they won or even whether the round was close. Aesthetically satisfying rounds are said to be characterized by high levels of *clash*; poor or unsatisfying rounds, by *mess*. The value of debate emerges from the clash of ideas.

Clash refers to the extent to which teams engage each other's arguments, rather than talk past each other. The two teams must agree on what the most central issues in the round are, understand these issues, and address them without letting extraneous issues interfere.[46] As one coach told a junior varsity debater: "The more directly you clash with the other side, the more likely you are to win" (field notes). When I asked about the best rounds of the year, debaters and coaches described rounds that had a high degree of consensus on the arguments:

> We lost by one point, and it was a very good, high-quality professional round with a lot of clash. Even the judge afterward said it was one of the best rounds she had seen all year. We all backed point for point on the flow. I dropped some disads, it was a loss, but other than that, the constructives went very well. . . . 1N matched our points, and I matched his points. (field notes)

> To me, [the quality] of a good debate is when on every single issue both sides have presented a fairly clearly defined position. . . . One of the things that really is a pet peeve of mine is when an affirmative speaker can give a speech . . . the negative gives a speech, and then the affirmative speaker comes back and merely repeats what they said the first time. It's like there was no intervening speaker. No clash. (interview)

It is now common for negative teams to attempt to win rounds by "spreading" their affirmative opponents: presenting as many arguments as they can in their constructive speeches in the hopes that their opponents may not answer one argument ("drop it"), leaving it on the flow for the judge to base the decision on. Negative teams have the advantage of being able to focus on selected affirmative arguments, while, in general, affirmative teams must respond to every negative argument. Some negative teams present a dozen different arguments with numerous subpoints, none well developed, but each an argument to which the affirmative team must respond. Many debaters understandably feel this strategy is unfair and "a scare tactic." In the process, the round becomes filled with arguments that are not fully developed, teams talk past each other, and the round becomes hard for judges (and opponents) to flow. While I do not claim that "spread" can never produce an aesthetic round, the assumption among most of my informants is that spread is intimately linked to mess:

> When you're in a round, and the idea is to make it a round that the judge can make an honest judgment on, meaning that every argument has been covered and is thoroughly argued, I think that spreading isn't a very good tactic. . . . It more or less leads to muddling the round. It's kind of ridiculous. Four points off their 3 points against every one of my points. You get 50 trillion points, and it gets muddled. (interview)

> Layton is the hardest team for me to watch. I always get upset watching them. When they're negative, they are coached to make a mess of everything. Just throw all this crap . . . because they always do that. I mean they just run oodles

of arguments that are awful. There's no evidence, they don't make sense, half of them contradict one another, the partners don't work together. They don't have complementary positions. They make such a mess of the round. They put so much crap out that the other team just can't deal with it. And so eventually they pull something out, and I was very angry because I had to vote for Layton, because they won some issue, and they pulled it across, and they explained why the issue mattered. . . . I was very angry, and I told them so at the end of the round. I just said, you know, "This is not the way to debate. . . . You win very ugly." (interview)

Often teams are faced with a huge array of brief ("blippy") arguments, lacking in substance, such as thirteen arguments against the ability of the plan to solve the problem, or a fourteen-point feminism disadvantage, or, in one round, twenty-seven claimed arguments. The affirmative team must attempt to impose some order. They may do this by stressing that the arguments lack links to their case (a frequently encountered weakness of brief arguments), lack brinks (indicating when the disadvantage might take effect), lack evidence, or lack analysis. Debaters often take these arguments and lump them together, providing a single, lengthier answer for a lot of small points, a procedure known as "clump and dump." Less effectively, they may ignore some points or claim that their partner will get to them—hoping that either their partner will or that the judge, being snowed under with the elaborate flowing that spreading involves, will forget that the points have never been addressed.

The point is that such strategies undercut the essential point of debate: confronting ideas—two teams presenting contrary arguments and, within the constraints of logic and evidence, determining which position represents the best or most effective policy. It is the aesthetics of rivalrous discourse that clash embraces and spread diminishes, and that when done well permits policy debate to be a thing of beauty.

Rebuttals and Storytelling

Although debate has moved from its oratorical moorings—speechifying is not a part of contemporary debate—it is hard to eliminate narrative. As students of discourse have argued, we think in narratives: concrete stories trump abstract claims.[47] All of the points and subpoints in the world cannot replace a clear and meaningful account.

In much of a round, storytelling has been replaced by arguing; the final rebuttals provide something of an exception to this change. In this brief period of time—four minutes during my research, now expanded to five—debaters are supposed to *explain* to judges why they deserve to win.

If not always narrative or storytelling in a formal sense, debaters must step back from the details of the previous hour and emphasize their important arguments. Rebuttals reveal tension between the demand to make points and to tell stories, between being specific and being global.[48] Indeed, part of the justification of the expansion of rebuttals to five minutes is, in the words of one coach, that it "would increase the storytelling ability," decreasing what is pejoratively labeled spewing (field notes). The second negative and second affirmative rebuttals cannot escape the need to address each of the issues that had been made previously (i.e., asking judges to "pull arguments across their flow"), as a dropped argument can easily mean a defeat. Thus, rebuttals do consist of a lot of brief claims about arguments, reading tag lines for evidence and extending the "two point" or the "five subpoint" and, as a consequence, can be tedious and confusing. While the better debaters are more effective at explaining, rather than telegraphing, much of the rebuttal is a reiteration or brief extension of previous claims.[49]

Still, the best debaters do something more in their rebuttals, described as "the most persuasive part of debate." They use this time to crystalize or weigh the issues that they wish the judge to consider in reaching a decision:

> A good 2NR will keep any judge awake. My strategy, especially when people drop stuff in the 1AR, is to tell a story about the position. Explain the argument, explain how it impacts the round, explain why it would be abusive to allow new answers, and mostly tell the judge why you win.[50]

> You set up all these arguments throughout the constructives and then [in] the rebuttals it's the job of the 2NR to get up and tie this all together. . . . You have to tie it all together in a package and deliver it to the judge. . . . You know, tell a story. At the end of the round you want to give this judge something to leave the room with. (interview)

The persuasive aspect of rebuttals is such that some judges, after having flowed the rest of the round, will put down their pens to listen carefully to these summaries, waiting for the debaters to explain what the round was about and how to vote. In particular, the introduction and the conclusion should have a rhetorical quality that sums up the debate. Even if these segments are sometimes only fifteen seconds, they attempt to present the big picture in a persuasive positive way. The second affirmative rebuttal speaker should reiterate the points made by his or her partner in the first affirmative speech in which the team's plan was presented. No matter how much debaters have become information processors, they cannot escape their role as homo narrans: storytellers by birthright.

Playing with Arguments

The practice of debate reminds us that this leisure world depends upon the strategic deployment of rival truth claims. Debate surely is a game—a contest—but in important ways it mirrors aspects of the world that are serious. The willingness of speakers to use whatever material they find to support a claim, in the absence of perfect knowledge, is congruent with the world of debate. Further, key institutional structures in American society—most notably the legal and political systems—are grounded in a fundamentally adversarial system, based on the belief that justice or policy will emerge from the clash of opposing ideas presented by intense defenders, as judged by neutral observers. High school debate represents an ideal type of system in which persuasion (the decision of the judge) emerges through conflict. In this, debate serves as a model for knowing in a world in which truth moves ever farther from those who purport to be its spokespersons.

Even argumentation is not simply the presentation of arguments. In this chapter I have not described the nuances of debate theory, an ever-changing set of perspectives on how arguments should be structured and how rounds should be organized. My concern is to explore the reality that arguments are given status and meaning apart from their formal content within this adolescent world, in which the arguments of collegians are given status by the fact that it is college students who are using them. Further, I note that arguments have aesthetic qualities: clash is beautiful, mess is ugly. Many arguments are grounded in the worlds of natural conversation, emphasizing quantification and dramatic example. Common sense, however much it may be sneered at in theory, is heavily present in practice. Stories have not been wholly eliminated by an emphasis on points and subpoints. The arguments that debaters use in a round reveal something about who they are, how they see themselves, and how others will see them. Claims making is not merely a cognitive domain, as scholars of argumentation increasingly recognize, but is a profoundly social endeavor.

Three

Evidence and the Creation of Truth

DEBATE, similar to other forms of persuasive discourse, involves truth claims: statements that attempt to describe the nature of reality.[1] One side presents a set of claims, and opponents dispute those claims. The affirmative advances a case and a plan, and their opponents argue that the case does not apply and that the plan would not work or would have undesirable side effects. How does one make one's view of reality stick? How can one convince an audience that claims about the world are justified? The key is "evidence."

Adults knowledgeable of policy formulation realize that evidence is critical to the arts of persuasion, but what are the implications of evidence for adolescent debaters? What is evidence, under what circumstances should it be used, and how should it be evaluated? While debaters distinguish between arguments and evidence, this division is not what it seems. Much evidence consists of nothing more than the opinions—arguments— of others, which have come to be published; much evidence is simply the blurbs of others that fit the claims that the speaker wishes to make. Even though evidence constitutes an essential building block of high school debate, evidence is distinct from truth, as it is, of course, in other forms of public argumentation. Rather than stating an opinion, a debater may find it is more persuasive to demonstrate that an expert or a large number of others hold that belief, providing one with implicit supporters.[2] The speaker becomes a conduit for the claims of others, and, as in much political or journalistic discourse, the speaker takes the role of an honest broker.

A piece of evidence—or a card, as it is sometimes known, because evidence once was typed or pasted on 3″ × 5″ or 4″ × 6″ file cards—contains three elements: a tag, a citation, and a text. The tag is a few words created by the debater that summarize the relevance of the evidence to the argument ("no support of systematic racism," "overcrowding decreasing," "drug legalization saves lives"). Not surprisingly, a strong tendency exists to overclaim what the evidence says, putting the best face on it. The citation describes where the evidence comes from. In Minnesota—and at the NFL national tournament—debaters had to provide full citations, with the name of the author, journal, date, and page numbers. In other venues, partial citations are legitimate since full citations are available if the judge or other team requests them, leading to a decreased likelihood of evidence challenges or "indicts," since the weakness of the source may be hidden. Sometimes citations are bolstered by qualifications, or "quals," which explain who the author is and why his or her truth claims should be trusted. Finally, and crucially, debaters present a selected quotation. The debater chooses the sentence or sentences that are most relevant to the case or argument. Typically, a first affirmative speaker presents approximately ten to fifteen pieces of evidence, although this varies as a function of the speed of the speaker, the length of the quotations, and the rhetorical preferences of debaters and coaches. Often debaters will use ellipsis in their reading, skipping words or sentences, an issue I will consider when discussing ethics.

Because evidence is so central to the practice of debate, and because adolescents have been little exposed to its use and collection, teachers lecture extensively on the types of evidence, techniques of research, and strategies for using evidence in context. Many students have not had the experience of conducting research (collecting evidence) in public or university libraries, or, nowadays, from computer databases, such as Lexis-Nexis. Research skills are key to both the educational value of debate and its competitive elements.[3]

Once gathered, evidence must be evaluated—a process of triage. Mrs. Miller explained to her class that evidence could be ranked on the following dimension: Experimental Evidence, Observational Evidence ("Statistics"), Opinion Evidence ("You have to look at why he said it. Is it his gut reaction? Is it just what he wishes would happen?"), and Layman Evidence ("the weakest because who cares").[4] The centrality of science and expert technocracy is evident from this ordering, which, if not universally held, would be seen as a reasonable division. The first categories are seen as "transparent" descriptions of empirical reality. Depending on the topic and the perspective of the debater and coach, evidence from government officials may be seen as more or less trustworthy; likewise, debaters are warned about evidence from "special-interest groups"—although the boundary between a "special-interest group" and an "objective source" is not always self-evident.

My Evidence

One way in which debaters judge peers is on the basis of their evidence. Just as professors may be evaluated by the number of books in their office and cooks by the quality of their knives, debaters are rated by the quality and (especially) the quantity of their evidence. Evidence is the material base of the activity. Among the reasons that summer institutes have become so influential is that they provide debaters with huge amounts of evidence by the beginning of the year, since participants at institutes share the information they have collected; students who have not attended an institute are at a competitive disadvantage, unless their team copies and shares evidence. Evidence is a status marker, carried in the large boxes, briefcases, or containers that are labeled "oxes," "bins," or "tubs":

> You go to a debate tournament and drag your huge tubs around the school to debate your rounds. (By the way, this is very uncomfortable since . . . I am wearing mile high heels and an uncomfortable wool Armani two sizes too small). Why? Because tubs . . . convey to a judge the psychological message that they [the debaters] are ready, prepared for anything, and completely cool and confident. . . . Humans being the primitive, carnal imbeciles that they are have a psychology that thinks "BIGGER IS BETTER!" . . . It shouldn't be that way, but hey . . . anything to give me an edge over those wackos that I'm up against.[5]

> One time in a round, the judge suggested that we just simply weigh tubs to determine a winner. . . . If you have two tiny tubs while the other team practically needs a U-haul, then it can definitely be intimidating.[6]

One tournament director jokingly told students that there was an elevator they could take, "if you have more evidence than you could ever use, and want to have it" (field notes). Laurie noted the status-enhancing qualities of having evidence by referring to a colleague from summer institute who had said that his goal was to leave with the most cards: he stayed up late at night cutting cards, and chose to stay and work while others played at the beach. Laurie noted drily, "That boy liked cards" (field notes). Colleagues on the Randall Park team described Doree as a "manic card cutter." Debate can be an activity well suited to compulsives.

The evidence that one collects becomes the collector's (modified by team policies on sharing). You own your evidence, and can refuse to lend it to others:

> Doree refuses to give Diane her briefcase of evidence for a round, stating, "You should work with the evidence you know. It won't help. You have most of my evidence anyway." I felt she didn't want her briefcase out of her possession. (field notes)

> Sean tells Ram that Ian has some of his evidence. Ram holds his head in mock dismay, clearly annoyed that his evidence is not in his file. In addition, Frank has forgotten to bring in evidence, having left it at home. Sean comments, only half-joking, "If he doesn't bring them in, I'll mash his head in." (field notes)

Given the psychological importance of evidence, the end of the debate year can be frustrating; all that work is now useless. While some material is included in a team's backfiles to be used in other years, the need for current evidence on new topics makes much previously cut evidence without value, particularly for those who are no longer active:

> A nondebater wanders into the debate room and, after looking at Doree's files, asks what she does with them after the season. Doree says that she will throw them out, adding, "It's kinda depressing." (field notes)

> Early in the year some Greenhaven junior varsity debaters were in the government documents room at the University of Minnesota library. A young man approached them and told them that he had coached at the Dartmouth Summer Institute the previous summer, and gave them a box of evidence. (field notes)

The work involved in creating these files is astounding and is very often tedious busywork, such as photocopying sheets and cutting out relevant passages. Some debaters spend evenings and weekends poring through sources at the library or downloading from the Internet or the Lexis-Nexis computerized document retrieval service. One noted:

> Cutting and pasting cards is a real bore. Sometimes it's just a royal pain. You have to suffer through the article, some are bad articles. You don't know if you're going to run across one where the only card is halfway through the fifty-page article or book. (interview)

Sharing evidence at summer institute is a significant help. With the need for evidence and the tediousness of obtaining it, an "industry" has developed around the edges of the debate world, providing evidence about the current topic.[7] Beginning before the 1960s, certain companies published "handbooks," collections of snippets from books and articles relating to a topic, structured to be cut up and placed on cards. Such ventures now provide summer support for recent graduates who are not ready to disengage entirely from the activity.[8] The reputation of handbooks is decidedly mixed, with some coaches and debaters hating them (one called them "evil, nasty things"), others seeing them as a necessary evil, and some, though rare in my research, finding them a positive good for the beginning debater. During my research, most Minnesota coaches did purchase a few handbooks for their teams, particularly to help initiate novices into the range of sources available and to help them begin to collect evidence. Because coaches worry about the accuracy or context of the quotations used, many encourage their students to check original sources and to use the handbooks primarily as an indicator of which articles are worth reading. Without an assured context, the evidence is questionable. Also, to rely on handbooks and other forms of "prefab" evidence diminishes the need to conduct research, part of the educational benefit of debate. While debaters do use handbook evidence, and consider some of high quality, handbook evidence has decidedly low status.[9]

Some debaters treasure this backstage work, tracking down, copying, and cutting evidence to put on cards or briefs, but for many the frontstage—the competitive rounds—is the joy for which the collection of data is a necessary evil to permit those peak experiences.

Cards, Evidence, and Briefs

Debaters are always searching for evidence of high quality. When they collect that evidence, they place it on cards, where it takes on a life of its own. "Evidence"—the statements and beliefs of experts—becomes "cards"—strategic claims that become part of the game, as their original context is put aside. At Randall Park, Mrs. Miller continually reminded her students that they were searching for "evidence," not "cards," an argument that she often lost, as references to cards were at least as common as those to evidence. Evidence is seen as something that is real and true, whereas cards, which *contain* evidence, are part of the game. As Mrs. Miller emphasized, "Cards don't prove anything, evidence proves things." Depicting reality should be the goal, not merely finding a claim that accords with one's strategy. It is evidence that is meaningful analysis:

> Doree refers to some material in her briefcase: "I have a wonderful card in my briefcase . . . uh, piece of evidence." On another occasion, Don, Randall Park's assistant coach, jokes: "I heard a couple of cards over the weekend. They don't deserve the word evidence." At one point Mrs. Miller asks Doree: "Was it a piece of evidence or just a card?" (field notes)

A tension exists between playing a game and attempting to get at the truth through the presentation of evidence.

A related issue is the relationship between cards and briefs. A brief is a sheet of paper with pieces of evidence—"cards"—connected through analysis that constitutes an argument. During my research, teams in Minnesota were moving from primary reliance on cards to reliance on briefs. Some regions (e.g., Nebraska) had moved earlier to briefs, while other regions (e.g., New Jersey) still relied on cards. The card files that were so characteristic of debaters during the late 1960s have been replaced by boxes that accommodate standard-size typing paper. The change is not merely aesthetic, but speaks to changing orientations to debate. The advantage of cards is that they are flexible. One creates an argument as one listens to one's opponents and thinks about their arguments, then selects those pieces of evidence (cards) that have the most relevant information. In contrast, briefs are more sophisticated as argumentation devices and may be more readable, as they enable the debater to rely less on spontaneous speech. When one is facing generic arguments, generic counterarguments may be desirable. However, it is difficult to revise a brief with new evidence or reshape a brief in the midst of a round. The best debaters are able to make these changes, but generally briefs decrease the flexibility to make good arguments. If the briefs are created prior to the round, briefs can potentially change every argument into a generic argument, even though debaters still must choose those briefs with the most relevant arguments.

The Perfect Card

The search for the "perfect card" is the Holy Grail of debate. Debaters look for evidence that will make a "kick-ass," "hot," or "nasty" card. Cards that are too good to be false. A journalist describes a summer institute by observing that "students . . . fan out daily across campus and city in search of the definitive statistic, the perfect evidence card."[10] Debaters are instructed that when they hear a powerful piece of evidence in a round, they must obtain the citation from the other team, so they can check it out. These specific and powerful claims can make or break a team:

> Brian says of Philip's Minnesota Sentencing Guidelines case that has been losing more than it wins, "They don't have the magic card that will work everywhere. Iris [an assistant coach] likes it so much, she can't understand why it's losing. It doesn't have a magic card." (field notes)

Magic cards make a point in a strong and unambiguous way, with none of the wishy-washiness to which academics are so prone. In a society as diverse as ours, a wide array of claims exist:

> "When I suggest that there is probably no evidence on a topic," Don jokes, "there's a card that says everything. You should know that. I learned that at the institute at Michigan when a kid came up with a card that said preventing nuclear war will be preventive medicine for the elderly." (field notes)

> Barry has a card, quoting a "person off the street." He notes, "He's just a schmuck off the street, but it's evidence. It's written. It's layman's evidence, but it's written." (field notes)

Some cards are "famous," such as one with a quotation from writer Jonathan Schell that suggests that any risk of nuclear war is potentially so catastrophic that it should be the central factor in making policy; or a card, from a book, *Christianity and Crisis*, written by Gary Macy, that suggests that nuclear war might not be so bad:

> Despite the multi-faceted appeal of a nuclear war, one must of course anticipate objections. The one that is most passionately voiced is that millions upon millions of people will die. While at first glance this appears to be a most compelling argument, upon closer inspection its force disappears, as it were, in a cloud of smoke. After all, most people don't know millions of other people, and in their hearts don't really care if millions die. Millions have died in the past. Millions will die in the future.[11]

Desired cards will not be simply "blurbs" or "blippy"—brief snatches of commonplace opinion with no analysis or empirical justification. Evidence should be recent (published within the last two or three years) and should come from credible sources. A coach notes:

> I look for a statement of opinion and a good reason behind that opinion. So if it's just a one-line statement of opinion, I don't like it. If it's a statement of opinion, then I look for the date. I look for the source. You know, the source is very important. What are the qualifications of the source? Who's the person saying this? (interview)

Aesthetic preferences are evident, as some prefer longer cards with more extensive reasoning and the ability to tell a story, while others suggest that many longer texts (some over a minute in reading time) may be redundant and may be no more effective than short, punchier evidence. Given the trade-off between the length of a card and the amount of evidence one can fit into a constructive argument or rebuttal, there is no single answer to the best length for a quotation. Some debaters prefer to use many cards from a single source, keeping argumentation consistent, while others conclude that using multiple sources suggests that many people hold the same perspective.

The recency of evidence matters. For social scientists who often cite publications decades old, this fascination with recent material may seem curious. Yet, in determining policy, the age of the information may matter. Evidence that was published more than three years previously is questioned:

> Don comments in September 1989 that they shouldn't use evidence [that occurred] before 1986. Brian, a varsity debater, adds, "It looks better to say 1989 than 1987." Don jokes to Brian about a citation of 1979 for a card, "Read that really fast." (field notes)

> Gideon Hafferty describes a debate that hinged on two pieces of evidence. The debate occurred on Saturday, and one piece of evidence was from the Sunday

paper (dated the following day). The second piece of evidence was from the next issue of *Time* magazine, dated the following Monday. The judge considered the *Time* magazine article a postdate, even though, because of the publishing deadline, it had surely been written before the newspaper article. Gideon notes, "It all depends on what's on the card." (field notes)

These instances suggest that judges evaluate reality as a moving sequence of events, with the latest snapshots the truest, no matter the model of the camera.

The Credibility of Sources

How should we weigh a truth claim? In conversation, the credibility of the source plays an essential role.[12] Debaters hoping to discover the "perfect card" may find themselves with a dilemma: those sources who are most extreme, less given to making nuanced pronouncements, may be those with less credibility. As one coach notes, "Sometimes I think it's scary that the 'best' evidence is often from idiots."[13] Which is to be preferred: a killer quotation from a kooky source or a balanced quotation from a recognized expert? The temptation for the former is hard to resist. Given the amount of information in a round, and given the reality that debaters do not have "indicts" on any but a few critical sources, this contributes to a culture in which one source tends to be as good as another.

Even the judge cannot provide a break on this use of source material, as judges typically believe that they should not intervene in a round. One judge claimed with regard to the evaluation of Nazi evidence, "I agree that Hitler is about the most deplorable human being to ever live, but I think that my moral judgments should not enter the round. This is for the debaters to settle."[14]

In practice, few pieces of evidence are indicted in the round over the qualification of the source, except for a few controversial individuals or organizations. As one debater noted, "It's getting less important. . . . I don't think people go for that quite as much any more. . . . Most of the sources the teams use they keep to themselves. A lot of the other teams don't have them, so they can't do much about it" (interview). A few individuals are known for "writing blurb," publishing material that debaters can use. In the topic on prison overcrowding, debaters frequently quoted criminologists Alfred Blumstein, James Inciardi, John DeIulio, and Jerome Skolnick, and occasionally my former colleagues David Ward and Dean Rojek. Particularly notable as a blurb writer was Ethan Nadelman, a Princeton scholar who was a major source for those with drug legalization cases. Nadelman was the butt of many irreverent jokes by these teens:

> The Randall Park team jokes about Nadelman being a "schmuck." Gordon adds, "This guy is a putz. . . . Ethan Nadelman likes to write evidence for debates" [noting that he was cited in the Latin America topic and the previous criminal justice topic]. Brian comments, "He likes to write blurb." To which Doree comments, "You like to read it." (field notes)

Nadelman writes dramatic comments that serve well in rounds; yet, they are so dramatic that he is tarred by his reputation, and student debaters use other evidence suggesting that Nadelman is a biased and misleading source.

Some sources are condemned for their political leanings. In my research, the Cato Institute, the libertarian think tank, was often indicted, whereas the Brookings Institute was not:

> Gordon, an assistant coach for Randall Park [and not a libertarian] comments: "Evidence is only as good as the people who said it, and who back it up. Flakes [he refers particularly to Cato's David Boaz] come cheap. Even when they do research, they do it to support their perspective. You can always tweak your statistics." Brian comments about more drug legalization evidence from the Cato Institute: "Do you want to read more flake ev? . . . We've got to find guys who aren't schmucks." Later, Mrs. Miller finds evidence on drug legalization, and comments, "This is from *The New Republic*. It's certainly better than the Cato Institute. . . . What you're looking for is good, objective, middle-of-the-road information that is based on research." Don suggests to Brian that when he does cite Boaz, he should refer to him as a "policy analyst," rather than as the vice president of the Cato Institute. (field notes)

The other major indictable source—a particular bête noire of Mrs. Miller's (and of other Minnesota coaches)—was Charles Colson, the former Nixon aide who discovered Christ in prison and who wrote passionately about the need for prison reform. She insisted that the team indict Colson as a convicted felon whenever they could:

> [The source is] the most important thing you have. If you base a case on Charles Colson, I think you're not being fair to yourself or to anyone else. (interview)

> In a round between Layton and Dover Heights, the Dover team quoted Colson. The Layton debater commented, "Colson was Nixon's adviser. He went to prison. He's not a very good source." (field notes)

Of course, what constitutes a credible source is a social construction: a function of how one views reality. Competitive policy debate in Nazi Germany or Soviet Russia (grotesque images) would rate source credibility differently than would American students in the late twentieth century. Indeed, sources rise and fall in public estimation. Should we prefer *World Marxist Review* or *Foreign Affairs*, *Vigilante Magazine* or the newsletter of Handgun Control? While some measure of consensus develops in any organized social system, these matters are tied to ideological preferences, and are linked to how we understand the world—empirically, and in terms of value choices. Such choices are inevitable, and even if judges prefer not to intervene, their standards for indictment may vary for different types of evidence. (How great an effort would one need to indict material from the KKK as opposed to the NAACP?) Thus, source credibility can be made an issue by debaters as well as implicitly influence the decisions of judges who are prone to vote for those claims that they find reasonable.

Evidence in Practice

Evidence, of course, does not speak for itself. Debaters set it in context within the round, and then describe its significance. At the same time, debaters cannot claim what they wish; they need evidence to allow them to make claims—under the assumption that "bad cards are better than no cards" (field notes). National championship coach Esther Kalenbach noted that "evidence is *anything* that might lead the audience to believe." Her point is that the presence of evidence to support a claim is in practice more important that the quality of that evidence.[15] Having some evidence is crucial, as personal claims are problematic:

> Sean and Barry are talking about how many people will be released from prison under some plan. Barry says that he can easily figure out the number, but Sean reminds him, "It doesn't matter if you can figure it out. Do you have any evidence?" (field notes)

> Frank argues that if one releases prisoners, the prison will immediately refill, keeping overcrowding constant. His opponent from Dover Heights points out: "You can't read one sentence somewhere in a card that says it will refill. . . . Can you read me one sentence that says that? . . . We want a card that says if you release all nonviolent [prisoners], it will all be refilled. . . . [You] never gave us a specific card that said that it would all refill." (field notes)

In practice, one piece of evidence suffices. Rarely do debaters use more than one piece of evidence per point.[16] However, reading cards is rarely sufficient: they need to be situated and interpreted; thus, the importance of having a tag that clues in the judges and other debaters to its significance:

> Doree says to the Randall Park novices, "Evidence doesn't say anything until you say what it says. You should make your evidence say what you want it to say. Here, you say here is the evidence. Here is what it says." (field notes)

Evidence waits to be interpreted, in contrast to the view often held by novices and junior varsity debaters that makes the card the reality.

In practice, in the hands of many debaters, evidence becomes an opportunity to say, "I told you so." While real analysis is possible, often interpretation seems more like that of the salesman who insists how wonderful his product is, assuming that the audience must know why the claim makes sense:

> Kiki, of Concord, continually emphasizes the value of her evidence: "This is a key card in the round. . . . That's going to be a key card. . . . This is another good card . . . a very good card." (field notes)

Even if the description of particular pieces of evidence is not all that could be asked for, the totemic quality of the evidence is impressive. Without evidence, policy debate would hardly be possible. The intersection of evidence and argument makes debate a compelling arena for serious policy education and for bizarre allegations.

Ethical Quandaries

Because of the centrality of evidence, the temptation to use material improperly is great. The push for the perfect card is hard to resist, even if one has to reshape that evidence. Yet, because one of the justifications of debate is its ability to teach adolescents how to conduct and apply research properly, ethical charges are taken seriously, and in severe cases can lead to disqualification of a team from a tournament or revocation of NFL membership. In this section I examine ethical problems that range from very serious and rare to understandable and expected. Adolescents are no angels when in pursuit of the prize of competitive victory. Specifically, I examine the fabricating of evidence, the taking of evidence out of context, overclaiming the significance of evidence, and stealing and misfiling evidence in libraries. While few have actually fabricated evidence, it is the rare debater who has never overclaimed a card. Like so many arenas of deviance, if one locked up everyone who has violated a moral prescription, the prisons of debate would be overcrowded.

Fabricating Evidence

One of the years that I was debating in the 1960s, the topic involved foreign aid. As it happened, the family of a classmate had a close friendship with General Somoza, then the dictator of Nicaragua. We used to joke that if we ever needed a quotation from the General, we could simply make it up, and then ask our friend to have Somoza say it. Sure, he hadn't said it yet, but he would if asked. Such is the lot of debaters, knowing what is needed, but not having the evidence to make the claim. Throughout my research, my friends (and later, my son) would ask that I create and publish evidence for them. It is reported that when Bob Shrum was a speech writer for New York mayor John Lindsey he inserted quotes in Lindsey's speeches that a friend could use as evidence for his collegiate team.[17] In other instances, debaters wonder about the legitimacy of using evidence that "moms and dads" have published, or even, given the range of publication outlets, those put out on the Internet, or whether they can publish material themselves (such as letters to local newspapers) that they can use in rounds.[18]

For many, nothing can be more destructive of the ideals of debate than fabricating evidence. As one coach said:

> There are certain practices regarded as unethical . . . by the larger debate community, period. If there is some Heideggerian or anthropological argument for forging all your evidence as ethical behavior, I'd like to hear it. (No, wait! I would *not* like to hear it.) Judges, especially in high school tournaments, are supposed to be educators. Tournaments are an extension of school.[19]

This being debate, some suggest that forging evidence can be a reason to reject a team *only* if the other team makes an argument that the violation is a "voting issue."[20] Significantly, the coach quoted above indicated that if the other team did not bring up the violation, he might not intervene in the round and might not vote against the fabricating team, although he claimed that he would raise the issue in other ways. Even something as serious as forging evidence might not cost a team a round if the issue was not raised.

Claims of "forged evidence" are significant:

> In a previous evidence dispute with a college in New England, I had two different libraries produce letters saying they could not verify that the source in question existed. I also learned that the university an author was supposedly affiliated with had no records of him ever teaching there. These documents were used in a round, demanding that the team prove that the evidence existed. When they could not, the judges voted for us. Continuing lack of cooperation

by the team led me to file a complaint with their dean, who then investigated and suspended the program.[21]

Nationals 1987, the team from ———— was in the semis and they were using a study that never was written. They had written all the evidence themselves. They were caught and they were kicked out. . . . Another team went out and tried to find it [the evidence], and they couldn't find it, and then they started calling all over the country, trying to find it. . . . And then they finally [tried to call] the so-called publication, and the publication didn't even exist. So they brought it to the tournament committee and said this is all fabricated. (interview)

In contrast, claims of forgery can be made inaccurately, maliciously or not:

Tylor Flatto [a coach at a rival school] did not like one of the kids on my top team for whatever reason, I don't know. And so he kind of started this rumor along with his kids that my kids were making up evidence, which was completely unfounded. . . . Once you're challenged on something like that, it changes your reputation. And word got around. (interview)

At nationals . . . summer before my senior year, a team in the tenth round was evidence-challenged, and they had fourteen pieces of evidence that were challenged in the round, and the negative team rested on the entire evidence challenge as the debate, and the students had 12 hours to find the original sources, or at least to show them where they existed. They were only able to find nine. . . . The NFL board made the decision of voting for the affirmative, because they felt that they had shown good faith. (interview)

Given the reality that debaters base their reputations on the evidence collected by partners, teammates, colleagues on other teams and at institutes, and handbook compilers, the threats to one's identity are real:

My junior year, Bert [her partner], I was totally convinced, had made up three or four pieces of evidence. They were just too good to be true, and as a partner, that's really hard to run that kind of evidence, if you just think maybe . . . It's not just his reputation he's putting on the line, it's your reputation, and I went back and looked through things. . . . All but one time I found it [the evidence]. (interview)

In the National Forensic League, the *team* is responsible for the validity of all the evidence they read in a debate. No matter its source, they vouch for it.

In practice, debaters sometimes make up minor pieces of information in the round. One debater admitted to me that he would occasionally make up a page number if the citation lacked that information:

"Everyone I think has done that once or twice. You can't quite read it or something. You know its there . . . you just go, like, 'page 63,' or something" (interview). Or:

> Brian is joking about his partner, Doree. In one round she was reading some evidence and noticed that there was no citation on the card: "She had to make up a citation." Mrs. Miller jokes: "You have to make up a cite that nobody has heard of. You don't want them to say, 'Oh, I know that article; it doesn't say that.'" (field notes)

Despite the humor, fabricating evidence, despite its lure, could undermine the activity, just as it does in scientific and journalistic communities. If forgery catches on, each card will be perfect, and policy analysis will become another genre of fiction.

Shaping Context

In the realm of art forgery, forgers often do not feel the need to create the entire work, but simply to alter those elements that make the object more salable: to massage the object to make it conform to what one wishes it meant. What is most important: the words or the meaning of the author? Given that the whole text will not be read, what is one's responsibility to an author's intention? Consider the following two cards, provided as a public service for debaters:

> Because of their increased sensitivity to unintended policy implications learned through high school debate, former debaters in positions of public trust are substantially less likely to plunge the United States into actions that could lead to nuclear war than are those who have never participated in this activity.

> Because of their openness to expressing a range of amoral positions and their desire to win at any cost learned through high school debate, former debaters in positions of public trust are substantially more likely to plunge the United States into actions that could lead to nuclear war than are those who have never participated in this activity.

I am the author of both of these quotations. Is it fair for debaters to use one or the other as part of their cases or kritiks of other cases? Would using one of these quotations be quoting me out of context? Both are strongly worded and have some measure of plausible analysis. What was my intention? Perhaps I only mean one, and the second (or is it the first?) is a joke. Fortunately, the material is here—assuming that both teams read this book!—to indict whichever card is run.

On one occasion, a team read a quotation that claimed that shoe production empirically destroys society. The author was a D. Adams in

T.R.A.T.E.O.T.U.: Douglas Adams in his fantasy satire, *The Restaurant at the End of the Universe.*[22] Aside from the overly cute and deceptive attempt to get away with this "evidence," if the full citation was given, without the explicit claim that this was satiric fiction, should opponents reasonably be required to know that this claim does not reflect the author's serious opinion? Is fiction out of bounds? If so, what does that do to the speeches of certain politicians?

Eliminating or changing a word can alter the value of the evidence substantially. Like the plastic surgeon, a nip and a tuck here and there can increase attractiveness, or so it seems—a process that makes one's argument "slimy," as coaches note:

> I think even really good teams will tend to edit evidence in such a manner as to seriously put in question whether or not the intent has been altered. . . . Taking part of a sentence, one paragraph and the last half of the sentence from another paragraph, putting them together as one sentence, and saying this author said this. They're the exact words. They meet the intent, but really when you start taking parts of sentences from different paragraphs and putting them together, even if you put the ellipses in, is that really legitimate? (interview)

Ellipses are an essential part of quotation, a reality that is recognized by reporters and sociologists. Yet, it is one that is evident only in *written* discourse, not in speech. In the quotations I report, some alterations occur through my errors as a transcriber, but others occur because I desire to tidy up the quotations, eliminating false starts and stumbles, and making the material more concise. Debaters can reasonably do the same. The use of ellipsis is a legitimate strategy in taming evidence.[23] However, there is an assumption that one will remain "true" to the author's intention, even if intentions are difficult for outsiders to know. Consider the following sentence: "Drug legalization will not be a very good policy." The debater who decided to strike the word "very" would probably be considered ethical; the debater who decided to strike the word "not" would surely be considered unethical. The Randall Park team discussed whether it was ethical to delete the phrase "I think that" from a card, not changing the argument, but only its certainty (field notes). Would it be legitimate to cut the word "conservative" from the line: "Conservative analysts believe that prisons should be privatized." Suppose the word was "right-wing," "numerous," "intelligent," or "foolish"? Even intonation matters. Consider the speaker who emphasizes "No. Money *should* be used to support this program" versus one who says "*No* money should be used to support this program." Since we do not speak punctuation marks, both readers can claim to have spoken the same evidence. Finally, is it fair to take a legitimately affirmative claim from a writer who supports the negative, as with a writer who claims: "While *it is true that legalizing drugs would reduce drive-by shootings*, the other costs would outweigh this policy." Can a team legitimately use the italicized passage without the rest of the sentence? Academics are very good (or bad?) at presenting every side of an argument: thus, the search for the one-armed economist who never adds, "but on the other hand."

Cutting is more legitimate than adding. Adding either a "very" or, especially, a "not" is considered out of bounds, even if the temptation is real:

> Brian finds a card that refers to "prison growth rate." Don says that he wishes it said "prison admission growth rate." Brian jokes, "Why don't we add that word in there?" Don jokes, "In the state tournament? They'd really like that." Brian adds, "Just like last year." (field notes)

Don and Brian are referring to an incident in which the team that won the state tournament on the elderly topic had read some evidence from the *New England Journal of Medicine* with words inserted that made the quotation specifically about the elderly. Eventually, the deception was uncovered and the team was soundly beaten at the NFL qualifiers, with teams ready to challenge the evidence. The card was not a forgery, but the team had added a bracketed comment that was not in the text itself.

Through all this, the question emerges as to what the responsibility is of the debater to the author, and through that answer what the responsibility is to the audience. Minnesota judges (and debaters) seemed more willing to countenance intervention by judges than by others; but the question remains that if someone does not realize that his pocket is being picked, do witnesses have a moral obligation to take action?

Overclaiming

When debaters present evidence, they "tag" it. They provide a brief synopsis of the implications of the evidence, as speakers often do in natural conversations as well. We tell what we are going to say. These descriptions are supposed to be a fair representation of the quotation, but often they are not. While slimy, these overtags are expected, and few debaters can claim that they have never engaged in the practice. Overclaiming or stretching is part of making a persuasive case. As the tag is not part of the evidence, debaters are not quite lying, as much as they are engaging in rhetorical exaggeration. If caught, they are likely to lose points, but they will not be disqualified, as in the case of fabricating evidence, although there are implicit limits. Overclaiming evidence is deviance that is winked at by debaters and coaches:

> I think they'll slant [evidence] enough to get their point across. . . . There's an example that a team ran against us that 95 percent of the prisoners were deemed nonviolent. That's what they said the card said. But if you looked at the

card, it said 95 percent were nonviolent or have been convicted of a nonviolent crime. But it didn't say that 95 percent were actually nonviolent. (interview)

You always want to have a good tag, because that's what the judges will remember. They'll remember your tag, rather than your evidence. And so you want to have a good punch with your tag and that tends to blow it up . . . and I think that is done just about by everyone, but that's the affirmative's job, and it's the negative's job to point out that they've blown it up. (interview)

Overclaiming is seen as a "tactic" in the round, rather than a lie, and it is then up to the opposing team to point it out while making their own arguments with their own overclaimed tags. Overclaiming evidence straddles ethical violation and tactical consideration.

Taking Evidence

The actual theft of evidence is a serious matter. Evidence is owned by debaters and is something to which they feel attached. The trust within the community, coupled with the weight of tubs of evidence, is such that debaters will, as a matter of course, leave their tubs of evidence unguarded in the hallways of tournaments between rounds, even overnight. Sadly, stealing evidence, while not common, is not unknown:

The stealing of evidence went on a little bit when I was debating. [Stealing?] I've never heard of that lately, but that used to happen a lot. We used to lock our briefcases because people would steal evidence all the time. (interview)

At one tournament, one team's briefcase disappeared, although it was found before the next round, clearly moved by someone. Coaches reminisced about stolen briefcases. One year three briefcases were stolen and were found only after a tournament. At a college tournament a team's van, with all of its evidence, was stolen, and was discovered with the files ransacked. (field notes)

While debaters are not all angelic, few steal or "misplace" the evidence of others. That clearly transcends moral boundaries. More common is the misshelving of library materials; such deviance is less condemned, perhaps because those materials do not truly belong to others (except the library, but institutions don't count):

Games are played at the library. Stuff disappears. It's misshelved. Microfiche is misfiled at Wilson [the main library of the University of Minnesota], so we find ourselves looking for alternative places to do research, because Wilson is usually decimated by the time school starts in the fall, unfortunately. And that is unethical, and it is done intentionally by some schools. (interview)

In December, Don says that he found an article on elderly prisoners from November 1, 1989. He says, apparently seriously, "We have it. No one else is

going to have it." Brian says seriously, "Don lost it." Don adds, "In the mari-
time records. We'll bring it back in a little while. Like the middle of February."
(field notes)

This is bolstered by a joking culture, suggesting hiding all of the central
articles for one's case. These actions, while not precisely criminal, remind
us of the ethical somersaults of which teenagers are capable when their
own personal interests conflict with ethical expectations that they have
learned as responsible citizens. Misplacing articles is a "natural and legitimate" mistake, and so, even if it is purposeful, it can still be justified as
accidental, protecting oneself from the implications of one's deviance.
Teenagers define their actions as part of a child's game, even when that
game has the effects of inconveniencing adults conducting serious research. In debate, evidence and cards are the coin of the realm, and, like
many coins, they are subject to the scams of counterfeiters, con artists,
and thieves.

Topics of Interest

Writing a book about policy debate involves a moving target. Not only
does debate theory evolve over time, but each year—with its own topic
area—is different from the previous year. Domestic topics differ from
foreign ones; narrow topics provide different challenges than broad ones.
The National Federation of State High School Associations, and its division on Interscholastic Speech and Debate, organizes the choice of the
annual topic, selecting possible topics and distributing a ballot. Topics
rotate, with an international topic chosen every third year or so. A year
ahead, a set of position papers are submitted, and from them several topic
areas are chosen. Eventually the final topic area is selected (for 1997–
1998, the choices were discrimination and renewable energy: the latter
was selected; for 1990–1991, the choices were the Middle East, Pacific
Rim trade, and space exploration: the last was selected).[24] During my
research, coaches from each state had a vote, plus a vote each from the
National Forensic League and the National Catholic Forensic League.
Finally, the specific resolution is written. When it is announced, debaters,
being the contrarians that they are, conclude that the topic and resolution
are poor choices. Complaints about the prison overcrowding topic re-
volved around its narrowness, claims that few cared about the comfort of
prisoners, and the fact that the resolution stated what the "benefit" had
to be (to reduce overcrowding in prisons and jails). Given the topic and
the resolution, the balance of affirmative and negative victories shift. In
Minnesota, in debating the prison overcrowding topic, negative teams

won as many as 75 percent of the rounds, because of the difficulties of proving that the problem was inherent, harmful, and significant and that the plan could solve the problem in the face of disadvantages.[25]

Each topic area is associated with both explicit and implicit political attitudes. The topic of prison overcrowding forced debaters to consider their attitudes about crime and criminals, shortly after the political usage in the 1988 election of the crimes committed by Willie Horton on a prison furlough. As debaters are predominantly upper-middle-class, well-behaved, suburban children, few had any significant contact with the criminal justice system. When responding to my interview questions, students were articulate and adept at providing thoughtful and politically correct responses, even if they lacked experience. For example, of the eight students who responded, seven believed personally that the federal government should reduce overcrowding in prisons and jails (eight of eleven coaches agreed). In general, students opposed capital punishment, had mixed feelings about drug legalization, and felt that crime was caused by social forces, particularly discrimination and poverty. When speaking in a relaxed interview setting, they held to the belief that "criminals" were like them:

> In general, I'd say criminals are people who haven't really had a chance to be successful in a legal sort of way. . . . Crime is still the only way to get out of whatever situation they are in, unless they're like some high white-collared criminal. . . . I don't think anybody is bad; maybe things that they do are bad. . . . You can't just toss them aside and forget about them. (interview)

> [Many are] people who are truly victims of society. . . . I think they're just people like us that got caught. (interview)

Listening to debate rounds, one gains a different impression. Perhaps debaters misstate themselves in the rush of talk, perhaps they are letting their true feelings out, or perhaps debate is simply role playing, but there is a hard edge to much discussion of crime and of criminals in debate rounds: forget recidivism, poverty, or people like us.

For instance, one debater who had claimed that criminals were like her, attacked a case suggesting that sentencing guidelines be used. She commented: "Just because a person is in jail because of drugs, that may be the actual crime he was convicted of, but maybe he's a Mafia figure who has killed a lot of people." With regard to Cuban Mariel prisoners, she noted: "Many of these [Cuban boatlift] criminals are bad people. They're horrible" (field notes). Another, quoted above, commented about a case to place female prisoners who were mothers in a halfway house, because they could be injured in prison: "So the women get hurt, so what? Aren't they criminals? . . . They could shoot each other for all we care." He suggests later, "Criminality is largely genetic anyway" (field notes).

There is a harshness in these claims that belie the kindly judgments that are evident in interviews. While recognizing that debaters have a case to make, these claims—and they are not uncommon in debate rounds—suggest a lack of sympathy, not technically necessary given the arguments. What are their true beliefs? First, these are adolescents whose views are being shaped as they mature. They have the judgmental perspective of children—those dogmatic tools that have served them well at earlier points of development—while they are acquiring the nuanced views of many policymakers (although, of course, the severe assessment of criminal character is by no means unique to adolescent debaters). Second, the interview provides a setting where, in speaking to a college professor, they might reasonably draw upon those views that they believe to be enlightened and suitable for adult discourse. As social psychological research suggests, we do not have permanent attitudes, but those attitudes that we express are shaped by the situations in which they occur.

Making a Case

The affirmative team has a responsibility to present a case that the resolution needs to be affirmed and then to present a specific plan to achieve this goal. While there are many ways in which cases are structured, each depends on a logical structure of interconnected arguments. Minnesota debate, during my research, relied in considerable measure on the "stock issues" paradigm, at least in creating affirmative cases. Each affirmative team argued that prison overcrowding is an inherent problem under the status quo that is unlikely to change, that it is significant and harmful, and that the plan presented is topical (falls under the resolution) and has solvency (substantially mitigates the problem). The plan consists of a set of planks that describes the proposed policy and its funding mechanism. In the 1989–1990 topic: *Resolved: That the federal government should adopt a nationwide policy to decrease overcrowding in prisons and jails in the United States*, the affirmative plan had to be a policy of the federal government, it had to be nationwide, it had to decrease overcrowding, it had to apply to prisons and jails, and it had to apply in the United States. Debate depends on the concept of *fiat*: the assumption that any plan (or counterplan) can be implemented, and that the apparent opposition of Congress or the Supreme Court will not block the policy. Many plans that are proposed could never be implemented in reality. Indeed, some suggest that the existence of "fiat," while necessary for permitting the discussion of a range of plans, may, in fact, blind debaters to the reality of policymaking, which involves complex negotiations and compromise. The vast majority of plans are impossible to imagine being enacted because of the reality of the political process that fiat obscures. Thus, while debate reveals some aspects of policy, it obscures others.[26]

Each word in the resolution is subject to definition. A team could suggest that the federal government referred to the President, Congress, the courts, or a federal agency. Overcrowding needs to be defined in light of numbers in the system, prison capacity, or number of prisoners per cell. The terms prisons and jails need to be defined, as do decrease, nationwide, policy, and the United States. However, it is not only the large words that can become issues. One team ran an argument (with "evidence") that the "and" in "prisons and jails" referred to "or." Would a prison built offshore be "in" the United States? The word "to" is often at issue: does it refer to "intent," as in "in order to"? Or does it refer to the outcome of a policy, whether intended or not? If "to" refers to intent, does it matter if the policy actually decreases prison overcrowding, if the intent was present and if other benefits result? In practice, few words are explicitly defined, but each is subject to arguments and evidence. As a result, resolution writers must be careful in their choice of wording, avoiding the word America (which could refer to the Western Hemisphere rather than just the United States) or choosing carefully between "policy" or "program." Debaters can dispute anything, and words are part of that anything. This is a world in which legitimate conflict can exist over what "is" is, suggesting how much we take for granted.

As noted, plans are structured in various ways. The drug rehabilitation case of Lakes Academy, a traditional case that the team was successful with during the 1989–90 season and at the national tournament, involves an introduction, a contention about the inherency (barriers to change) of the status quo, the plan, a second contention about the significance of the overcrowding under the status quo, a third contention about the harms of this overcrowding, both to prisoners and the general public through early release programs, and a fourth contention that the plan solves the problems. In this eight-minute, five-single-spaced-page argument, twelve pieces of evidence were presented from such sources as *Crime and Delinquency*, the *New York Times*, the *Bureau of Justice Statistics Bulletin*, the court report of *Palmigiano* vs. *Garrahy*, and *USA Today*. With the exception of one piece of evidence from 1984, all sources were published from 1986 through 1989.

The case begins and ends rhetorically:

> Imagine that a family member was diagnosed as having cancer. Would you lock him in a prison cell and deny him access to medical care? Certainly not. Most likely, you'd send him to a hospital where doctors would provide the best

treatment possible. Unfortunately, the current penalty for chemical dependency is incarceration. This unjustified denial of treatment manifests itself in increasing rates of drug-related crime, which can easily be prevented by curing the disorder which perpetuates them. Even more distressing is the subjection of these diseased individuals to the inhumane conditions of overcrowded correctional facilities. Because the crisis in our criminal justice system cannot be remedied until we start treating drug abuse as a disease, Dina and I firmly advocate the adoption of this year's resolution: THAT THE FEDERAL GOVERNMENT SHOULD ADOPT A NATIONWIDE POLICY TO DECREASE OVERCROWDING IN PRISONS AND JAILS IN THE UNITED STATES.

Indisputably, drug addiction is one of the most pressing issues our nation must face. The time has come to stop incarcerating sick people, and to provide these victims of drug addiction with the treatment they deserve and require. By confronting the problem at its root, crime, violence, and the pernicious overcrowding in our prisons and jails can be reduced. Please affirm the resolution.

Teams work hard on creating dramatic openings and closings that capture the attention of judges, and they typically read these sections in a slower and clearer voice than the rest. In between these rhetorical flourishes is the heart of the case, but even here the arguments are clearly written. Were it not for the speed at which they were presented, most mainstream cases that present "reasonable" policies would impress adult audiences.

The plan provides for a specification of the case, although plans are often sketchily presented. In the case of Lakes Academy, they presented a two-plank plan:

PLANK ONE: LOGISTICS

A. ADMINISTRATION: A 7-MEMBER BOARD, endowed with all necessary information, trained staff, land acquisition, and funding, shall be established and oversee implementation of the plan mandates.

B. FUNDING: AN OPTIMAL MIX of the following: nonessential military cuts, a two-percent tax on alcohol and cigarettes, and other revenue-enhancing measures.

C. ENFORCEMENT: ANY AND ALL NECESSARY MEANS.

PLANK TWO: MANDATES

A. DECRIMINALIZATION of nonviolent drug-related offenses by requiring treatment.

B. MANDATORY TREATMENT PROGRAMS will be modeled after the PHOENIX house program.

C. EXPANSION OF TREATMENT FACILITIES as needed.

D. PRISON CAPACITIES SHALL NOT EXCEED 95 percent.

In most rounds, the vague logistics are not subject to criticism by the negative team; attacks on administration, funding, and enforcement are not considered very effective arguments.

Other Minnesota teams order their contentions differently, sometimes placing the plan either first or last, but typically having the same rhetorical opening and closing and the same set of contentions dealing with inherency, significance, harms, and solvency. Whether or not the plan is topical will be referred to only if the plan is attacked by the negative. The now current desire for affirmative disclosure of a case before the round permits the negative to begin to construct their counterarguments early, but even in Minnesota, before disclosure was practiced, teams kept careful track of the cases run by their opponents and would prepare for them. As a result, some debaters changed their case each week, slightly but significantly, in order to keep their opponents off balance.

The resolution is constructed to provide a range of cases. During the prison overcrowding topic, teams ran cases that called for building more prisons (the public favorite, but a rarely used argument), drug legalization, drug rehabilitation, community corrections, halfway houses for women, sentencing guidelines, programs of transcendental meditation, restitution and fines, capital punishment, diversion of mentally ill prisoners, release of elderly prisoners, boot camps, repatriation of foreign nationals (especially Cuban boatlift prisoners), corporal punishment or electrical shocks, penal colonies, creation of employment opportunities, establishment of prison industries, expansion of the size of prison law libraries, privatization of prisons, prisons modeled on Japanese corrections facilities, and the transfer of prisoners to the then Soviet Union. The cases ran from the plausible and thoughtful to the bizarre, trivial, humorous, and grotesque. Many squads, such as Randall Park's, presented several cases throughout the year, and different sets of partners ran their own cases. While on some teams everyone used the same case, it was more common that all debaters (or at least each set of partners) had their own case that, like their evidence, "belonged" to them, and that could not be used without permission.

Good Cases and the Real World

Those cases that were defined as the most serious (although not always the most successful, in this year in which negative teams usually triumphed) were those that were technically proficient and that "made sense" as policy. It was rare but not unheard of that a varsity final round involved a bizarre case. Coaches noted that cases had to be logical:

> I think [a case] has to put the best point forward. It has to be clear. A lot of plans are vague.[27]. . . . I really get frustrated as a judge listening to things that I . . . don't understand. . . . I think there are all sorts of different ways to organize a case, but it has to be structured . . . and it has to follow logically. (interview)

> I think it should tell a story. I think it should outline a significant problem, that there are clear mechanisms to solve. (interview)

Even more significant is the appeal of the case.[28] Good cases are those that, as one debater put it, are "honest and sincere." Judges vote for cases that they believe to be poor policy if the arguments have not been effectively countered, but judges prefer to vote for cases that they *like*:

> I love cases where the inherency is very solid. Where it just says, you know, this isn't done for political reasons, or isn't done for financial reasons. And to come out and have a very strong emotional appeal, whether it be because a lot of people are getting hurt or a lot of people are potentially going to be hurt. Say, "Hey, look, there's a simple, simple way to solve this. All you have to do is do it." (interview)

The cases that were particularly admired were those with policy appeal: removing mothers from prison to halfway houses, establishing restitution policies, legalizing or decriminalizing drugs, or establishing rehabilitation programs. These were in contrast to cases whose solutions were thought poorly of, such as corporal punishment, establishing programs of transcendental meditation, or sending prisoners to the Soviet Union.

Key to the recognition that a case is a good one is that it is "real world." This phrase echoed throughout my interviews:

> I think [releasing mothers from prison] is a very real-world case. And the closer your cases are to reality, I think the easier they are to defend. (interview)

> If you can find something that's a good idea but just hasn't been done yet for whatever reason, you can make your case for change that much better. . . . So, I mean in a real-world sense you have to look at issues like that. (interview)

Whatever happens within the round, high school debate should be about considering serious policy options. Those teams that take that task most seriously have an advantage, particularly with judges who emphasize a real-world policymaking paradigm.

Dangerous Cases

Just as some cases are respected, others provoke laughter or even anger. These cases are not considered "real world" and may be poor policy or squirrelly (described below). Some cases (corporal punishment, for example) are simply dismissed as "dumb." They may win some rounds, but against strong teams with evidence and logic, they rarely triumph. Judges consciously or not look for reasons to vote against them, maintaining their moral sense of self. What a judge votes for potentially reveals the judge's character and can be stigmatizing. Thus, judges who vote for bizarre or offensive cases will make the point that they *did not want to* vote for the case, but that the weak negative team left them no other choice. With some judges a team that argued for extermination camps could win a round if the negative team did not address reasons why genocide would not "work." One judge, more open to all arguments than most, noted:

> [The women's case] was really good. I mean that appealed to me. . . . Why discriminate against women? The guy comes off really as, "I'm a progressive male," real understanding. The girl obviously comes across as being very progressive. . . . On some level we're all human and we're all influenced by that. And I try very hard not to be, but we all are. . . . [Male judges who are progressive] are going to like voting for it. . . . They're put in a position of, If I vote against this case it's gonna look a little funny. I mean they're gonna feel awkward just voting against it. (interview)

In contrast, judges feel "dirty" voting for unpleasant cases, and in extreme cases they may simply refuse to vote for a case that they find morally offensive. Adolescents, embracing their power to shock, sometimes force judges to make these choices, enjoying the range of outrageous policies to which they have been recently exposed. In expressing the inexpressible, adolescents are liberating themselves from those beliefs handed down by parents and other guardians.

An example of this problem occurred during the 1995–1996 season, in which the topic involved changing U.S. policy toward China. In a break round at a major midwestern tournament, a team ran a case that suggested that the United States should launch a first-strike nuclear attack on the People's Republic of China, referred to as a spark case. The three judges (two of whom were from Minnesota!) unanimously awarded the round to the affirmative. The response was a firestorm of protest. Could a case that advocated the death of hundreds of million people ever be justified? Even if the arguments of the negative were not very effective, did the judges not have a responsibility to the educational function and the public perception of this fragile activity? Or were all arguments worth pursuing, especially issues such as nuclear strikes that have been considered by defense agencies? Was this case, even with its strategic advantages, too extreme, like cases advocating genocide to achieve population homogeneity?

Opponents of the decision were unsparing in their scorn:

> The biggest problem most people have with this case is the utterly senseless and random violence and destruction with no regret whatsoever about its targets. . . . Why would you even consider writing this case? What service are you doing for your debaters to have them run an abysmally bad strategic and moral case. Has high school debate fallen to the point where this is all that is left to innovate with?[29]

> Our words matter. . . . NO ONE is ever required to advance such a position, and I would exercise my right to reject it out of hand. . . . THIS WAS AN AFFIRMATIVE. No one boxed these two into a corner. They asserted that an unprovoked nuclear first strike was a good thing. They involved us all in their tragic "reasoning" when they noted that the only reason to do it to the Chinese was that our debate resolution required it. It requires no such thing!!!![30]

In the discussion, no one advocated this policy, but some suggested that the debate served a valuable educational purpose, as the discussion surely did. The use of free speech and playing with ideas in a setting that is not "real world" has merit in itself; further, who is to draw the lines of what policies are acceptable? Many find some killing acceptable. If a first strike of China is unacceptable because of the death toll—and the affirmative argued that a first strike would ultimately *prevent* deaths—what about capital punishment?:

> Debate may be more than just a game to some people, and I agree that words are important. Having said that, I maintain it is absolutely essential to any democracy. . . . By extension, *any* public policy position should be fit subject for examination. That taking the ab initio position advocated by some people in this thread is akin to censorship and prior restraint. . . . Everyone needs to be held responsible for what s/he says and the way in which it is said. That is educationally responsible. But there is no educational value to telling people in a democracy that there are public interest or public policy subjects that may not be discussed.[31]

> My responsibility is to keep my personal beliefs out of the round. I will judge the round based on the arguments made in the round. When judges are allowed to automatically reject a case or an argument that they find disgusting, this activity will be destroyed. It's a slippery slope. . . . Debate is a game. Nothing

more. When I voted aff. nothing happened. I think that the educational value of this round will have far lasting effects. That's what's important.[32]

These quotations could easily be duplicated as the debate raged over the significance of advocacy in a round. Does a case reflect the character of those who make it—are they tarred by their advocacy? Similarly should judges be linked to their decision? Or are cases merely technical claims that lack broader implications? These issues will continue as long as adolescents continue to taunt their elders by presenting positions that no reasonable person could endorse, even while the position can not be defeated without considerable effort.

Squirrels and Nuts

Just as debaters sometimes test the moral limits of advocacy, others create strange, narrow cases, called "squirrels."[33] While the label squirrel refers to the fact that these cases are out of the mainstream of the resolution, some suggest that the name is apt because the cases are "nuts." Affirmative teams enjoy coming up with unusual, surprising ideas and then searching for evidence, which, given the diversity of opinion in a heterogenous society, is sometimes plentiful. Negatives face the challenge of dealing with a surprise for which, when they first hear the case, they have little evidence and must rely on logic. A fan of squirrel cases noted:

I believe in the Ringgold High School model, which is live and die by the squirrels. I don't like running straightout boring cases. . . . [Squirrel cases] take people by surprise. It puts more of a thrill as a negative. I like squirrels. They make me think. . . . Read the first affirmative and see the faces on the negative when they see they have no evidence. They add spice to life. (field notes)

Squirrel cases during the prison overcrowding topic included mandatory birth control (reducing overcrowding in twenty years), expanding prison libraries, sending prisoners into space, building prison barges, using cryogenics on prisoners, establishing penal colonies, building more shopping centers (less crime occurs in malls), and giving guns to prisoners (so they can shoot each other).

The appeal of squirrels is such that one evidence handbook bills itself as *Squirrel Killers*, although some squirrels are so strange and esoteric that they are outside the range of this handbook. While debaters enjoy creating and opposing squirrel cases, these cases are usually defeated. As Mrs. Miller noted, "It's hard to win over a long time with a case that is counterintuitive." The best teams and best debaters reject these cases, unless they run them as a lark. Thus, it was a shock that one squirrel case involving sending American prisoners to the Soviet Union was presented in the final round of a novice tournament. That the case was bolstered with evidence from a satirical article in *The New Republic* (the negative—and perhaps the affirmative—was unaware of the humor) made the debate that much more surreal. One of the three judges actually voted affirmative.

Most squirrel cases are based on a single article, but in some cases the evidence can be compelling, even if it derives from self-interested groups. One case involved establishing programs of transcendental meditation in prisons and jails, in which the central article was based on research describing how the program could prevent harms from overcrowding and could lead to decreased recidivism. Best of all was the fact that other teams did not have evidence on the case, as the material was published in an obscure journal.

Unlike the dangerous cases described above, squirrels do not outrage coaches and judges. While coaches may become exasperated by the childishness of their charges, squirrels represent a teenage form of *playing* with ideas: simultaneously sophisticated and childish. If these cases do not dominate debate, they provide an intellectual charge and, lacking evidence, force both negative and affirmative teams to rely on their wits.

Creating Cases

Creating cases is central to the educational mission of debate. If debate rounds are a game, the creation of cases should provide the educational backing, involving thought, logic, and writing skills. Much time in class and team meetings is consumed by the consideration of what cases should be run. Most coaches insist that students participate actively in this process, and, on those teams in which individual students do the work on writing affirmative cases, students own the rights to these cases. The owner, due to his or her knowledge of the area, is likely to be the second affirmative speaker, able to extend the arguments, while the partner gets to read the typed speech.

The process of creating cases may be complex:

> A lot of it starts at the summer institutes. . . . Students go to these institutes and then come back with ideas. So, we work with those. . . . Often cases come out of those. And then just go and browse around the law library, and who knows what you may come across. . . . Ideally the students write [cases]. Now, I don't write cases. I will take cases students have written and go over them, and suggest revision and editing and like that. (interview)

This example underlines that the creation of cases is grounded in the social networks of debate. It is rare that a debater will come up with a case in total isolation. Even if one writes a case, it is tested in the crucible of team evaluation, with criticisms leading to major alterations or even to shelving of the whole idea. This is particularly true for novices, where older students may be assigned to work with younger ones in creating cases. Teammates push and prod the "author," suggesting possible disadvantages and weakness of evidence, looking for the right transitions, tags, and cards. Cases depend on a community assessment that may encourage or discourage the creator. Most cases eventually become collective products, even if one student remains the "author."

Coaches and Cases

Coaches differ in the extent to which they believe that it is proper—educationally and competitively—to be involved in the creation of cases. Some coaches let students write and research cases, while others see writing and researching cases as equivalent to creating plays for a sports team. The first set of coaches emphasize that it is not their responsibility to do anything more than advise and consult with their students, even if the outcomes are less satisfactory than if the coach had done most of the work. For these coaches, writing a case makes no more sense than having an English teacher write a student's term paper:

> One coach of a small team told me that he had a student who went to debate institute and brought cases back with him. The team worked with these cases, including a prison-building case. He said, "It did zilch for them all season, but it was theirs." His varsity team chooses what cases they will run, and he takes them to the university law library to do the research. He explains, "I don't believe in writing cases for them. Kids need to learn to do things for themselves, critical thinking, research on pretty esoteric topics. I do them a disservice if I do the work for them. I owe them my honest opinion, but if they want to run it for a week and then I'm proven right, we can change it." (field notes)

> I make the kids write their own [cases], and they are abysmal. They are atrocious, but they believe in them, and they come back and they fix them and they fix them and they fix them, or they get tired, and we talk about what they're doing and why. And I think that one of the strengths of our program here is that the kids learn how to do all of these things for themselves, where in some programs the coaches write them, the coaches hand them their arguments; they hand them their cases. I absolutely won't do that. (interview)

Other coaches, particularly younger assistant coaches, justify heavier involvement:

> We came up with [a case] because I gave it to them. . . . I went out and I spent the week before the Concord tournament and I researched the heck out of that

case. I, me personally, I did it in the law library. I came back with a whole huge sack of stuff and that week we wrote the case. I did most of the writing. [The varsity debaters] helped me a couple of times. . . . I was the one that could stay up all night writing the case. These kids have homework. . . . We're not talking educational here. Coaches design the plays in football. The players don't design the plays. (interview)

The closer that one is to being a teacher, the less willing one will be to write cases for students. The closer to being a coach, the more the writing of cases is seen to be legitimate. The question involves a trade-off between competitive success and personal growth. Given that these adolescents have not had experience in making adultlike claims, it is easy to see why some coaches would wish to provide their "kids" with texts to read, and it is easy to understand why other coaches feel that the greatest gift they can give their charges is the ability to create arguments, however imperfect the final outcome.

Presenting the Real World

Debate is predicated on the possibility that adolescents can represent the world in a plausible way through evidence and cases. Of course, debate also assumes that differing perspectives on the empirical world exist, but evidence is assumed to be more than random remarks, and cases are expected to be reasonable, considered policy.

This chapter suggests, however, that the social world is at least as influential in the creation of debate as is the world of facts. What counts for good evidence is a social construction, particularly given the inability of high school students to check the accuracy of expert claims. Some claims seem within the world of debate to be more legitimate than others. This perspective is also evident when teenagers talk about the topic: emotional responses to criminals and crime are balanced against those things that one believes that one should believe.

In the construction of cases, one selects the extent to which one will define debate as an intellectual game as opposed to policy analysis. Dangerous cases, posing morally challenging scenarios, even if arguably backed by long-term benefits, exemplify this game perspective. More "reasonable" cases, perhaps boring when repeated again and again, may provide the satisfaction of success and the satisfaction of feeling that one has insight into adult policy deliberations: a heady experience for one who only recently was defined as a child.

Four

In the Round

Before the round the guys are your friends.
They laugh at your jokes and chat.
But as you walk in the room the pleasantries end,
And your pal is now a brat

They look at you like the hawk at the hare,
As you answer their arguments clearly.
Their eyes seem to ask you: "How do you dare?
Fool! You will pay for this dearly!"

Next, he gets up, all haughty and proud,
With a smile on his face,
Deconstructing your logic and taking it out,
He finishes off with grace.

It is their last speech and they rub it in;
They are winning, there is no doubt.
What do you do? Lift up your chin,
Get up and lie your way out.

> *Debate Round* (e-mail from seregil9@ecity.net
> to cx-1@debate.net)

So FAR I have focused on the preparation for the round. Here, I examine
how students actually debate: the practice of competitive high school debate. Opening one high school tournament, the principal of the host
school, welcoming the participants, began his remarks: "As one talker to
another group of talkers . . ." (field notes). To understand this world is to
understand talk, although it is not only the "quality" of talk that determines the outcomes of rounds; talk is situated in special settings that provide the criteria for judging.

At its heart, debate is simple. One participant noted that there are only
three fundamental rules: (1) there are two teams, affirmative and negative; (2) these two teams must debate the resolution, one supporting it,
one refuting the claims of the other team; (3) a judge evaluates the debate
and determines a winner.[1] Some even suggest that these three basic rules
can be modified. Thus, one team ran an argument that both teams should
lose ("a double loss"), and the judge accepted the idea: accepting the

idea that debate is about "ideas," not creating a winner and a loser, emphasizing the educational aspect, granting the team whose argument won, the loss. Even determining a winning and a losing team can be questioned.

Of course, surrounding this basic structure, a large set of rules, norms, practices, and expectations have developed to which students must adhere for success. Debate is not simply topical argumentation, but a patterned activity, involving, as noted, standards of argumentation, speaking, and evidence. Talkers do not only speak for themselves, but have partners: a team of talkers. At times, these additional rules are explicit, sometimes they are taken for granted; occasionally the rules that operate in practice differ from the rules that are formally prescribed.[2]

The Tournament

To understand how debate is done, one must focus on the organization of the activity. Debates do not just happen, but happen at venues called tournaments. These vary in length from one day (for tournaments early in the season and for novices)[3] to three days (for major national tournaments, like the Tournament of Champions, Barkley Forum, or the Glenbrook Tournament). Tournaments can range in size from eight teams to two hundred. The national tournament of the National Forensic League occurs over five days in the middle of June. In 1997, 208 teams qualified from districts around the country. Most of the local Minnesota tournaments that I observed covered Friday afternoon and evening and all day Saturday, with each team debating four or five rounds, before breaking into the quarterfinal, semifinal, and final rounds. At any one time, approximately forty to sixty teams participated from twenty to thirty schools. While some of these tournaments had schools from neighboring states, none of the Minnesota tournaments were truly national. Most were held at high schools, although a few were held at local colleges.

In Minnesota, tournaments were held each weekend (excepting holidays) from late September until early February. For many coaches, the season was too long (or, as one coach put it, "inhumane"), and plans were discussed to shorten the season by two weeks. For debaters, these are exciting festive occasions—educational parties—but for many coaches, tournaments represent something else, much as they value the educational outcomes and socializing. As one coach put it, when I asked about the least enjoyable aspect of debate:

> The time of the tournaments . . . When you have to be ready to go at noon on Friday, and you don't get home until nine or ten, and you're up at the crack of dawn on Saturday, and you go all day. That's a really hard, rigorous schedule

for anybody to deal with, and it messes up a lot of things. It messes up getting enough sleep, because if you're a debater, you go home, and you work for two hours, and then you go to bed, and then you get up at the crack of dawn, and then you start the day over. By Saturday afternoon, you're exhausted, which means that had you planned anything else besides debate, it's thrown out the window, because you can't move. You're too tired. (interview)

Students can run on adrenaline, but coaches have no such option; it is remarkable that most stay awake listening to debaters spew. Championship debaters may live on four or five hours of sleep during tournaments. Lifting heavy boxes of evidence and speaking at rapid rates require stamina and conditioning, reminiscent of athletes.

At the beginning of the season, tournaments are designed to train novice debaters. Rather than having novice debaters switch sides, a novice team might consist of four young debaters: two debate every round as affirmative, and two debate as negative. The success of the team depends on the combined record. Tournaments for novices in Minnesota often have case limits. Affirmative teams are given a small number of case areas from which they can draw (e.g., drug decriminalization, building more prisons, changing sentencing guidelines), so that novice negative teams need not prepare for every possible case: a Herculean task.

Tournaments differ in the number of "break rounds" scheduled after the preliminary rounds have concluded. Some large tournaments begin with "double octos" (the top thirty-two teams), while others begin at semifinals. In Minnesota, sometimes quarterfinal, semifinal, or even final rounds are hidden, so that the top teams will be scheduled to face each other without learning that they are the top teams, while the other teams have meaningless rounds.[4] On other occasions, final and/or semifinal rounds may be canceled, with the top four teams receiving trophies and permitting the tournament to end early.[5]

Tournaments have their own character. This is particularly true of those events that move from location to location annually. The NFL tournament has a different tone, depending on its location: part of this is due to the abilities of the hosts to arrange an attractive space,[6] and part is due to variation in the judging pool and in the teams that can afford to attend. Because of the more conservative Minnesota style of debate, state teams tend to be more successful in those years in which the tournament is held in regions that have similar styles, since many judges are selected from local coaching pools.[7]

Other factors provide tournaments with distinct cultural meanings. One Minnesota tournament is held the weekend immediately preceding Halloween. Debaters are encouraged to wear costumes, an option of which some of the younger teens take advantage, although varsity debaters, drawing from adult standards of decorum, typically find this childish or "stupid." A Wisconsin school used to hold the "Superbowl of Debate" on Superbowl Sunday, in which teams were invited from National Football League cities and were asked to wear the appropriate football jerseys. Other tournaments, such as those held at Macalester College and Concordia College in Moorhead, Minnesota, are known to be more accepting of odd cases, rapid speech, and extreme arguments, because of the presence in the judging pool of collegiate debaters. Further, since Minnesota typically holds two tournaments each weekend, attendance at one or the other will often reveal the coach's network. Dentin High School used to hold a tournament at which they presented the "Governor's Cup." Some coaches disliked Dentin's coach and felt that the pairings were not random; they organized a tournament the same weekend at Greenhaven, diminishing the attendance at Dentin.[8] Some tournaments pay room and board to have desirable out-of-state teams attend, or arrange to have out-of-town debaters put up by team members (as Grand Rapids [Minnesota] High School did when Randall Park attended their tournament, or as New Trier High School [Winnetka, Illinois] did for students from Woodward Academy of Atlanta, Georgia).

Dress and Decorum

An observer visiting a debate tournament would surely be impressed by how well dressed the adolescents are; they often look like young attorneys or politicians. The torn jeans and raunchy T-shirts seemingly standard issue at public high schools are rare. Most boys, particularly those on the varsity level, wear jackets and nice slacks or even suits. Occasionally, a student will wear a sweater and slacks. T-shirts, jeans, and shorts signal that the wearer is not committed to debate. Girls typically wear blouses and skirts, sometimes with jackets; varsity debaters may wear pantyhose and, possibly, tasteful earrings or a necklace.[9] Those who are dressed more casually are likely to be novices, judges, or assistant coaches. Even though debate rounds are judged on the content of what is argued, dress matters.

Some coaches feel this strongly. When Lyndon Johnson was a high school debate coach at Sam Houston High School:

> He picked out your suit for contests [or] how much lipstick and what dress you wore. Nothing was too small. Everything had to be made perfect.[10]

For boys, with the relatively limited male wardrobe, the choices are relatively easy. For girls, the issues are more complex. Short of wearing a tuxedo, there is little a boy can do to be "overdressed." Girls, in contrast, must avoid the dangers of being too feminine or too overtly sexy, although some sex appeal is considered desirable, since many judges are young men. One varsity debater noted, "One time I did something kind of risqué; I wore black nylons with the line down the back. That was just about as risqué as I would possibly get" (interview). Adolescent girls often ask their female coaches about their outfits:

> Laurie is planning to buy clothing for the Tournament of Champions. Its importance is evident by the fact that she tells us that she is selling some old riding equipment. She asks Mrs. Nyberg for her opinion about the dress she is considering: blue and white silky material, with a V-neck. (field notes)

Mrs. Nyberg explains:

> If winning were my only objective, I would probably try to come up with *the* formula dress. But first, that's tough to identify, and the other thing is, I think there has to be a place for individuality too, and the personality to come in. I think forcing a female to always wear a suit, always wear heels, always no jewelry, always hair back and very conservative . . . Again, you want to avoid the extreme. [Question: What would you tell female debaters?] I would say good taste is the overriding factor. . . . I do have to describe it to students. . . . Straight lines on girls are usually more attractive and draw less attention to themselves . . . as opposed to ruffles and frills. (interview)

"Dressing up" is part of debate culture, and is believed to benefit character, even if, in theory, it should not influence outcomes.[11] Coaches hold strongly to the idea that proper dress matters, even while denying that they take it into consideration in their decisions:

> Your credibility [is determined] before you ever open your mouth, and subconsciously think that happens, and I think the fact that you are dressing up and going that little step to dress up shows a little bit of pride in yourself and a little bit of pride in the activity. One of my pet peeves is in men who wear a sport coat to a tournament or a suit, and then in the round, they roll up their sleeves, loosen their tie, and take off their jacket, even when they're speaking. Why did you wear it? It doesn't matter in a decision, but to me that's a pet peeve. (interview)

> If you have a kid up there who's dressed up real nice, and a kid who is not, I think the perception is by a lot of judges, Who's taking this more seriously, who has more experience in the activity, who has more respect for it? I mean that's kind of bizarre, because none of the judges ever dress up. We're always in jeans and T-shirts. (interview)

Many, though not all, debaters prefer to dress up for tournaments, marking their adult role, and may even conclude that it helps them debate:

> If you're a slob, it makes your arguments look like slobs. I mean, it's the impression you give them. If you look very businesslike, you tend to sound more

businesslike. And it also gives you a little more feeling. I like standing up there in my full suits. I'm a businessman. I'm a debater. (interview)

I kind of enjoy dressing up. . . . There's a feeling of professionalism almost to it. . . . It adds to the confidence factor. It makes you a little more aware of what you're doing if you're dressed up. (interview)

Even though one might expect teenagers to be opposed to dressing up, in fact it adds an aura to the activity. Such display makes the parallel of debate to trials and legislative debate self-evident. To dress up is to take on the costume of the attorney or lawmaker. One can argue—were cost not an issue—that education might improve if we could return to the days when students, as a matter of routine, dressed in coats and ties to attend high school. Those days have long passed, but debate suggests that perhaps their passing should be mourned.

The Round

The basic unit of debate is the round. Here, two teams face each other in heated conversation for an hour. Not including "prep time" (five or ten minutes in most tournaments), during my research a round consisted of sixty minutes of talk.

When a round is going well, it can be a beautiful, even thrilling, occasion. Developmental psychologist Mihalyi Csikszentimihalyi writes of the concept of flow as being particularly important for the actualization of talented teenagers (see chapter 9).[12] By this, he refers to a subjective state by which a person is completely immersed in an activity, losing sight of surrounding mundane events. Flow constitutes intense concentration in an activity: a perfect state of focus. In the best rounds, debaters are "high" from talking; they are flying. The thrill of flow, along with the various social rewards, makes it difficult for some to leave the activity, even when their "confinement" in the institutions that sponsor debate has ended.

Debaters speak of flow as well. In their usage, flow refers to keeping track of arguments (as well as the pad on which these notations are made: "on the flow"). The flow is not a natural part of discourse, and so debaters are instructed how to flow and as to what a flow should look like. The concepts of flow—technical and emotional—merge when in the round the debater stands before the judge, taking brief and cryptic notations and transforming them into a polished performance, rhetorically and logically. The words flow in sequence in a form that convinces the audience that the speakers' claims are correct. One varsity debater explained that in some of his best rounds he doesn't know precisely what he will do or say next. All the pieces fall together in a seamless analysis. This is exemplified in linked "points" that can be placed on the flow; talking persuasively without making specific points or arguments simply does not count. The successful skein of words contrasts with rounds in which the speakers felt that their arguments did not mesh, or they were poorly organized, or they were confused about the opposing team's case, or otherwise stumbled through a turn at talk. Perhaps one of the more significant aspects of a round is that it is hard to recover poise in the face of error or confusion. The turn at talk is so brief and so rushed that errors may pollute the whole turn or make the immediate circumstance humorous.

Although rounds are supposed to focus on arguments about the validity of the resolution, that continuous focus is difficult. This is particularly true because debaters are forced to respond viscerally and without full consideration. The round is a breeding ground for Freudian slips and other forms of frame breaking. Speeches are never as smooth and flawless as debaters wish them to be: a danger of all speech that is not fully scripted.[13] Often, debaters make gaffes or embarrassing claims that on some fundamental level reflect what they really believe. Thus, in one round, after being closely questioned, a speaker responded, "Do I look like a retard?" (to which his partner helpfully suggested, "Don't ask that.") (field notes).

Most debaters indicate that an outstanding round depends on an excellent opponent. Participants often distinguish between "easy" rounds against poor or incompetent teams and their best rounds in which the abilities of their opponents contributed to their own sense of satisfaction. One described his best round as being one in which he was debating affirmatively against a team that used a very similar affirmative case:

> We were hitting Covina, and Covina ran a case that was identical to mine. . . . We were running it affirmative, and, like, they knew every little argument to try to pin down on us. We won it by only a couple of points. They knew every point to argue, and we had every response. We clashed perfectly. No stupid disadvantages, no stupid topicality, no counterplan. (interview)

Some will even name a round that they lost as their best or favorite round, precisely because it had this element of "pure" debate: the direct engagement of ideas.

Competitive Tongues

High school debate assumes that students desire to win, not just learn. The outcome is as important as the process. While participants often pay obeisance to the virtues of learning and having fun, the driving force is competition, as it is in other scholastic domains, such as mock trials, chess, and academic bowls. Strategic gamesmanship can characterize debate; for example, "psyching out" one's opponents, such as waiting until the last minute to decide whether a team will be affirmative or negative. Within the rules, winning is crucial.

One highly competitive coach began a round by stating, "Ladies and gentlemen, the fun is about to begin. . . . Our main purpose is to have a good time in this debate. The rest of this doesn't matter much" (field notes). Yet, his ability to make this statement depended on the fact that while debaters know that it is not false, it is not wholly true; not for him and not for them.

The importance of competition was evident in the reaction to a coach's suggestion that at the beginning of the season his school would hold a novice tournament in which rounds had no winners or losers, but only explanations from the judge. Only three teams showed up. One of his colleagues—ironically the one who wanted debaters to have fun—noted, "I couldn't find anyone who lacked those juices. They wanted to know who would have won." Another coach joked, "This would have been the ballot. These would have been the comments" (field notes). Competition is such that, as a result of Minnesota's open enrollment policy for high schools, some students transferred from one school to another in order to participate in a better program.

Some comments about competition reflect adolescent desires and self-centeredness, forgetting that in rounds between two excellent teams, only one can triumph:

> If you Debate to just play, then leave, you should do nothing in your entire life. You do every thing to WIN!! I do everything and anything possible to win. I do WHAT EVER IT TAKES to win. There are no POINTS for SECOND place!!![14]

> My feelings are that if I don't win a tournament, it wasn't worth going to. I like to think I am the best and I therefore must have failed if I don't win. I also get frustrated when I feel those around me aren't doing their fair share.[15]

Although coaches and other (less fierce) debaters proclaim that education is the most important outcome, competition provides the juice, even if lasting impacts are elsewhere. Winning provides the reward that makes competition seem reasonable. As Mrs. Miller told her class, "I'm not saying I don't like to win. I'm very competitive, but there are some things more important than winning. I want to teach you skills that you can use for the rest of your life" (field notes). The virtue of debate is that participants do not have to accept this line to gain the benefits. Those recruited to the activity tend to be those whose competitive urges have been finely honed:

> I get a thrill out of competing, arguing against people, mental challenge. . . . I can debate through rounds where the people are really bad, and I can kind of

enjoy it, but it really makes a debate tournament when you hit the top team, and you have a really good debate, even if you lose. . . . I wouldn't be in debate if I kept on losing. (interview)

As one debater noted about his own success, "I was willing to go the extra mile to get better, to improve. I think it's basically just willing to do what it takes to win" (interview). Without the desire to prove oneself, to test oneself in fire, debate would simply become a lot of fast speakers reading evidence past each other. Competition transforms a round into a community of shared interests.

Emotion Work

Whenever one gets adolescents together, these novices in the world of public self-presentation are likely to display emotions. Behind whatever placid exterior the teenager can muster is a roiling set of feelings: anxiety, pain, excitement, depression, joy, and exhaustion. This is particularly true in the case of public speaking, a scary domain in which one's personal mastery of the art is continually evaluated. For a fifteen-year-old to stand before an adult and put his or her self on the line—rhetorically naked—is a considerable test. Although the display of calm sophistication may, in part, produce that deep feeling, such feeling rules do not work fully.[16]

ANXIETY

We speak of individuals as having a case of nerves on those occasions in which they will be judged in public situations in which the possibility of failure looms. The evaluation of one's public face is threatening. Giving a speech that has not been fully planned or rehearsed can be daunting, similar to acting in an unscripted drama in which one must give an eight-minute soliloquy in front of critics. Of course, teens have some experience in this matter as their storytelling and other conversational abilities indicate.[17] Given that one recognizes a direction for our talk, this skein of words is not impossible.

Still, this recognition does not eliminate stage fright. The feeling of uncertainty is palpable during the opening hours of important tournaments; until the first round begins, the participants are keyed up, subdued, or serious. I was struck by how quiet the Minnesota State Tournament seemed as I walked the halls. Not surprisingly, novices consider tournaments to be "pretty scary," and at Randall Park several novices made excuses for why they were unable to participate in the first tournament. One varsity debater comforted the novices by explaining, "If you go in confident, you're stupid" (field notes).

For important rounds, such as final rounds, participants may battle nausea, the likelihood that they will "lose their lunch." As debaters explain:

> Every round I feel very nervous unless I know what case they're running or I know what arguments I can put out against it. . . . At the Layton tournament [early in the season] I felt really sick [to my stomach]. It got better right after I read the affirmative case. (interview)

> [At the final novice round of the Boston Heights tournament] I felt sick to my stomach, 'cause there were all those people in there. And having to debate in front of an auditorium made me extra nervous. (interview)

Other debaters find that they cannot eat anything at major tournaments, get little sleep,[18] have nightmares (imagining oneself naked in a round is not uncommon), or even shake or shudder. If only one could bottle adrenaline. Some use the restrooms frequently, so one tournament director in his introduction gives directions to the toilets, noting, "I know in the nervous moments before the round starts, bathrooms are very important." A coach explains, "Every time you hear a toilet, we should cringe." Even coaches, not themselves on the line, admit that they pace the halls or feel ill. One coach joked that at the sectional tournament, "I spent all that day hiding and praying," which her assistant described as being "Catholic at the tournaments," noting that people discover their faith at times of stress (field notes).

Sometimes, the effects of stress can be clinically evident, particularly headaches, magnified by stress, lack of sleep, and minimal food:

> My problem . . . is that even though I love debate, I get really bad headaches and my head gets really foggy for a round or two. So I spend most of my time at tournaments really not feeling well.[19]

Our bodies may subvert the pleasures that one should take from competition with friends in an activity that one treasures. The social psychology of self-presentation can cause pain in debate and in other venues where evaluation matters for one's identity.

EXCITEMENT

Excitement represents the other face of adrenaline, and at times can hardly be disentangled from nervousness. Debaters can be "up" for rounds, using the rhetoric of "flying" or being "high." One coach even suggested that some students are "addicted" to the activity, as evidenced by an excessive intensity and an inability to leave the activity after graduation. She notes, "It gets in your blood, and it's hard to get out" (interview). As with all intense commitments, going "cold turkey" can be difficult. Others, not using this dramatic metaphor, note that an emotional "high" is part of debate: "Sometimes you get that debate high. You just keep going and going. I feel happy. I feel good. If you feel you're doing well, you feel high" (interview).

As Mihalyi Csikszentmihalyi notes of flow, emotions may make one forget where one is. Action becomes the essence of the moment, the opposite of nervousness in which self-consciousness dominates. One acts in the present, bracketing the past and one's self-conscious realization of the constraints on action:

> Coming out of the round I can barely remember the round itself. I remember before the round has started, but I can't remember the round. I kind of think of it as another gear. Just kind of like shift gears. . . . I know what I'm going to say . . . but when I'm up there it just kind of flows out. (interview)

> You are no longer conscious of the outside world. . . . You could have had so many things on your mind before the round and they're gone. They're absolutely gone. . . . You're so focused in. You are not in the real world anymore. You are in this debate round, and I'm sure the same thing happens for athletes too. (interview)

> [After winning a final round in a novice tournament] I was extremely surprised because when I was up there I really didn't know what was going on. . . . I didn't even know we won first place until we came back and Doree said, "You're screaming your head off." (interview)

This energy dissipates in the aftermath of a round, and it is common to see debaters, having finished their speech, take a deep breath, put their head on the table, or even collapse into a chair. The exhaustion is palpable.

The final opportunity for emotional release occurs as an outcome of the tournament. While competition has many virtues as a motivation, it produces an emotional wake. The joy that debaters feel is powerful, but after a brief moment of exultation, they must tame their joy to appear pleased but modest. In contrast, others must cope with their frustrations, but do so in a way that suggests that this outcome that clearly matters, does not really matter. Sadness and frustration must be hidden, and tears must be held back—often a difficult assignment for adolescents, who find their reputations on the line. This emotional management is particularly evident when a team believes that they should have won, have mentally prepared for joy, and discover that they have been vanquished, in their minds, unfairly.[20] As much as performance skill is involved in a round, the real acting may be after results are announced.

While occasionally tears reflect frustration—particularly for females for whom such expressions are more culturally legitimate—these talkers typically rely on words, however impolitic, with the words often phrased in ways characteristic of childhood. One adolescent, after a loss he felt was undeserved, commented about the judge, "I could kick that guy right in the head. . . . I'm going to kick out his lights. . . . I want to pull out his hair" (field notes). As this is a "sophisticated" senior, the threat is not serious, but the anger was quite real. Despite claims that debaters throw chairs or tables, these expressions are known by their absence. Although we imagine debate as a cognitive world, emotional forces can no more be excluded than they can be in any circumstance in which reputations are on the line.

The Politics of Respect

Activities gain their meanings from how they are treated and defined: from surrounding ritual activities. Sociologists, such as Erving Goffman, refer to this as the "frame" of the situation: what kind of event is going on, and how is this definition maintained by the behaviors of individuals that support this frame.[21] What activities support the meaning of the event? For debate, the illusion is that the event is a serious intellectual evaluation of particular policy issues. The metaphor of a courtroom or congressional chamber is real for these future attorneys or politicos. At a tournament, the dress code of debaters supports this frame; in the round itself, the demand for politeness and policy analysis becomes crucial, part of the emotion work of debaters: the ability to achieve one's goals and create interpersonal smoothness through the public display of emotion.[22] This is particularly striking when the frame is broken—not uncommon when one is dealing with teenagers, whose strategies may include those they learned as children.

On the surface most rounds are polite. "Please" and "thank you" are common. Debaters typically introduce themselves before the round, and routinely shake hands at the end, no matter the outcome. Overt rudeness is often noted by judges on their ballots, sometimes lowering speaker points and occasionally changing the decision, providing for social control. One judge wrote, "I hate to have to say this, but I can't believe how rude you two are. You talk loudly during your opponents' prep time, you make derogatory comments about their arguments, and you generally make the round unpleasant" (field notes). These comments greatly upset the team's coach. Some varsity teams can barely control their scorn for novices:

> I was at my first varsity tournament. In an early round we hit a team that was varsity (I mean real varsity). They were laughing amongst themselves that we were just novices, and this would be nothing. Our case was pretty weak, which didn't help our cause any. But, instead of just rolling over us, they assumed one of the most condescending tones I've ever seen in a round. They spent most of their speech time flashing us dirty looks, and in some cases pointing at us between cards.[23]

While the status differences might seem enormous to this more sophisticated varsity debater, for the adults involved in the activity both teams comprise adolescents struggling with maturity. Some instances are dramatic. One team's members took off their trousers and debated in their skivvies against a female team. On another occasion, it was said that "the negatives took off their shirts and made farting sounds in their armpits."[24]

Teams are expected to demonstrate *respect* to their opponents; even if they do not feel that way, they must behave as if they did. This demonstration of respect is more difficult than it might appear, as debaters, still learning the impression management strategies of adult society, may display their superiority by denigrating those they feel are less worthy by making sarcastic remarks, rolling their eyes, or giggling at poor arguments. Striving to be adult makes them seem more like children. Coaches note:

> If they're doing something that's truly offensive or inappropriate, I will try to communicate that on the ballot. . . . Like the Dentin girls completely destroying some sophomore debater.[25] They could be just as effective being nice to this kid, but they feel they have to rip them limb from limb to get the win in the debate round, and I don't like to see that. . . . People need to have a certain humility in terms of it could just happen to them as well as they can do something like that to another debater. (interview)

> [I'm embarrassed by] kids who pick on other kids in a round, making them cry, or, you know, just call them dumb. [Tell me about when a debater was brought to tears.] It was awful. . . . He just badgered a girl until he made her cry. . . . It was a matter of "Is this right? Is this right? How can this happen? This can't happen." It was just like somebody just keeps asking questions, and the girl obviously didn't know. (interview)

Yet, these demands for decorum may be easier said than done; not only does incivility seem to serve a communicative function in that on the surface it is an attempt at persuasive speech, but it also serves a boundary maintenance function to solidify the uncertain status position of debaters. Thus, a student joked, emphasizing the underlying meaning behind the veneer of politeness, that the negative should begin his speech, "The affirmative is stupid" (field notes). One debater noted candidly:

> When you're standing there making a speech, you don't want people snickering at you. . . . And I'll admit, I've done that a few times, too. Especially in that one round where Barry and I were against that Braverton team, and they were reading evidence to support my case. I was doing everything but outright laughing my head off. It was just so funny listening to them read evidence. And then sometimes I would be really stupid and do stupid things, like, well, I don't know what "topicality" means. (interview)

This debater recognizes that in the status hierarchy of high school debate, as in other venues, the perpetrator of disrespect might in other circumstances become its target. Teenagers may feel that such remarks persuade a judge that their arguments are superior, despite the fact that such tactics often boomerang. This can be evident in the three minutes of cross-examination in which debaters ask their opponents questions. Many inquisitors are arrogant in such situations, indicating that the opponents' inability to answer a question accurately, briefly, or directly casts doubt on their fitness. One coach advises her team about cross-examination:

> Be nice. It's so important. You want to judge to sit back and say, "He's a nice guy. She's a nice girl." You want the judge to feel good. It really does make a difference. . . . I know it's sometimes fun to be nasty, but being nice helps you win. . . . You really need to ask them [questions] at a professional level. . . . You want to nail somebody to the cross in a nice, pleasant manner. If you stick in the knife, you don't want to leave it in because they can pull it out and survive. You want to turn it, but in a nice, polite fashion. (field notes)

This reflects one of the more difficult things for adolescents to learn: how to be "tough" without being "nasty." The subtlety and implicit meanings that are part of adult competitive discourse are opaque to adolescents, who, as children, are used to saying what they mean, even exaggerating in the process. The image of polite discourse that is integral to debate makes these adolescent excesses all the more jarring.

"Sex" in the Round

According to my survey, approximately one-third of all debaters are female. Compared to such activities as Little League baseball, fantasy gaming, race-car driving, or hunting, this is a significant number. Further, the number of females in debate has apparently increased over the last few decades. Indeed, some tournaments now give trophies with statuettes of female debaters to all winners, just as all the figures used to be male. On one level, claims that there are walls preventing the participation of girls in debate are misleading. Many coaches, as is true for teachers generally, are female. Whether there are barriers to the participation of girls and women at the highest, most competitive levels of the world of debate is not a question that my research addresses. My concern here is how girls are treated within debate rounds.

While some data are dramatic and disturbing, it is not the case that discrimination occurs on every team or in every round. The one allegation of rape at a tournament (the accused was not brought to trial and, so, remains innocent) is an aberration.[26] Sexual harassment occasionally occurs, although the boundaries between compliments and offensiveness can be cloudy. Once, prior to a round, a coach from a rival school placed his hands on a female debater's shoulders, noting pleasantly, "Some of the guys on the team would like a date with this hot one" (field notes), ostensibly complimenting her, but ensuring that she realized that while she was speaking, her body would be on public display. Humor, likewise, reveals the boundaries of attitudes. Sometimes debaters joke about rape, as when one female debater kidded another about a disliked male judge, "Rat probably wanted to rape you after the round" (field notes). On another occasion, a male assistant coach referred to the writer of a piece of scholarly evidence as "Ellen, babe," adding good-naturedly that he did that "because I'm a sexist asshole" (field notes). A "sexist asshole" is apparently still a role that males can jokingly play with their female debaters.

More to the point is the normal use of gender in the round. Being male is unmarked; being female is notable. Thus, females are compared to their male counterparts, not males to females. Female voices are judged too high, whiny, and difficult to listen to. (It was suggested that the two female varsity debaters at Randall Park should engage in "team whining.") Tough female debaters are considered "bitchy." Attractive female debaters are "wenchy" or "slutty" or "ho's." Females are said to flirt and to use their sexual appeal in rounds to persuade judges. That often these views are also expressed by female coaches and students demonstrates how culturally ingrained they are. The evaluation of female voices and bodies is, of course, subjective and not susceptible to objective evaluation. Flirting is a judgment made by an observer, but not all females deny these strategies; it is part of a strategic balance for those labeled "bitches" or "witches." Males may be poor speakers or overly aggressive, but that evaluation is not linked to their gender. No one jokes with these young men about unbuttoning their shirts strategically or wearing tight slacks.

Likewise, few suggest that males flirt with (older) female judges, or even conceive of the possibility.

THE BITCH

Successful debaters are tough, giving no quarter, denigrating their opponents' arguments. The dilemma for female debaters is that these traits can lead to the claim that they are "bitchy," complaints that some judges make explicitly on their ballots. While girls can win with this style, as the so-called "Dentin witches" did, they do so at a cost. What is considered appropriately aggressive for males, is bitchy for females. The female teenager can not just debate, as can her male colleague; she must be nice and feminine while destroying her opponent—Rambo in chenille:

> Two Randall Park assistant coaches were talking about their female debaters. Iris commented to Don: "I got the girls not to be bitchy. Sweet and kind." Don, thinking back to last year with his male partner, noted: "We didn't have that problem." Later Iris reminds Doree: "Don't be so tough. It looks bitchy, and you come off badly." (field notes)

This was a problem with which Doree struggled, as she wanted to be effective and yet avoid the label of bitch. So, when Iris warned her, "You need to be careful not to be too . . . ," Doree filled in the word "bitchy." Iris "corrected" her by inserting "feisty," adding, "It looks bad for all-women teams" (field notes). The term "bitch" can be pronounced in many ways. Doree worried to me and others whether she was coming across as bitchy, and sometimes defined herself in that way. As one coach noted:

> I think there is less room for girls to be very aggressive in debate. Judges see this much more negatively. I think that we teach girl debaters sometimes directly and sometimes indirectly that they cannot be aggressive because they will be bitchy. I think that's both spoken and unspoken. Boys can get by with more things that way. (interview)

These definitions, incorporated into the self-image of female debaters, constrain their behaviors, and thus are not seen as a problem by male debaters. Some coaches take this so seriously that they will not pair a team of two girls. Avoiding bitchiness is seen as part of decorum, politeness, and respect.

THE FLIRT

While it may be distressing to learn that female debaters trade upon their sexuality, this is not only widely believed, but acted upon by some. There is considerable discussion of using one's body for competitive ends. That much of this is joking in no way eliminates the realization that this constitutes part of the "advantage" of being female in a world where males dominate. One male coach notes:

> If a judge is sitting in the back of the room, and it's obvious that this judge is what we might call a dirty old man, and that he could be persuaded by a pretty girl with a pretty smile and some sweet talking, then you smile and you talk sweet. And that's where the bitchy gets balanced out. . . . I've had a couple of girls that were just knockouts, but gorgeous girls, incredibly bright, and they understood that one of the monkeys that they had to carry on their back was that on occasion a male judge would accuse them of being bitchy, and their counterbalance was on occasion if they had someone in the back of the room who was susceptible to a smile, you would use that smile. That was where the balance came. (interview)

The choice for the teenage girl is between being maligned for toughness or being ogled: a dilemma that is linked to the problems that some young women have in maintaining self-esteem in a culture that denigrates them for precisely those actions into which it pushes them and in denying them credit for those actions for which their male colleagues are honored. The presentation of sexuality in ostensibly nonsexual domains reflects this dilemma. Coaches are convinced that girls choose short skirts to impress collegiate judges and older men who will evaluate them, and some young female coaches consider that a strategy for success. One female coach speaks of a "woody judge":

> There's a term called a woody judge, which is a young male college judge, who sees, you know, . . . somebody up there who's this gorgeous debater, and there's all sorts of jokes about, you know, it's a woody panel, meaning the team of the girl will win because these judges are gonna cater to the attractive young female. . . . I had an all-girl team last year that would joke about that kind of thing, you know—put on the bright red lipstick this round. (interview)

Other coaches jokingly make the same strategic point, always in the guise of complaining about flirting:

> I don't like them wearing miniskirts, and I tell them that, unless there's one judge I know. If that judge is there, I say, "Unbutton the top button of your blouse and hike up your skirt" [he laughs]. . . . This is a judge who is very taken by female debaters. Attractive female debaters, and you flirt with him a little bit, and he loves it. . . . I think with that individual, he likes an attractive female debater, so I try to make her more female for him. I suppose there's a question on whether that is legitimate or not. (interview)

> I mean if you've got a cute girl with a young college guy, that influences decisions. It really does. I mean, I've played that up. I've used that. I will go and I will tell the girl, you've got a guy who, like, is into cute girls. You are good

looking; don't forget that in the round. I would never ask her to, like, prostitute herself and, like, show a leg. . . . I mean, you can be discriminated against because you're a woman, or it can work to your advantage. (interview)

Discussion about the use of sexuality is routine:

Doree jokes to Mrs. Miller about the tournament next weekend at which she will debate with Diane: "We're going to wear short skirts and black nylons, and keep crossing our legs." One young judge jokes to Doree: "I always vote on legs." Don later tells Doree: "Show a lot of leg." Doree insists that she doesn't flirt purposely, and therefore it is not unethical. Another debater says of an attractive female: "She shows off her legs." Doree says of another debater: "She's trying to impress the Concord judge [an older man], so she's wearing a miniskirt that was so high. I was going, 'Way to look professional!' I wonder if it helps their scores. She didn't know how to wear it, so she was mooning everyone in the cafeteria." (field notes)

We had jokes about the girls from Concord wearing tight pink sweaters with low-cut necks and always dropping evidence cards and then bending over to pick them up. (interview)

Randall Park debaters claim that Wendy, one of the Dentin debaters, deliberately exposes her legs to the judges in the final round (all five of whom are male). She is a very attractive girl, wearing a long skirt with buttons up the front. When she debated against Randall Park with a female judge, Brian claims that three of the buttons were undone. Now six are, and one can see her calf as her legs are spread apart. When she stands, the dress hikes up, so the judges can see her thigh. As the debaters are seated on stage, one can look up her dress. The debaters I am seated with claim that the display is deliberate. Brian whispers: "Watch what she does when she sits down." Philip notes: "It's pretty hard to miss." Doree adds: "Good view." Brian responds: "That's why I picked it." (field notes)

While these strategies are aimed at judges, they may also be aimed at male debaters (in the views of male and female debaters). Adolescents are attempting to master their raging hormones; some have had more experience than others. Attractive girls can use this to their immediate advantage in ways that are ethically questionable:

[A male assistant coach tells me], We know what Pamela Taylor told Gina Hearn at institute. Wear the blouse, fluster the guys by using it, and distract [them] enough, and then because there's a little sex bias very subconsciously in the judging, and if you're starting out equal, you can fluster them enough to bring them down to overcome the sex bias. (interview)

[A female debater tells me], Ms. Taylor was telling us about how at nationals she was up against someone who she had known all year, who kind of liked her, and who was a very shy person. Well, when he got up for his speech, and she had just gotten done with hers, she said, "Let me help you with the microphone." And she went over to him, and she played with him, and she put the thing around him, and she gave him a little pat. She left, and, boy, his speech was lacking, and it was simply because of what she had done. (interview)[27]

Doree, an attractive and mature eighteen-year-old at Randall Park, haltingly sensitive to the political ramifications of her actions, had to deal with this dilemma. Her coach and teammates were convinced that she flirted deliberately:

[Female debaters] wear short skirts and wear black clothes, and, you know [she laughs], the way it's been going on for centuries. . . . I think it's like listening to Diane and Doree. You know, they laugh about it, and joke about how short she's going to wear a skirt. . . . They do it! Sure they do. [GAF: They didn't wear any really short skirts.] Doree once in a while does. Sure they do it. Women have been manipulating men for centuries [she laughs], and if they have one thing going for them, we're not going to change that. (interview)

Doree would sit, like, cross-legged, and then she would move her chair over a little bit, so that her skirt went this far, and it would be facing the judge. And Brian would say, "I saw how you moved over, and you were facing toward the judge." (interview)

This young woman is tagged with the label of being a flirt, based on her use of her body. From Doree's perspective, as expressed in her interview, she was frustrated and uncertain about the label. She notes:

A flirt is a flirt. I'm just not, like, that [wearing short skirts and flirting]. I can't relate to it by any means, As a matter of fact, I tend to stay away from that kind of dressing, because I don't want to get that reputation. . . . I know I have gotten kind of a reputation sometimes, not often, but sometimes flirting with other people. And I guess I can see that, and I guess maybe to some extent it could be true. [To] quite a bit of an extent it could be true. But I know when I am coming out that way, and I know when to draw the line. Brian, he seems to think I'm this huge loose woman. (interview)

Doree struggles with her reputation: Is she a flirt? Does it matter? Does it help? She sees herself as having "conservative ethics," but few seem convinced. She is criticized for being a bitch and for being a flirt, while she is only attempting to be a debater and to have a social life. This is not to say that her teammates and coaches are fantasizing, but they are understanding her behavior in light of how *girls* act in debate rounds. Doree can do nothing that is not interpreted through the lens of gender—as is true for all females, but not for males.

The Challenges of Cross-Examination

When I was debating in New York City in the late 1960s, cross-examining one's opponents had just recently been introduced in that circuit;[28] today, these three-minute breaks are found in virtually all tournaments. Yet, these periods have not been fully accepted as an integral part of debate. While in Minnesota cross-examination is seen by most coaches as being very important, in other areas of the country, and particularly on the "National Circuit," some joke that it is time for the judge to step outside for a smoke or simply that it constitutes "prep time" for one's partner to prepare for the next speech.[29] In theory, one debater is supposed to ask the previous speaker a set of questions; today, "tag-team CX" is becoming more common, with either member of a team able to ask and answer questions, downgrading the activity as a means of judging debate, and permitting one debater to know little about the argument.[30] Even in Minnesota, most coaches do not "flow" the answers in cross-examination on their debate pads, although they occasionally take notes. The ambiguity of this time is such that there is no consensus on whether the participants should look at each other, modeling these minutes on "natural conversation," or, as in Minnesota, face forward, looking at the judge, maintaining the image of debate as a performance for an audience. While theorists such as Jurgen Habermas, and before him John Dewey, argued for the democratic value of dialogue within the public sphere, they imagined talk based on reciprocity and engagement—processes that are absent in the round itself, even while participants are questioning one another, where dialogue seemingly belongs. Debaters are talking *at* each other, not *with* each other, and this is evident in cross-examination, which ostensibly brings dialogue into the round. If debate involves democratic models of engagement, they occur outside of the round, as do so many other forms of socially valued education.[31]

Those who believe in the importance of cross-examination suggest that its value is twofold. First, the questions allow a team to specify what was unclear in one's opponent's speech, a task that may be essential because of the speed and lack of clarity of some speakers. Second, the questions can place traps for one's opponents, setting the stage for future arguments. The team answering questions often tries to refrain from giving information, even to the point of deliberately not answering questions, answering vaguely, or wasting time. Coaches emphasize both aspects of cross-examination, although the second is of special importance:

> I think it is fairly important for the debaters to set up to find out exactly what
> the other team is going for, find out what they're talking about, get the ins and

outs of the cases to set them up for later argumentation. A good CXer can really do that—sets people up well, gets the answer, and then says, "OK, so this is your position in the round," and they will say, "yes," and you'll say OK, and then you can get them. I mean really nail them. (interview)

One coach continually asks her students, "What are you going to do with that [question]?" The answers are supposed to build on each other to create a meaningful argument. One debater claimed that through an effective cross-examination, he was able to destroy an opponent's case:

[Question: What was your most effective cross-examination?]
That's easy, the prison law library case. . . . I asked them in cross-examination, "Find a place in your entire case where it mentions just once the word jail or jails." . . . They never could find it during cross-examination. They never could find it in time for any of their speeches. They never did find it, which the judge caught, wrote down on her ballot, made me feel great. We totally destroyed them. (interview)

Cross-examination represents the closest approximation to argument as it occurs in natural conversation: the opportunity for give-and-take. It also represents an analogy to the legal trial in which traps are set and sprung. Perhaps it is this "game" aspect that makes cross-examination the aspect of the debate round that receives little respect.

Timing Issues

Whether debaters are giving constructive speeches or rebuttals, they have little time in which to work. Eight minutes is a brief period to build or destroy a case. While today, debaters have five minutes to rebut all the arguments in the round, during my research they had but four minutes.[32] Given the flow of talk, how are debaters able to time themselves to ensure that they present all of their information. For novices, timing is a major challenge. Some find they can think of only two minutes of talk out of eight possible minutes; others are only halfway finished before they are out of time. Novices are taught how to triage their analysis, that is, cut out those arguments that they cannot fit in. Likewise, some debaters create extra arguments for security's sake, should they run out of ideas, an embarrassing lapse for a varsity debater. The amount of evidence and the number of arguments affect the speed of the speech, and consequentially its rhetorical force. Hearing varsity debaters finish their speeches to the second is impressive for one who has never had that experience. Similarly, figuring out how best to use the few minutes of allowed-for preparation time can be a problem for young debaters.[33]

One of the first pieces of equipment that debaters purchase is a reverse timer. This timer can be set for a length of time, and then counts down, buzzing at the ending. Speakers take these timers to their podium or desk, and measure their speech against what the machine is reporting. In addition, in many rounds debaters receive signals, sometimes "verbals" and sometimes hand signals. These signals can be given by partners, the judge, or a member of the audience, and can be arranged at various schedules (every minute, thirty seconds, etc.). Debaters lacking their own timers place themselves at the mercy of others. On one occasion, the judge forgot his responsibility to time one of the speeches, permitting that speech to go several minutes over time. On another occasion, a judge said to the debaters, "You should keep time for yourselves. I may miss a few minutes, particularly in rebuttals, but you should assume that time will continue" (field notes).

Aside from help from machines and persons, varsity debaters develop what they refer to as "an internal clock": a sense that derives from experience as to how much time they have spent—a phenomenon much like how professional cooks are able to specify with remarkable accuracy how long dishes have been in the oven.[34] This timing is part of the sense of flow that the best debaters feel during the round. One varsity debater told me when I asked how she timed herself: "It's more or less natural. . . . I just know the rate of speech and how much I can cover. It's just a question of how much to put in it" (field notes). However, she tells me that, as a trick of the trade, she leaves thirty seconds for a conclusion, which she can compress to ten seconds if needed. A coach noted:

> It's an internal clock, very much, and I don't think I coach that, to be quite honest. Kids develop that really quickly; even novices develop that. They get a sense quickly after . . . a couple of tournaments; you get a quick sense of what's eight minutes and what's four. You know, when I was varsity, I don't even remember looking at the timekeeper. I mean I always kind of knew how much time I had left . . . I mean you'd look to see for sure, but it's an internal clock. (interview)

That this involves socialization is clear, as one sophomore debater told me when I asked him how he timed his speeches:

> That's one of the things I was kind of worried about. When I first started I thought, How will I fill up eight minutes? How do I know when it's eight minutes? I think that's something that just has to come with experience . . . you've done it so much that you have a feel for it, how long a 2AC is, how long the eight, four minutes, three minutes is, and it's kind of a security blanket to have a timer there with you. It gives you an idea, but it's more a matter of knowing, having kind of a feeling how long it is. . . . Part of it is coordinating

where you are in your speech, like having little kinds of signposts in your speech, like where you have to be by a certain time. (interview)

Timing involves a combination of experience and education. To some degree, the use of time in a speech is a function of the number and quality of the arguments put forth by one's opponents. An affirmative facing ten disadvantages by the negative must answer each one so that none stands at the end of the round, even if this means that the subtlety of the arguments is lost. The negative, for its part, has more flexibility to determine how many arguments to run against the affirmative case and how much detail to present, as a single argument can defeat an affirmative case. These choices shape the elaborateness and speed of the argumentation.

Timing sets the boundaries of debate. While almost everything can be altered within the round, the clock is an obdurate master. Although timing may not be considered at first to be one of the key abilities that debaters need to master, it is a tricky skill, and when successfully achieved indicates that debaters truly have gifted tongues.

The Perils of Judging

Some claim that debaters never lose a round in which they participate; they claim it is judges who steal victory from them. Although winning a round is not an objective matter, like winning a hockey game, with the reasons for winning easily recognized by a naive observer, differing evaluations are easily understandable. Unlike most decisions of sports umpires and referees, a judgment in debate is not about particular plays, but involves an evaluation of the entire event. A team could win every argument but one, and still lose the round. In the need to reach a conclusion, the debate judge acts similarly to judges at boxing rings and figure-skating rinks.

Despite the variability of evaluation, the outcomes of most rounds are fairly clear, but it is frequent for debaters to contend, in effect, that "we wuz robbed." Being picked up (for the win) or dropped (for the loss) can be disputed. Because outcomes are not objective, it is common to feel that the outcome of a round does not involve the evidence and arguments, but some form of politics or personal affiliation.

Doing Judging

The judge sits in the back of the room, listening to the two teams and evaluating the arguments, a task that demands different skills from those of the speakers. With the exception of timekeeping, judges have no formal role other than to decide the outcome of the round on a printed ballot. Judges must decide how many points (out of thirty)[35] each debater deserves, determine which team won, and provide a reason for the decision, along with a set of comments. Judges should be unbiased, knowledgeable, friendly, and good listeners, as well as be educators by providing comments after the round or on the ballot.[36] For many judges, these evaluations of evidence, arguments, and presentation underline their role as teachers, leading some to prefer judging novices, where their advice may have more impact. Coaches are often frustrated that the debaters have little interest in the comments given on a ballot, but only in the outcome.

In Minnesota, the team with the higher point total was supposed to win, although in other parts of the country teams could receive "low point wins," if the most skilled debaters did not win the argument. Minnesota judges were discouraged from announcing their decisions or providing oral critiques immediately after the round in the interest of efficiency, thus insulating judges from the frustration and pressure of losing teams, and communicating more directly to the coaches, who could train their debaters from the written comments. However, these critiques have become commonplace elsewhere, as they support the image of debate as education.

Judging a policy debate does not involve precisely the same skills as evaluating a debate between political candidates. In the latter, one lets the waves of heated talk wash over one, perhaps not listening to each point, but basing one's evaluation upon a sense of which points were most important or most personally relevant.[37] Furthermore, in political debates one is expected to evaluate the candidate's character from the talk, a basis of judgment that would be suspect in policy debate. Judges are expected to follow the arguments by writing the points made by each speaker on the flow.[38] This notation, typically written on a legal pad, allows the judge to determine what arguments have not been answered. An attempt in northern California to outlaw written flowing in order to diminish the importance of technical and complex arguments proved to be a disaster, according to one judge (field notes). By judging the arguments and responses to them, the judge can determine the outcome of the round. Without this written record, it is hard to recall which arguments have been dropped or expanded. Of course, each judge has the obligation to weigh the significance of what material has been dropped and how effective the answers are. Debate theory describes the basis on which judges should make decisions, but for many judges the time pressures prevent a full evaluation of each argument, and decisions are often based on the outcome of a few arguments that the judge feels are crucial. One judge told me that he has two modes of listening: one when he attempts to think about the material and evaluate it globally; the other is just to flow the material and to check it for consistency. He hopes to use both in his judging (field notes). Despite the utility of flowing for keeping track of arguments, the act of writing is distracting: one listens or one writes. Flowing emphasizes a quantitative analysis of arguments, while critical listening is qualitative, and, so, may lead to different decisions. Flowing is a skill that can be mastered, although it remained a challenge for me as I found myself noting the previous argument while trying at the same time to process the current one. One cannot focus completely when one flows. This may be complicated when, as a judge, one must *appear* to be paying attention, which takes one's focus away from actually doing so.[39]

The practical creation of the flow differs among judges. Some judges use a separate page for each major argument; others use a separate pad for each team; still others attempt to use a single page. Some write horizontally across the page; others, vertically. Some use different colored pens for the arguments raised by the two sides. Some flow cross-examination; others stop their flowing before rebuttals, focusing on what is said. Some judges complete their ballots during the rebuttals; others, immediately after the round. In other words, even among trained judges, techniques may vary widely.

In order to judge a round "properly," one must remain focused. Even a few seconds of daydreaming can disrupt the flow. Given the fact that some debates are, frankly, boring, some speakers are difficult to listen to, and some judges do not get enough sleep, this paying of attention may be a considerable challenge. In the round, debaters may share their written case and evidence with their opponents, and, as a result, the judge may be the least knowledgeable person in the room. I have observed respected judges staring out the window or doodling on their flow. Perhaps they were concentrating, perhaps not; perhaps they were thinking about what *they* would have argued. Judges do daydream occasionally, as do psychoanalysts and air-traffic controllers. For a male judge to attend only to the topicality arguments of an attractive eighteen-year-old in a tight sweater and miniskirt presumes a cognitive discipline that not all can manage. In practice, of course, judges have an out, in that debaters cannot know for certain what arguments judges have missed or misunderstood. When I was asked to judge, I did not understand or write down every argument, although I was always able to propose some plausible reason for my decision.[40] As long as judges have heard enough to make a case for what they consider to be the essence of the round, they can escape with having a few private fantasies. While it is desirable for the judge to provide a decision that is "right," reaching *some* decision is essential.

One of the challenges for debaters is that unlike most speakers (but similar to psychiatric patients and auditioning actors), they face a blank audience. A key feature of most face-to-face discourse is that one can shape the talk as a function of audience response—smiles, nods, grimaces, and yawns matter. Judges, often head bowed, scribbling on a pad, typically provide little feedback. This is consistent with the view of the judge as a neutral, dispassionate observer—a fly on the wall. One can almost imagine debates being held in rooms with a one-way mirror, behind which sits the evaluator. Of course, judges cannot totally hide their responses, and some are more expressive than others, a trait that many debaters, especially nervous novices, appreciate. One novice told me, "I like a reaction from the judge. I tell jokes to feel good about myself. I don't like it when the judge doesn't respond." Another novice told me before I judged a round that, when appropriate, I should nod or look puzzled. (field notes).

Debaters are advised to watch the judge for clues. One judge, a retired speech teacher, would nod vigorously when she agreed with an argument. Another judge told me that he would hold up his pen when he felt the debater was speaking too rapidly, suggesting that he was unable to write fast enough (field notes). Any breach of the wall between judge and debater transforms logical accounting into persuasive activity. Judges, however much they wish to be unobtrusive and objective, leaving the debate to the debaters, cannot escape the actuality that they are in the room and in the round; and just as the judges are evaluating the speaking, the speakers are evaluating the listening.

Judge Adaptation

Whether judges respond in an observable fashion, debaters know that judges have individual preferences, and much of the coaching before rounds consists in describing the propensities of judges ("Are they friendly to our style?") and strategizing what arguments to use. This becomes a challenge when, in the final rounds, one faces multiple-judge panels. Some teams keep files on judges, describing their preferences based on the coach's knowledge or on previous ballots: debaters desire, in the words of one, "a judge catalogue," providing predictability. Before a team goes to an out-of-state tournament, they may call acquaintances to learn the characteristics of judges and their preferred paradigms—the theoretical choices from which they judge rounds. During my research, the most popular paradigms included stock issues (judging harms, significance, solvency, and inherency), policymaking (viewing the affirmative plan as a possible policy), and "tabula rasa" (open to any argument of the debaters). The recognition of differences among judges is institutionalized at some tournaments, such as the national tournament, in which booklets are distributed, detailing judges' views (in 1987, this included attitudes toward communication versus substance, decision-making paradigms, speed, counterplans, topicality, and generic disadvantages).[41]

The existence of these categories demonstrates how diverse debate is as a national activity. Even within a region, considerable differences of opinion exist. What is acceptable for one judge is inappropriate for another, and there may be joking resentment about judges with disfavored paradigms. Minnesota debate was still quite conservative, allowing fewer types of arguments. At the sectional tournament, held to determine who would qualify for the state tournament, the coaches in Randall Park's region deliberately selected judges ("old fogies") who would evaluate the debates based on their favored stock issues perspective. In contrast, debaters at one school placed a poster of dinosaurs in their room with the name of prominent old-fashioned judges next to each dinosaur (field notes). A few years later a group of younger coaches sent around a flyer with the headline "Dinosaur Debating Is Dead," angering the older coaches and revealing the challenges of paradigm change.

In many activities, this diversity of perspective would be considered a substantial disadvantage. Imagine a baseball game in which umpires create their own strike zones (in fact, they do, but that is seen as an unavoidable problem). In debate, this difference of perspective is considered by many a benefit: that debaters do not have an objective standard, but must adapt to different audiences, contributing to the idea that debate should be *communication*. This argument assumes that participants will be aware of the judge's perspective and that the judge will be able to state his or her own paradigm. While the best teams engage in *judge shaping*, convincing the open-minded judge that their perspective deserves to triumph, judge adaptation is hard to avoid. Even in national-circuit debate, which has a reputation for being more open to different arguments, judges have preferences, and in those circumstances debaters who emphasize stock issues often have little success; ironically, especially among judges who claim that they are open to whatever speakers want to argue.

Judge adaptation is crucial to success. To win a round, one must win the judge. In the words on a debate T-shirt: "Adapt or Die." One

Minnesota team constructed seven or eight versions of their affirmative case, tailored to particular types of judges (interview). Judge adaptation is seen as a profound benefit of debate:

> [I use judge adaptation] to teach audience analysis, know your audience. . . . It's a basic theory of communication and persuasion to understand and know your audience and adapt to them. (interview)

> [Judge adaptation] is critical. Critical to being a successful debater and I think critical really to learning a lot about debate. Kids who don't understand judge adaptation have missed a big part of what you learn when you learn how to debate. . . . One of the main reasons I think it's desirable, particularly for high school kids, is that they tend to be egocentric and they tend to think . . . that everybody should see the world as they do, and I think if they can figure out that other people see the world and experience the world a lot differently than they do, and that they need to accommodate that, that's life's lesson. (interview)

Of course, judges do not have random standards for evaluation, and so what holds for one judge holds for others; differences may be subtle, but are critical in achieving success.

The flip side of judge adaptation is what might be labeled judge insertion. To what extent should judges insert themselves in a round? Some judges, particularly those who define themselves as open to tabula rasa [blank slate], claim they judge whatever the debaters choose. This stance is in practice an illusion, if for no other reason than that two teams might choose to make different kinds of arguments, pleading with the judge to give priority to those that they find important. Further, adolescents, devoted boundary testers, create juvenile arguments simply to test the judge's willingness to accept anything. Even judges whose philosophy is to deny that they are the center of the round, and that "You debate, I judge," cannot help but intervene, even if it is the "debater's round."[42] One male team, facing two female debaters, argued that the team wearing the nicest ties should win the round. Another team presented a kritik that debate should be "a theater of pain," justifying sadism. On another occasion, a male team stripped to their boxer shorts while debating two females (who could have, but did not, run a feminist kritik on male hegemony). Are there no limits to what can occur in a round? As one judge, sympathetic to the tabula rasa style, noted in regard to this incident:

> I have begun to think that judges must take a stand. . . . When it comes to the point where it says: "we will sexually harass these young women because we think it is a 'cool' paradigm!" I personally, am not tab [tabula

rasa]. . . . The judges must take a stand on what is acceptable and what is not acceptable.[43]

Debate is supposed to represent mature behavior, so childish strategies must be policed and repressed. In theory, most judges support the ideal of letting the debaters choose the issues on which to clash and not intervene in deciding what issues are most important in the round. Yet, the dichotomy between intervention and nonintervention is false. Even conservative, stock-issues judges know that it is up to the teams, not the judge, to make the case; yet, in my interviews, almost all judges recognized limits, even if there was not complete consensus on the location of these lines:

> There are some issues [on which] I will [intervene] . . . if there is . . . unethical behavior going on. . . . There has been a situation where I had a team that was reading evidence from an article that I had just read, and I knew they were massively misquoting the article, and that [the] particular piece of evidence they were using from that source was what would have won them the debate . . . I voted against it because that was something that I knew was unethical behavior in the round, and I did insert myself. (interview)

> I consider myself a reasonable person, and I would probably use the reasonable person's standard. And if the links are too tenuous, I would step in, even if the other team had not. (interview)

> If you're totally obnoxious . . . there are some rules that you can't go beyond. You know, if you're rude and you're downright nasty, you're not going to pick up my ballot whatever the round was like. (interview)

These coaches each raise different issues that would allow—or require— them to intervene. Whether or not one accepts these particular justifications, the judge cannot escape the responsibility to monitor the round and to make a decision on what occurred and what the implications were for the education of debaters and the future of debate.

War Stories

Given the control that judges have over outcomes, it is common for debaters to believe that they have been cheated by an incompetent evaluator. Such a perspective protects them from the uncomfortable realization that, compared to their colleagues, they are less talented. Even such an objectively mediocre debater as this author managed to persuade himself that his record should have been more impressive than it was. Of course, for every team that loses a round unfairly, it stands to reason that another team must have won a round unfairly, although finding *those* victims is difficult indeed. Thus, coaches try, usually unsuccessfully, to comfort teams by telling them, "Sometimes you win when you shouldn't. It all evens out." Yet, conversations among debaters are filled with horror tales at which tolerant friends nod and share a comparable story. These constitute the "war stories" shared among colleagues, reminding us that rhetoric is not wholly lost from the world of debate.

Part of the problem of evaluation is tied to the organizational structure of the debate world: there are not enough *trained* judges, particularly because of the modest pay they receive. As a result, untrained lay judges, who know little about the rules of this esoteric activity, are often asked to judge rounds. In such circumstances, debaters—quite reasonably— feel that they know more than those who hold the power. As David Cheshier, former director of Georgetown's summer high school debate workshop and currently director of debate at Georgia State University, asked: "Should students who devote all that time immersing themselves in these arguments be judged by people who don't have a very sophisticated understanding of these arguments? The prevailing feeling is that they should not."[44] As debate has moved from a model grounded in persuasion and communication to one grounded in argumentation theory and information processing, the need for specialized judges has become evident. Lay judges, according to many, may be able to evaluate Lincoln-Douglas values debate, but not policy debate. The basis of how these outside judges make judgments, while similar to how citizens evaluate political candidates, undercuts the standards of this social world. Debate like many other activities (such as calculus, auto mechanics, or gymnastics) is subcultural. A debate judge could no more referee a basketball game than the reverse. If it were only the case of assigning numbers of points to teams, lay judges could, perhaps, escape some scorn; yet, it is in their explanations that they reveal their outsider status. Still, perhaps it is a tribute to the public image of debate as essential to democracy that many assume that any well-informed citizen is competent to evaluate a round.

Encounters with naive judges emphasize that debate is not a transparent activity, but requires specialized knowledge of the rules of the game. The accounts are humorously memorable, even if some stories are elaborated and reworked, as good stories always are:

> Ever had a judge come into the round and say, "Do you guys have a topic to debate, or do I have to give you one?" Or when [cross-examining] the 1A, have the judge ask, "Are you asking me or her?"[45]

> Once, the only comment I got from a judge was that he felt no one "made love

to him" with their speaker [*sic?*]. Then there was the judge who voted us down because "she just didn't buy the plan."[46]

> We were at [a] tournament that was using parents to judge rounds. We were neg, and the judge gave the round to the aff. On the neg ballot, the judge wrote, "The use of 'Cards' was distracting." He then went on to write something to the effect of "I gave the affirmative the round because they didn't use many of these 'Cards.' "[47]

Complaining about judges involves the same emotional release that complaining about umpires or referees has in sports. In an activity in which one's success rests outside one's own hands, these complaints produce empowerment and a recognition that uncertainty can be managed through talk—as it is, in another sense, in the round.

Debate Politics

Although judges do not always admit it, decisions in situation of ambiguity and uncertainty are shaped by factors that are extraneous to the event itself. In other words, debate rounds are not only won or lost on what happens in the round itself: politics, in the broadest sense, matters. To be clear, I am not alleging conspiracy or bribery. I am not suggesting even that judges insert politics consciously; nor is it possible to disentangle all of the factors involved in a decision. Excepting the rare unethical occasion, there is no way of knowing whether decisions are political. For instance, how does one decide when a judge evaluates the debaters of a coach one dislikes. As a coach noted about a personal dislike:

> Before [a financial dispute] we'd been friends on the circuit, and our teams worked together . . . then it got to be a very political thing in terms of would he vote against my team because we had this falling out, would I vote against his team. . . . Who's voting against whose team for what reason? Can you get a [favorable] ballot from this person? . . . That's very unpleasant . . . the kids are just pawns in some kind of adult game. . . . I remember in high school debating a round once where this guy voted against us, and it turned out that he and my coach had a lawsuit. (interview)

If politics is all there is, then what is the point of having the round? Tournaments could be decided in the judges' lounge; the outcome is out of the control of the debaters. Yet, sometimes decisions are complex. On occasion, the judge must decide between the more skilled team and the team whose arguments *in this round* were better. It is difficult not to give the win to the former.

The presence of politics becomes particularly difficult to determine be-cause some judges "lean over backward" to be fair; but the very act of leaning over backward is itself political.[48] As one coach noted of a col-league, "We will lose a [judge's name] ballot every time, but it's not that it is political. . . . I think he likes those kids so much he's afraid to vote for them. People overcompensate" (interview). On another occasion, a coach emphasized that in one round he gave a win to a female debater he dis-liked, noting, "I wanted to down her, but I just couldn't." The question, then, is how did his attitude—of which he was painful aware—play into his decision? It certainly mattered to him; there was no way that he could judge the round as if he had no feelings toward this girl—just as we can never treat blacks or women *only* as people in a society in which these are important and marked social categories.

In my research in Minnesota—a fairly ethical debate community—consensus existed that politics influenced many decisions, and there was considerable concern about this perception. One successful coach startled me by explaining that, in his view, "I think you have a fifty-fifty chance of getting a fair decision at the end of the year" (interview). As usual, joking reveals the heart of the matter. One judge kidded a debater by claiming, "I wanted to tell you that I thought you were awful, but I voted for you because your coach is my friend" (field notes). On another occasion, in a late round at the national tournament, a South Dakota judge gave a Min-nesota team a courtesy vote, since he knew they were going to lose, and did not want the decision to be unanimous (field notes). Judges worry explicitly that when they give debaters from a school losses several rounds in a row, the school's coach may perceive that they are biased; so, on occasion, they will make a point of telling the coach that their deci-sions were not political. One judge told me how badly she felt because she "dropped every Covina team I judged. I felt so bad" (field notes).

Stories abound alleging favoritism.[49] Some judges are considered to be friends of a team, likely to "pick them up," while others are opponents, likely to "drop them." While these decisions can sometimes be traced to judging paradigms, often they are linked to personal or political factors. Cliques in a community in which people have worked closely together over years are real and powerful:

> There's something going on in the state right now, and that's that five or six coaches get together and [have] a pact of some sort. Their teams work together, they're real effective, they share a lot of information. . . . But I think in some ways that might alter their judgment later. . . . Their coaches have been part of this network for a really long time. . . . Judges selectively choose who they want to win and rig their decisions. . . . Judging varsity, I feel a lot of intense pressure to make the right decision, and [to make] that right decision . . . a political decision; and I felt a lot of times that's not fair and in some respects have . . .

probably gone the other way. Maybe this other team didn't deserve it, but I was sick of the politics. . . . Sometimes I've regretted the decisions I have made. (interview)

I found it hard for my kids to win in Minnesota when I first started coaching, and . . . I see . . . a little bit of a cliquishness or something. . . . There have been times when I first came in this activity [when I would] pat you on the back, and you [would] pat me on the back. The old boys' kind of network. [Question: You mean, I'll vote for your team, you vote for my team?] I think those kinds of things sometimes happen. . . . I think there were some that were fairly explicit. I know for a fact that I had a team in the final round for national qualifiers one time, and there was a fellow who was a friend with another fellow, and this fellow had two teams. There were two debates going on, and two teams were gonna go on from those two debates, and this coach who was judging our debate told me as much as he waited until the other debate was decided before he made a decision in my debate round with my kids, because he wanted his friend's team to go on, and if the other team didn't go on, he was gonna let the team that debated my kids go. He told me that. (interview)

Instances like this remind us that although ostensibly debate is an activity for the kids, it is also an activity for adults whose reputation results from what happens in those rounds over which they have little control.

In addition, given that the decision that a judge—often a self-interested coach—makes in a round between teams *A* and *B* may help his or her team advance to final rounds makes such claims plausible. For instance, Randall Park debaters were angered at a coach of another school who gave them an upset loss against a poorly regarded school at the NFL tournament qualifier. This loss eventually had the effect of having that coach's school qualify for nationals, instead of Randall Park. The Randall Park debaters and some of their coaches were convinced that this decision was strategic, not based upon the arguments in the round (field notes).

On occasion, bitterness can become a matter of public display, injuring the image of debate as a community of friendly colleagues. The rarity of these public disruptions make them memorable in the lore of the community:

I was told by another coach that the year Mrs. Miller was given the award for Minnesota coach of the year, a frustrated rival "walked into the judges' lounge and said it would be a cold day in hell before I'll vote for any of Annette Miller's teams." (field notes)

Politics may not be beanbag, but it can be a powerful force. Part of its insidious quality is that it is hard to know when it is present, with judgments easily shading into paranoia.

REP BALLOTS

No matter how much a judge wishes to be a blank slate, upon entering a round typically she or he knows the teams by reputation. The social context of the round is known to the experienced judge. Even at the NFL tournament, operating by code, these codes are easy to break. The judge facing a prominent successful "rep" team versus an unknown team can hardly help but have certain expectations of the outcome of the round: to deny that is to delude oneself. The presumption of what is likely to happen in a round can be overcome, but that overcoming is part of the round. Again, one may choose to lean over backward, but that stance still takes reputation into account.

The prevalence of reputation ballots is hotly contested, believed more by coaches and debaters from losing schools, who are not the most unbiased of observers and have reasons for wishing to believe that reputational ballots are common. Teams do not receive strong reputations randomly, but because they are talented, work hard, debate often, and have excellent coaches and large budgets. Separating skill from reputation is impossible, and assumes that judging decisions can be objective, which is also impossible. Yet, for all that, reputations are believed to have power separate from ability. For instance, a coach from a school without a strong reputation told me:

> I lose lots of debates that we [really should] win. . . . You get . . . strange judging at the varsity level, because it's [already] decided who the winners and who the losers are. We've always been a loser school. . . . You asked me for a number [of ballots lost because of reputation]. I bet between 10 and 20 percent. (interview)

Others agree:

> At major national circuit invitationals, you deal with a pool of teams and judges that become very close after attending the same tournaments all year, and this creates the potential for decisions [based] on reputation. For a judge who has attended three tournaments in a row that have been won by Greenhill or Caddo, it is not hard to justify in their minds, one of those teams beating "Eastjabumfuck Central."[50]

Given the dispute over whether teams with strong reputations get more "leeway" in a round, it is striking to learn that some coaches—a minority view—believe that reputation ballots are, in close rounds, legitimate:

> I do think in some ways programs, by being fairly consistently good, earn some reputation, which maybe people take more seriously when a team walks in. And they may take them a little more seriously or something, and part

of that's what you work for as a team . . . to have some respect as a team. (interview)

I think that people got some wins because of reputation. But I don't think that it was done undeservingly. They may have won a few close ones on reputation, but I think it happened every year. I have done it. (interview)

Since reputations are dynamic, linked to effort and the paying of one's dues, certain teams can gain reputations and be the recipients of those wins and trophies. Indeed, one might ask whether, in qualifying tournaments to select schools to attend national events, it is more desirable to send the better team or the team that happened to triumph in that round. Again, this expectation effect is a function of the power of a tight-knit community; one is not only "downing" anonymous teams, but one's close friends, an issue with which coaches struggle, especially in break rounds or at important tournaments:

I think we try and be as fair as we can be. I think year after year, the more you're involved, the more difficult it becomes. I find it more and more difficult to be fair, only because you know the people involved. You know the coaches involved, and after a while you begin to know the kids involved. And it really becomes difficult to be subjective. I think sometimes, as a coach, you find yourself in a no-win situation in that no matter how you vote, no matter how, on a close round, especially if the teams are not as well prepared or well coached or well trained, they're not going to see this as, well, it could have gone either way. They're going to see it as a personal affront to them, and then it becomes more difficult. You have to consider [that] Janice Nyberg's teams or Annette Miller's teams are prepared to lose a round . . . then as a critic do you go, well, did I give them the loss because I know they can handle it better than the other team? (interview)

As this coach recognizes, there is no "truth" in a round in which two sides are arguing opposite positions. If it is a game, what are the rules? The expectations of how the world usually operates set the stage for understanding how that world operates in any given instance. Thus, the expectation that the judge brings into the round colors perception, shaping the outcome.

Life in the Round

The round is the fundamental unit of the debate world. Good teams debate more than one hundred rounds during the course of a season, feeling victory, tasting defeat, making friends, scorning poor judges, and, hopefully, learning about how to argue. Even those who suggest that debate is no longer a persuasive activity must recognize that, in some ways, it still is: there is a judge who must conclude—because of what debaters say and who they are—that one team or the other deserves to emerge victorious. These judgments never occur in the rarified world of truth, but are infected inevitably by the world in which they are made: with the friendships, enmity, respect, and scorn to which all social worlds are subject.

Surrounding the round is a social event: the tournament. This is the place in which the social networks of debate develop and flourish: a world simultaneously of teenagers and adults, a rare location in which teens and adults share some of the same values and attitudes. Teens are training to be adults, drawing on adult knowledge, while not giving up entirely some of the childish behaviors that served them so well when they were younger. The tournament is a world of emotion: honor, fear, exhilaration, love, nausea, brutal anger, and profound sadness and discouragement. Teenagers in the halls may be loud and boisterous, but debaters also draw upon an adult-sanctioned code of decorum and formality in dress that is rare in high school corridors. These strains provide us with insight into the struggles of teens as they expand the range of behaviors of which they believe that they are capable.

Five

Our Team

DEBATE is not just talk and research, but it is talk and research within an organizational and social structure. In this, debate is like all activity, and compares to other forms of voluntary behavior.[1] Debaters participate on a team: a group that provides a safe space within the hectic world of high school life. Their peers and coaches constitute their social world, the cocoon from which they emerge to meet other teens.

Teams demand considerable *social investment*, and must generate commitment strategies. First, a team requires a *temporal commitment*: participants give their time for the achievement of collectively valued and measurable ends. Second, joining a team means that one has decided to be involved in the lives of others. Belonging to a team demands *relationship work*. Third, groups routinely develop a *status structure* by which individuals are ranked in relation to others on significant dimensions. Finally, to engage in activity that is perceived as meaningful, participants develop a *group culture* or *idioculture* through which experience can be processed.

Within policy debate, the most important and delicate relationship is with one's partner. For adolescents, this is uncomfortably close to being a marriage. Success in this competitive world depends on taking into account the interests and concerns of another person. Some partners develop close relationships; others have relations that, like many marriages, are rocky, sometimes leading to separation. Sometimes a relationship may be tinged by eros, a problem when passion cools. Partners may experience love, respect, scorn, or disgust. If the two are not approximately equal in ability and commitment, tension can result, sometimes infecting the whole team. The dynamics of these dyadic relations are central to how adolescents debate. The partnership may be the first extended instrumental relationship in which an adolescent must deal with a status peer. Adolescents base these relationships on adult models, cribbed from the media and the observations of family and friends.

Team Life

As high school debate is organized through a team or club, the activity is a form of small-group behavior.[2] Teams vary from a handful of participants (for policy debate, only two partners are required) to several dozen.[3] Debate constitutes a smaller group within the larger high school: a place of refuge, a haven from a sometimes harsh and heartless social scene. The team serves as a home space for its participants—a space of powerful and intense relationships. It is a setting that, in practice, amounts to a "lifestyle enclave," providing support for interests and practices that may be scorned in other high school domains.[4]

Teams differ as to whether they are centered around a formally constituted high school class that may either be voluntary or compulsory (at some schools, teachers require debaters to enroll in the same class each year), or may function only as an extracurricular activity. While teams succeed under either system, having a class with the team run by a teacher provides a structure and stability not found in many other high school leisure domains. With the decline in the number of schools offering debate, and with fears for the future of the activity, some interested observers have discussed the possibility of organizing debate programs outside of the aegis of schools, permitting students from several schools or neighborhoods to participate—just as Boy Scout troops are organized. Indeed, at some tournaments, unaffiliated students debate as "mavericks."[5]

At both Randall Park and Greenhaven, debate is taught as a class. The class at Randall Park, taught by Mrs. Miller, is not required, but most debaters attend it. It is an easy way to receive a high grade without doing work over and above the work expected from being on the team. Teaching this class, in place of a required English class, also benefited Mrs. Miller in that it did not require extensive preparation or much formal teaching. The class met during the final period of the school day, permitting work to continue after school. It also meant that on those Fridays in which the team attended a tournament, one less class was missed. Typically, students worked in the school's debate room—Mrs. Miller's classroom—for two to three hours, often not leaving until after five o'clock. There were originally sixteen students on the class list, but two of those students dropped out early, and one of the most active debaters was not registered in the class. The team consisted of fifteen students: two seniors, seven juniors, and six sophomores—three females and twelve males. The team varied considerably in their commitment and interest; four of the students were distinctly marginal members, rarely attending tournaments and doing relatively little work.

While the Randall Park team had a generally successful year, they were particularly respected for the strength of their novice debaters, clearly the best in the state; and within two years, they were highly successful at the National Forensic League tournament. While there were some intense friendships and dislikes, the team was not characterized by either a powerful closeness or a profound interpersonal hostility. Despite occasional flare-ups, the team functioned successfully; the school's top varsity team was one of the stronger teams in the state, although not one of the very best.

Debate is an intense activity, with a six-month season in Minnesota. It begins at the start of the school year; the first tournament is held in late September. Tournaments are scheduled each weekend, except over Thanksgiving and Christmas. The state tournament and the national qualifying tournaments are held in February. Unless a school's team is invited to the National Forensic League tournament in June, most teams disband in February. The debate class at Randall Park was held only during the fall semester, with students selecting other extracurricular activities in the spring. Yet, in Minnesota—and in most other states—the debate season is twice as long as that for other "sports." States and school districts operate with different rules, and in some areas debate activities are more limited. In contrast, for schools that participate on the "national circuit" (see the appendix), tournaments continue through May. The time together builds an intimacy not found in many other high school activities; this intimacy also potentially produces emotions that affect achieving their common goals.

To understand the power of these small groups, I examine several components of team life: temporal commitment, relationship work, a recognized status structure, and the development of a group culture. Each contributes to group life and to the powerful identity that results. Although teenagers can find these elements elsewhere, debaters have chosen a particular social space in which to participate. In meeting team expectations, they are moving into a world that has features of adult social organization, while still providing a zone of childish exuberance.

Temporal Commitment

Debate requires belonging to a group that depends on the commitment of members in a competitive setting. The desire to win generates pressure for demonstrating that commitment through spending time participating in and preparing for the activity. As a result, debaters have an obligation to their team.[6] The most committed adolescents spend enormous amounts of time, occasionally, as noted in chapter 8, to the detriment of their schoolwork. This places pressure on those not equally committed. Not only do students at Randall Park take the debate class, but they are expected to remain after school each day, visit the university library, attend weekend tournaments,[7] spend their evenings cutting cards or downloading material off the internet or through Lexis-Nexis, and develop strategies with their partners. When a school hosts a tournament, family members may become involved; parents are encouraged to participate by staffing the coaches' hospitality suite or by preparing and selling food.

The most active, committed debaters can spend upwards of forty hours a week. To some extent this is a personal choice, but it also is a group activity with pressure to match the commitment of one's teammates. One junior on the Randall Park team wanted to succeed as a debater, but was continually frustrated by the demands of his family:

> Darrin calls his parents to see if he can go with Doree, Phillip, and Brian to the University of Minnesota library. He reports back that he has to babysit for his younger siblings, while his father goes out to dinner. Mrs. Miller is clearly disappointed because she wants Darrin to become more integrated into the team. He jokes that she can babysit in his place. Darrin explains that his father doesn't like him to do work for debate after school, even when the work can be considered "homework." (field notes)

Students and their parents must select the proper level of activity, given the other commitments and demands of family life. When one's child is part of a group that depends on his or her presence, discipline poses a thorny problem. Parents must select the proper punishment for debaters (or, indeed, for any teenager who participates in a collective activity), knowing that one's child will not be the only one punished. Thus, one parent grounded his son for hitting his sister, a choice that also punished the young man's partner, coach, and teammates. In this instance, the partner was paired with a novice who had never debated at a tournament (field notes). A coach reports:

> I had a girl last year who snuck out and went on a date when she wasn't supposed to, purely socially, and came back, and her mom said, "Well, as a punishment, you're grounded, including you can't debate this weekend." [Question: How did you feel about that?] Oh, I disliked it. I think parents should discipline their kids without using school as a weapon like that. . . . These kids are part of a team; they've made a commitment. (interview)

Such scenarios, by no means uncommon, emphasize how dependent teams are on family politics over which they have no control. A more extreme case, not unknown in other competitive realms, is the debater who resides during the senior year with the coach or the family of a fellow debater, as did Iris, the Randall Park assistant coach, when her parents moved out of state. The possibility that one of the sophomores might live with Mrs. Miller was discussed briefly when it was learned that his parents were moving.[8]

Yet, despite social pressures, debaters set different goals for the amount of time that they wish to devote to this activity. Coaches must structure the team to provide for these levels of interest and commitment and ensure that more committed debaters do not resent those who devote less time:

> I do have a program that makes room for students who like the debate activity, but aren't addicted to it, and want to improve their skills, as well as the student who wants to spend a great deal of time on debate. (interview)

Yet, organizing a program for distinct groups of students whose needs may be dissimilar and who may resent the choices of others is not always easy.

Linked to time is the work space available to the team. Many high schools set aside a debate room, frequently the classroom of the teacher who coaches the team. To increase team spirit, coaches make this room a second home for their adolescent charges.[9] The room is a place to "hang out." Excluding sleep, team members may spend almost as much time in that room as in their bedroom at home. The messiness of the room is a mixed blessing, indicating the team's comfort level. The existence of a special space motivates students to spend more time on their debate work than they might otherwise have done. It is a place of both work and play: a place in which debaters feel that they *belong* and where they wish to be. It is a space in which they can be, at the same time, both adults and protected children.

We can think of commitment to debate in light of role distance.[10] To what extent will one make this activity one's exclusive calling? To what extent will one be defined by debate?[11] How tight should one embrace the activity? How are these choices affected by the pressures of others, and how do these choices affect others? I examine the problems of undercommitment, overcommitment, and the struggle to obtain a sense of balance.

UNDERCOMMITMENT

In some sense, undercommitment is the most obvious problem for a group; an individual may decide not to meet the standards that others have set. She or he does not live up to the stated or implicit expectations for group behavior. Surely a lack of commitment is evident among students who skip class, do not hand in assignments, do not attend tournaments, or get bored and leave the tournament before the end. These teens have found themselves in an unsatisfying environment and attempt to escape this onerous burden. That this has consequences when the school has some measure of direct social control, as in the case of classroom attendance, is obvious; however, it is less obvious why there is a concern for extracurricular work, apart from the embarrassment to the coach or the frustrations of one's fellow teammates. Yet, these pressures of social control are quite real:

> Don, the Randall Park assistant coach, jokes about Barry and Frank who missed the tournament this weekend: "They wimped out." Later, when Ram and Sean miss a debate because of the school's Sadie Hawkins Dance (to which girls invite boys), Don teases, "They're wimps. . . . They're not worthy of debate. . . . I think it is very unprofessional, undebater-like," and jokes that "we should pay off their dates to make sure they have a horrible time," so they would never make the choice again. He humorously, but revealingly, remarks, "I never did it because I was never invited." Another coach complains about two female debaters who chose to attend their school's Sadie Hawkins Dance rather than attend a tournament, indicating that "the level of motivation is poor." (field notes)

At times during the season, Mrs. Miller pressured her team, forcing them to give the attention to debate that she found lacking. On one occasion, she threatened: "I'm not going anywhere with you if you're not willing to work. Things are not going well, and we must work. I shouldn't have to beg. . . . I'll set up a schedule, and if you're not interested, you're not interested" (field notes). Part of the problem of these speeches by the coach is that they are directed to some members of the group more than others; they can lead to resentment on the part of those who feel that they are doing their share and to cynicism by those who feel that they are contributing at the level they feel proper, even if others believe that they are insufficiently committed.

OVERCOMMITMENT

Overcommitment would seem not to be a problem, at least within the activity itself. How could there be too much commitment? One coach emphasizes this point in suggesting that coaches and students need to be fanatics:

> A fanatic is a . . . student who is totally committed 100% to what they are doing. . . . They are the "type A" person who devotes time and energy to their . . . event without thought of immediate reward or acclaim. They are the ones who not only profess, but live the creed of success. They are forensics—its past, its present, and its future.[12]

Yet, this coach is extreme. Most would agree that for adolescents debate should not be the totality of their lives. Some teens cross over that line, becoming "debate bums." Perhaps the most dramatic instance of this was a day on which a part of the Randall Park High School building caught fire (a small and contained fire). Despite the clanging of fire bells and the evacuation of the building, team members continued to stay in the debate room and work on their cases. Mrs. Miller, knowing nothing of this choice, commented that had she known, "I would have had a fit" (field notes).

Some abandon any pretense of a normal high school life in order to pursue their activity. As one champion debater told me, "I debated and just went to high school on the side." This young man explained that by college he was totally burned out, a frequent complaint, even among high school seniors. Another former debater remarked, "I spent a whole year working harder than ever. I mean that's all I did. I spent all of Christmas break working in the library. So I killed myself, and then I graduated" (interview). Mrs. Miller commented:

> [To] kids who take debate too seriously . . . winning becomes so important that they lose perspective. . . . That's the kind of kid who worries me. . . . Jay Brown never graduated from high school; [there were some kids] who did nothing but debate and that was it—their whole thing. . . . I think that it's stupid. You have to have other things to do, too. . . . I try to impress upon the kids that schoolwork comes first and then debate. (interview)

For some, this leads to an unbalanced life, as debaters comment about their fellows:

> Charles, for example, he will not go to dances, he will not go to parties, he will not do anything. He would much rather work on debate. . . . I feel . . . it's almost like he's trying to build himself into a little wall and cocoon, so he doesn't have to get involved with anything else. . . . You lose out on so much of your social life. (interview)

> It's kind of mean, but a lot of these kids don't have a social life. I have been trying to get Tom to ask this girl out all year long, but he won't. He's afraid to. I mean he is sixteen; he ought to be dating. You've got to have a social life. It is important. You can't destroy yourself at sixteen. (interview)

Choosing some adult skills, these teens ignore others, keeping those childish areas of their behavioral repertoire. It is not for nothing that a coach quipped that "debate is an excellent birth-control device."[13]

Some even find themselves dreaming about debate, or, more worrisome, have nightmares, as one former debater noted: "I relive certain rounds that I won, and I have this nightmare about final round at Nationals my senior year that I go in and forget what I'm supposed to say. I've had it a bunch of times" (interview). One student joked that he dated a young woman from a school with a strong program because he wanted her file, a successful strategy, giving new meaning to getting into someone's briefs.

STRIVING FOR BALANCE

Too little commitment places a student outside of the world of debate, leading to resentment from one's fellows. Too great a commitment, while on the surface less damaging, has other drawbacks, leading to burnout or regret at what one has missed. Balance is needed. Participation is not an absolute; one can select an appropriate level of involvement, as long as one has the support of one's teammates and coaches. Yet, in practice, choosing this balance often involves tension. One assistant coach half-joked to his team: "Let me tell you a secret. You can be a good debater, or you can have a social life. You can't do both at the same time. You can be a bad debater and have a good social life" (field notes).

A marginal participant on the Randall Park team explained that he enjoyed the tournament he attended, but added half-jokingly, "I can't keep this up every week. . . . I just want to go to the fun [tournaments]," a comment to which his coach commented, "You have to pay your way." Evidently this young man decided that the cost was not worthwhile, as he participated little after that tournament. When I asked this young man at the end of the season about the least enjoyable aspect of debate, he remarked:

> Having to go to all the tournaments all the time, because I do a lot of other things beside debate. I mean if I devoted my full time to debate, I could have been the state champion if I tried. . . . I could have won easily, but I have a job. I like to skateboard a lot. And so I just really never had time for it. (interview)

He added that it required too much commitment, particularly given his commitment to skateboarding. Others left because of track, theater, and romance (giving up debate for "lipsuck"). One coach had to face the resignation of one of her top varsity debaters because he was a champion fencer. She commented that, one year, a top debater, also a star wrestler, wrenched his arm, allowing him more time to debate. Like many ambitious coaches, she said, "Thank God" (field notes).

Of all the students I met, no one struggled as hard with the question of balance as did Doree, the female senior debater at Randall Park. Doree felt she had made a commitment to her partner, Brian, but it was not a commitment with which she felt entirely comfortable. Throughout the season she struggled with her commitment, and would have reduced her involvement if Brian had had another partner. Doree explained:

> I guess I didn't realize how much work it was going to be. I also didn't realize it would take up so much of my time that I would become so strongly tied to it. . . . I think it's kind of self-destructive. . . . I mean looking at some of the people on the team, I feel like, "Gee, they're missing out." I look at maybe I

missed out on a lot of things too, although I tried not to. . . . [Doree explains she almost quit the team.] First of all, I can't quit my job. That was really number one; I couldn't. I ended up doing so anyway because I just couldn't handle it. But I said, "Brian, I'm not going to quit my job. I will quit debate before I quit my job." And I said, "Unless you help me, I'm going to quit debate." I wasn't threatening. I was just saying unless we come to an understanding, it's just not going to work. I wasn't going to quit Junior Achievement because I need a scholarship from Junior Achievement. . . . I had to keep my grades up because I'm going to have to apply to college and have to apply for scholarships. . . . After all that, I'm not going to have much time to go to libraries. And I said, "Don't push me into doing that," and he really didn't this year. I said that another thing was, "I don't know what you know about me and my mom, but she's very strict," and one of the things was I can't get my license until I was 18. I said, "Brian, there's no way I'm going to get to tournaments." He goes, "I'll drive you." I said, "Do you swear to God you will drive me to the tournaments, and to the library occasionally? . . . Otherwise I can't; it's just not feasible." He said, "Yeah, no problem." He didn't do any of that. Even one day when I was really sick, I said, "Brian, please take me home. I have to go home." He said, "No." I'm like, "Come on, you promised last year." He's like, "No, I didn't." I just got really mad. It's [as if] he did all this to get me not to quit, and then now that I'm in it, and I can't quit, he wasn't following through with it.

[Question: Why couldn't you quit?] If I had quit, right about the time when I was really getting drained out of things, Mrs. Miller would have been mad at me, Brian would have been mad at me. I would have felt like I had let the team down. It would have decreased morale. . . . I realize that I was probably a bitch most of the time, but it had come to the point where I didn't care. (interview)

In the next section, I discuss the problem of having partners with different levels of commitment. Here, I emphasize Doree's problems in achieving balance in her life, facing competing commitments, attempting not to let down a partner who depended on her. At the low point of the season in December, Doree, who was ill, getting five hours of sleep a night, vented to Diane: "I hate debate. I hate my life. I don't want to go to college" (field notes). While her acute despair passed, the ambivalence never did. This talented young woman found herself in a no-win situation. Add to this the facts that she had a meaningful social life with a boyfriend, was reserved, and was careful in not revealing her emotions to teammates and coaches. Her torment throughout the season was evident, eventually leading to her missing the state tournament because of a longstanding kidney infection. At one point, during her pain, Doree wondered half-jokingly, "Maybe I need to go to see a psychologist" (field notes). Mrs. Miller recognized her conflicting demands, but still commented:

"Sometimes she's more worried about how it looks on her résumé than she does [about] what really is happening." One assistant coach felt that Doree was "trying to figure out how she could please everybody in her life and not really alter herself too much. Not really put too much into it, but not make anybody mad" (interview). Another assistant coach, feeling that Doree's social life was the main problem, attempted to motivate Doree to qualify for the NFL tournament in California by reminding her that she could wear her bikini on the beach, and joking that they should buy her boyfriend a ticket (field notes). Fellow teammates, even less sympathetic, became adept at reading Doree's moods. If she prepared her arguments between tournament rounds, it was seen as a good sign: "That means she really wants it" (field notes). Often, she was seen as not wanting it. Children can get away with setting the terms of their involvement in ostensibly voluntary domains; adults are less able to. Doree's multiple commitments contrasted with the time-management tools available to deal with them.

Relationship Work

Any group of teenagers is a potentially fiery, unstable mix of hormones, anxieties, and tight allegiances. Bringing a dozen young men and women together, forging a team, is a daunting task. While this challenge applies to all groups, adolescents are at the age when they have recently acquired knowledge of the intense relationships of adult life—relationships that help to define their budding selves and public identities. Friendships should occur naturally, and while they can be encouraged by adults, the group determines its conditions of association. Some teams have regular parties; others would not dream of such events, preferring to separate their friendships from their extracurricular work. One coach notes the importance of social gatherings for his squad:

> I think [for] those students in particular [for whom] debate becomes a real focus of their high school education, the social atmosphere is necessary for their social growth, because even by going to debate tournaments, they're eliminated from a lot of the social interaction with other high school students sometimes, and that interaction with other students from the debate team within their school and from students from other schools I think fulfills that void that they might experience. (interview)

As part of a team, one becomes involved in an intersection of lives. One suffers the frustrations and joys of teammates. At times, this sharing of lives is intense. One Minnesota team lost their coach to a sudden heart attack; and shortly afterward one of their assistant coaches, who worked with the novice debaters, was involved in a serious automobile accident on the way to a tournament, suffering major brain damage. These teenagers were forced to deal with human mortality, while continuing their extracurricular activities. The success of the team throughout this personal turmoil was impressive.

The Randall Park team did not have to cope with such drama. As a group, they were generally friendly, although not especially close. The two top varsity debaters—a talented junior boy and a senior girl—were partners, a relationship I describe below. Although Brian and Doree had an amicable relationship, they were "not the greatest of friends." The prickliness of their relations affected the entire squad. As noted above, Doree was torn over the amount of time she had to devote to debate. More significantly, she never desired to be a leader: a role she left for Brian to fill. Despite sympathy for her difficult situation, at times the coaches considered her aloof and selfish in her decisions to limit her involvement. She chose not to attend the state tournament. While there was medical justification for her decision, other more committed debaters might have competed. For his part, Brian lacked the authority or maturity to direct the team; the coaches felt that, as a junior, he had not emerged as a natural leader. The second varsity team—a senior boy and a junior girl—while good debaters, though without the "raw debate talent" of the first team, lacked Brian's intensity. The three junior varsity debaters, all juniors, not a particularly talented group, had lengthy and complex relationships. Each was irritating in some way to his or her teammates. Although they could often be friendly, they made their resentments public; none had the ability to take a leadership role. The four sophomore novices, while collectively the strongest group, at times were frustrated by the time they had to devote to the activity and by decisions concerning the choice of partners.

By December, after a few disappointing tournaments and as the qualifying tournaments for Nationals loomed, Mrs. Miller, becoming increasingly frustrated with the bickering, dissension, and lack of work ethic of some of the debaters, switched partners. The two varsity boys debated together, as did the two varsity girls; the junior varsity boys each debated with a novice. This shook things up, but after Christmas the team members returned to their previous partners. The ambivalence among the team members continued, exacerbated by Brian's feeling that Doree was not doing her share and by his uncertainty over whether he would have a competent partner the following year.

Comparing the Randall Park team with others, the team, though never in turmoil, came up short. Assessments of the team in the postseason interviews were generally positive ("Everyone on the team was pretty nice to everyone else"), but the team did not measure up to the previous year in which two seniors had been charismatic leaders and had been extremely successful. Several students commented that they felt that team spirit was lacking, and Mrs. Miller described it as a difficult year. The success of the novices did not compensate for a sense of malaise.

Life outside the team affects what occurs inside. During the season, debaters fall in and out of love. Many of these relationships influence life on the team, affecting both mood and commitment. One coach reflected:

> We had an interesting situation this year where one of the debaters had a girl-friend, and . . . she had even been in debate so she knew the situation, and she became upset because she felt that she was being neglected once we got into January. . . . I just said to her, "You know the nature of the game, and you know that he's not running around with other women; he's with me every night after school until ten o'clock; so, he doesn't need that pressure right now. He doesn't need you to be saying to him, 'Spend more time with me,' especially when you understand this is important to him to be successful because this is his last year." Eventually they broke up, and she found somebody else. (interview)

The Randall Park team, despite stresses, functioned adequately, but other teams were not so fortunate. Consider an example from a coach who had the misfortune of coaching a team with his talented daughter and several headstrong boys:

> This was a very traumatic year for me. . . . Two of my best four debaters quit their senior year. It was further aggravated by the fact that my daughter . . . was one of my best four policy debaters . . . pretty much the rest of the varsity seniors were all boys; they could not deal with this really incredibly bright young lady, and I had a sexism problem on the team. Nobody wanted to debate with my daughter, which is one of the reasons I decided to move her into Lincoln-Douglas [one-person] debate. . . . I was very, very involved in that from the very personal position as a parent, not only as a coach. . . . So, it was after I moved my daughter out . . . my two other boys decided to quit because . . . they wanted to pick their partner and they would say, "Coach, I'll debate, but I'll debate if I can debate with X." And I'd say, "No, no, that's still my decision." . . . They said, "Well, if I can't pick my partner, then I won't debate." And I said, "That's your decision." . . . Losing teams have a problem in that they're always looking for someone to blame for their losses, their failures. Winning teams present a whole different set of problems. You have a problem of arrogance, you have a problem of over-inflated self-images and egos. That was one of the problems I ran into with this group this year. (interview)

Although this coach was willing to accept the demands of his debaters and switch his daughter to another style of debate, perhaps because of his guilt over being simultaneously a father and a coach,[14] he was unwilling to accept the seemingly more minor demand that the boys choose their own partners. (If debate was an activity in which winning and losing was not crucial, such a choice would not pose a significant problem.) It was this latter decision that the coach considered a threat to his authority, and which led to the breakup of his powerful and successful team. For the debaters, friendship overwhelmed the authority of the coach, emphasizing the importance of relationships. The choice of partner influenced the season for the entire team, transforming what appeared a promising and happy year to one filled with frustration and anger.

More generally, outcomes impact small-group life. A successful team has a different emotional tenor from a team that must lower its expectations. There is nothing like victory to provide a soothing and healing balm. On those weeks that the Randall Park team did well, the team was more congenial than when the weekend was a source of frustration. The successes or failures of one's colleagues shape the quality of life. Ultimately the commitment that debaters bring to their activity cements them as part of this small, dynamic organization with others who share that commitment.

Team Status

Any group develops not only a division of labor but also a status structure through which participants can order each other on meaningful dimensions.[15] These statuses can be powerful in determining one's emotional attachment to the group and in channeling permitted behaviors. While in other groups, race, gender, and age are salient—and they are not absent in the world of high school debate—in competitive activities one's skills, commitment, and success define one's position. One's identity is shaped each round. Each victory ratifies one's standing; each loss provides an opportunity for an account that legitimates one's ability in the face of negative feedback. While some debaters have their own "groupies," followers who watch them debate, others receive little but scorn for their efforts. While it is reasonable that high status often buys rewards,[16] I focus on poor reputation and the strains of competing for scarce status to examine how status concerns shape the internal life of team activity.

COMPETITION FOR STATUS

Given the legendary precariousness of the adolescent ego at a time when position seems to matter, status can become of great significance to the emotional life of the debater and of the team. Who you are is how you do.[17] For this reason, coaches may play on the vulnerabilities of teenagers to motivate them. For example, the coach of the Denton team switched his "A" and "B" teams to motivate the top team, which he felt was not debating as well as they should, and to reward the second team, which had reached the semifinals in the previous tournament. Significantly, the label of A and B teams had no practical effect, as both teams were debating in the varsity division. Yet, the switch was seen as being highly meaningful, and may have impelled the former A team to work harder to regain their rightful place, as both Denton teams reached the semifinal round at the next tournament (field notes). Jealousy can impel action, but it is a dangerous game. Such attempts to pit one pair of debaters against another can backfire, undermining team spirit and unity, as when one debater told me that he was no longer interested in the success of two younger teammates who were going to participate in the national tournament (field notes).

It is common for teenagers, even in the face of continual feedback from judges, to be uncertain and anxious of how they rate on the team and in the activity. Even a highly successful and praised novice like Ram, whose record as a novice was 32–2, admitted to feelings of insecurity, wondering if his streak of victories would continue. More problematic was the other novice team—Barry and Frank—who at most tournaments were not as successful as Ram and Sean. Frank, in particular, was marginal. Even though he and Barry did quite well, even winning a tournament, he was edgy about his status, particularly as compared to the other sophomores. In fact, Frank was not as effective a speaker and did not work as hard as his peers, although he devoted considerable effort to debate. His performance varied considerably, weak one day and relatively strong the next. Throughout the season, he was not respected by the other novices, and on occasion Barry wanted a new partner. At each tournament, the varsity debaters and assistant coaches would ask Barry, "How's Frank?" Never the reverse. Novice status was a continually touchy subject for this team. When Barry and Frank reached the finals of a junior varsity tournament, Frank turned to Barry, asking with some pathos, "Are you proud of me now?" He told me later, "He said last week that he wasn't proud of me" (field notes). This reached a head at the tournament in which Barry and Frank reached the final round. A coach at another school, seeing them in the finals room, assumed that it must have been an error. Frank, disgusted, told Barry, "What a jerk!" For Frank, fighting for his status, this was no innocent mistake.

While debate was important to Frank, and the approval of his teammates mattered a great deal, he felt that the other novices were too "intellectual," and did not have the same interests in sports, music, dating, and hanging out. He recognized that he was at least partly responsible for their losses, remarking sadly, "It felt like when we'd lose a round, and you get on the ballot, and it would say 1AC is at fault, you know. It's kind of, 'Oh, it's my fault again,' so it's kind of hard" (field notes). Frank wanted to participate in a world in which he was not fully a member. He was always on the edge of slipping to a lower rung. Eventually his father took a job in another state, and Frank told me that he did not expect to debate again. The status he wanted on the team was too difficult for him to achieve.

COPING WITH LOW ESTEEM

For many coaches, telling a student that he or she lacks the skills for varsity debate is particularly painful. This is necessary in that many tournaments place a limit on how many varsity teams from any one school can attend. Even after a student has debated for several years, a coach may feel that the student has not reached the level necessary for varsity competition, a decision that may be made harder if less experienced or younger debaters have reached that level. Yet, at least these debaters have an escape. Participants who do not find themselves successful and esteemed can leave the activity, finding something more suited to their abilities and motivations—impossible in academic classrooms. To be sure, they will have lost investments of time, energy, and some money, but many in this situation simply cut their losses.

The Randall Park team had several individuals for whom the rewards of debate were less than the costs. These four young men and women were fully marginal in the activity, and by the middle of the season did little work. Perhaps some of them would have succeeded with intense effort, but most likely they would have remained marginal. Their behavior and status were consistent, if discouraging for those who believe that debate has profound benefits for all.

More interesting were three juniors, each active in debate, who professed to enjoy the activity. None of the three was very successful, and individually and collectively they received little status. At most tournaments, these boys debated junior varsity in contrast to their teammate, Brian, also a junior, who was regarded as one of the outstanding debaters in the state. One of the assistant coaches noted the problem by remarking: "If I were a JV person, and I wasn't very good, but I had seniority, I think I would have felt really angry if I were passed over by novice kids to go to the state tournament. . . . That would have kind of clued me right there."

Danny Melton was a bright and enthusiastic boy, slowly losing his vision—a nearly insuperable obstacle for one who would have to read quantities of evidence—and he had not learned braille. He was convinced that he could be an outstanding debater, and he became frustrated when he was forced to debate with partners that he considered beneath him.[18] The fact that he lost his first fourteen rounds of the season did little to change his self-esteem. Like Danny, Darrin Sisk had a large ego, and was convinced that he should be on a varsity team. Teammates felt that Darrin was arrogant, and he was scorned for his unique views as to what would make a good case. Carl Dayton was not as self-confident as his friends, did not work as hard, and preferred to debate on the junior varsity level because he would have a better chance to win rounds. Carl loved to speak, but cared less about doing the preparation before the round. Typically, two of these three would debate together, and some weeks they attended tournaments as a team of three, trading rounds.

"The Juniors" were a standing joke and a problem. Mrs. Miller, having two strong varsity teams, had no desire to let these junior boys debate on a level at which they would fail, and, more than that, embarrass her. She and the other coaches joked about the boys' lack of ability, referring in October to their poor performance, "I think I have the wrong team in novice" (field notes). With two strong novice teams, she had to be somewhat careful not to offend these three juniors by having the novices debate varsity, while the juniors were still in junior varsity, although by the end of the season that happened. As one of the boys noted when I asked him about the least enjoyable aspect of debate, he responded:

> Some of it's the in-team politics. Who gets paired with who, and how [coaches] decide who the teams are and which bracket [varsity, jv, novice] they'll go in. That sometimes seems to be a bit unfair in the way that's arranged. . . . [The novices] came in, and here I was with a year of experience plus institute, and then these exceptionally good novices come in and just take over, and take the slot that I was supposed to have, and so I had a little problem with that. (interview)

He convinced himself, however, that the problem was that he just did not work as hard as he could have.

Don Davis, the assistant coach, was particularly annoyed at these juniors, continually making jokes about them and fantasizing about how he could get them to quit to keep the team "pure." At one point, he commented, "They live in their own world." He asserted that they would never leave junior varsity and wistfully suggested that they be forced to deny that they debated for Randall Park. He joked that they should burn Darrin's letter jacket. One day he took a toy gun, pointed it at the back of Darrin's head, and pulled the trigger. Later, he saw Danny and told him that he would attend one of his rounds, joking, "As hard as it is to listen to you, I will" (field notes). For Don, the problem was "cooling out these marks," to get them to leave voluntarily. In our interview he described the problem:

> We were saying, How can we get rid of them? Or how can we track them to where they will be satisfied and they won't pose any real difficulty. . . . Danny is saying he's going to go to institute. . . . Danny says, "Well, I'm going to institute, spend $700 for it, I expect that I'm not going to spend the whole year in JV. I want to go varsity." . . . Darrin's not going to go to institute, and that's better because he often would use things like that as a leverage, or he would turn out a couple of briefs and then . . . would dangle that in front of [Mrs. Miller]. . . . How to get him to make peace without disturbing the whole thing too much [was a problem]. (interview)

It is easy to appreciate the perspective of these juniors who are taught that debate is based on effort and is an educational activity in which competitive success is not the primary criterion. The presence of these young men reminds us of the difficulty of creating an ordered status hierarchy when the values of the activity are based on a claim that is only partially held. The difficulty is how to achieve one's competitive goals while not bruising adolescent egos too badly. On the one hand, winning and losing should not be crucial, but, in fact, coaches want their teams to have a reasonable chance of success, and so must be placed at the right level of competition, despite the personal affronts that may result. Team harmony and justice may conflict with task orientation.

Group Culture

Every group develops a culture that comes to symbolize the group to its members. I have termed this local set of meanings and traditions a group's "idioculture,"[19] defining it as a system of knowledge, beliefs, behaviors, and customs shared by members of an interacting group to which members can refer and that will serve as the basis of further interaction.

Traditions can involve nearly all aspects of one's debate life. Nicknames are a prominent, but by no means the only team tradition. For example, the assistant coach of one team brought a hard-boiled egg before a major tournament, which the debaters and coaches shared, tying them together through their shared consumption, a tradition that was to become memorable and significant for the team during the season (field notes). Another assistant coach asked those debaters who were staying late to form a "circle of death" (field notes). As the season progresses, events become memorable and enter teamlore. For instance, the fact that Doree routinely used to convince her partner, Brian, to lug around her evidence at tournaments was often recounted (field notes). Another instance widely referred to was the day at summer institute when Danny was arguing against a women's prison case that his Randall Park teammate, Darrin, was running, and commented, "If I were a man, I'd object to special treatment for women." As Darrin narrated the story, the audience began to giggle without Danny understanding why. Danny added: "I was so intent on thinking. Then I said, 'Well, I am a man, so I would be pissed.'" (field notes). One assistant coach at Randall Park described the elaborate traditions that emerged when she debated:

> Where we ate was always important. We couldn't eat at the same place twice. . . . Always we bought new pens. Every weekend we had new pens. . . . Thursday night we'd always go to the store and buy them. . . . One of my debate partners always wore the same socks. He washed out his socks every Friday night and always wore his same lucky socks. . . . And then we never took down the pictures in our briefcases if we were winning. Once a cartoon went up and we won that weekend, the cartoon never came down, but if we lost that weekend the likelihood is the cartoon was gone. (interview)

As in any group, these traditions define the group; however, high school debate teams differ from other groups, in part because of the age of the participants (a reality I discuss in more depth in chapter 6), but also because the team, like other competitive groups, has goals that are simultaneously task-oriented and socioemotional.[20] Cultural elements serve not only as ends in themselves, but to help the group achieve specifiable goals as well. Team spirit, an intangible feeling that is exemplified in particular cultural traditions, creates cohesion and directs tension outward.[21] Team culture serves not only to define individuals, but to exemplify a moral order. At my son's first high school, Woodward Academy, the assistant coach, a fan of professional wrestling, borrowed the label of a wrestling group, "New World Order" (itself borrowed from American politics), to refer to his team as the "New Woodward Order." All members of the team received an NWO cap, making them recognizable at tournaments. The metaphor of strength, power, and a desire to win at all costs was deliberate. One day, Mrs. Miller posted a picture of the Maharishi Mahesh Yogi along with an article describing his plans to build a town in Oklahoma. Next to it, she placed a telling note, which became part of the team culture: "The last-place person this weekend gets sent to Oklahoma to serve the Maharishi" (field notes). Not only did this serve as a joking threat and as motivation, it also related to a case that two novices planned to run to force juvenile offenders to practice transcendental meditation to direct them from a life of crime. In another example, at one overnight tournament, the Randall Park team staged an ice-cube fight at a motel as an initiation for the novices.

Successful or colorful phrases that one teammate may use in a round or practice can be used repeatedly. After Ram used the phrase, "The affirmative is attempting to hang the status quo, but they don't have a rope," Frank was so impressed that he used the same phrase in the next three rounds in which he was on the negative. The phrase entered the culture of the team, both because it was amusing and because it was seen as persuasive. Eventually, Frank decided that the line was so effective that it should be used only on special occasions.

It is not only that culture is recognized internally, but that outsiders may recognize a "team style," a style modeled by the coach or senior debaters. One coach informed me that he believed that teams reflect the personality of their coach, detailing how different teams were extensions of the men and women who led them (interview). During my research, the Denton varsity team—all female—had the reputation of being bitchy and sarcastic. One team from an elite private school had the reputation of being stuck-up and snotty. Another team, Whitbridge, had a reputation for dressing alike, leading some to label them the "Whitbridge clones." A fourth team was known for its preppie style, with each debater wearing a collegiate sweater. Still another school was known for the fact that their male debaters wore stylish bowties. The range of typifications is impressive, as most prominent teams had stereotypes in the world of Minnesota debate.

Over the season, each team develops its own cultural traditions, which fit the background knowledge, normative standards, functional needs, status relations, and experiences of the team. This recognition indicates to participants that they belong to an organization that has collective meaning. Group culture makes belonging satisfying and identity-enhancing. The fact that these debaters are adolescents, recognizing the power of organizational life, adds piquancy to their traditions, but even adults cement individuals into an organizational structure.

The Challenges of Partnership

As complex as team life is, nothing can rival the intimate power of a dyadic relationship. Few things can be as satisfying for an adolescent as knowing another with whom one can share one's hopes and desires, who is fun to be with, who shares one's emotions, and with whom one wants to spend time. Who would not wish a marriage with these characteristics? Yet, when there are disagreements, tensions, and hostility with another person that one has been yoked to, and on whom one depends for one's identity, satisfaction, and reputation, little can be more painful and frustrating. The relationship is reciprocal: just as you depend on another, another depends upon you. Rejection can be matched by another's rejection of you. In these ties, teens can be adults, while still not jettisoning all the egocentrism of childhood.

The closest to such relations that are to be found in the teenage years is the dating relationship ("going steady"), but at least with dating relations, if the experience proves unsatisfactory for either partner, they can break it off, perhaps finding another who better meets their needs in a dating market. Such is not the case with one's debating partner. Putting aside the decisions of the coach, not many potential partners exist on any team. Further, unless the potential partner wants to switch, unless one's own partner feels the switch is desirable, and unless the partner of one's potential partner also wishes to switch, such changes, unless mandated by the coach, bring trouble in their wake. For most debaters, the success and satisfaction of their debate career is intimately and inextricably linked to the characteristics of their partners. While some teams routinely switch partners, in varsity debate partnerships are relatively stable and emotionally complex. The choice of who will be partnered with whom—in practice, one of the most sensitive issues that a coach confronts—is hardly a casual matter. Despite the talk of education, virtually all participants want to be paired with the strongest debater possible. All too often failure is attributed to an incompetent partner. Given that individual debaters may have a higher estimation of their abilities than their peers and mentors have, choices of who will be partners can be perceived as unfair and offensive.

To explore the world of debate partnership, I examine positive ties, negative relations, whether partners need to be friends, romantic entanglements, and negotiating a disparity of commitment. I conclude with a discussion of the division of labor in light of positions in the round. While the analysis is based on much observation and interviews, I particularly draw upon the relationship between Randall Park's top varsity debaters, Doree and Brian, which serves as a model of the strengths and weaknesses of partnerships.

Partnership as a Positive Relationship

Two teenagers who enjoy the same activities are likely to become and remain friends when impelled to spend time together. Friendship is not merely a random choice, but the pressures of social circumstances tend to produce positive relations. In workplaces, people strive to be friendly, and these attempts typically, although not always, are successful. In other words, it is in the interest of partners to make every effort to become friends, and to define a mixed relationship as a friendly one, hopefully convincing themselves in the process.[22]

A classic instance of a positive partnership was that of Don and Ravi, the previous year's champion debaters from Randall Park. They began debating together their first year, and continued successfully for three years. Both were bright and articulate, but more significantly they had the same goals and worked hard to achieve them. Don had a superb analytical mind, and Ravi was a graceful and persuasive speaker. Although no relationship is without its strains, this dyad represented to many what debate partnerships should be. The relationship between Sean and Ram, Ravi's younger brother, friends since fifth grade, seemed likely to become a strong partnership.

During the year I observed, the ideal partnership was that at Greenhaven between Vic and Laurie. These successful debaters had been teamed for three years. They never had a romantic relationship, had different networks of friends, and were not emotionally close, but as their coach put it: "They have a true respect for each other. . . . They know each other so well. . . . It's a very complementary partnership." According to the assistant coach: "They know they are different people, and they like each other a lot, but they don't like each other. They have no interest in being friends outside of the debate context" (interview). Vic was the more persuasive speaker and wrote the cases, learning everything about their affirmative case on women's prisons; Laurie, faster, highly competitive, and more intense, did a large proportion of the library research, collecting negative evidence. While the relationship between Doree and Brian was complex and mercurial, both indicated that they liked the other, and did not see their disagreements as personal clashes. They often teased each other and cared about each other's successes and failures. At one point, Doree explained to Brian that she liked to debate with him, because over time she could guess the arguments that he would present. Their minds were in sync. Although their goals differed, they admired each other, and, had Doree more free time, they would have been even more successful.

Negative Dimensions of Partnership

Tolstoy remarked that all happy families are happy in the same way, while unhappy families have their unique forms of misery. So it is in debate. Although most partnerships work, failures are memorable. At Greenhaven one of the better younger teams broke apart because of personal dislike. One of the debaters was so frustrated with her partner that she wished to leave an out-of-state tournament in the middle. She was convinced to stay, and made it to the final round of the junior varsity tournament, but she stopped debating after that weekend (field notes). Another debater, intensely frustrated with his partner, angrily told me that this boy "is coming closer and closer to death" (field notes).

This kind of relationship is particularly dramatic in those instances in which the anger flares in a public situation, such as at a tournament round:

> One of the strangest rounds I watched involved two debaters who clearly hated each other. They argued before the round was over about who should give the first affirmative. (Both wanted to.) Throughout the round they made cutting remarks to each other. He told her: "Sit down and stop your whining." She retorted: "I hate you." Then she added sarcastically, "Oh, fine, do what you want." (field notes)

While this represents an extreme example, rarely found among committed debaters, what is here said openly is sometimes felt or expressed privately. Needless to say, such relationships are unstable. For successful task orientation some commonality of values is essential.

More frequent is the oscillating relationship between Doree and Brian, which at some times did appear to be hostile. Their teasing often merged with insults; their joking discussions often seemed like fights; their bickering could seem like dislike. Thus, Doree said to Brian, only half-joking: "You know what I really hate is when you look at me when I'm giving a rebuttal. It's as if, if I drop anything, you'll hit me" (field notes). Theirs is occasionally a high-conflict relationship, larded with jokey talk, which, given Doree's ambivalence about her debate commitment, led one teammate to express bitterness:

> It really made me angry at the end of the year. She was treating Brian like dirt. . . . They could have gone to Nationals, but I think that she sort of sabotaged that last round. . . . I think she did it deliberately. . . . I think she threw that round, because she didn't want to debate anymore, and she goes, "I am so glad it is over." (interview)

Although this debater is probably not correct in the sense that Doree did not consciously decide to lose that round, he does recognize strain in the relationship.

Friends and Partners

Given the benefit of being friends, and the drawback of distaste, one might ask how important is it that partners be friends. Indeed, a similar question might be raised about marriage; can one have a powerful task orientation without an associated tight intimacy? Most people, certainly

most couples in an age in which spouses are supposed to be best friends
and lovers, would suggest that friendship is a necessary characteristic of
a relationship. Under the positive aspects of partnering, I described two
successful partner relationships: one in which the two debaters were close
friends, and the other in which they were personally distant. The extreme
example of a distant relationship was that of a Minnesota team that won
the national championship in the 1970s. One observer exaggerated that
the girl never spoke to her partner except to ask for directions to the
bathroom; yet, they succeeded, because they had the same drive. This
debater, now a prominent coach, described the situation:

> My partner that I ended up with at the end of the season, we were the top
> debaters, but we couldn't get along. . . . We just had severe personality
> conflicts. . . . It was a big joke on the debate circuit. . . . We had very sincere
> ideological differences. He was a very conservative Catholic Republican from
> a high-income family and I was a liberal Democrat, no religious background,
> from a low-income family and . . . we just could not get past our political
> differences to get along. . . . I think by the end of our senior year we decided
> that, you know, we wanted to be successful, and that, you know, Edwin was a
> fantastic debater, one of the most eloquent people I've ever heard, just a natu-
> ral, and I certainly wanted to be his partner, and I think he had similar feelings
> about me in terms of if we want to take a shot at the national championship,
> this is the team to do it. (interview)

This example reminds us that partners can agree to transcend differences.
The team was able to create a chemistry necessary for victory, although
how long that chemistry could last is unclear. Group life without personal affiliation is an unstable mix.

In contrast, debate puts pressure on friendships. Some friendships do
not stand the test of competition, even when the partners are ostensibly
on the same side. Such debaters compete against each other, rather than
against their opponents. Consider the following instances:

> Before the tournament, we were best friends. We got along great, and were
> really good friends. Now, when we debated, we were so mad at each other, we
> didn't speak for a couple months. Something just happens when we debate
> together. We have tried to work it out, but it just isn't going to work. . . .
> Should I just debate with [this partner] and be miserable? I am on the verge of
> quitting it altogether.[23]

> My partner . . . and I both had the same problem. . . . Our novice year we
> didn't debate together, and we were really close friends. We began debating our
> sophomore year, and we've been relatively successful since. We had to compro-
> mise our friendship to allow us to debate together, though. We are both very
> competitive individuals, and at times it seemed as though we were competing

against each other, rather than the other team. We still remained friends . . . but it was a different friendship. . . . It was more of a working friendship throughout our sophomore and junior years. Now in our senior year we are a lot closer than we were the past two years, in part because we are a lot more relaxed. We are more confident, and it has helped our debating and our friendship. . . . You understand your partner a lot better.[24]

These two young men were attempting to deal with a fundamental dilemma of friendships. It is difficult to maintain a friendship in which one's status is judged at the expense of one's friend's; when that status or power balance begins to change, as when one partner is seen as doing better, the friendship is under strain. Jealousy, that green-eyed monster, intrudes itself when the relative standing of two equals is altered, and when that alteration is publically acknowledged. When the unit is forced to make consequential decisions, as in a debate round, tension occurs over who should have the decision-making priority until a resolution is found. In the case of teenagers, who do not have much experience in linking expressive and instrumental relations, problems are often magnified.

Romantic Entanglements

As hard as friendship work is for adolescents, love is that much more difficult.[25] Heated though they are, the romantic relationships that develop when one is fifteen are not expected to last until one is sixteen. Often these relations cool in months, weeks, or days. Teens have learned some of the tools of love, but they have not lost the egocentrism of childhood. Both the exclusivity of the romantic relationship and the public display of the breakup can affect the partnership and infect the team. Of course, romances off the team often have similar effects. Yet, when attractive, hormonally intense young bodies spend time in the same space, developing shared understanding, romance is understandable. For boys and girls, sex is the frosting on the cake of friendship.

Most in the debate world warn against romantic relationships, difficult as they are to avoid entirely:

Don't debate with your girlfriend. It puts so much stress on your relationship, especially if one of you is a measurably better debater. . . . I have seen a lot of debater love, but I am hard-pressed to think of successful boyfriend/girlfriend debate teams.[26]

Where there's love dynamics on the team, that is the worst. . . . The last two years, I've become a regular Dear Abby, Dr. Ruth, or something. . . . I had a boy/girl team and they were doing fine. The girl had a boyfriend . . . but then as we got ready for regions we spent a lot of time together, and they took first place at regions . . . and really felt a bond that one had supported the other, and I could see this really did happen. So then, as we were getting ready for state, we had this love triangle, because we have this relationship on our team now where love is in bloom, and then the girl, her boyfriend helped out a lot with the team, who had been sort of a presence all year . . . so he was calling me and was upset, and he didn't know what was happening with his girlfriend, and [the team] did not work well at [the state championship]. (interview)

From the perspective of coaches, who are held responsible by parents, principals, and school boards to keep the team harmonious, it is easy to see romance as a threat. One coach explained:

I strongly discourage romance on the team. I tell the kids, you may be in love now, but when you break up you're going to have an enemy, and now you've got an enemy in the team you may have to debate with, and you hurt the team. So, if you want to have a romance or fling, keep your hormones in check, and find someone who does not debate. (interview)

Yet, from the stance of the teen who has no time for a social life outside of debate, the appeal of a social life *inside* debate is clear. At least while the romance is in flower, one can have one's cake and eat it too.

It is notable that not all boy/girl partnerships are explicitly romantic. For instance, Doree and Brian never had a romantic relationship. Doree was a senior and was more socially mature than Brian, who I never heard talking about girlfriends. Like many brothers and sisters, they would tease or tickle each other, and would, on occasion, wrestle playfully. Doree, who had a boyfriend off the team, felt that there were sexual undertones:

I don't know if he would ever admit to this, but I had a feeling for a while that he had a crush on me. . . . I definitely didn't have a crush on him. Well, in some ways I very much like his personality. There's a lot of things that are very attractive, and he has a lot of good qualities. I'm not attracted to him by any means, simply because he's a year and a half younger, which doesn't usually pose a problem with me, but it did in this one. . . . He seems younger. He was very immature, especially in male/female relationships. . . . He is still very little-boyish in that manner. . . . *I knew it would never work out even if we did act upon it.* . . . I liked him and I found him to be a very good friend at times, and he was fun to wrestle around with. It was like he was pretty much my little brother. (interview)

The power of romance is evident in the fact that even though this relationship had no potential to become romantic, it was a possibility that Doree thought about before rejecting it. Not to fall in love is a considerable achievement when coupling is normative.

Negotiating Commitment

Just as differing levels of commitment can affect team life, they have the possibility of raising havoc with partners. Adolescence is a special time, a vista of opportunities has newly opened: romance, parties, driving, even a work life. To the extent that most varsity debaters are males, this often relates to the significance of male bonding. To what extent should allegiance to a partner take precedence over other uses for one's time? How does one judge one's behavioral alternatives?[27] Is a tournament worth missing out on an important date, a job, or a family outing? Committed debaters tell horror tales of betrayal by those less committed:

> One of my best girlfriends went to [a tournament] with a sophomore who was being hailed as "our little prodigal" and considered, despite his inexperience, to have a real handle on debating. So they went, and started doing exceptionally well. . . . Yet midway through the tournament, in a round directly following lunch, [she] walks into the round alone, expecting [her partner], the glorious sophomore, to show up. He doesn't. After about fifteen minutes of anxious pen-twirling and throat-clearing, she has to forfeit the round. This cost them any hope for a placement showing. Apparently, [he] had decided that seeing the campus was more important than debating, and he'd gone for a stroll about the grounds. He wasn't lost, he wasn't upset, he just didn't want to debate.[28]

> I was eagerly awaiting my senior state tournament. . . . Wednesday night I went to get on the plane to Anchorage, and could not find [my partner]. . . . Finally, I had to catch the plane without my partner. We later found out his reason: he just did not want to come. . . . The moral is, never count on a partner too much.[29]

While the debaters reading this will certainly be sympathetic to the betrayed partners, it must be admitted that for adolescents, as for others, it is painful to confront a friend and say that one cannot do something that is important to that person, even though both had made a commitment. Commitments and desires may conflict. By disappearing, we hope the problem will vanish. Even when one's reasons for disengagement are legitimate, the pain is palpable. One coach explained about a star junior debater who chose to quit to spend more time with his ill father. His partner had to struggle with a sense of betrayal:

> It was sort of a struggle for him to be mature enough to understand that there was a good reason for it, and at the same time I think there was so much

bonding with partners that he felt a little bit of, you know, he never said betrayal, but maybe . . . Debate was his number one commitment. . . . You do get
kids who are do or die with it . . . and it's hard for them to understand a partner
that's not. (interview)

Like many troubled partnerships, the dilemma between Brian and
Doree concerned the centrality of debate in their lives, and the amount of
time that she could reasonably be expected to commit. For Brian, debate
constituted his social life, his passion. Not so for Doree. As Brian noted,
having watched the successful partnership between Don and Ravi: "She
didn't have the commitment that I did toward it, which creates a problem.
It frustrated me a lot" (interview). Doree wanted to quit, but could not
because of her commitment to Brian: "He was my partner, because we
had worked so hard last year to do well, and we did do okay. I mean not
exceptionally well, but for him to do what he's done is very incredible,
and I felt like I was letting him down. It's like after working so hard to get
him to the point he was and then just dropping and leaving him felt like
I was abandoning him, and I felt that was like a traitor" (interview).
Doree's commitment was taxing to her, and every limit she placed on her
involvement only served to increase Brian's frustration. It is common that
the weaker or less involved partner continues precisely because he or she
does not want to let down the other partner, supporting a tyranny of
commitment and leading to insoluble feelings of despair,[30] and in the process increasing the partner's frustration since the commitment is never
sufficient.

Partners and the Division of Labor

Team participation in most sports and other collective competitions presumes a *division of labor* in which participants specialize in different
roles. Although it might seem to the outsider that debaters simply debate,
in fact in two-person policy debate the two individuals have significantly
different obligations. The position in which one specializes affects the
relationship with one's partner. As described in the introduction and in
chapter 4, there are two positions in each partnership. One can be a first
(1A) or a second (2A) affirmative speaker and a first (1N) or a second
(2N) negative speaker.[31] Debaters do not often switch their positions,
particularly with the same partner and within the same tournament, as
different skills are necessary; it becomes difficult to switch after one becomes accustomed to a position. The partnership typically involves a stable division of labor, and some partnerships are chosen because the
debaters in question wish certain positions. In Minnesota, the 1N was
typically the faster speaker, having to present the range of negative

arguments, while the 2N has to outline the "fundamental claims of the negative case,"[32] as does the 2A for the affirmative. In general, the 1N focuses on the specific arguments against the affirmative case (case-side arguments), while the 2N makes broader arguments. As one debater, who enjoyed being the 2N, told me: "2Ns have more fun. 2Ns are abstract thinkers. They're conceptual thinkers." Those who debate 2A or 2N will usually be more "persuasive," since they have the broader speeches, and these are often considered the "power positions" in debate. Debaters change positions only when it is apparent that one is faster or more persuasive than the other. One debater exaggerated by suggesting that "2A is mainly speaking style." Because the first affirmative speech is a "canned" speech, previously written, practiced, and repeated, the less experienced debater is assigned that task. In general, the debater in the second position has the higher status on the team and in the debate world, and will receive higher speaker points.

Debaters become typified in terms of their position, both to themselves and to others, and partnerships are successful when the two identities do not clash. So, as a team, Doree and Brian fit together nicely in that Brian was the faster speaker with a better knowledge of the evidence (and, thus, was the 1A and 1N), and Doree was the smoother and more persuasive speaker (and enjoyed being the 2A and 2N). Doree could say, "I'm not a 1N. That's all I have to say." Likewise, at one tournament at which Brian debated as the 2A with another partner, Doree joked to Brian: "Iris [a Randall Park assistant coach] was probably sitting there saying, 'Gee, I wish Doree had done the 2AR [Second Affirmative Rebuttal].' You're a 1AR" (field notes). In a successful partnership, one person will become skilled in one position, while the other will learn the other position; that this decision may have implications for status, reputation, and success potentially creates tension.

The partner relationship is central to competition. Unlike the use of arguments and evidence, it is not something that can be taught. While claiming that great partners are fated to be together may be too strong, these relationships are fragile and dynamic, adding an element of chance affiliation that an objective competition might not be thought to have.

The Personal World of Debate

Prior to this chapter, I focused on the practice of debate itself. However, the reality of team life suggests that debate—as any activity—is grounded in personal relationships. To be a successful debater, one must adjust to one's social circumstances: to carve out a place on the team and then to develop a relationship with one's partner. These ties, particularly for adolescents for whom identity work is so crucial, are considerable challenges. The ideal relationship is rare. Most debaters must adjust to others, while they themselves change in this most dynamic, complex transition. They are learning the flexibility of adult relationships, while maintaining some of the dogmatic egocentrism of childhood.

Perhaps it is the challenges of these relationships that provide the life values of debate. While we should not neglect what individuals gain intellectually, high school debate constitutes a community: a dyad, a small group, a social network among schools, and a subculture of individuals with similar interests. In the next chapter, I turn from the practice of debate to those elements of adolescent life that, whether adults like it or not, are central features of teenage culture in a society in which official morality and the demands of adults conflict with the underside of adolescence.

Six

Debate Culture

TO UNDERSTAND high school policy debate, one must understand adolescence. In the reams of analysis of teenage social organization, most scholars emphasize that the teenage years are a time of transition: a period in which individuals must navigate the shoals separating childhood from adult life. This transition occurs in the context of powerful biological changes (the mischief of puberty), a recognition of new goals (needs for achievement, self-esteem, and affiliation),[1] the acquisition of cultural knowledge (creating niche marketing for film, music, and clothing) and economic responsibility (becoming wage earners with access to disposable cash), and changes in institutional commitment (dropping out of high school and being treated as adults by the criminal justice system). Although changes are not simultaneous, comparing a thirteen-year-old with an eighteen-year-old is startling. While biologically these changes do not match the changes from birth to age five, in altering one's place within an institutional order they are arguably more significant. These changes have led many to conclude that this period is a bounded stage, a claim given support by such labels for this time as "adolescence" or "the teenage years." This division of life into periods or stages constitutes an example of what sociologists speak of as boundary work.[2]

Clearly, adolescence involves social and institutional transitions, but in contrast to a model of adolescence as a sharply defined stage, I emphasize how adolescents in their distinctive cultures and social systems draw upon behaviors of childhood, while expanding their behavioral repertoires to incorporate those activities seen as constituting adult behavior. As a cultural sociologist, I focus on how cultural options affect one's self and public identities. By the end of preadolescence, contemporary American children are exposed to a range of adult behaviors and attitudes from which children had previously been relatively sheltered, a change in American society that some find distressing and dysfunctional.[3] Sociologist Ann Swidler has argued that one can conceive of social change as involving the metaphor of a "cultural toolkit,"[4] suggesting that change in one's behavioral options are particularly likely to occur in unsettled times, when previously successful behavioral routines are now defined as not working well. Although her analysis was originally linked to societies undergoing dramatic political, economic, or technological changes, it can also be applied to change among those maturing, being treated differently, and facing new social and institutional demands. Our ex-children are exposed in their teenage years to new "tools" or "strategies," which slowly, but inevitably, they acquire.[5] Given the biological, social, and institutional unsettledness, teenagers' use of these tools is defined as increasingly useful and status-enhancing, and explains why adolescents are likely to engage in those behaviors (sexuality, alcohol, tobacco) that adults have set aside for themselves, based upon artificial social, political, and chronological boundaries, or that even have been declared illegal, but are commonly found (drugs, theft, interpersonal violence).

These changes do not immediately replace the strategies of childhood; in practice, they are incorporated into the teen's toolkit alongside those techniques that had proved successful earlier. Adolescents can draw upon the tools of both childhood and adulthood in establishing who they are and creating an indigenous, authentic culture. This helps to explain how teens can seem simultaneously and alternately very sophisticated and very childish. Part of the "problem of adolescence" is that these young persons do not have full allegiance to the tools of either childhood or adulthood. Part of the problem of teenage pregnancy ("babies having babies") is that these teenage mothers, who once were common, normative, and successful, are not fully committed to adult strategies of organizing parental life. Social organization provides little help, given the structure of our occupational and marriage markets. We are amazed when teenage mass murderers or drug dealers cry for their mothers when they are thrown in a cold cell, drawing on distinct and seemingly incompatible tools—some sophisticated, others immature.

Many adolescent activities have these features. It is not that adolescents have reached a plateau that is halfway between childhood and adulthood, but rather that they oscillate in their behavioral choices, while struggling to create a communal identity. Adolescents are both adults and children. This reality is a central part of what makes them unpredictable and often difficult for adults to control. They slip from our grasp by their ability to embrace several age-linked personas. By sixteen, a boy or girl can do most of what adults do, and may do these things quite well; yet, in our culture at least, they have not entirely jettisoned techniques of childhood; nor do we expect them to. Consider a case, not from the world of debate, but from fashion modeling—a journalistic account of a successful sixteen-year-old model:

> James seems quite childlike at times—she's easily distracted, prone to slouching and staring into space, then snapping to attention in a fit of enthusiasm. She's physically affectionate in a sweet, unself-conscious way, always hugging people and leaning against them. She can be insecure, like the time she accused a Com-

pany Management driver of preferring to drive another model rather than herself, then stalked away, looking as if she might cry. Yet other moments she seems much older than 16, so jaded as to be unshockable. She has a pierced nipple . . . and frequently invokes her "whole life," as if this were an endless expanse of time.[6]

While this journalist adds a psychological interpretation to the story, the girl's "contradictory behaviors" can be seen as resulting from an expanded set of behavioral options. Only slowly are the effective skills of childhood impression management set aside, and even then not completely.[7]

For its part, high school debate, although not as exotic as modeling, is also a crucible in which adolescents develop adult skills. In contrast to Seventh Avenue, this world has been designed by adults for teens. In the early chapters of this book, debaters have been depicted largely as serious students of policy, even if their strategies and techniques may appear quirky or bizarre. However, to overemphasize this sense of purpose, this analytical gravitas, is not to do justice to the fact that debate is situated in youth culture, a teenage ghetto. These are not adults, but "kids," with childlike enthusiasms and irresponsibilities.

Consider a message that appeared on the e-mail debate discussion list (I have changed the person's name):

John Smith is the biggest mother fucker this side of the mason dixon line [*sic*]. He is on this list. . . . he thinks he is cool but he is just a big conceited bastard. If you ignore his posts he might leave. He never has anything to say, he only wants to use you gays to do his research for him.

In an e-mail message commenting on this one, the young man added, significantly (emphasis added):

I made a typo I said gays instead of guys take no offense. *Also this is High school debate, we are free to be as immature as say, high school kids, maybe.*[8]

Receiving messages from this list is to be thrown into a world in which serious discussions of Foucault, alternative energy sources, and inherency merge with claims that rival debaters are "faggots," "sluts," or "sickos." Debaters enjoy engaging in what they call "trash talk"—"talking smack" or "talking shit"—a linguistic pleasure, stemming from playful "grudges" that connect them with the irresponsibility of childhood and with adult skills at derision, learning techniques of malediction. Adults may, reasonably, be dismayed by the obscenity and scurrilous character of this discourse, and by the ability of debaters to wrap themselves in the mantle of the First Amendment while doing so, but the reality is that talking trash is fun, just as are insult games such as "playing the dozens" or "signifying" in other cultures. As a result, one contributor to the e-mail debate list can send the following message under the forged name and address of another who vehemently denies it:

> You know over the last few weeks i have noticed that the debate world has a lot of homosexuals and i was wondering if any of you would like to share your homoerotic activities with me. i guess what i'm trying to say is i'm gay.[9]

Presumably this message was vastly amusing to the sender, possibly a teammate or friend, and notably juvenile to much of the rest of its audience, even as it proclaimed awareness of "homoerotic activities." Examples of childish self-presentation emerged repeatedly:

> Carl, Frank, and Jimmy are taking sharp pens and scissors and sticking them in their legal pads during debate class when they are supposed to be preparing their arguments. The substitute teacher finally orders them to stop. Frank tells the others: "We gotta think about a new game to play, because we can't stab flowpads." I have seen debaters walk on desks and play frisbee with a roll of masking tape. On one occasion debaters place a teammate in the large trash can or toss a koosh ball in hotel hallways late at night. (field notes)

> While they are researching in the school library, Vic, a senior debater, places two books in a younger debater's backpack, so that when she goes through the library's detector the alarm rings. The books are *Fifteen Minutes: The Story of My Abortion* and a book about becoming a teenage mother. (field notes)

> Frank tells his teammates that he and his partner Barry are writing a book, entitled *The Best Ways to Win a Debate*. It includes such techniques as pouring kerosene on an opponent's briefcase and lighting it, and passing gas in cross-examination so that one's opponent has to smell it. (field notes)

Perhaps the most memorable instance of childish behavior was sitting at a restaurant with an assistant coach, a college freshman, and watching him casually switch the tops of the opaque salt and pepper shakers. Another young assistant coach brought in a water gun, squirting debaters, coaches, and researchers alike. Childhood is too much fun to be wasted on children.

The Power of Oscillation

These instances of childishness do not constitute a moral disengagement, but an attempt simultaneously to escape and to embrace adult expectations. As one coach noted:

> In some ways they're very sophisticated, but so naïve, and they play like little kids. I think it's more typical of debaters that sometimes when they're doing

things for fun, they'll go to doing silly little things, maybe sixth-, fifth-grade kinds of things. (interview)

Another coach noted that debaters are socially mature, but not always socially wise. Sometimes this involves childishness breaking into a serious discussion of issues: "The first affirmative, claiming that mentally ill prisoners should be released, notes, 'The status quo policy to the mentally handicapped is retarded'" (field notes).

These teenagers are given responsibility and are expected to use it well, a battle between superego and id:

> One senior debater remarked: "I don't know any other activity that gives you that much freedom. They take you on overnights, but you're basically on your own." Her adult coach notes: "You don't get a second chance." Her partner, referring to negotiation between adults and teens, adds: "When [our coach] says you're in bed by midnight, you're in bed by 2:30." (field notes)

Nothing is wrong with these adolescents other than that they do not consistently fit into either a world of childhood or a world of adulthood. They have sets of skills from both worlds, but without always having the experience or desire to use the skills in the way adults define as proper.

Successful coaches recognize that their charges cannot be given full responsibility, although they may seem like adults in many venues. Adult coaches are supposed to stand in loco parentis. This gives the "mature" adult coach an advantage over the younger coaches, who are often charismatic and proficient in debate theory, but who may themselves still be working through their own self-image of being adults, teenagers, and children, and who are expected, despite their own personal oscillations and uncertainty, to convince a group of rowdy, randy teens that they represent moral authority.

Adult coaches, often having raised their own children, can better adopt a stable authority role—negotiating the gap between peer and authority. In the words of one coach, their charges remain "ex-children":

> A speech coach planning the final banquet asks Geri, Laurie, and Vic if they mind being called children in the program. At first they jokingly object, but then agree that it will be acceptable since it is for their parents. Laurie says, "We're children to our parents." The coach jokes: "You're children to us, aren't you?" Laurie says, joking but half-serious, "No." Geri adds firmly, "We're your students." (field notes)

Debaters joke about the advanced age of their mentors, implicitly accepting and magnifying the differentiation of child and adult:

> The Randall Park team jokes about Mrs. Miller's age, suggesting that she lived before typewriters, or that when she wanted to write debate cards,

she had to carve them on stone tablets. Carl talks about leaving his debate briefs in Mrs. Miller's classroom; she asks him, "Do I look like your mother?" Carl responds: "Do you want to know?" Mrs. Miller, laughing, retorts "No!" On a third occasion, Mrs. Miller says something that Phil considers old-fashioned; she retorts, "You're looking at me as if I've died." (Phil laughs.) (field notes)

In a society that defines adolescence as a distinct social category, adolescents look for ways to differentiate themselves—culturally, morally, politically—from both adults and children, attempting to find new tools or strategies. These strategies produce some of the freshness and vibrancy of the youth culture, but at the same time it makes this culture dangerous, particularly in those cases, as in high school debate, when its display occurs within a system in which there is institutional responsibility. As a result, whatever debate coaches might think of the actions of their debaters (often what we wink at is more than what we claim that we permit), the awareness remains that principals, parents, and sometimes attorneys are looking over their shoulder.

Childish Deviance

Adolescents, our children with adult abilities, behave in ways that are too close for comfort to the ways that adults behave. Deviance in the world of debate often consists of engaging in "status crimes," behaviors that are legally acceptable, if not desired, when engaged in by adults: smoking, drinking, sexual intimacy, and minor vandalism.

It is not that debaters never engage in actions that are criminal—rumors were plentiful that some consumed mind-altering substances—but I was surprised, despite my close observation of the Randall Park and Greenhaven teams, that I gleaned no direct evidence of such behavior on these Minnesota teams. Most rumors dealt with marijuana, which seems to many high school students to be illegal with a wink.[10] Joking also occurred among debaters about using "speed," a double entendre for the name of a stimulant drug useful for staying up at tournaments, as well as a metaphor for rapid speech. It is not that high school debaters do not use drugs—some do—but drug use was not perceived as an immediate problem that coaches had to confront.

These forms of deviance involve for debaters, as for other adolescents, a coming to terms with their anticipated adult self. When will they permit themselves the luxury of engaging in adult pleasures? Teens continually adopt and shed cultural personas, developing a *generational self*, along with their personal one.

Such activities challenge the coach's responsibility to maintain social order—not always because all coaches are convinced that this is necessary, as many recall their own indiscretions with nostalgia, but because each overnight stay is a potential disaster that could affect one's reputation and career. Many coaches told me that, at the beginning of the year, they "read their debaters the riot act," informing them of the rules and explaining the consequence for disobedience, and at the same time insulating themselves from the charge that they did not attempt to maintain discipline:

> Mrs. Miller tells her debaters: "Over the years I've had such good kids. They've been very responsible. I've had very few problems. There have been a few cases. One time a kid [was forced to return] to school by bus. This was at 2 A.M. in the morning. I think we were in Duluth. Another time there was a girl—this was at 3 A.M. in the morning—who didn't come back by bus [in the middle of the night], but I made sure that she would never travel with us again. She would have been a good debater. I don't like to play games. I don't like to be woken up. I know all these people, and I don't want to be embarrassed with my friends." (field notes)

Just as debaters constitute a cultural and reputational community, so do coaches, and it is important that these adults publicly enforce those rules that their peers proclaim. The bus story—about an event that happened many years before—is part of Mrs. Miller's repertoire; a single instance of discipline that serves in place of continued threat. Further, the threat of sending a participant home on the bus gains power not because of its punishment value per se, but because of the stigma and the secondary punishments likely to be meted out by one's parents. These threats seem universal.

> I started coaching three years ago. I started the program from scratch. I kicked everyone off the team that was on it. There were some discipline problems, some attitude problems. I just started over. (interview)

> We told them that when we were out on the road they were expected to behave themselves. They were expected to listen to what I said, and do what I said, and if I said back into the hotel room at 11 [P.M.], they were back in their hotel rooms at 11 . . . discrepancies would not be tolerated. If a kid was caught doing something that they shouldn't be doing, they probably wouldn't go on a trip again. [I was] very firm about that early, you know. You have to really establish that. And the kids will think you're being a jerk and an asshole and a hardliner, but you have to be. (interview)

As sociologist Howard Becker noted, studying the professional life of public school teachers, one must be strict at first, if one is to be more flexible later in the term. Becoming more strict over time is a challenge, as students do not believe subsequent threats.[11] Of course, one of the most effective ways of enforcing social control is to require that the participants discipline themselves, and, thus, coaches pressure their adolescent lieutenants to take on this responsibility, widening the net:

> One way I handle that is to make the seniors be the models, and make the students discipline one another. And the idea of team captains is pretty effective. . . . Peer pressure and the kind of respect that the senior debaters have garnered works pretty well. And then, of course, if the problem goes beyond that, why I would have to deal with it. But having that for structure, I think helps control. (interview)

Yet, despite what coaches may state to their charges, going "on the road" involves a party atmosphere, which coaches realize. One coach is more explicit than most about her ambivalence in the roles of both disciplinarian and facilitator:

> I sometimes have a real difficulty with traveling tournaments because part of me is sort of a strict authoritarian person who thinks I should be able to say, "In bed at twelve and no messing around," and all this stuff, and that they should just do it, and I know they don't. I mean there's just no way to monitor, and kids will be kids, and they're going to stay up until four in the morning, and talk. . . . That is real hard on me. . . . I don't want it to be a party. I want them to have a good time, but I want them to be there for the debate, and I want them to get their sleep, and I want them to perform their best. . . . When you take a whole bunch of kids to a hotel, it's almost impossible not to have a little bit of excitement and slumber-party atmosphere. . . . Sometimes I would like to have a small traveling team, and just pick those people who are do-or-die debaters, you know, and, yet, on the other hand, I guess I think it's silly not to have some occasions where the kids see it as a social occasion. (interview)

This coach struggles with the merging of the instrumental and the expressive aspects of debate. Tournaments can often seem like parties, in which teenagers are simultaneously serious and silly, moral and willing to engage in those activities that adults feel are inappropriate. How coaches manage this dilemma goes a long way toward determining how they are viewed by their debaters and supervisors.

Up in Smoke

Given the knowledge of many debaters, the subculture of smoking is startling. While this is not a phenomenon much found in Minnesota, a state in which smoking is not permitted in high school buildings, and in which the weather is not conducive to puffing outdoors, it is evident elsewhere. When I moved to Georgia, one of the first questions that was put to me as a sociologist was why so many debaters—in college and high school—chose to smoke cigarettes. I am uncertain whether the rate of smoking is higher among debaters than elsewhere, but it is certainly recognized that smoking is a characteristic of this scene; and because of the intelligence, knowledge, and social-class background of many debaters, this is surprising. Smoking seems an odd form of teen resistance to adult demands by these gifted and talented youngster. Yet, the prevalence of tobacco, more than marijuana, is noted by many debaters:

> I think debaters try rather hard to fight off the "nerd" stereotype, and in doing so, adopt as many behavior traits as un-nerdlike as possible. I think debaters try harder to be "cool" than any other group of people I've seen. . . . I also happen to think that debaters are a whole hell of a lot cooler than most any other group of people I know, but that's 'cuz I find a lot less idiots in debate than anywhere else. . . . I smoke an ass-load of Marlboro Mediums daily.[12]

Somehow this message is not fully persuasive. Debaters could choose any number of antisocial, self-destructive activities that they do not choose. Perhaps smoking provides for debaters, as for others, a pacifier, a means of diffusing the tension in the round, and is something to do with their hands. Perhaps smoking is simply a cultural form that has spread from a set of high-status cultural actors, and that with a new cohort will fade. Smoking seemed particularly prevalent for debaters on the National Circuit, where unpopular arguments give the arguer status. It may be precisely because it is so difficult to make a case for cigarette smoking that the activity is so appealing.

A Drinking Culture

I do not doubt that debaters drink less than most students. Tournaments are not characterized by drinking binges. I never observed a debater who was hungover, although no doubt there were a few who hid their problem. Yet, of all the forms of teenage deviance, adult coaches find drinking the most serious, and the most threatening to their positions as adult chaperons and school agents. Over the years, many coaches have had to confront the bottle on road trips:

> At the national tournament, one of the Minnesota debaters went to dinner with a teenage friend who ordered margaritas. She [the debater] claimed to have had only a taste. (field notes)

> I think of . . . the schools that won the Governor's Cup at the Dentin tourna-

ment . . . the teams that won that filled it with beer and drank it with their coach. (interview)

Most coaches strictly oppose drinking while teenagers are under their supervision, whatever they might think of the occasional beer. Punishments and reprimands can be severe, a fear that dampens the drinking that might otherwise occur:

[Some debaters who did not make the state tournament] got a room at the hotel where the state tournament was, and they had liquor in their room. There were other debaters in the room. . . . They were not under my chaperoning at the time, because they were not there with the team. They were there on their own. . . . I was not even supposed to know they were there, and so I disqualified them from the national competition, which was a couple of weeks later, of my own volition, because they had violated [the] Minnesota state high school rule, which was that you don't drink during the season. (interview)

We were staying at a hotel for a regional tournament, and one of the students had brought a bottle of liquor up to the room. . . . I heard noise coming from the room at night, and found the bottle of liquor, and at that point all of the students in the room were on the team. . . . The kids know I have a very strict policy. . . . I will not condone it under any circumstances. (interview)

We ran into [drinking] once. . . . The head coach took care of it. He kicked the kid off the team. . . . He booted him off for a month. . . . He [the boy] had liquor in a bottle. (interview)

This assistant coach noted candidly that the student involved was not one of the best debaters on the team, and he surmised that had he been a particularly strong debater, the outcome might have been different. The status and number of individuals involved surely shapes how coaches judge nocturnal goings-on. Sometimes closing one's eyes does make problems disappear, at least for the moment.

For younger coaches, these rules may have a special piquancy, in that they believe that the drinking constitutes "no big deal." Enforcing these rules, while necessary because of institutional demands, does not have compelling moral force for them, in the same way that baby-boom parents often have difficulty convincing their children that marijuana is *really*, *really* wrong. One young coach notes the contradictions in his position:

When I debated, we drank. . . . If my kids did what I did when I was in high school, I'd kick them off the team. [Question: Why?] Because it was wrong. [Question: Did it hurt you?] Well, I don't know if I'd say for sure. [Question: Was it illegal, maybe?] It's illegal and it shouldn't be. . . . You know it's a double standard. . . . I would say most coaches, especially the ones that are successful—and this is a stereotype, but I think it is true—have at one time or another either given explicit or implicit approval of drinking or actually drank with the students. Not necessarily at a tournament, but at their house, at a party. I think it goes on a lot. . . . I have mixed feelings about it, but it's just a job security thing for me. . . . See, when I was assistant coach they had a drinking problem, and some kids on the team were drinking and they got caught, and it was bad news. People were fired, and kids were kicked off the team. I was just like, "No, never again, am I going through this." I mean, yeah, if I had it all over to do again in high school, I think I'd probably do the same thing I did. . . . It's kind of unfair [he laughs], but as a coach, I'm not prepared to deal with it. . . . Gene O'Connor is this 52-year-old teacher. He's been around for a long time. He's had a lot of success, but if some kids get caught drinking, he's not going to get called on the carpet. I mean he's going to say, "Oh, these are some bad misfit kids, kick them off the team," but if it happened with me, I think my overall ability to lead would be questioned. (interview)

This coach cogently notes the situated quality of team discipline. I do not suggest that coaches are insincere, but even those who are sincere see drinking in light of institutional demands and in terms of the culture of teenage life. The realities of what adolescents do when they have the chance—and what we did when we had those chances—undercut the rules we are required to enforce. High school debate, composed of free-thinkers and individualists, operates in an institutional world.

Strange Bedfellows

The number of students who leave high schools untouched by sexual intimacy continues to decline: debaters, not all of them nerds and outcasts, are part of this trend. Not every debater is sexually experienced, but enough are. The issue for coaches is not what pleasures teens choose to pursue in their bedrooms or the backseats of cars, but their behaviors on the road.[13]

"Relationships" are common on the debate circuit. One debater referred to the "Mark-Diana saga" and "The Bizarre Love Triangle of Nathan, JT, and Danielle."[14] Coaches tend to be more tolerant of this sexual behavior than of drinking (or drugs). Many coaches are amused, even when discipline is required:

My favorite story is of [a former debater]. [While in high school] he had this thing with this girl two years younger, and he was giving me all kinds of information, you know, that they were sexually active. . . . It was just a stitch [she laughs]. So I got all this birth-control stuff . . . and we started this conversation, and he thought I was coming from, "Don't do it." And I was coming from, "If you're going to do it, for God's sake be responsible." . . . I had a girl pick up a guy at a bar in Moorhead one time. She didn't go with us to the nationals [she laughs]. I've had good debaters that I wouldn't take out of town. . . . You can't watch them all the time. (interview)

[I say to my team] "If you guys have a boyfriend or girlfriend on the circuit, I don't care. I think that's great [he laughs]. I mean, I had girlfriends on the circuit, and, you know, I'd hang out with them in the hotel lobby, go down to the pool. If you want to be in your room, that's fine, but at 11 [P.M.], you're gone. . . . I'm not as concerned about the sexual thing as I am about the drugs and alcohol. If that's going on [sex], unless it is getting a little out of hand, I'll probably just kind of turn the other way. I mean, they're kids, they're dating [he laughs]. It's part of growing up. I don't see that as evil. (interview)

The standards that separate sex and drinking are striking, and connect to the moral codes of adults as they apply to adolescents and to the institutional pressures that force coaches to keep order. Sexuality is accepted as part of normal teenage activity; drinking is not. Fifty years ago the expectations at debate tournaments, as elsewhere, would have been reversed.

Little Vandals

Vandalism can be fun.[15] Sometimes, though, things get out of hand as adolescents choose to stretch the bands that bind them. Hotels know that whenever they host a conclave of teens the cost of redecorating and cleanup must be included in the price of the rooms. Teens steal towels and signs, and collect other personal "souvenirs." On occasion—not often, but frequently enough to be recognized—teens "trash" their hotel room. One debater kids about his memorable experiences at the national tournament:

We had more fun than anyone out there. I hope they didn't have to replace all the carpet. It wasn't our fault the sink and shower overflowed. The toothpaste wasn't even that obvious.[16]

The year before my research, the Greenhaven team apparently had "trashed" their room at a hotel:

Maureen and her roommate decided to trash the room. They didn't do anything permanently damaging, but they strewed toilet paper over and wrote on the mirrors and things—that happens all the time. Generally it's harmless, and you just make the kids clean it up [he laughs]. You say, "Well, you did it, you clean it up. We're not going to make the maids do it." (interview)

The incident passed into team lore, and the following year the team wondered if they would be allowed to stay at the hotel again. While limits exist as to what kind of vandalism coaches tolerate, there is a sense that coaches feel this is part of the natural exuberance of youth—part of their immaturity and, unlike drinking, not an embrace of the privileges of adulthood.

Teenage deviance is part of the debate world, but how it is seen and dealt with results from its situated context, the status of the individuals involved, and institutional pressures on coaches. Teenagers can get away with a lot, but they must sense those uncertain, hazy lines that separate kids from malefactors. Debaters, resting on a stereotype of virtue, have more leeway in this regard than other adolescents.[17] In a community that attempts to socialize teenagers into a serious adult world of policy discourse, adolescent rebellion is ironic and disconcerting. However, the fact that most debaters seem so committed to sturdy adult values sometimes encourages adults to "allow them a pass" when faced with deviance, which, often, in its way, suggests that debaters are accepting values of which adults are less proud.

A Community of Talk

The world of debate transcends local boundaries. Over time, teens come to know others with similar interests and skills throughout their region or the nation. Debate consists of more than a string of local cultures. Members of the debate community feel a strong affiliation. This is institutionalized in the ritual of shaking hands after a debate round—a ritual so established that if novices choose to break it, symbolically, when they reject the hands of their opponents, the scandal will reach the ears of their coach. After one well-known debater was killed in a traffic accident, the notice of his funeral and the address for condolence cards was placed on the Internet, with a friend, writing: "It's times like this when I feel close with everyone in our community."[18] The observer of a round might conclude, given the occasional nasty comments, that participants are not particularly close. Like the actions of opposing politicians and attorneys, this does not reveal the whole story. Surface rivalry does not translate into personal dislike. These are individuals who meet each other frequently. They are repeat players in a social world.[19] In the round, the need to differentiate competing positions for a judge is real, but this leaves open a space for affiliation after the round. For example, when Don and Ravi qualified for the national tournament, an opposing team sent them a handwritten note of congratulations. A surprised novice reported:

> I think it's kind of astounding like, when in the debate round, [debaters] are real vicious to each other in cross-x or when they're speaking—just direct attacks—but outside the debate round it's a total turnaround. They're real friendly to each other, and they can totally attack someone's character in the

round, and then like ten minutes later out of the round, they're friends again. . . . Finals at Carroll Falls, it was Greenhaven against Denton, and Denton was like really vicious in some of their stuff, some of their attacks. Greenhaven was almost returning the favor. Then after the round they were all friends. . . . I've noticed that a lot of rounds, you can still be in a good round, real competitive, fierce round, but you can still come out being friends with the other team. (interview)

A transcendent community surrounds the competition.

It is surely true that some teams affiliate with other teams and keep a distance from still others, but the debate network is thick for the more active participants, who realize that what connects them is more significant than what divides them. The strength of the network is impressive, and it is particularly evident at tournaments early in the year when old friends and adversaries rekindle acquaintanceships and share summer stories about debate institutes or about the cases that they have been researching. A coach reported:

> The Brookfield [Wisconsin] debaters spend a lot of time coming over here [to Minnesota]. I found out that my kids on Easter vacation their senior year, after debate for high school was done, went over to Brookfield and spent a couple of days with the kids there. (interview)

In some cases, the connection permits a student to fill in as a debater for another school, if local rules permit, as they do in Minnesota. Brian was asked to debate for a nearby school that was short a debater, a connection made because their assistant coach had previously debated for Randall Park. A second Randall Park debater, Darrin, also debated for another school, and claimed that it was his most enjoyable experience of the year, making a new friend through the crucible of competition (interview). The power of these friendship networks makes it difficult for graduating seniors to disengage. Some continue to debate in college, others sign on as assistant coaches, and still others work part-time at a summer institute or compile handbooks. The margins of the activity are filled with those whose heart remains on the flow. For many the break is gradual and uncertain, having to slowly tear oneself away from one's friends. A young coach noted:

> I thought for a while about teaching in high school, but I'm not gonna go that route. And I found it kind of hard to tear myself away from debate, and when the opportunity arose to get a coaching position down here, I decided to take it. (interview)

His network was more important than his future career.

Most often the networks that develop among debaters have an instrumental component, as they are used, in part, for gaining evidence and learning about creative arguments. New cases quickly spread within the community. Thus, when Danny wrote a JV case about establishing penal colonies, by the next week many of the teams he faced knew of it. Diffusion of information has become more rapid with the growth of electronic media: e-mail discussion lists and Internet pages. Some social networks are extensive. Don Davis, Randall Park's assistant coach, informed me that he was in regular contact with students and coaches from eleven schools. Before major tournaments, members of the Randall Park team called friends to determine what cases other schools were running.

Dating Debaters

Networks may be established through romantic affiliations. Adolescents from different schools may see each other socially. One star debater asked a girl from another school to attend his school's prom, a fact that was laughed about among their peers. As one young man who has dated his rivals explained, "Debate becomes your social life. . . . Once you debate, it consumes your life, and you need another debater who understands it" (field notes). A former participant reported:

> I really like the crowd much more so than anything else. I've never gone out with a girl that's not a debater. You can go to an art museum if you want or go to a movie and have a good chat about what the movie meant to you. Because when you feel that you're smarter, or if you generally are, [or if you] have a better grasp than most [other] high school students, you don't want to hang around with them. (interview)

A coach notes that not only do these relationships have their emotional side, but they also serve as an identity marker, a source of prestige. As it is the most intense adolescent relationship, romance cements debaters, and teens who spend their weekends together will see each other as appropriate suitors.

Instituting Friendship

No factor is more important in establishing networks of relations in high school debate than the summer debate institute. The first summer institute was held at Northwestern University in 1931, and later the University of Iowa organized an influential institute in the mid-1950s. The primary motivation was to provide teaching opportunities during the summer for high school coaches, but the possibility for a college or university to make money from underutilized dormitories and classroom space also proved powerful. The summer institutes at Georgetown University and at Northwestern in the late 1960s and early 1970s were particularly influential in forging and fostering the rapid-fire, evidence-intense national circuit style that dominates debate in many regions. By the 1970s, as many as fifty colleges had established summer programs. Programs range in size from several hundred participants (e.g., at Michigan or Baylor) to several dozen, with costs ranging from several hundred dollars to several thousand, depending on the length of the camp and the quality of the faculty.[20]

Participating in summer institutes has proved to be crucial for serious high school debaters, especially those who hope to participate on the national level. Participants learn "debate theory" (orientations to debate that are explained at the lectures by experts) and how to develop cases, get a feel for the topic, and collect and share evidence. While this training may not be essential for participating, it does provide students with an advantage. Some institutes focus on novices, others on the most advanced national circuit debaters; others teach Lincoln-Douglas debate or speech events; and still others have a regional focus, such as the Minnesota institutes previously held at Winona State University and at Macalester College.

Aside from the economic benefits to the colleges at which they are held, institutes provide summer employment for underpaid high school teachers, former high school debaters, and college debaters. The close connections among collegians and high school students has altered the world of high school debate, making it more collegiate. As James Copeland, the national secretary of the National Forensic League, explained: "In states that tended to send their kids to these kind of camps, the kids would come home with a very evidence-oriented, spread-oriented style of debate that mirrored what was going on in college, because they were taught by college kids" (interview). Nowhere but at summer institutes was debate theory taught. Students were taught that it was not enough that one just argued the issues, but one needed a theory to justify them. As these theories became more elaborate, the activity changed to become increasingly unrecognizable to the general public, unaware of such terms and usages as hypothesis testing models, tabula rasa, deontology, counterplan theory, and humanism kritiks.

Debate institutes are intense times; participants want to "do debate," with sleep and leisure secondary. According to one participant, fifteen hours a day of debate work was common. One debater at an institute explained that she generally awoke at 5:30 A.M. and worked until breakfast at 7:00. After breakfast she worked on her research until 8:30 A.M., when she attended a general meeting and then a theory class until lunch at noon. From 1:00 to 3:00 she attended a research class, followed by research in the library, then dinner. After dinner, the individual lab groups met. In the evening she worked in the library, and from 10:00 P.M. until midnight she met with friends and worked on her projects. From midnight until 1:00 A.M. she worked in her room. At 1:00 A.M. was lights out but she "found ways to keep lights on, flashlights, to keep working." Given the amount of work and lack of sleep, it is worth noting that when I asked about her most enjoyable experience, without hesitation she responded "institute" (interview). At institute, participants have nothing to do but "deal with ideas." I do not suggest that every student enjoys the rigors of institute life, or that all are equally successful—horror stories exist—however, working eighteen hours a day can be a peak experience, when coupled with a deep and profound sense of community.

This intensity worries some organizers, who demand balance. A debater, having attended the Coon-Hardy Institute at Northwestern, told me of the presence of "forced fun"; organizers insisted that everyone attend a movie (field notes). The Concordia (Minnesota) camp institute organized what they called "Labletics," in which participants in each "lab" or group had to spend an hour each day in sports, a rule made necessary because adolescents had no interest in shelving their desire to cut cards or prepare briefs (field notes). Stories are spread about the student who had to be taken to the hospital after using Vivarin, a drug to keep one awake, or about the debater who had not slept in five days.[21] Whether these accounts are apocryphal is less important than that they are believed as events that could reasonably have occurred. These debaters are seen as much as heroes as victims.

Whatever the virtue of summer institutes as intellectual centers, they are crucial in knitting adolescents together into a loose national network. Participants at a summer institute share a link to their alma mater; further, debaters are typically assigned to small groups, sometimes on the basis of ability. Being in a top lab at a major program, such as Michigan or Dartmouth, is a mark of status. Lab partners are expected to remain close throughout their debate years, building a network.[22] At national tournaments these acquaintances enliven debate rounds when opposing friends make private references. A coach explains:

> A lot of [the value of institute] is a networking kind of thing where kids get to know [each other] really well, and see [each other] on a weekly basis. They become people you have as friends for a long, long time. Don had a good networking after going to Michigan, which was really helpful when we went to nationals, and all kinds of contacts to trade with them. (interview)

Before the national tournament, Laurie from Greenhaven contacted acquaintances from summer institute to learn what cases were being run in other areas. She called friends from Tennessee, Illinois, Nebraska, and California, and was called by an acquaintance from South Dakota. Coaches encourage their debaters to attend different institutes, increasing the amount of evidence available and expanding their social networks (field notes).

Friendship Circles

Some look at the activity and see a world that is far less socially integrated: a world of cliques, a circle with a well-defined boundary. Needless to say, outsiders see this wall more clearly than do insiders. A first-year coach at a school with a newly formed team revealed that he found Minnesota debaters uncivil. He noted that often, in a round, students did not even trouble to learn each others' names, commenting, "No wonder they are hostile." This view, from a man outside the region, is not shared by most of those in the state. But his concern with status and arrogance is not unique. Some allege that the elite participants look down on those around them, "scorning the little people." This tight circle of friends results from competing together in tournaments and meeting in institutes, as well as in the evaluation of skills and records of success. It may be hard to break into a peer group if one lacks a sponsor or a record of success. Most people, even those who are gregarious, are shy in their dealings with strangers and draw boundaries, preserving the self-enhancing nature of the group. Making new friends is not always easy; sometimes shyness appears to be arrogance. Opening oneself to another leaves one vulnerable to rejection. One coach asserted:

> What bothers me is the attitude that many of these debaters take that they are somehow better than those who are not competing at this level. This causes them to look down on their competition, teammates, and even their coaches. . . . Since I have seen the nicest debaters take on this attitude, I am convinced that there is something inherent in the activity which spawns this arrogance.[23]

One cannot deny that elites develop here, as in every other pursuit in which individuals are aware of the ability and commitment of others. Nor can it be denied that these groups, like others, display preference for their peers and distrust or disparage those outside their boundaries. These processes are sociological universals, virtually impossible to eliminate. The question is the extent to which circles are open and flexible. The answer, to some degree, is an answer that provides little balm for the individual who feels that he or she has been excluded and can find no way to breach the walls. Networks in voluntary social worlds assume that everyone does not have the *right* to know everyone else, but that the strands of acquaintanceship spread throughout the activity.

Putting Networks into Practice: Ethics of Sharing Evidence

The success of debate teams is linked to the quality of their evidence. A team spends thousands of hours in libraries, on computers, and poring through handbooks and articles, searching for the most potent evidence. I discussed the evaluation of evidence in chapter 3. Here, I examine whether sharing evidence with those outside one's team is legitimate.

Rules for sharing evidence connects to how one views the activity. In most forms of sport it would be unethical to obtain the playbook of the opposing team. In education, plagiarizing another's efforts is wrong. Yet, if one sees evidence as the background against which competition is played, sharing provides a better test of how one can use arguments.

Minnesota teams take a more conservative attitude toward the sharing of information than do teams in other venues, who have other traditions, most notably those in the national circuit. Although the standards have changed, during my research most Minnesota coaches believed that one should not disclose one's case to opponents before the round or give evidence related to one's own or one's teammates' cases. After suggesting that she believed in trading evidence, one debater remarked that affirmative cases were different: "I found a case, and I knew whose it was. I wouldn't read it. I would not look at it because I feel that's very unethical. Affirmative cases are secret" (interview). When information is released about a team's case, dissension can result. The year after my research a related incident shook the Randall Park team:

> Barry was sort of dating the girl from W. B. Packer who was their varsity debater. THAT caused some huge conflict with Sean, because there was the suspicion, for which Barry was very apologetic, that he leaked a bit of information to W. B. Packer about what the teams were running. This was particularly bad because Ram and Brian had the same case, and this was high treason as far as we were concerned. (personal communication, 1997)

As espionage agents know, pillow talk can be effective in gathering information, and debaters who are dating may claim that as their primary or partial motivation, provided that they can convince their teammates that, in terms of evidence and strategy, they get as much as they give. For some, the desire for evidence outweighs other pleasures:

> The first time Suzy and I met outside of a speech tournament context was for lunch on a Saturday at the Village Wok, and the supposed reason was that she

was going to give me her files. . . . Fastforward a month and a half to a night in May that was Prom Night for both of our schools. We went to Randall Park's first in downtown St. Paul, then drove across town and went to Lewes's. I was probably as naive and unsexually-aware as a high-schooler could be, and Suzy was my first girlfriend. . . . Well, we ended up in my car in her house's dark driveway in a rather reclined position across the front seats, and after a long hour of canoodling, with her making more forward motions (such as unbuttoning my shirt partly and not minding that the top of her dress was falling a little below the ideal level, not to mention her lying more or less on top of me), she moaned between her breaths, "What do you want from me?" "How about the rest of your evidence?" I replied, to which she let out a frustrated sigh. (personal communication, 1997)

Don jokes to Ben about his girlfriend on the Carroll Falls team, "How much [evidence] is she giving you?" Doree comments, "Every time they needed something, they went, 'Go seduce Allen' [a debater from another school]." (field notes)

Secrecy is required in those circumstances in which one has collected evidence that can attack another team's affirmative case. Thus, Randall Park developed negative arguments against Layton High's successful computer case to decrease prison overcrowding by employing more efficient prison management. Members of the team were explicitly told that they should not trade or even discuss their evidence, in order to surprise the Layton debaters. One student was criticized for telling friends from another school about a discrediting article they had found (field notes).

These expectations conflict dramatically with the current norms of national circuit debate, where it is expected that teams will disclose their cases, sometimes sharing the first affirmative speech prior to the round—a useful practice since the words flow so rapidly that taking notes is difficult. In turn, negative teams often share the generic arguments or counterplans that they plan to run. The strategy selection in the later speeches, coupled with the quality of these first arguments, determines the outcome. With the growth of the Internet, debaters can share on-line details of cases that they hear at tournaments.

As a result, distinct cultures exist that typically do not conflict, but when they do sparks may fly. By behaving morally, given one set of expectations, a debater can find himself punished by a coach with another set:

I am a former debater from Millard South HS in Omaha, NE. . . . A couple of weeks ago I shared with the list a situation where I had posted a caselist from a regional tournament at Augustana, SD. After posting the list, several prominent SD coaches faxed my coach, complaining. . . . Apparently, this sharing of information was not seen as acceptable conduct. My coach . . . became enraged that I had posted this list and took me aside and reamed me. . . . I explained that I didn't know that this was seen as unacceptable practice in this region. . . . I also explained . . . how caselists were actually beneficial to the activity as a whole. [The coach and principal] felt that possible retaliatory action could have been taken against our school for my posting of the list and implied that my actions were not within the bounds of good sportsmanship. [This debater was forced to endure a two-tournament suspension and decided to quit the team.][24]

Whatever the justice of the particular claims—other coaches would have supported this young man—this sad tale underlines the differences in styles and expectations.

Most coaches and debaters support the trading of evidence, at least in some instances:

Several years ago . . . that was a big issue in debate, whether information and flows should be traded. . . . And at that time I even gave copies of our affirmative case to a couple of other coaches who were complaining the loudest, and said, "OK, now beat us." They didn't. I think, if anything, it makes for a better argument. (interview)

The promiscuous sharing of institute evidence is a case in point. Certain Minnesota teams developed trading relations with other teams, such as those between Randall Park and Carroll Falls, where friendship and dating supported the sharing of evidence. Indeed, the connection of friendship and evidence trading goes in both directions: trading evidence creates networks. One coach told about the relationship of his debaters with students from another state:

We had a very close relationship with Hoover last year, and we traded all kinds of evidence, fostering a wonderful social experience from kids making friendships. . . . We went to Hoover one time, copying some of their stuff. They came up here. I think it's wonderful for the kids to see teamwork in research. (interview)

In this coach's view, information is not proprietary; the sharing is more important than the strategic use of surprise. Another coach concurred:

One of the great things about debate when I was in high school was you develop really strong, personal relationships with other people, besides people on your squad. And you learn how to work with other people. And, you know, kids aren't just giving other kids evidence; usually it is an exchange, it's an even trade. . . . And I think there is just so much information and so many case areas, especially when the topic is broad. I don't see anything wrong with kids helping each other out as long as it doesn't turn into a situation where people are ganging up on one team. (interview)

The trading of evidence does not speak to the quality of the evidence involved, and a team that merely "uses" the evidence of another team without getting to know or understand it can find itself in trouble. As one coach noted, referring to her debate years: "I really felt that it wasn't my stuff that I was reading . . . and you weren't comfortable with it, and you didn't run it as well, and you didn't have the right answers for it" (interview). As noted in chapter 3, all evidence is not created equal; nor can all be used equally well.

Of course, teams that are not part of this network, such as one inner-city Twin Cities team, can be put at a disadvantage by being excluded from these networks.[25] As in so many other areas, money and social class powerfully affect reality.

A more sensitive concern than the general issue of sharing evidence is the sharing of evidence *during a tournament*. The team from Greenhaven was appalled by the fact that, during a round at the Tournament of Champions at the University of Kentucky, their opponents received evidence against their case from previous opponents. Mrs. Nyberg explained:

> The girl from a team we had met previously came into the room where we were then debating another team, and gave that opposing team, whatever it was—if it was a flow or some pieces of evidence to use against us—while this round was in progress. I think that is blatantly unethical. . . . [Trading information at tournaments] would be destroying good sportsmanship. . . . Once you get to the tournaments, then the rules of the game come into play. (interview)

Other Minnesotans speak of a conflict of interest in helping one team defeat another. As a consequence of this attitude, Minnesota coaches prohibited the trading of evidence and flows of other rounds during a tournament. This issue became heated because of an event during the 1995–1996 season:

> At a tournament held in Minnesota last weekend, Team A was debating Team B in one semis and Team C was debating Team D in the other semis. Before the semis round, the coach from Team A went to one of the debaters from the school of Team C not competing in semis and asked for some evidence to use against Team B. This debater gave the coach of Team A the evidence. . . . The evidence was inherency cards from a few days ago suggesting that Team B's plan had been done. Team A and Team C each won their semifinal debate. Team B protested the exchange of information from school C to school A

which it argued was used in order to gain an unfair advantage over team B. The tournament ethics committee initially decided to disqualify Team A and Team C from competing in final round and hold a final round between Team B and [Team] D. After further discussion and further appeal, the tournament decided not to hold a final round and recognize Teams A, B, C, and D equally as semifinalists. . . . One comment made about this incident is that there is a "generational" difference here. The older, more experienced coaches view this conduct as unethical and unfair to teams. The younger, less experienced coaches believe in the free flow of information and the educational value gained by the exchanges.[26]

For many Minnesota coaches, this behavior was obviously unfair, slanting a level playing field. One can surely imagine the anger of Team B at their defeat through the connivance of the rival coach. Yet, on the national circuit such behavior would be unremarkable (other than the fact that Team A was arguing a conservative stock issue, like whether there was an inherent barrier against instituting the plan!). One prominent national circuit coach observed:

I don't understand why borrowing or exchanging evidence with another school for specific use in a specific round gives a team "an unfair advantage." Is it unfair to read evidence that your team did not research? Then no one should read handbook evidence, or evidence that they personally did not cut at institute. Why is the unit of the school so sacrosanct? Why is it OK to borrow from my teammate but not from my friend from another team? . . . It seems to me that one of the best things about debate in the northeastern region and national circuits is that there's some real fellowship about sharing and trading evidence and ideas.[27]

The tension between these models is real. For debate as a quasi-educational activity in which learning plays an equal role with competition, sharing information may be considered legitimate and even desirable cooperation. Yet, one could equally claim that receiving advantageous information for short-term competitive gains is undesirable, particularly in a community in which some teams are better networked than others. The choice is ultimately grounded in the moral images that decision makers prefer.

This choice, in turn, connects to larger cultural issues, such as the importance of individual enterprise versus cooperative action. Throughout the worlds of education and work, one finds this tension evident. Should groups work together, blurring personal accomplishment in the name of collective attainment? For American institutions that value both individualism and communal support, such a cultural tension is potent.

The Subculture of Debate

While the social network is powerful, it is given meaning by a set of cultural traditions that connect individuals. Stories, rituals, customs, beliefs, and jargon link debaters, and are spread at tournaments, summer institutes, and now on computer lists and Internet pages. Students, by virtue of the boundaries of their culture, participate in a distinct universe of discourse. A sign at Randall Park put it, "Remember, we're not in the real world, we're in the debate world." As one observer noted:

> Asked to describe high school debaters [David] Cheshier [then director of the Georgetown summer high school debate workshop] notes that "intellectual competition turns them on. They're the same kind of kids who would play fantasy games and war games." Debate as "Dungeons and Dragons"? It's not that farfetched a notion when you consider what debate and D&D have in common: arcane lore, a premium on quick thinking, and the thrill of combat in an imaginary universe. Between rounds at the Georgetown summer workshop, I chatted with a voluble tyro from one of the country's debate powers, the Bronx High School of Science. Did he enjoy debating? "Sure," he said, "but it has nothing to do with the real world."[28]

Whether or not debate competition has to do with the "real world," its culture is meaningful to its participants. If not a real world, it is an ordered world.

One of the challenges of creating a culture of debate—as is true of youth cultures generally[29]—is that the participants keep changing. This reality is reflected in the fact that former debaters are recalled in collective memory by the topic of their year (water, Latin America, prison overcrowding, space, homelessness, and so forth). The reality of graduation means that each year skims off the oldest and most knowledgeable cohort, replacing it with a green and ignorant one. The process of subcultural socialization must be continuous for the culture to continue. Debate, like many other subcultures, promotes continuity. Coaches are the most obvious example of this continuity, but, as I mentioned above, it is often difficult for successful participants to disengage entirely, remaining on the margins, further cementing debate culture. These individuals keep alive the memory of those stars of past years—even recognizing that those individuals' fame will fade with time. An assistant coach attempted to list the "ten best Minnesota debate teams of the 1980s." Today, those teams would no longer be known, just as a list from the 1970s (or 1920s!) would have been obscure: the subculture is too transient, too lacking in an institutional history for a meaningful "hall of fame."[30]

   The difficulty of institutionalizing leisure history does not mean that
no cultural traditions bind debaters. War stories are routinely shared,[31]
just as they are by mushroom collectors,[32] Little League baseball players,
and others who recognize a shared commitment. During the year that I
observed, frequent mention was made of the fact that at the state tournament the previous year, the lights went out. The event was mentioned
both before and at the 1990 state tournament, with the coach of the
school that hosted the tournament both years handing out a black post-
card, allegedly a photo of the previous year's tournament, and a book of
matches, labeled "emergency lighting." The president of the Minnesota
Debate Teachers Association joked, "Much of the discussion [at the last
meeting] is what is the best way to run debates in the dark." At the annual
meeting, the coach of the host school commented: "I'm going to call the
meeting to order by lighting the candles." Stories were spread among
debaters about how one participant burned incense in the hall. Doree, in
arguing against a case that called for electronic monitoring of prisoners to
reduce overcrowding, noted the possibility of power failures, commenting that "it even happened last year at the state debate tournament."
   Likewise, entrepreneurs provide cultural artifacts for this subculture,
not just briefcases for cards and briefs or timers, but bumper stickers:
"Honk if you're prima facie," or "Debate—If you can't convince them,
confuse them," or "Real debaters don't need briefs. Want to check?" Another feature, seemingly trivial, that links debaters is pen-twirling, an act
of fine motor coordination that I was never able to master; perhaps it
serves some of the same functions as cigarette smoking in using the body
to drain nervous energy. One day I took my son to buy shoes; the clerk
immediately recognized him as a debater because he was absently flipping
his pen. A key informant felt that this skill was sufficiently important to
mention during our first week of acquaintanceship, and he taught the
members of the Randall Park team how to do it that week. Often the skill
is learned at summer institute. One debater joked: "I didn't go to an institute that taught pen spinning." This seemingly mundane behavior served
as a public identity marker, dispelling the image that debaters are klutzes.
Its status is such that one debater shared his skills on the e-mail debate
list: "I can twirl back and forth over my thumb (continuous), I can twirl
over [my] middle finger and catch with thumb (two different ways). I can
do the drummer's twirl on both sides of my middle finger and in both
directions."[33]
   A final cultural domain that cements community is the creation of verbal indicators of membership, establishing boundaries of meaning for insiders in contrast to those outside the activity.[34] These creations can be
instrumental, directly related to the *doing* of the activity (in which case
they are labeled "jargon" or "technical talk"), or expressive, playful re-

minders of a moral order (labeled "slang").[35] Debate is notable for the creation of these neologisms; indeed, part of the criticism of the activity is that it is too filled with such esoteric phrases. Yet, it is easy to parody *any* group for insider speech—a point sociologists ruefully recognize.[36] Socialization involves learning the meaning and use of such terms. While affiliation mechanisms are found in all groups, they are intense in adolescent groups, where the issue of identity management is central, and in which such specialized terminology mirrors adult life.

Learning the correct names becomes central. One participant explained that for his first two weeks as a novice, he was confused, thinking that "briefs" meant underwear, instead of written arguments (field notes). Using such speech reveals that one is an insider; it is an identity marker, as surely as flipping one's pen. The desire to employ technical terms is so overwhelming that coaches must remind their debaters to use "ordinary" words. Mrs. Miller commented to her Randall Park charges, who wanted to run a counterwarrant (a claim that the affirmative case is not representative of the resolution), that they should counter the argument without using that label. She notes, "You guys are so into calling things" (field notes). Debaters take a simple argument and assign it status through a technical term. This becomes notable when debaters confront those outside the activity. One must be prepared to translate: "I go in [a stationery store] and ask for a flow pad. They say, 'What's a flow pad?' I'm laughing and laughing, and I say, 'Legal-size pads'" (field notes). On one occasion, a male debater who asked for flow pads was directed to the feminine-products aisle.

In instrumental speech, debaters use such terms as flipping the PMA (turning the "plan meets advantage" argument against the team that made it), kritiks (moral criticism of one's opponents' presentation in the round), T (topicality; whether the plan falls within the scope of the topic), Hasty G (a hasty generalization), a squirrel (a trivial, narrow, or silly case), or iso (isolationism). These terms are in dynamic tension, and new terms are added as others disappear from usage.

The creation of expressive language, more directly tied to the community than to the activity, similarly distinguishes insiders and outsiders.[37] Some of these terms are stable, but because they lack institutional support they may change more rapidly than instrumental jargon, and may be more regional or local. During my research, debaters spoke of a honto (a person consumed by debate), a hummer (a strong case), a meatball (a large generic argument), slug (a short point in rebuttal), road-kill (teams in a tournament, easily beaten), to drop or to down (to receive a loss from a judge), and an old stone or dinosaur (an old-fashioned judge). The line that separates technical and cultural speech is hazy, as much of the subculture is focused on the activity; yet, as always, being able to "talk the talk" can be as meaningful as being able to "walk the walk." In high school debate, there is no walking without talking.

The Cultural Domain of Debate

High school debate is a meaningful social world, both nationally and locally. More than that, high school debate is an adolescent world. It is necessary to understand debate in light of the oscillations of adolescents: oscillations of moral value, of affiliation, of identity, and of a toolkit that contains behaviors that characterize children and adults and that differentiates adolescents from both. One is simultaneously a child, a teen, and an adult. Human societies set the rites of passage differently, and in other cultures and other times, boys and girls at the age of novice debaters have full adult rights and privileges. Our society sets the bar for adult membership high, and, thus, these adolescents have some adult skills, but, because of our socialization, not always adult judgment. The forms of adolescent deviance, mild compared to other adolescent worlds, are often precisely those activities that are legitimate for adults. The guardians of these debaters are ambivalent, and their ideas differ about how seriously to police these activities. After all, they are confronting students who in most respects have embraced their expectations, and now are embracing their own pleasures, if before their time. Further, in an activity that encourages teens to question everything, should not these domains of deviance be questioned as well? The decisions of adult guardians are shaped by the forces of social control that stand behind them. Teens will be teens, but what this means—what the zone of acceptable behavior should be—is determined in practice. That much of this deviance occurs on the road in a transitional world in which debaters are given additional freedom and additional responsibility makes the pressure on the adult supervisor greater.

The world of debate has a structure that transcends the boundaries of the individual team. Because of social networks that have developed through tournaments, romantic affiliations, and summer institutes, debaters know each other, with the most committed developing an extensive set of linkages. This creates relationship clumps within the activity, where some individuals come to know each other well, and consequently develop what seems to outsiders to be an impermeable circle that, given boundary maintenance mechanisms, permits those outside the boundaries to define the group as arrogant or exclusive.

My evidence suggests that the world of high school debate is a powerful social scene, yet this is not a comparative analysis of teenage leisure groups. Other activities have, in their own ways, tight-knit groups.

Within high school, sports teams, musical ensembles, and other extracurricular activities can be powerful forces. Outside of the institution, adolescents can become closely linked to church groups, political movements, or community service organizations, and these groups, often with significant numbers of teenagers, shape identity. Indeed, some participants attempt to balance debating with other activities—Junior Achievement, drama, fencing, tutoring, or religious fellowships. Each group has the potential to fully engulf a self,[38] although the time commitment of tournament participation surely makes debate particularly intense. Some participants live for debate; others enjoy a modest involvement, leaving time for the media, socializing, and other domains. Such competing activities, draining free time, limit one's emotional and instrumental investment. Such balance may not be undesirable.

As is true of any social group, a set of cultural elements are created in debate. Just as groups create an idioculture or group culture, networks create subcultures based on communication and shared interests. The creation of history, customs, beliefs, stories, and jargon serves to establish the content of the relationships that constitute the network. Culture and relationship structure are intertwined in the creation of a world to which people desire to belong and in which their cohesion leads to interpersonal caring.[39] Removed from their world, debaters (and other high schoolers) lose part of their selves, and this, for many, explains an intense sadness on that glorious day of graduation.

Seven

Teachers and Coaches

DEBATE exists within an institutional world. That debate is situated in schools is essential to understanding how the activity operates. This is an activity that schools teach and in which their teams compete. In contrast to many forms of voluntary adolescent activity, forensics is controlled by teachers, school-hired coaches, principals, school boards, and state educational agencies. In this, it contrasts with Babe Ruth baseball, Eagle Scouts, religious assemblies, gymnastic clubs, fantasy gaming groups, and youth gangs.

The organization of debate within schools means that the presence of a team or class is tied to organizational politics. *Without institutional blessing*, a group of students cannot create such a group. The actions of the larger institution constrain the doing of debate. While some have suggested that, because of the absence of programs in many schools, private clubs should be organized, there is little movement in this direction.[1]

The uncertain standing of debate—and of the key roles of principals and supervisors—means that the activity may be present or absent in any given high school. While certain factors predispose a school to have a program (e.g., suburban location and the social class of the parents), some schools that might be expected to have strong programs, do not. Of the four major private schools in the Twin Cities, only three offered debate at the time of my research; the same was true in Atlanta. It is common for a program to be viable one year and nonexistent the next, often because the teacher or coach has retired or resigned.

Institutionally, those interested in debate must mobilize resources. Unlike football, band, or chemistry, debate is not now seen as essential for a high school. A high school that does not teach forensics will not be decertified. For debate to thrive, its constituency must encourage decision makers to provide an appropriate structure and sufficient resources.

In this chapter, I begin by examining the process of obtaining institutional support. I then examine the economics of high school debate. How can programs succeed, often in the face of marginal resources and bureaucratic indifference? I then turn to those figures—teachers and coaches—who mediate the relationship with institutions. What does being a teacher or a coach involve, and what are the different implications of these two roles? Finally, I turn to the organization of debate classes within the high school: a course that can be a combination of lecture, workplace, playground, and study hall.

Support Systems

Given the precarious state of debate and its self-evident justifications (as participants see the matter), some call for more vigorous lobbying for its support. When times look bleak and the respect one deserves is lacking, public relations is in demand. A well-funded coach noted:

> In some years past I've been sort of angry that administrators don't know what's happening or what's going on at the time, and I get upset at the fact that I have to be my own publicist. I don't like to blow my own horn. I want to coach the team, and I would like someone out there caring enough about it to put the articles in the newspaper. . . . My one complaint is that if I don't publicize the team, then it may not get publicized, and . . . that's not a real happy situation. (interview)

For an activity to be on stable footing, a constituency must proclaim its value. Without a vocal constituency, debate—or any domain—can be an easy target:

> [Debate] doesn't have a big constituency. It doesn't have a big following. It's not a revenue sport. It can be replaced. Its primary selling point [is that] it's an educational activity, and the school says, "Well, don't kids get enough education during the school day anyway?" You're not going to get a lot of public outcry when you do cut it. The only people that are going to cry out are debaters, and the coach, and maybe a few parents. But even the parents don't fight all that hard [for it] sometimes. (interview)

One prominent debate coach noted that "even a few parents, pulling the right cords and making the right vociferous noises, can help quite a lot; a lot of parents can work wonders."[2] A relatively small group of parents, caring deeply about a program to which few object, can have a significant effect; these squeaky wheels demand grease.

School districts that have had a tradition of success have an advantage. In Minnesota, South St. Paul High School, located in a working-class suburb, formerly home to the city's meat-packing plants, has historically been a debate powerhouse, and it remained so during my research. Between 1944 and 1987, the school had won the state championship eleven times. Debate had been institutionalized in the school, and was a claim to fame. The school board protected the program. This partially resulted from the school having had several very influential coaches, and from the fact that a member of the board had a son who was a debater. The long-time coach taught nothing but speech and debate. With so many students being exposed to debate, it was relatively easy to create a powerful team and to provide institutional support among administrators and alumni. Long-term success builds upon itself, making debate part of a school's self-image and making cuts difficult. Yet, after a series of problems with the coaching staff, no classes in debate were taught at the high school for several years prior to my research. While the debate team was not decimated, the current coach had to rebuild the program and to persuade the administration that classes should be reinstituted. Even in a location in which debate is so important, the possibility of elimination is real. St. Francis High School, another working-class-area high school, located in the exurbs of Minneapolis, also has had considerable institutional support. The successful, popular coach, whose teams won three state championships and a national championship in the 1980s, mostly teaches debate classes. Perhaps most significantly, he was able to get his school named a government document repository. The existence of this resource not only helps the team do research, but also makes it more likely that the school administration will continue to support the program, given their investment in maintaining these documents.

In contrast, consider the cases of Harvest High School and the Greene School. Harvest is a public school in a rapidly growing part of the Twin Cities, an area with a number of strong debate programs; however, the fact that Harvest's theater program is one of the best in the state made debate less appealing, and it had no debate team. Likewise, Greene, a top private school, lacked a debate program, even though a teacher was willing to teach debate. Again, competition existed with strong music and drama programs. Greene also had the misfortune of once having a coach who, I was told, was "a pretty slimy guy." His reputation seemed to rub off on the activity (field notes). Perhaps more typical was the case of a prominent Twin Cities coach, previously a coach for two rural high schools. After she left, the schools were unable to find a suitable coach, and the debate programs at both schools died. The memory of the success of a program dies quickly without an active supporter. Ultimately, many schools feel that there are only so many voluntary activities in which they can excel; the strength of one decreases the desire and support for others. Although writing, reading, and calculating are defined as central to the mission of schools, public speaking is not; such "esoteric" topics as chemistry and European history receive more institutional support.

As is often the case with social and political movements, personal relations matter. Those schools in which the principal is enthusiastic or is a former debater have a built-in protector, at least during the tenure of that administrator:

Penny is a former debate and speech coach, and still helps out with both, and I mean as the assistant principal. . . . Her being an administrator is just so helpful. I mean I don't have to do any paperwork. She takes care of that. (interview)

At Boston Heights, I found the three elements that I perceived a successful program needed, which are kids, administration, and budget. . . . Our head principal, he is what I would call a man of vision. . . . He's very proud of the fact that we offer cocurricular programs or activities that over 80 percent of the student body has something to participate in after school, outside the regular school day. He firmly believes that not all learning happens in the classroom, that some of the best quality learning actually happens outside the classroom, and that's why I think he supports some of these programs. (interview)

The fact that Mrs. Miller had a long and positive relationship with the Randall Park principal is said to explain why the team has support. For instance, when her old copying machine finally died, the team could have faced difficulty, as they copied up to five thousand pages per month. Fortunately, the principal gave the team a copier from his office; disaster was averted. His generosity underlined how dependent debaters are on equipment and on those who control that equipment. Likewise, Internet or Lexis-Nexis access can significantly benefit a team's ability to be competitive. Of course, limits always exist to the beneficence of administrators, faced with their own constraints. The superintendent of the St. Paul public schools is a former debater: "He makes reference to it every time he gives a talk to the teachers as a whole. I think [the board of education] knows it's important, but we have so many other things that are ahead of debate in importance" (interview). This former debater provides little support for the single debate program under his jurisdiction.

Although relations with other members of the faculty are not as crucial for the team's standing as is the relationship with the administration, the resentment of teachers in having their students absent from class on Fridays, and the perception that the debate teacher has found a good deal by teaching speech class and missing school days, can provoke resentment. I was told that one coach, notably poor at confronting internal politics and in establishing positive relations with his colleagues, almost destroyed a program because, as a college student successor noted, "He didn't play the games he had to play . . . sucking up." In fact, at Randall Park not everyone supports the debate team:

They [teachers] have a meeting with parents [of ninth graders] before [the ninth graders] come over here to the tenth grade. . . . [The department chairman] had told them that it is lots of work, and they'd better make sure that they know what happens before the sign-up for the [debate] class, because [the debaters will] have no Saturdays, and they'll have no nights after school, and so forth. So there are those people [who oppose it], and math teachers hate it. [Question: Why?] Because we're always taking their kids out of class. [They are] the kind of teacher who thinks that all the time that she or he has everyday is the most vital thing in the kid's life. . . . I always laugh and call it the Catholic grade school syndrome [she laughs] that you have to be there. (interview)

When the faculty must decide priorities, these political reactions may influence the outcome. The frustration may be with a colleague, but it is the careers and life chances of adolescents that are affected.

Because of the link between debate and the institution, the existence of a program is closely tied to internal school politics, leading to healthy programs in some places and sickly ones in neighboring schools.

Debating for Dollars

For any activity to exist, resources must be available. Debate costs and, unlike basketball or football, is unable to support itself. Schools differ widely in the level of funding and support available, and the size of the budget is correlated with the success of the team. At some schools—mostly those on the National Circuit—the debate team may receive tens of thousands of dollars, not including the salary of the teachers. Plane fares, hotel rooms, and tournament registration cost money. Even teams that compete on a local or regional level require some institutional support. Copying and tournament registration must be paid, and the coach typically receives a small compensation.

How do teams acquire resources? How does a team survive in an educational world without unlimited resources? In a national survey of coaches that Patrick Schmidt and I conducted in 1990 (described in more detail later in the chapter), of seventy-nine schools responding, nineteen (24 percent) had annual budgets, excluding salaries, of under $2500; twenty-two (28 percent) had budgets between $2500 and $5000; eleven (14 percent) had budgets between $5000 and $7500; and ten schools (13 percent) had budgets between $7500 and $10,000. An additional seventeen schools (22 percent) had budgets above $10,000, including one school with a budget above $30,000. Most coaches whose teams attended the national tournament (56 percent) required additional fundraising for their teams.

Compared to other areas of the country, and excluding public and private schools that debate on the National Circuit, many Minnesota schools are adequately funded, although few would describe themselves as well funded. During my research in 1989–1990, the additional stipend for a teacher or salary for an outside coach ranged from $1500 to $4500, or as one coach jokingly exaggerated, "about ten cents an hour" (field notes).[3] Considering the hours and opportunity costs (activities missed as a result of involvement in debate), the dollars motivate few. Team budgets ranged somewhat more widely. The best funded program had a budget of $10,000, with several funded at about $6000, and still others at $2000–$3500.[4] While these budgets prevented much out-of-state travel, it meant that teams were not continually fund-raising or dependent on the largess of parents. Many schools received additional revenues from hosting their own tournaments, from fund-raising, and from costs hidden within the school budget (e.g., copying costs, buying note cards). To put the budget in perspective, a single out-of-state bus trip for twenty students costs $2000. According to one coach who runs a well-attended regional tournament, her costs run to nearly $6000, including $1200 for custodians, $1300 for awards, and $2500 for judges,[5] although tournaments can be run for less, and some or all of this may be offset by registration fees.

When compared to the wealthiest debate programs, Minnesota programs were modest affairs. During my research, I was told that one national circuit team had a budget of $34,000; another school's budget was $40,000. Most incredibly I was informed that a prominent national circuit team had a budget of $120,000–$150,000, which included $20,000 from the school and additional funding from a discretionary fund controlled by the Board of Education. The coach receives no salary for coaching, and claims to spend over $10,000 of his own funds annually.

In contrast, some teams receive minimal support—at least from direct school sources. One school program had received $7000, a reasonable amount, until after three districts had merged. The following year the debate team was defunded. Because the coach was able to obtain $5000 in grants, and to charge debaters for each tournament, the program was able to continue at least temporarily.[6] Reported cuts of half to two-thirds of a budget are not uncommon, even among strong, competitive regional programs. Since the American education system is largely funded locally, a patchwork of support is evident. There have been no attempts by Congress—filled with former debaters—to establish a federal mandate for debate or by large corporations to create an endowment for individual programs.

The question emerges how to cope with these limits. Many programs cannot survive cuts, particularly without an adult mentor who is committed to the continuation of debate. Once a program disappears, reviving it is considerably more difficult.

When budgets are stretched, individuals and organizations attempt to survive at the same level of activity through "making do." By trimming and conserving, the activities can continue. The ability to make do is the fond dream of all politicians who hope that, by cutting budgets, the same services can be maintained, at reduced cost. Up to a point, such a perspective is clearly correct. The first cuts involve rethinking expenses. Randall Park attempted to conserve money by having students place article extracts on cards by means of rubber cement, rather than tape. Further, the team purchases rubber cement in gallon containers. Another school packs more students in their school van than is legally allowed; the coach jokes that whenever they pass a state trooper, they must duck. Taking two vans or a bus would be too expensive. When teams travel, they often stay at a cheaper motel, even if the room is less comfortable and the establishment is less convenient or safe. Of course, once you have switched to that least expensive motel, the following year that is no longer possible as a means to save additional money. Sometimes the coach exceeds the budget, hoping that the school administration will cover the extra expenses or take the shortfall from next year's budget. The ultimate in making do is to decrease the size of the traveling teams, perhaps cutting the number of debaters entered at a tournament from twelve to six, or even eliminating overnight tournaments. Such a strategy ensures that only the best students get to participate at the cost of making debate even more of an elite activity and harming team morale.

If one is not able or does not wish to reduce costs, an appealing option is to increase support. Such funding can come from the school administration, the coach, parents of debaters, or money raised from the public, nonprofit agencies, or businesses.

Lobbying the school administration is the most efficient strategy, but one with limited success, given other demands for funding. Some coaches simply pay for expenses out of their own pockets. In wealthier schools, parents may be asked to contribute, although that makes debate more exclusive. For example, at South Eugene High School, a school that the children of faculty at the University of Oregon attend, some parents contribute upward of $1,000 per year for the opportunity for their offspring to debate, and many see this as a good investment (field notes). At private schools, these expenses may be defined as part of the high cost of a quality education.

For some teams, fund-raising is a major part of their yearly activity. This may involve sponsoring a tournament in which registrations more than cover the costs. A large part of the tournament in budgetary terms is the refreshment stand, which, if the food is prepared or contributed by parents, is pure profit. Teams sell poinsettia plants, discount coupon books, or magazines and hold bake sales or car washes. One former debater suggested selling doughnuts in the morning and Rice Krispy bars at lunch.[7] If too intrusive or time-consuming, this fund-raising can distract from the practice of debate.

Some schools are entrepreneurial enough to raise funds from charitable or fraternal organizations. One underfunded program received a $1000 grant from the local American Legion post. A second team combined money from the Legion and the Veterans of Foreign Wars to fund their travel to the national tournament in California. A third team relied on support from a community foundation that had been established to help fund educational projects, including scholarships and cocurricular activities. Creative applications to local foundations can, in some cases, provide needed support.

Finally, teams may rely on corporate support. Just as the National Forensic League receives funding from Phillips Petroleum and Liberty National Life, individual teams receive money. A team in Wyoming was supported by local coal companies, and a team in northern Minnesota by local lumber companies. We have not reached the point where debaters, like some Little League baseball players, wear their sponsor's name on the back of their jackets, but some teams encourage local entrepreneurs to provide tax-deductible support. Perhaps someday debate tournaments, like football bowl games, will be known by the name of their sponsors: the Honeywell Little Nationals or the Pillsbury Round-Robins. While there is something troubling about the constant drumbeat of corporate advertising, benefits may outweigh the disadvantages.

As many have suggested, the lack of institutional support for high school debate advantages the rich schools and wealthy debaters against those without resources. Some observers see a "wall" decreasing the likelihood of success for minorities and working-class teens.[8] No playing arena, despite our field of dreams, is truly level. This is an example of what sociologist Robert Merton has labeled the "Matthew Effect": that is, those with more to begin with are continually advantaged.[9] In chapter 8 I describe a "Doughnut Effect," whereby public school debate programs are found in the ring of suburban school districts surrounding urban areas but not inside or outside that ring.[10] If we examine the strongest programs, the effect is even more pronounced. Since debate may have particular benefits for those who enter without extensive cultural capital, this reality is deeply disturbing. For poor school districts, money is not to be had from the administration, parents, community fundraising, or local businesses. The only hope for these programs is a commitment from charitable funding agencies. An alternative solution is to impose limits on high schools as to the size of their budget or the amount of travel, creating more vigorous local leagues (or to create, in effect, different classes of debate: say, AAAA, AAA, AA, and A, stratified on the size of the budget).

The Teacher and the Coach

The man or woman who teaches debate has several yardsticks by which to judge outcomes. Is it crucial that students learn the skills of how to research, speak, and think, or is the best assessment the team's record at the end of the season? In fact, although some might say that only the skills are critical, both—skills and success—connect to the appraisal of a debate program and the evaluation of its leader. These multiple means of judging outcomes suggest divergent models for determining how one sees oneself. Being a forensics director is not easy, and involves a great investment of time and a variety of skills: one must be not only a rhetorician, but also a psychologist, social worker, parent substitute, bus driver, travel planner, publicist, and bookkeeper.[11] One 1965 study of forensics directors found that, according to self-reports, they devoted eighteen hours per week to debate—a figure that, including weekend tournaments, is probably fairly accurate. Even if some of these hours overlap with school hours, they indicate a significant time commitment: devotion that administrators or significant others do not always appreciate.[12] Yet, the dedication of coaches cannot always outweigh the time demands, fatigue, and lack of compensation.[13]

Before discussing the tensions and role conflicts inherent in the act of training a group of adolescents, I present a group portrait of debate coaches/teachers, focusing on the men and women who lead high school programs.[14] In the spring of 1990, Patrick Schmidt, an undergraduate at the University of Minnesota and former high school debater, and I distributed a set of questionnaires to a sample of coaches.[15] Two groups of coaches were sampled: (1) the approximately 150 coaches whose teams competed in policy debate at the 1989 NFL national debate tournament in Golden, Colorado, and (2) a random sample of another 150 coaches of National Forensic League–affiliated programs.[16] For purpose of this analysis, I combine data from these two samples.

The demographic results were somewhat surprising. Despite claims that men dominate the activity, we found that, nationally, coaches were almost evenly divided by gender (51 percent were male; there was no significant difference between the two samples). The typical coach was 39 years old, and had been coaching for eleven years and teaching for fourteen. Their teams had, on average, thirty-four students, although this may represent a generous assessment of who was on the team—the number of active students would surely be significantly lower. Approximately half (51 percent) of the coaches had assistants. This is one area in which we discovered a striking difference between the more and less competitive teams. Just over 60 percent of the coaches who participated at the NFL national tournament had at least one assistant, whereas only 34 percent of the less competitive teams did.

A large number of coaches had participated in debate in high school or college.[17] Slightly fewer than half were debaters in high school, and 43 percent had debated on the collegiate level. In fact, 57 percent of the coaches said that a major reason they accepted the position was that they had enjoyed participating as a student. Clearly, the continuation of high school debate depends upon the existence of programs of high quality. Not surprisingly, coaches continued their involvement because they "enjoy teaching debate" (68 percent). This is also reflected in the fact that 56 percent of the coaches considered their students above average in intelligence, and an additional 43 percent said that their students were exceptional. Only one coach found students "average." It was not surprising that coaches were unanimous that debate teaches important intellectual skills. Beyond the claim of enjoying teaching debate, only 11 percent cited the additional payment they received as a significant motivation for coaching.

Within the school setting, recalling that these respondents are primarily teachers, 69 percent taught speech, and 47 percent taught English. The only other sizable group of teachers were the 20 percent of coaches who taught social studies. Within the school, debate was seen primarily as speech, only secondarily as part of English or social studies.

One last issue deserves comment: the political stance of debate coaches. As a group, American educators are politically left-of-center. It is not that teachers are brainwashing their students—unlikely with such an inquisitive group—but that their position as role models matters. In our sample, 41 percent of the respondents defined themselves as liberal or very liberal. (This was during the period that liberal was being referred to as the "L-word.") An additional 39 percent defined themselves as moderate, and only 17 percent saw themselves as conservative or very conservative. Among the fourteen Minnesota coaches I asked, twelve defined themselves as liberal, one as conservative, and one claimed mixed views. Of the sample, 46 percent were Democrats, 22 percent Republicans, and 28 percent Independents. Although no questions were asked about whether debate coaches were libertarian in orientation, that approach would certainly have some appeal. The evidence suggests that in their politics, coaches are not a representative national sample.[18]

Mrs. Miller, for instance, made no secret that she was a liberal Democrat, and often would criticize then–President Bush,[19] and would warn students against appearing racist or chauvinistic in debating prison overcrowding. She encouraged students to challenge conservative evidence as biased (she routinely disparaged Nixon aide Charles Colson), but I never heard her suggest they should attempt to do the same for liberal evidence. When the Lincoln-Douglas debaters were discussing limitations on pornography, she noted: "I'm a really liberal-minded person. I don't think I can judge a round like this. My mind is set" (field notes). The fact was that most of her students (eight of ten had similar views) did not object, although it is possible that her views helped to shape theirs.[20] Thus, when one student, discussing guidelines for prison sentences, ventured the opinion that "I think that racism isn't as big a problem in Minnesota as in Alabama," she responded, "Racism is racism. It's found everywhere." When a black student noted, "It's true that black people commit more crimes than whites," she responded, "On a percentage basis. Remember that people who commit crimes live in poor, urban areas, and blacks, Hispanics, and Asians live in those areas" (field notes). Mrs. Miller felt a responsibility as an educator to provide students with political information and opinions. These views were not forced on students, but were openly and forcefully expressed.

Some (mostly liberals) feel that this political stance to debate is appealing to people who are "open-minded" and trains them in being open to ideas; to some, this is linked to liberalism or libertarianism. In the minds of Minnesota coaches, liberalism is linked to a set of educational virtues:

> I think that if you're debating and involved in a question, and understanding it, that has any connection with human services and kindness and people things. . . . I think the more you know, the more liberal you become. (interview)

> I think debate makes them liberal. . . . Debate makes you have an open mind. It means that you have to see things from a lot of different viewpoints, and because you are able to do that I think it gives you a more liberal feeling about things in general. You're more accepting of difference. (interview)

One outspoken coach put the matter directly, if humorously:

> I think it probably tends to make them more liberal. That's at least a hope—but anyway I think it does, because . . . you're at this stage in your life when you are developing those views about things. And I think debate tends to form students' political views. . . . Of course, liberal is where the truth lies. No [he laughs], it tends to make you more modern. Let's put it that way. (interview)

Debate is not politically neutral, and, no doubt, conservatives will shudder to hear these assessments. However, according to one coach, bias may be built into the structure of debate. Most resolutions (particularly those involving domestic politics) call for government involvement. While teams present both the affirmative and negative sides of the resolution, the affirmative position is the one that they develop as their case, the position with which they most identify:

> Affirmative cases tend to be liberal because, after all, they're fixing something that's perceived to be wrong in current society, and, of course, conservatives say, "Well, there's not a lot wrong with current society," so you have to be liberal to say there's something wrong. . . . With negative, you rely on hand-book evidence. You don't deal with it as much. When you're affirmative, you really get into it. You do your own research. You come to believe in your case. (interview)

Whether the bias is structural or personal, there is no doubt that in Minnesota, and seemingly nationally as well, conservatives are challenged as they are throughout the academic community. There are, of course, prominent conservative debaters, coaches, and judges. Yet, for conservative adolescents, forming their views, this is another challenge of competitive debate.

Teacher or Coach?

As noted above, disagreement exists on whether the *primary* role of the forensic educator is as a teacher or a coach. The issue emerges when groups name themselves. Thus, when a group of well-established national circuit coaches decided to form an organization to address their needs as forensic educators, they chose the name National Debate Coaches Association. In contrast, in Minnesota, in part because of the pressure from several leading figures, the forensic organization changed its name from the Minnesota Debate Coaches Association to the Minnesota Debate Teachers Association. The fact that this move was self-conscious and agreed-to after considerable discussion, symbolizes the different perspectives that the labels bring. The dispute is linked to the question of whether college students or recent college graduates—seen as coaches, not as teachers—should run debate programs. The idea was not to exclude these individuals, given that the option would be to shut down these programs, but to legitimate the hiring of more debate teachers. College students could provide neither the educational value of debate nor the institutional stability.

Those who prefer the label and the self-image of debate teacher point to the educational aspects of the activity, arguing that their most important goal is to teach, not win rounds. One told me that as far as his school was concerned in hiring a "coach":

> The person is first and foremost a teacher. The primary purpose of that person is not to train debaters, as supportive as I am of that, but to teach them. . . . The

worst that happens is that you wind up with one-year-college coaches, a new one each year. (field notes)

Others emphasize that this role of teacher is central to their self-image:

[Question: Do you think of yourself as a debate coach or debate teacher?]
Oh, teacher, without question. A teacher first, and then a debate teacher as opposed to a debate coach. . . . My career is not being a debate teacher. I mean, I am a history teacher. I'm a teacher first, and then a debate teacher after that. . . . It wasn't that way with my coach in high school. I mean he was a debate coach, and then he got this job teaching school because he wanted to coach debate, and that gave him a means of doing that, and I think that's some-what true for people on the circuit, that they're teaching so they can get their debate thing. It's a way to make a living while you coach debate. (interview)

Teachers, many of whom are exceptional educators, do not necessarily share the perspective of their students who are motivated primarily by the game aspect. For teachers, "competition is a motivational tool to produce learning on a scale that most high school classes can't produce"[21]: a means to an end. These educators, who demand serious, plausible, or logical arguments, are sometimes derided as old-fashioned, "buffaloes," "old stones," or "dinosaurs."

For others, the label debate "coach" is fine, not because they believe that students are not learning important skills and knowledge, but that their role is to coach their debaters in acquiring these skills, with the out-come being success in debate rounds—an objective criteria to which all can relate. While most of my interviewees preferred the primary label of teacher, not all did. Some, of course, were not formally teachers, and they typically defined themselves as coaches, the position for which they were hired. Given that most coaches were once debaters themselves, the ele-ment of competition so necessary for success and commitment seems cen-tral. To claim that one is only a teacher misstates reality. As one "coach" explained:

I do more coaching than teaching. I mean, I'll help them with the strategy, although they have to teach themselves how to do it. I don't think it's some-thing you can necessarily teach. I think you have to learn it yourself. I mean I can't teach them to read fast. I mean I can't teach them to understand things or to make arguments necessarily. I can help them. I can coach them more than I can teach them. (interview)

For many, the role involves some of the duties of both coach and teacher. The two terms operate in a dynamic tension, depending on the issue or on the stage of the debater. As one put it:

I see it as an evolving and changing relationship. When they're sophomores, I really am a teacher, and I guide them pretty heavily, and I'm pretty controlling. . . . I don't always give them a lot of freedom. . . . As the three years progress, I think that if I've done my job well . . . I am a coach. That means that I'm there to answer questions, I'm there to suggest positions, . . . I'm there to hear debates and critique, but I take pride in the fact that I think my kids by the time they are seniors can think of issues on their own, can develop them, and can think in a round. (interview)

The designation of the role of coach or teacher is a sociopolitical issue, having to do with occupational ideology, but it is simultaneously rhetorically situated in the range of practical tasks that is implied by the assignment of directing a team.[22]

Limits of Engagement

Related to the question of whether one is seen is a coach or a teacher is the issue of how much help should the adult provide, an issue discussed in chapter 3 under the creation of cases. One would hardly expect the quarterback, much less the tackle, to create the playbook for the football team. Plays are developed by the coaching staff: that is their job. In contrast, an English teacher would never write the term paper that a student is required to hand in as an assignment. High school debate falls somewhere between these two poles. Teachers demand that students do their own work; coaches require players to follow their professional suggestions. The game image of debate presumes an active and strategic involvement of a coach; an educational image downplays this image.

Some coaches feel that it is wrong and even unethical for coaches to do most of the work on a case or on creating arguments. Opponents of intense help argue:

I think it's improper and unethical for coaches to write their students' arguments. I think it's great for coaches to revise and edit and discuss them, but when you come down to writing them, I don't think it should be a coach as author. (interview)

It is WRONG to write anything for your students. Regardless of whether or not you are a teacher, as a debate coach you are an educator and have a responsibility. In my mind, writing things for your students in debate would be exactly like writing their paper for English or history. It is unethical and in terms of competition, I think it is cheating.[23]

One coach who had hired a talented assistant found that her debaters resented the fact that he did much of the research and the writing for them, creating cases and briefs. She notes, "Three of the four that had been on the varsity team last year were real frustrated by this. First of all, their feeling was, 'We can read an article, you don't need to tell us what's in it, and what's important'" (interview). The sense of personal accomplishment was taken away from these debaters; further, because they were not intimately familiar with the arguments, they may have been less able to respond to counterarguments.

To state these criticisms is not to suggest that others do not hold differing opinions. In some sense, there is a trade-off: greater skills and education in mastering the cases that are created, as opposed to the satisfaction of working from scratch. The efforts of the coach can motivate the students to work harder; some define the involvement of the coach as collaborative education. Proponents see this as "leading by example" and role-modeling.[24] With dozens of esoteric cases on the national debate circuit, having students learn by themselves how to answer each and every one would pose an insuperable obstacle. Indeed, the assistant coach for one of the educators cited above prepared the arguments against an opponent's case at a regional qualifying tournament. His strategy was successfully implemented (field notes). Given the reality of top competitive debate, where education blurs with sport, the involvement of coaches seems inevitable. As one coach notes: "Virtually every national circuit coach I know has [his] hands in the brief-writing game. Saying that brief writing is unethical is like saying that sex for the fun of it is sinful. You may be right, but everyone's doing it."[25] It is an open question as to whether if the National Forensic League ruled that coaches could not create arguments, it could be reasonably enforced.[26]

Coaches and Students

The relationship between coach and debaters is often intense: wonderfully intimate or disturbingly hostile. These students are smart, and like many smart children may be provocative. Because of the amount of time that debaters spend with their coaches, this relationship is highly salient, multistranded, and tinged with emotion. Being a coach is not a role, but a bundle of roles, for which, rhetorically and often in reality, the welfare of the student comes first:

> The ideal coach [has] to have the student concern foremost, not win/loss record, but is this kid . . . getting something out of it? . . . You look at somebody like Ray Goldhagen, who's just a tremendous coach. I mean he looks out for his students. I mean he's as competitive a person as I've ever met, and the guy's just out for blood, but . . . I've never seen it come down to a situation where he didn't think about the kids first. (interview)

> I modeled my relation on the relationship I had with my coach. . . . I mean I have a very special relationship with him. He is almost like a second father to me. I still see him every time I go home. Because you spend so much time with

your debate coach . . . I just think [it is good] that if you can have a relationship where your authority is respected and you're respected as an older person who ultimately must have the say, but yet you're still a friend, you are still somebody that can be confided in. (interview)

These are statements of how coaches ought to behave, and individual coaches live up to their ideals more or less well, but the comments remind us how morally central coaches consider their presence. They matter in the lives of students. Some coaches even refuse to drink alcohol at coaches' parties while traveling with their teams, because they feel that it sets the wrong example.

On the positive side, coaches can essentially adopt three roles: parent, friend, or professional leader. These roles are, of course, found among teachers generally, but because of the amount of time that debaters spend with their coaches, the intensity of these roles may be greater. On the negative side, the dangers are abuse and manipulation, indifference, and lack of respect. In reality, a student's relationship with the coach involves a mix of these themes. Indeed, one respected veteran coach explained that each coach, as a consequence of personality and debate orientation, can recruit and retain a different group of students: he believes that his team is different in style from that of other coaches he admires: what might be called "the cult of the coach" in team culture. Not everyone can reach each kid:

Every kid needs something different. Every coach has [his or her] own style. . . . Kids that I could reach here at Boston Heights, someone like a Henry Fuller wouldn't even look twice at. And Henry would get a whole different group of kids. . . . It's just some of those peripheral kids. A kid might not debate for me ever, but a Henry Fuller could come in and [help that kid] be a great debater. . . . He [the coach] knows how to handle that kid, where I would just look at him and say, "Go away, I don't even want to see you." Every team, I think, really reflects their coach. . . . I know for a fact that most of the people think the Boston Heights [debaters] are incredibly arrogant. . . . Part of it's the community and a little bit of it is me too. (interview)

Male teachers often are seen as playing the benevolent "father figure." Females are easily seen as mothers:

Barry throws a pen at Brian that almost hits Mrs. Miller, and she says, half-joking: "Why are you throwing that at me. I can still change your grade?" Barry jokes in response: "Mrs. Miller, I love you." Doree adds: "You're my second mother." Mrs. Miller says: "Oh, God!" Barry says: "You're the mother I never had." (field notes)

Mrs. Miller, she's kind of a symbol, like my grandmother . . . she's like a grandmother to me. She always wants to know how your day has been. She wants to know everything that happens at home, and anything she can do to help, and then she's always there. (interview)

From the perspective of the coach, particularly those who have reached middle age, and particularly women, seeing debaters as their children seems natural. Coaches worry about "their children," when the young people feel they are being neglected or mistreated by their biological parents. The coach from the inner-city school told me that at times he feels he is doing "social work," including on occasion providing his students with food or money. References to adolescents as "my children" are common:

> Mrs. Nyberg is looking for her debaters. "I'm going to find my children." Later, when Mrs. Nyberg received the Coach of the Year award from the Minnesota Debate Teachers Association, Mrs. Miller said of her: "This person has an open heart to all debaters." Someone else said of her, "Oh, a kid person"; i.e., she takes her relations with her students personally. (field notes)

The relationship is such that coaches sometimes ask their students to pick up their children from day care, and in turn these students may ask to borrow the coach's car or may express concerns about sexual intimacy. Not every coach is comfortable with this role, but few can avoid some entanglement, despite desiring a measure of distance. The significant other of one coach died suddenly in the middle of the season, and this coach, who had served for many as a surrogate parent, had to rely on her team as a support system. One of the members of her varsity team spent considerable time with her young daughter, taking her to the movies and baby-sitting in this time of loss (interview). While the flow of information is not equal, debaters learn about the strains and traumas in the lives of their coaches.

The teacher's or coach's role "in loco parentis" may create discomfort for biological parents who find their adolescents have become more distant while another adult has assumed the role that they had once treasured. One's child's affiliation is now tied to the public sphere (the team), rather than to the private one (the family):

> I do think you develop into a friendship because you share experiences you don't share with other students when you travel with kids, when you are in motels with kids, when you are in a sense their caretaker, like their mother when they're away from home. I have on occasion had mothers come and say, "You know, I'm kind of jealous of you, because my [son or daughter] thinks so highly of you," or "They spend so much time with you." . . . Kids share with me things they don't share with their own parents. I know about their boyfriend and girlfriend. I know those kinds of things, whereas

maybe their parents don't even know they've got a boyfriend or girlfriend. (interview)

The danger is that these relationships can become so close and intense that the parties see themselves as being "friends," with moral authority and discipline lost. The ability to maintain distance, while fostering trust and intimacy, is both a challenge and a necessity:

> Sometimes the students want to see you as their friend, and that's something I resist a lot. I don't like them to become too familiar. I start out with new students actually being very strict, real firm. . . . A few will call me Hank, but only because they know I don't accept it, and they'll do it to try to get at me. They know I'm Mr. Fuller, and a few will call me by my first name, and I will ignore them. I just won't say anything. . . . We end up being usually with students, having a pretty close relationship. These kids end up coming to me with problems at home, with friends. I become in many ways a counselor with them, because I am with them so much. (interview)

> The nice thing about being a teacher is that there is some distance involved. I mean I can be a friend of theirs and we can talk and tease each other and mess around, but there is still a distance that I think is real important, and important to preserve. I don't have to operate at their social level. . . . I think I am their friend, but in an adult kind of way, as opposed to [being a] peer. (interview)

This issue is particularly salient in considering the relations between young debate coaches and their teams. The transition to authority is not easy, particularly if one is hired at the same school one has just debated for: one is a student to one's former teachers and a peer to one's former teammates. One debater returned as assistant coach at his alma mater the year after he graduated:

> Don tells the debaters that, after sixth period, they can start their debate work, missing class. Mrs. Miller says to him half-joking, half-annoyed: "You've changed roles. You don't tell them things like that." He is supposed to be an adult, not a fellow student. A few months later, Mrs. Miller said to the team, "It's really ironic, and it's really fun to hear Don tell you things that I used to tell him." (field notes)

> [A junior explains to me,] it's been interesting to see Don go from a debater last year to a coach. He doesn't have quite the respect [from us] that Mrs. Miller has, but then he's also a little bit easier as a coach as well, because we knew him last year, and he's one of our equals, and we can still relate to him. (interview)

Walking that line between being a peer and being an authority can be difficult, particularly if one does not have authority of one's own, but only derives it from association with the coach.

Overly close friendships can create political problems, but intimacy is more dangerous. The most troubling issue for young coaches is the possibility of sexual relationships. These relationships are not unknown with coaches of any age, but with young coaches these relationships outside the confines of the team are not deviant. It is one's power that makes the relationship awkward and unethical. In their discourse, young coaches emphasize their recognition of the inappropriateness of intimacy:

> When I was a freshman [in college], my wife was a senior [in school] . . . and still debating. She was a year younger than me, and we weren't going out then. I would have not let that happen. I mean I'm real opposed to [that]. You've got a lot of college students coaching, and sometimes relationships evolve, and sometimes they're between coaches and students, and I am just totally opposed [to all that]. (interview)

> I like to have a comradery with the kids. I don't want to be their friend. It's clear that we're not friends. I mean they're not going to invite me out to a movie or anything, but while we're together I'm joking around with them. . . . Virtually every single year I've been a coach I've had girls who have had crushes on me, and that's tough to deal with as a head coach. (interview)

From the perspective of the coach, social relations are an essential part of both teaching and competition. Yet, because they are so emotional they can be deeply troubling as well as deeply satisfying.

The Limits of Commitment

Coaching is a role that sociologists speak of as a "greedy institution."[27] There is *no limit* to the amount of effort that one could spend on coaching, if one wishes. Some coaches, such as one who claimed to spend thirty-one weeks on the road, are examples. One coach embraced the idea of being a "fanatic":

> We as coaches must be *fanatics* about our academic discipline. We need to be so involved and concerned that we become 100% intellectually and emotionally involved. . . . Students must learn that this is their activity, but my profession, my life.[28]

This claim is striking in that it is so different from the perspective of most Minnesota coaches, who are continually troubled by the need to achieve balance in their lives, just as their debaters are. It is not only that they must deal with bookkeeping or with the occasional irate parent who pressures the coach to place a child on the top team or change partners, but even pleasurable activities can be draining. How can one be a responsible coach, while still having a family, a life? One coach, who decided to resign shortly before I interviewed her, explained:

> My children are becoming older and more involved in extracurricular kinds of activities, and I wanted to be there for them. I got to one soccer game that my son was in this year. . . . My daughter wanted to start dance, but that was on Saturdays and my husband was taking my son to karate, so then I couldn't [take her to dance] because I was gone on Saturdays. . . . I wanted that time to spend with my family. (interview)

Most coaches with families have thought about whether coaching debate is worthwhile; arranging that block of time to be away from home suggests mislaid priorities.

A Battle for Respect

Adolescents edging closer to adulthood often believe they have acquired all the tools of adult life. While coaches can create distance and provide warmth, they cannot always buy respect. This is particularly true when the rules or strategies of the coach are contrary to those arguments that are status-enhancing among teenagers, often inspired by the more esoteric positions learned from collegiate debaters at summer institute. Even a well-liked coach such as Mrs. Miller was seen as hopelessly old-fashioned. One of her debaters noted, "I said I'm going to do it my way in senior year. . . . I never used what she said during a round" (field notes). Needless to say, coaches resent that their students violate their instructions. On one occasion, a coach was half in tears because her team was running counterplans and other esoteric arguments. Coaches speak of the arrogance of their debaters, and are offended by the lack of respect for their input, sometimes demonstrated in class or at tournaments. The experience of the coach should not be lightly ignored, even when debaters have more knowledge of current arguments. One coach sighs: "I often feel resentful over the way I am treated by some of the students, and their attitudes often lead me to question why I put up with this."[29] In a later note, this coach remarked: "I have never seen members of any athletic team treat their coaches the way I see many debaters do—I wonder if that is because athletic coaches have the power to make their students run until they puke when they are disrespectful."[30] Of course, sports coaches are supposed to set strategies and develop plays, using their players as agents for their abilities, and some sports coaches would reject this rosy image, also finding a lack of respect by their players.

From the perspective of the debaters, ignoring the coach makes perfect sense, turning the metaphor of education to their advantage. Putting aside the claim that some debaters are more knowledgeable than their coaches, these students believe that the ultimate decision as to what they run in a round should be theirs. The debater should have been taught sufficiently well to make a judgment. As one debater rather arrogantly puts it to peers: "You are the one who will be running the case. If it is horrible, then you will be the one embarrassed. Even though she may be your coach, if she has no idea what she is talking about, then blow her off. She can't give you an F without a good reason. Run the case, and if she fails you, then go to the principal."[31] Another debater—another "brat" according to some—noted, "I ran [a case] even though we were told NOT TO, [my coach] never did figure out what we were running from the ballots."[32] Debaters convince themselves that making their own arguments is educationally justified. A student who ignored the advice of a teacher on an Advanced Placement exam would not receive a poor grade for ignoring the advice, although he or she might well receive such a grade should the advice of the mentor turn out to be valid. The argument, as it appeared on the debate discussion list, sometimes appeared to be a battle between "somewhat hysterical, vengeful, authoritarian coaches" and "debaters who think no one can or should restrain them in any department."[33] The ideal situation involves a meeting of minds under circumstances of respect, with debaters recognizing what experience can teach them and coaches recognizing that students may learn more from their own failures than from the coach's success. That this does not always happens suggests the challenges of an activity that is part sport and part education.

The Dangers of Coaching

Within any community, one finds individuals who do not live up to general standards. I have mentioned coaches who are sexually intimate with their students and, given the broadened definition of sexual harassment, others behave inappropriately as well. Some coaches misappropriate or embezzle funds from debate programs or from summer institutes. Not every coach has the leadership skills, good judgment, or emotional balance to lead a team, at least as viewed by the team, by parents, or by other coaches. Some coaches, particularly those with their own children on their team, are plagued by the same issues that Little League coaches face: personal favoritism versus team success. This can become sensitive when coaches must decide who should be partnered with whom and who should be able to attend the most desirable tournaments.

Some acts stand outside the boundaries of legitimate public behavior. Even if coaches wish to win at all costs, they must pretend that this is not the case. A current coach reflected on a coach whose frustration exploded:

> I remember one incident when I was in ninth grade where I saw a coach slam a kid up against a bus and scream and yell for two hours because they didn't win, and I thought that was really, totally uncalled for. . . . It started outside of a bus. . . . They got on the bus, and the coach spent the next hour and a half reaming the kids. (interview)

One is reminded of the behavior of some infamous and highly successful college sports coaches. According to some, such anger can motivate players.[34]

Creating strategy and tactics to influence students ("playing mind games") may be part of the game of debate, which sometimes involves manipulation that strikes some observers as inappropriate:

> I really think that there are teams where the kids are just treated poorly and taken advantage of, and pushed way too hard, and not cared for. . . . If you're on the top team, great, you'll get all the attention and love you deserve, but if you're not, you're treated as a subhuman being. (interview)

> Iris tells about the time she was at a tournament and was feeling very ill. Her coach made her continue, even talking with a hoarse voice. Her partner had to write her whole 2N speech. She says, "I was really sick on Friday, but [the coach] stopped at a pharmacy to get me medicine. The coach said that if they won the quarterfinals, they could forfeit semis, then when they won quarters, the coach said they could forfeit the final round if they won semis. They eventually won the tournament. (field notes)

Sometimes the desire to control can be a powerful force for success, but at what educational and psychic cost?

A Confederacy of Coaches

Just as students have networks and community, so do coaches. Because of long-term involvement in the activity, the community can be intense. It is routine, for instance, for coaches to have parties at overnight tournaments, where adults can share common interests—and, not incidentally, smoke and drink. Most coaches appreciate such zones of privacy. For outsiders, such events make the community seem like a secret club from which they are excluded, either deliberately or by being made to feel unwelcome. Time certainly helps one to become accepted, but so does demonstrating that one understands the problems of debate coaches when coping with unruly teenagers.

The existence of a community of common concern, arising out of competitive rivalry, different philosophies of debate, and varying levels of involvement, became clear when the "clan" gathered after the sudden and untimely death of a long-time member. His funeral was well attended by debate coaches from throughout the state. At the banquet of the Minnesota Debate Teachers Association, his significant other received the award for coach of the year. She was certainly an appropriate candidate, but one suspects that the timing of the award was designed to make a statement, as she recognized, referring to the difficulties of the past year (field notes).

A Class of Their Own

In chapter 5, I discussed the team as a voluntary association. Debate programs vary in their formal institutionalization within the school structure: some programs are purely extracurricular, while others are cocurricular, tied to a formal class. In many schools, debate class is printed in the catalog and receives a budget line. Entropy serves to ensure that the activity continues. One participant noted:

> [Make] your forensics program curricular. Better cocurricular than extracurricular. Better curricular than cocurricular. In times of tight money, cocurricular gets saved over extracurricular, and curricular over cocurricular. Make forensics count as part of [the] curricular job of the director of forensics. . . . When the program is integrated/grafted totally into the school curriculum, when credit is being given, when the program fits the school/district mission, when the program has good p.r., and especially when the director of forensics is an educator/teacher, not merely a competitive coach, the program is on solid grounds, and will be saved, and can also get some money, which many have been saying is the savior of programs.[35]

A few high schools, such as Greenhaven, require that every student enroll in at least one speech class, which provides a strong institutional base for competitive speech and debate, and is ideal from the perspective of forensic educators.

Many schools, particularly those that have debate coaches who are hired as teachers, have debate classes, although the total number of schools with debate classes seems to be a minority. Some schools maintain two classes: one for novices and the other for advanced debaters. A few have multiple sections, with one coach teaching debate to over 150 students each year. Some schools have classes devoted to Lincoln-Douglas debate or other forms of speech. These classes provide a route for recruitment to the team, as well as being a perk permitting teachers to teach in their area of specialization.

Just like English or math, every debate class is structured differently and, depending on the skills and motivations of the teacher, can be either scintillating, boring, or in-between. Further, classes can be mandatory for members of the team, allowing the teacher some measure of control, but also decreasing students' curricular options and forcing them to take a redundant class. Teachers also differ in the emphasis on specific content learning as opposed to practice. Are debate classes exercises in "doing," or do they involve the direct and intentional transmission of a body of disciplinary material?

The class that Mrs. Miller taught at Randall Park seems fairly typical. In part because Mrs. Miller had not done a large amount of personal recruiting the previous year, only fifteen students had enrolled. The class met the last period of the day during the first semester. Of these students, seven were taking the class for a second year, and, in one case, a third year. Three of the new students became active debaters, the heart of the team in future years. An additional four students were enrolled, but had relatively little interest in competitive debate, although each attended several tournaments.

In the early weeks of the semester, Mrs. Miller lectured on the elements of debate, including issues of practice [how to cut evidence], topic content [prison overcrowding], and debate theory [topicality], but these lectures later became infrequent, and she rarely lectured more than twice a week. The rarity of the lectures was evident a month after the beginning of school. On this day, Mrs. Miller handed each student a large lollipop as they entered the room. She indicated that she wanted to lecture about evidence and objectivity and, wanting the class to listen, told them to "put [the lollipop] in your mouth and leave it there" (field notes). For the novices and less expert members of the team, these were particularly valuable occasions: the "learning time" of the class contrasted to the "research time" after school. Although students also had a textbook, little referred to, the lectures were a significant way in which information was transferred, second only to the informal conversations after school and at tournaments. At various times, class members were asked to perform practice debates or affirmative speeches, critiqued by the teacher, assistant coach, and other class members. However, many days the class simply consisted of time for students to do their debate work (copying and cutting evidence); the class, in essence, ran itself. Mrs. Miller frequently reminded students, sharply sometimes, that they had to work, and not chat about personal matters.

Debate class—at Randall Park and elsewhere—should provide a time when students can focus on their work. Yet, those who criticize these courses suggest that in reality they are little more than a study hall for which students receive academic credit and high grades:

> We don't learn a whole lot in debate class. [A fellow debater] learned more in three weeks in institute than he did all year here. . . . It gives you an extra hour in the day; other than that it has no value to me. . . . I use it as a debate study hall. (interview)

> It's great at the beginning if you have novices because you meet with them every day, and you get that hour. You get that class time. . . . The seniors taught the novices, so they would lecture to novices, which was a great experience for us as seniors. . . . As the year went on, not much happened in class. It turned into kind of a rap session. (interview)

Those who support the idea of having a class use this same justification: the value of time that members of the debate team spend together, creating cohesion. As one debater noted:

> When the majority of the team can be in class, or, even better, if all of the team can be in class, then you know that there is some time you guys can all be together. . . . I've been in the class all three years that I was in debate, and it was a nice time when I could relax and talk to the team. . . . We quite often didn't do any work. And that's not necessarily bad because it wasn't class or anything. . . . [It] kind of makes you tighter knit. (interview)

Even those who do not emphasize the bonding ritual that the class provides recognize that having the time is essential—referred to as quality time. A coach explains:

> I think [having a class] is crucial. Only because you don't have enough time to spend. It helps coaches because you're there one less hour of the day to coach high school debate. . . . A class gives you a structured time where you get to demand students' attention. For at least fifty minutes, they can't run out the door. (interview)

The intellectual justification for the structured use of time coincides with the pragmatic interests of teachers and students to have a period of free time carved out of their busy day.

Just as debate itself is both an educational activity and a sport, debate class at Randall Park and elsewhere has a marginal status as an academic class, a practice, and a study hall. Whether this constitutes a "real class," and whether it fits the teaching mission of the school, depends on educational philosophy. Those who emphasize the value of "hands-on" education have less problems with such an approach than those who emphasize direct knowledge transfer.

The School and the Debater

The institutional location of high school debate shapes both its funding and its organization. The advantages are obvious in having an "educational" activity tied to educational institutions. However, this places the fate of debate in the hands of those whose interests do not necessarily coincide with the desires of those who participate in the activity. The fate of debate is largely outside the hands of those who are most committed to it. As a result, adult sponsors must engage in political strategies to maximize their resources. Programs in some schools succeed in providing resources, while others are continually at risk.

A key feature of a team's success and survival is linked to the adult leader's skills. While many leaders are tenured teachers, well situated within the school, others are college students or former collegiate debaters whose employment is shaky and is reviewed annually. If these coaches are unable to establish institutional networks, even competitive success may not save their position or the program's existence in the face of complaints or budget cuts.

These leaders are situated in a world in which they are simultaneously expected to be teachers, committed to education, and coaches, committed to winning and character building. Given these two alternative models, how should adult supervisors see themselves? Some individuals are hired by schools on a temporary basis without having teaching credentials or course involvement; these individuals, while they may teach their charges information in preparing them for competition, basically are coaches. Other adults see themselves as teachers, balancing the desire to win at all costs with the educational mission of the institution.

Whichever role is selected, these adult leaders must establish relationships with their charges. Are they surrogate parents, ersatz friends, or instrumental leaders? Given the talents and arrogant self-confidence of the adolescents with whom they labor, how can they gain respect from their charges, especially when these charges act in ways that the adult sees as contrary to the educational mission of the activity? Establishing a balance between trust and respect and permitting students the freedom to make choices and mistakes is difficult. These are vulnerable adolescents with needs for guidance and direction, but they are also bright teens with a strong desire for personal autonomy. With the school administration and parents on one side, and "children" on the other, the teacher/coach must negotiate a relationship that satisfies everyone: a significant challenge that not everyone manages.

One way in which debate has become established in some school systems is through the creation of a course. While this institutionalizes the activity as a curricular or cocurricular program, it raises the question of whether a significant body of knowledge is taught. These courses, in effect, start after-school activities one hour early. Debate class as study hall is a real challenge for those who claim that the activity represents a legitimate branch of learning.

The placement of any activity channels its options, limits, and opportunities. Since high school debate is situated in schools, the reality of the American educational system determines the growth or decline of the activity, however much individual students and coaches feel that their activities should depend on their own choices. Schools remain the primary provider of resources and so, ultimately, set the terms of debate.

Eight

Gifted Leisure and the Politics of Debate

> Society suffers from the lack of educated citizens
> who accept the uses of debate, who want to be
> persuaded, and who have the sophistication to
> avoid being manipulated.
> (*Jay Heinrichs*, "How Harvard Destroyed
> Rhetoric," *Harvard Magazine* 1995)

How SHOULD the public respond to the world of high school debate? Is debate vital to the future of the American polity, is it merely an odd expression of adolescent enthusiasms, or, worse, could the gamelike argumentation divert us from the serious consideration of public policy? Is high school debate a form of gifted education? Is it an educational tool that is valuable for every educated citizen? Is it a bizarre activity, no more worthy of public attention than, say, the game of Dungeons and Dragons? Or does it contribute to an atmosphere of contention, dominated by facile elites? In this chapter, I explore the value of debate. How should we read this voluntary adolescent activity?

Participants in debate, as evident from the previous chapters, are an unusually intelligent and articulate group of boys and girls. Playing with serious ideas in whatever form—and playing is the operative word— should easily be justified, even despite the adolescent uses to which participants sometimes put this knowledge. Given other forms of education, seemingly less playful, is debate the best, most effective use of an adolescent's time? Further, could playing with ideas, transforming arguments and evidence into a game, mold these citizens into cynical adult players on the field of policy?

The View from Outside

Most Americans believe that American education has failed—or at least has not been as successful as it might be—in teaching the rudimentary skills necessary for being a productive citizen. The crisis of education in America has been, at the least, evident for some twenty years. Debate could be seen as one answer to this problem. As Michael McGough wrote in his critique of high school debate, published in 1988 in *The New Republic*:

> Mention high school debate to most Americans and the image evoked is a pleasing one: fresh-faced youths out of a Norman Rockwell scene expostulating in breaking voices about the meaning of democracy and pleading with the audience to reject the contentions of "our worthy opponents." Inform them further that thousands of high school students take part in interscholastic debating, and that top debaters are courted by elite colleges and law schools, and you've spawned the hopeful impression that here is an oasis of liberal learning in the intellectual desert charted by Allan Bloom and William Bennett.[1]

The conclusion that McGough and others draw is discouraging; to wit, the less one knows about high school debate, the better one likes it. Debate, from this perspective, is something that we admire in the abstract, but not in the particular, at least not as debate has developed. Indeed, previous chapters might provide ample support for this view of high school debate as esoteric, bizarre, or even dangerous. The decline in popularity of the activity over the past several decades reflects in part a concern with its peculiarities.

It is surely true that, for observers, the antics of many committed people appear decidedly strange. As an American, imagine watching cricket, sumo wresting, curling, or cockfighting. The fact that other individuals find such activities to be endlessly fascinating, worthy of song and poetry, reminds us of the cultural relativity of leisure preferences. Likewise, the joys of the all-American activities of football and baseball require socialization, as many women can attest.

The unwary spectator at a tournament, often a parent or a school administrator, may leave with a sense of profound bewilderment, a feeling exacerbated by the dashed belief that they thought they knew what competitive debate entailed, based, perhaps, on popular images of the Lincoln-Douglas contests. McGough, a former debater, suggests: "Today's budding Buckleys traffic more in bizarre jargon than the telling bon mot."[2] Similar charges were being brought as early as the 1940s. Competitive debate involves specialized speech, not designed as a spectator sport for the general public, a fundamental problem in creating a base of popular support. The development of a corps of judges, knowledgeable about the activity, rather than permitting an outsider ("lay") audience to determine the outcome of the rounds, has emphasized subcultural standards of evaluation.[3] Add the possible cynicism of arguing anything and everything with passion, and one finds a basis for criticism.

Today, these charges seem pervasive. Public confusion is real. I once sat with a high school senior, watching for the first time her boyfriend debate and finding herself totally lost. More politically significant than the mystification of lovers are the concerns of employers. One veteran college debate coach asked his college's president to attend the final round of the collegiate national tournament as his guest. Much to his dismay, after listening to the collegians spewing and spreading, making "silly" arguments, the president left in disgust in the midst of the round (field notes). These reactions are salient when coaches arrange demonstration debates for parents. One Minnesota assistant coach notes about the father of a star debater:

> I remember talking with Rajiv's father when Rajiv first started and we did a demonstration debate for them, and he came up to me afterwards, and he said, "They talk so fast," and I tried to explain to him that it really wasn't fast for debaters, . . . and he said, "Well, I think you lose something." . . . If we could set them up into a round that was gonna be real mild-mannered and easy going, you know, temper what they see, they would be more receptive. (interview)

This coach suggests that the way to gain public support is to distort the actual performance, creating an aural Potemkin village. Would we attempt to demonstrate football by setting up a game of touch? Perhaps high school debate is not a spectator sport, never to be seen on ESPN (or CSPAN!), but its subcultural features limit its appeal.

The frustration in being unable to understand one's child's activity, and finding that one's offspring has outmatched one in argumentation, is magnified by life around the dining room table, an experience of which almost every debater is aware and which the more self-reflexive ones agree has some justice:

> At first [my parents] thought it was great, but now they're starting to dislike it. They think I get too argumentative with them. (interview)

> My mom . . . appreciates the quality of [debate] and what I've gotten out of it, and she looks highly upon it, but then she also says, if I'm arguing with her, "Stop debating me." And that pisses me off like you wouldn't believe. Seriously, I'm not debating her. My God! If I was debating her that would be totally different. . . . Boy, I really hate it when she says I'm debating her (she laughs). (interview)

I recall that my parents made the same charges after I joined the debate team, and in turn I say the same thing to my glib son. That participation can be used against the participant is ironic, but it recognizes that debaters are skilled at arguing passionately and at great length on any side of an issue. Debaters recognize that they use their skills to get their way, a charge that feeds the belief that debate contributes to cynicism and loss of moral grounding, even if participants maintain strong political commitments.

Yet, despite complaints, the public does have a vaguely positive, if uncertain, view of debate, and most parents are well-pleased if their child chooses to spend time in this way, especially if it does not affect their grades negatively. Debaters report that parents and other adults are supportive:

> [Adults] think it's the greatest thing a high school kid could do. Finally people are using their brains. . . . Kids using their minds in school and debating. Oh, what a great thing. (interview)

Coaches note that most parents are supportive, once they understand the purposes of debate:

> I had a parent write a letter, and he's totally amazed that his son . . . would want to spend Thanksgiving vacation . . . or Christmas vacation in a college library. They had never thought that they would raise a son who would consider a Saturday afternoon's enjoyable trip to some library as a highlight of a weekend. (interview)

> Parents don't know anything about debate when the students first join, so they don't know the commitment involved, they don't know the reading requirement, they don't know that it's such a scholarly kind of thing, that it takes in-depth study. . . . Once they start to see some of the gains that their kids are making, then they understand. . . . And maybe that goes back to our athletic mentality [she laughs]. If their kids can bring home something that says they won, boy, that enthusiasm just spreads. (interview)

Administrators, for their part, use a successful debate team as a marker of the academic standing of their school.

This support can spill into the political arena. The Montana state legislature unanimously passed a bill of congratulations for the Loyola Sacred Heart speech/debate team, which had won the Montana state championship for the fourteenth year in a row! The legislature gave the team a standing ovation, and the team received praise from the governor.[4] It was not reported whether legislators wondered why there had been so little competition in the state, and whether state support for competitive debate in public high schools was justified.

Debate within Student Cultures

How high school debaters are viewed among their peers is difficult to answer, as it is different in each school, changing over time, dependent on the participants. Adolescents can be cruel if behavior is stigmatized. At other times, teens may be consumed with envy, and at still other blissful times, more frequent than stereotypes suggest, may be supportive of their peers. What leads to these judgments is often tied to local norms, rather than to a global sense of what constitutes proper adolescent behavior. Some adultlike behaviors are accepted, others not. School culture, always in flux, matters.

In some schools, debaters receive an athletic letter as they represent the school in intermural debate competition; in others, such recognition would be inappropriate as debate is not considered a sport and debaters don't sweat.[5] In one high school, debate might be seen as high status; in another—perhaps in the same suburb—debate can be an activity for nerds, scorned by high-status members of the student body. In some schools, debaters are treated with the respect accorded athletes; in other locations, such an analogy would be ludicrous. These attitudes may change annually: perhaps a function of the team record, the success of other teams, the esteem in which the coach is held, or the personality or social standing of individual members.

At some schools, debaters are respected. One participant compared other schools to Randall Park:

> I know some schools where debate is looked upon very highly and people actually go and watch it. . . . Carroll Falls says that they have quite a few people, especially during tournament time, that just go and watch. They have a little rooting section. (interview)

At Greenhaven, which has a strong and long tradition in speech, debaters have high status, even though Mrs. Nyberg notes that sometimes their intellectual ability separates them from others in the student body, who "let them go off and do their own thing" (interview). At one school in a Twin Cities exurb, a community still largely rural and working-class, the coach has diligently and successfully fostered pride in the team, establishing a parental support group. In the only inner-city school in the Twin Cities, debaters have gained status in their multiethnic community. Their coach remarks:

> I think at first maybe they might have been looked down upon, if I think way back, but then we won. And as these kids go on and they become speakers, and even in classes they're more aggressive, they're more logical, I think they get some respect. And now this year my debaters, it's funny, they got their own briefcases, they wore attire more correctly on debate days, and maybe they were teased a little bit, but I think they took it as a badge of honor. (interview)

In contrast, adolescents at other schools do not give debaters esteem. Coaches report:

> I don't think [most other students] understand it. I don't think they really think much about it at all. . . . It's a bunch of geeks that get together and talk about boring things. (interview)

> Well, when I first started a program here I got the distinct feeling that kids were trying not to admit that they were on the debate team. I had one boy who wanted to date a cheerleader, and he would never carry his briefcase with him or anything, and I think he felt that way, and I felt that when I first started. I don't feel that way now. (interview)

At Randall Park, a well-regarded suburban high school, debate is considered a low-status activity by most students, at least as reflected in the eyes of team members:

> We're [seen as] a bunch of people who talk fast, and don't really think about what we're saying. Usually very eccentric. [Students] do not look at it very favorably at all. . . . Very low status. (interview)

> [Debate is] one of those kind of things that for years has had a really negative stigma. . . . In Randall Park there's still a negative feeling among students because they think that debate is one of those really academic activities, and academics is still kind of downplayed and shunned. . . . I think it's a negative thing only because, wow, that's just too smart a kind of thing. (interview)

I have only the debaters' view of their fellow students' attitudes, views that are surely diverse, and largely based on ignorance. Debaters, like most people, are convinced that they deserve more credit than they are usually given, and they play off the stereotypes that they feel others harbor, as in this playful reminder:

> Anyone wishing to become a member of the Debate Nerdz Clubs of America, please send an 8 × 10 glossy photograph of yourself (taped glasses, pocket protector, armfuls of flowpads, action shot of pen-twirling ideal) and a 10,000 word essay (with a minimum of 500 obscure yet devastating impact cards) to DNCA, c/o Thom Bray, MENSA, and Erkl, 1 Million Googleplex Avenue, Infinity, CA 90023. Membership is free, but we do ask for a donation of 10 IQ points from each member, to be placed in a security pool for members experiencing a barrage of pejoratives.[6]

These teens support the views of observers of student culture that intellectual activities do not—at most schools—have high status.[7] Schools are not bastions in which intellectual achievement is prized, at least among their inmates.

Education and the Value of Debate

The images of debate—pro and con—often emphasize that debate involves intellectual engagement, part of the core of education. That it is seen as a quirky form of education—distinct from what many adults consider education to be—leaves open the question of whether it achieves its goals. Does it produce insight, or only sophistry? Most grant the educational benefits of debate; the political commitment of many debaters suggests that they do not learn only sophistry. If debate were only fun, it could hardly be justified, as is true for most voluntary worlds.[8] Yet, part of what gives debate its power, allowing the activity to trap teenagers within its web, is that it is fun. Competition is essential for motivation. One adolescent, suggesting a linkage between debate and sport, muses: "All the sport takes place in your brain, which makes it educational" (interview). Another linked sport and education:

> Sport . . . a lot of it is in the round, and education is out of the round. You learn how to research, and you learn how to speak better. You learn to organize yourself better, and while you're performing the sport, you learn things. . . . The main objective in debate isn't education, that's not the main thing . . . but you should have fun, and that's what the sport part of it is. (interview)

The game of debate makes education palatable for teens.

The benefits claimed for debate are diverse, even if it is difficult to demonstrate these benefits conclusively, because of selection bias. Debaters, after all, are not a random sample of the student population. Central is a belief that these skills serve students well as they leave academic precincts: debate inculcates life skills:

> I have a son who is going to start debate next year, and the reasons I want him to be in debate are for the skills that I see as lifelong skills that he will gain. Whether he wins or loses, I think he will come up better for it. (interview)

> You can treat it as a sport only, and you say, this is a sport . . . this is not intended to educate, but in the nature of the game it does. And that's what the beauty of it is, you know, it is a sport where you can get the same highs as you can doing any other competition, any other sport, and yet you're helping yourself in later life. (interview)

One former debater describing his debate experience concluded humorously and poignantly:

> So what advice would I give to coaches and current debaters? Don't leave! Fail as many grades as possible. It's not worth it to graduate. College is too easy . . . most of my classes have 2–3 papers a semester. Just three years ago I was writing that many each day. Debate is a subculture of people that communicate with their own language; it's quite an elite club. Make sure you all enjoy it for the fun of it, but also keep in mind you are learning something.[9]

I divide the claimed benefits of debate into four categories: thought and analysis, organization and research, citizenship, and self-confidence. I do not discuss speaking skills specifically, although they are implicated under self-confidence. I do not demonstrate that debate actually has these benefits, but that these justifications are claimed. Testing these plausible claims demands a different methodology.

Thought and Analysis

The single most prominent justification is that debate improves thinking skills. The motto of the Minnesota Debate Teachers Association is "Reason Is God's Crowning Gift." *Critical thinking* has become a mantra among educators. Debate is nothing if not critical and, when done well, thoughtful. Ted Belch, the respected coach at Glenbrook North High School, sees a direct relation, arguing that the activity's popularity is "a spinoff of the critical thinking movement in secondary education."[10] Debate demands intellectual dexterity. As one participant explained, "I like the idea behind debate. . . . The idea that you can take an abstract problem and make it concrete in your mind" (field notes). Coaches make this explicit:

> It's [enjoyable] seeing how excited the kids get about thinking. I am just amazed at the energy that occurs with the students. . . . The fun part is . . . when we are preparing for [tournaments]. . . . It may be ten o'clock at night, and we're still at school chomping on chips and popcorn, and putting our arguments on the board, and talking about how we're going deal with this. . . . Just seeing them think and coming up with their ideas, I get excited about that. (interview)

> [Debaters] learn how to think, and, if you can think, you can succeed at anything you do. . . . Debate is unique in anything I have every done . . . the only thing that taught me how to think. . . . Just in a round thinking, being able to see how things are going back and forth, being able to follow that, being able to think of ways to win the round, thinking of ways to win the argument, but also before rounds, thinking of arguments that you want to use against a particular case. (interview)

These quotations could easily be multiplied, but they indicate the significance of the image of thoughtful engagement in the minds and the rhetoric of debaters.

Organization and Research

In addition to developing critical thought processes, participants are said to be able to learn how to use their time efficiently and to develop research skills. Debate is not simply talk, but is talk that is grounded in evidence. There is potentially unlimited time that one could spend on debate, and one must choose how to use available time wisely, while making time for schoolwork. This need for temporal organization is surprising to some. One boy enthusiastically explained in the middle of the term: "This is awesome. Debate has taught me to schedule my time. Last year I was getting mostly C's. This year I got all A's and B's" (field notes). A coach was similarly euphoric about the organizational skills she had learned:

> I got to college and realized that everybody doesn't know how to write. Debate provides some basic, fundamental ways to write. It teaches you organizational skills, it gets you organized in your personal life, it gets you organized in your academic life. . . . In their mind [debaters] have created file cabinets for everything, and they don't miss things. They don't miss appointments and they keep things on schedule. (interview)

> First of all, [I learned] organization. Not only organizing arguments, but just actually organizing things, knowing where things are. A year ago this room would be in a mess. (interview)

> Research [is] probably the biggest [benefit]. If somebody had asked me before debate, I want you to research something on the Georgia ISP program, I'd be sitting there. I'd have no idea where to go. [I'd say] "I don't know what to do. What do you want me to do?" No ideas. And now I know how to research. (interview)

Teaching teenagers to organize themselves, as any parent can attest, is no mean feat. That this is a salient part of debate is easily recognized as a virtue. The large tubs of evidence carried to tournaments would serve no purpose without a system by which relevant information could be retrieved. To be successful depends on the ability to organize information in order to make it readily available.

The Gifts of Citizenship

Some allege that learning citizenship is an important value, noting that "the language of democracy is the language of debate."[11] As noted in chapter 2, a compelling feature of policy debate is that participants are forced to defend both sides of an issue. This contrasts with a model in which one commits oneself to a single idea, deeply held, and then develops arguments to defend that position. In other speech events, such as original oratory or extemporaneous speaking, one selects one's position and presents that stance with vigor and passion. In fact, some teams run affirmative cases in which they do not believe, but they are persuaded that these cases can win. In the prison overcrowding topic, drug legalization or expanding the death penalty were such cases.

While some suggest that cynicism could result, in practice the demand to take both sides involves one of the grand perceived virtues of debate: the ability to understand multiple perspectives. This connects to the role of a citizen in a democracy, displaying respect for opponents. To recognize the grounding of an opponent's position implies empathy. To the extent that the halls of Congress are populated with former debaters, it explains why American political parties often seem so nonideological and flexible, while at the same time partisan and disputatious: oriented to victory, but not absolute truth.

From this perspective, debate promotes tolerance. A coach at an elite private school told me that the father of a former debater told him that his son had experienced anti-Semitism in other parts of the school, but not on the debate team.[12] Another coach explained that she valued that her students start "realizing that there's more than one version of the truth. There's lots of different ways of looking at issues and they're multifaceted. Things are complex, not simple, and it's interesting to look for complexities" (interview). An obituary for a long-time debate coach noted that "he realized that the abilities to speak and think clearly were of the utmost importance in a democratic society."[13]

Proponents argue that the ability of adolescents to participate in the political process augers well for democracy, and that their capacity to defend all sides of an issue leads to tolerance that supports our political principles. The experience of winning and losing political arguments provides a basis for participation in the public arena, implying that every student should experience debate to create a more active citizenry. If some students believe that debate for its own sake is valid, most distinguish between those positions that they believe are morally compelling and those that are "only" debater's arguments.

Self-Confidence

The final virtue of debate transports us from the enshrinement of reason to that of emotion. Debate transforms callow youth into confident social actors. By learning adult skills adolescents can, in part, tame those childish skills that have previously served them well. To see ninth graders confidently standing before a roomful of adults and peers, arguing a position with passion, is impressive. Students themselves, recalling how unlikely that scenario seemed months before, are astonished. Coaches refer to shy, mousy students, transformed through the power of forensics, becoming assured and poised:

> The ones that I remember the most aren't the stars of the team, but they are the students that are perhaps introverted, who, over three years, gained confidence

so that they were able to raise their self-esteem and carry on a debate, and do so with full confidence. (Interview)

> It teaches you how to be self-confident. Every debater that I know [feels this is true], once they've gotten through that first, initial debate round—those first rounds are awful. I mean you're totally scared, and you can't believe that you'd mess up so badly, whether you won or lost. [I've] only had one student who ever said, "I will never do this again . . . take me home. I've been sick for three days preparing for this." Just to know that you can stand up in front of a room and talk for eight minutes . . . makes everything else so much easier. You come to school and you have to have a presentation for five minutes; that's nothing. (interview)

One coach describes a student who blossomed:

> This kid who started out in ninth grade . . . a little kid, hadn't hit puberty yet, real short guy, real quiet, smart kid . . . just sat there and didn't say a lot. But he was a junior last year. He all of a sudden just took off. . . . Over the course of the year, he became popular, outgoing, confident. . . . He really just sort of blossomed, and I think a lot of that had to do with debate. (interview)

The debater conquers stage fright, feeling, like the actor, that public presentation is a peak experience. In a society that depends on public personas and impression management, such skills have real virtues. For adolescents, whose self-consciousness is legendary, the ability to transcend oneself is striking.

Of course, most coaches can tell stories about kids who, for one reason or another, they were unable to reach—suicides, drug abusers, dropouts, single mothers, thieves. To be a high school teacher forces one into the role of social worker. While teachers look with pride at most of their charges, some "get away." Even its most fervent defenders do not claim that the activity is a panacea for the troubles that ail society.

The Ironic Relationship of Debate and Schoolwork

Given the many encomiums for debate, it is surprising that, if grades are the measure of success, the picture is ambiguous. While there is nearly universal agreement that debate aids students in bolstering their educational skills, this does not always translate into higher grades, particularly for the most committed. Preparing for next week's tournament can conflict with preparing for this week's test. For elite debaters, the season lasts as long as the school year. Assignments are postponed until after the tournament—a never-ending cycle. Of course, many participants are highly motivated students, whose career goals and beliefs in what is necessary to be admitted into highly selective colleges pushes them to maintain their grades. Given the nature of the high achievers who participate in debate, a ceiling effect is evident. A straight-A student can only keep the same grades or see them decline. A student who was tenth in a class of over 400 students claimed that debate had harmed her grades and forced her to drop a class. One coach, commenting on the decline of grades, noted, "Last year I had a team that probably, instead of having a B+, A– average, could have had a straight-A average, but they got so involved in debate that it affected them a little bit" (interview). Does this "little bit" matter in the trade-off with life skills? With the exception of the few who become "addicted" to debate—what one coach describes as "debate bums"—the trade-off is typically manageable.[14]

The benefits to schoolwork are real, as noted above. For many students, debate makes them become more organized and better able to write papers:

> They learn so much from the debate activity that what takes another student for writing a paper a great deal of time, they can do it quicker. . . . Teachers make comments, "We can tell when you've had kids in debate, they speak up in class, they participate." (interview)

> Debate was one of the hardest things you ever did, and if you could write a debate case, you could easily finish your French assignment. You could easily write a two-page paper for your sociology class, or you could read a chapter. (interview)

Whether the learning comes from the preparation for the round or in the round itself, it is apparent that the activity can be a potent force for learning.

The paradox, then, is that some students find that their grades do not improve or even decline. Whether grades matter remains an open question, although most parents and school administrators take grades as an indicator of learning. Indeed, one set of parents at Randall Park gave their son an ultimatum after he had received two F's his first semester in debate: either improve your grades or quit the activity. This occurred precisely when the debate season was becoming intense, and the demand forced this student to consider how to budget his time.

Yet, if learning is the goal, debaters whose grades have declined may in fact be learning more than if their grades remained higher without debate. Further, to the extent that debate serves as a credential for college admission, a student with debate participation might do better in this market than a student with higher grades who lacks participation.[15]

Part of the explanation is a function of the competitive urges of adolescents to be the best. Debate provides a vista of infinite work. There is no end to the number of cases that can be written, the number of briefs that can be prepared, or the amount of research that can be done. Debate can seduce the unwary. Students regularly comment on how difficult it is to keep up with their schoolwork and still perform well:

> [Debate] probably hurt my grades overall. I'm constantly leaving my math and science classes. . . . Last year I was constantly leaving to go to the debate room because we had tournaments. . . . I would say last year that it hurt my grades, this year [it] probably helped my grades. . . . I got efficient at it. (interview)

> Debate becomes an obsession . . . then it distracts them because they don't spend as much time as they should on their homework to get their correct grades. . . . It affected me in the homework sense. . . . In one class it did. I was virtually a straight-A student. . . . In physics I got a B for the year because my homework grade was like a D– (he laughs), because I handed in about half of my homework assignments. I just plain ole didn't hand in half of them, and that was partially because of debate. (interview)

To some degree, these students admit using the activity as an excuse not to work as diligently as they might in classes that did not motivate them. These students did well in the course they loved, and simply did not have time for the classes that were unappealing to them because of the press of debate work. In terms of learning valuable skills, debate helps students' academic careers. Yet, the grade point average is often a shorthand for one's academic identity.

Debate and the Career Ladder

As children, we dream about an imagined occupational order: romantic, fantastic, or mundane. We have hoop dreams. By adolescence career paths open, close, and become more or less plausible. When asked about their career trajectory, most adults can cite some person or event from their teen years that directed them toward their future occupation. If adolescence does not fully determine how we place ourselves in the occupational order, it does set the tone for decisions that may have severe or serene consequences. The ecology of high school life opens up a range of possible career options: options that reverberate for years. One coach says simply, debate "is an open door." Opening options characterizes teenage activities that mimic or transform adult ventures:

> I think [debaters] begin to think higher. . . . If you ask a kid what they are going to do and what they want to be [they might say] I wanted to be an astronaut until I was, well, a senior in high school probably. . . . So kids don't really have set career plans. . . . Most kids say, "Well, I think I'm going to college, and I'll

get a job." I think debaters after debating [will] say, "Well, you know, I might
go to law school, and I might go to graduate school, and I might get a Ph.D. I
might become a teacher," but certainly their goals and expectations expand.
(interview)

[Debate] sharpens the career plans of debaters and brings them into
greater focus. They still flounder a bit; they still have to go out and explore,
but I think they're going to explore avenues that they were unwilling to explore when they were freshmen or sophomores, because it was not within their
realm of thought. They didn't even dare to dream about some of the things
that they can seriously think about when they're seniors, and when they're
young in college and they have the confidence that they can really achieve it.
(interview)

Precisely for these reasons, some are anxious to expand the world of high
school debate so that it includes students in inner-city and rural areas
who might not otherwise share these dreams. This leads to the formation
of urban debate leagues. In Chicago, such a pilot program is supported by
Phi Beta Kappa and Northwestern University, and has involved elite suburban schools serving as partners with poor inner-city high schools.
Emory University has a program with the Atlanta public schools to foster
debate, even at the junior high school level. Programs such as the Fuller-
ton Daniel Webster Project in southern California attempt to link college
debate programs with inner-city high schools. If debate is expanded in
this way, it might short-circuit the reproduction of the social class structure that leads the children of poor parents to be limited in their career
aspirations.

The occupational arena to which high school debate is most closely
linked is law. A large proportion of active, successful debaters consider
attending law school. As one debate coach asserts, "At some point or
another in your debate career, you're convinced that you want to be a
lawyer." In no other occupation is the image of evidence, argumentation,
and cases of such relevance as the law. Indeed, as I noted, high school
debate reflects a transformation of the American legal system:

We see an awful lot of kids go into law firms. I think that when they see the
kinds of skills they have and they see the success . . . it gives them the confidence to do that. . . . My husband's an attorney . . . I sat down and read his
briefs, and he had me comment on his briefs. They're exactly like a debate brief.
You have to state a position, and you have to find the evidence to support it,
and you have to give rationale for why your position should be adopted by a
judge. (interview)

Coming into high school in ninth grade, I really wanted to be an architect, and
then after the first year of debate with all the arguing, and liking all this, and

reading the law, and getting into politics, that's what changed my mind toward law and politics as a career. (interview)

While debate inspires participants to practice law, public policy, politics, or education, not everyone is so affected. Several students, by no means a majority, but enough to suggest that the process of career shaping is not inevitable, found their career possibilities changed in other directions as a consequence of their contact with debate:

> Debate turned me away from law. I've read all these laws, and all the bull that flies everywhere with these laws, and I don't like it. I don't want to get caught up in that kind of scene, because it's bad. I just want to do something that helps a lot of people. (interview)

> I have decided that I do not want to be a politician, but that I do want to go to med school like I originally planned. . . . I had this idea that I wanted to be a politician . . . It would be fun as a sport, but not a profession. (interview)

As a result of high school debate, adolescents have a clearer view of these worlds of work. Given the choices of participants, debate contributes to a reputable social standing as adults. If all teens were debaters, schools could easily reproduce social elites, although we might worry about the ability of society to reproduce a broader social order, with manual laborers and clerical workers as well. A society of debaters would be littered by mounds of broken dreams.

Debate as Gifted Education

The label gifted (or gifted and talented) education is in many circles a loaded and political term.[16] What is a gift or a talent, who has these gifts, how should we determine this, and after it has been determined, what should be done with these children?[17] This is not a treatise on gifted education, but rather the story of some very bright adolescents—teens who may or may not be labeled gifted. Both the reality and the stereotype suggests that if there is a class of gifted students, many debaters would be in that group. Not all high schools have a formally constituted gifted and talented program—Randall Park did not during my research—and some educators have ideological objections to these programs, although parents typically support them. Given the content and context of debate, is it reasonable to suggest that high school debate is a form of gifted education?

I have previously detailed how, despite their intelligence, these young men and women remain "kids," oscillating between serious policy analysis and sheer childishness. Yet, no one who has spent time in debate rooms and at tournaments can fail to be impressed with the intelligence and skills of these students. During the discussions on prison overcrowding, students raised important questions about how our criminal justice system should be organized, recidivism rates, paternalism, and possibilities of rehabilitation, while at the same time joking about the efficacy of torturing prisoners or sending them to outer space. Hearing the policy discussions, often more sophisticated than my understandings as a sociologist and university professor, suggests that these students are gifted.[18]

Before discussing the implications of debate as gifted education, I emphasize that debate as a voluntary activity does not recruit only students who do well in school or who are very bright, and perhaps for these other students debate is particularly valuable:[19]

> [Question: Do you think most debaters are gifted students?] Not necessarily. Because I have a real problem with the term gifted. . . . Academically, I'm an average student, not because I'm an average student, but because that's the amount of energy I put into it. But in debate, I thrived above and beyond, and I've seen other kids like that. You know, Cal Johnson is like that. . . . Is he gifted? I don't know, maybe he is, but in the traditional sense of the word, he wouldn't be labeled that. (interview)

> I told you about the girl from Iowa. She wasn't talented and gifted, but . . . she took away [a great deal of learning] from the activity. . . . Sometimes the kids that we will have the most profound impact on are the kids that will never be the Albert Einsteins, who will never be the big lawyers, the big doctors, or the big engineers, but they're going to take a potentially wasted life and do something really, truly successful with it, because of what they've gotten from this program. . . . It's not necessarily [the] talented and gifted. (interview)

The point is that debate is not only a program for gifted and talented teenagers; partisans claim that anyone can benefit from the exposure to the world of ideas, evidence, and public presentation. But, given this, can debate be seen as a form of gifted and talented education—a program that a school, wishing to serve its gifted population, might institute?

Developmental psychologist Mihalyi Csikszentmihalyi argues that one of the key elements of gifted education is the ability to foster a sense of flow.[20] Csikszentmihalyi refers to "a subjective state that people report when they are completely involved in something to the point of losing track of time and of being unaware of fatigue and of everything but the activity itself."[21] In this sense, as well as in the technical subcultural meaning, flow characterizes high school debate. Within the round, as detailed in chapter 4, a complete focusing of cognition should occur, and, as noted, on completion of the final speech of the round, a debater, after speaking with remarkable speed and concentration, may literally collapse into a chair. In this sense the experience of debate constitutes part of what Csikszentmihalyi considers important to the development of adolescent talent. Csikszentmihalyi couples this need for focused concentration with the presence of charismatic adults, memorable teachers:[22] the creation of a supportive and inspiring community. In addition to these social and behavioral components of gifted education, debate is also connected to thinking skills—the thinking and evaluative skills of which contemporary educators are so enamored—although it must be admitted that often critical thinking skills depend on whether the conclusions arrived at are those of the instructor or the debater. (Would the teen who endorsed racial prejudice, colonialism, traditional sex roles, or drug use be admired as a critical thinker?) Still, debate ranks highly in teaching students how to question and debunk the taken-for-granted: to say no, when it might be tempting to say yes:

> If indeed the goal of gifted education is to teach critical thinking skills, I think that debate is a primary area for gifted education. It draws those students, it teaches the skills that a lot of the gifted educators look at, and I think it's overlooked in a lot of schools as a building program for gifted education. (interview)

> It certainly is [gifted education]. It does all those things they tell us gifted education should do . . . [develop] critical thinking and problem solving and research and communications, and so forth. It's the one that's been around the longest. (interview)

Of course, because debate has been taught for so long—nearly a century in Minnesota—it may lack the cachet attributed to educational innovations.

A further element in debate is the creation of community. Part of gifted education—arguably the most significant aspect—is that it provides an arena in which bright adolescents can find each other, share problems, and develop a public identity that validates their abilities in the face of a school system that may otherwise place obstacles and of a student body, often oriented to athletics, that may be unsympathetic or scornful:

> Debate tends to draw a lot of students who . . . may not have a peer group where they can stand out. It gives them that need of achievement. I think in some ways, for the more intellectual student, it creates the peer group for them. A lot of students, I think, [who] get in debate in many schools tend to be the "nerds" in the school, and they feel comfortable [in debate]. That's a new place for them. (interview)

> [Debate] teaches you to accept your brightness. Most of the students that I've ever run into as a debater and as a coach were really bright students who were

bored. . . . I was in a gifted and talented program . . . and all of us were also debaters. . . . After debate was over, I couldn't go to school five days a week because it was totally monotonous. (interview)

By providing a home, a space, a community, and a network, debate opens opportunities for students to create their own education outside the constraints of syllabi and lesson plans. Along with one's teammates and coach, one organizes one's education.

High school debate, as currently practiced, cannot be considered a program for gifted students in a formal sense. Further, the benefits of this activity apply to those who are not narrowly defined as gifted. To be sure, some alternative programs—academic teams, mock trials, Model UN— also encourage similar skills, in some cases at lower cost to the school. However, it is likely that there is no other institutionalized program than debate that better serves many students who are labeled gifted and talented.

The Troubles of High School Debate

I make no secret of my admiration of high school debate. Thus, it is a paradox that in many regions the activity is in decline. Some even wonder whether it can survive the next few decades. Whether one believes that the arguments, evidence, and skills of competitors have improved in the past few decades, no doubt exists that the number of policy debaters and the number of schools have declined over the past several decades.

It was not always so. During the early 1960s debate programs grew rapidly,[23] although how much of this should be attributed to the schooling of the baby-boom generation is uncertain. Some 200 Minnesota high schools sponsored policy debate in the 1960s. By 1990, the number had sunk to approximately 40 high schools (out of nearly 400 high schools in the state).[24] Since the large majority of these schools were in the suburbs of the Twin Cities, tournaments were still possible. In Indiana, the number of debate schools sank in under two decades from 110 to 40 (in a state with 385 high schools), with the number of tournaments declining from over 50 to 7.[25] The effects build on themselves. Fewer active schools in a region lead to smaller tournaments or expanded travel costs, leading to higher budgets in the face of lower community interest, producing further declines.[26] The decline of Catholic education, once a mainstay of competitive forensics, has also hurt. Even the growth of Lincoln-Douglas debate has not fully compensated for this decline. While there has been concern about the decline of debate for some time (one coach moaned, "You don't have to learn for the twenty-fifth year in a row that debate is dying" [field notes]), the decline is real—paradoxical for an activity that most people see in principle as beneficial.

How has this situation come to be? Three classes of explanations are proposed for this precarious state, each having structural components: (1) the decline of the number (and commitment) of debate teachers, (2) the growing complexity and esoteric quality of debate, and (3) the absence of adequate financial support from school districts.

Where Have All the Teachers Gone?

While there is surely some nostalgia and illusion in asserting the existence of a "Golden Age" of debate, this is the most common explanation given by Minnesota debate educators. As noted, Minnesotans hold that their debate tradition results from gifted teachers. As these men and women find themselves sliding into middle age, the schools look for—and do not find—replacements. Their favorite students have chosen other occupations. To coach is hard work without much appreciation. One experienced coach notes:

> Our best and brightest are not, for the most part, going into the field of coaching. In fact, many are dissuaded from coaching and [want] to do things that are more lucrative. Additionally, why would most people want to emulate some of the things they see? Some of these things include seasons that never end, hassles from administrators, 2am returns home from weekend competitions, missed time for religious worship due to tournaments, broken or nonexistent relationships, and a general lack of appreciation for all of the things that we do.[27]

What person would choose such a life?

Coaching debate is surely easier for younger teachers without family. Being both a teacher and a coach at the same time is like having a job and a half, without full compensation. These teachers, like their students, frequently miss classes on Fridays, retarding their class preparation and forcing the school to find replacements. The burnout rate is high; those coach-teachers who remain committed often find assistants—frequently former debaters—who help by staying after school and judging at weekend tournaments. With the aging of the teaching profession and the lack of hiring due to cutbacks in education funding, there has not been an influx of new, young teachers.

Further, the educational benefits of debate itself, coupled with greater economic opportunities for women, have diminished the pool of teachers. Debate provides excellent training for the professions, notably for law and for teaching. Given the divergence in material rewards between these occupations, one teacher asked rhetorically, "Why would anyone who could be a lawyer be a teacher?" (interview). The expansion of law schools and other professional schools has diminished the pool of debaters going into education. Further, teaching was once a preferred occupation for bright, articulate women. With the opening of the economy to women, law and business schools proved to be more attractive than schools of education. If our society limited lucrative career options for women, the pool of debate teachers would surely increase!

One solution has been to replace tenured, long-term teachers with college students or with former students, making debate an extracurricular activity. This solves the problem for the moment, but it has several unintended effects. With these younger ex-debaters bringing in their style of collegiate debate and serving as judges at tournaments, more established teachers feel even less interested or capable of participating. Further, since these young men or women are not full members of the high school community, they do not have the credibility with the faculty necessary to build a program or to protect it in battles over resources. Finally, as most of these individuals are not committed to a long-term career in teaching, their presence denies the program stability. Several programs in Minnesota—even successful ones—changed coaches every few years. With each change, the possibility of the termination of the program is more likely. Debate, unlike football, is not seen as an activity that needs to be continued.[28] One coach remarked:

> The schools we have are more and more into control of college kids with no educational degrees, with no teachers, very transitional programs, you know. Kids will be around for a couple of years, and [schools] have to scramble to find a new [coach]. (interview)

Once a program closes, starting a new program is difficult.

The problem is recursive, feeding on itself. To be a coach, it is helpful to have debated competitively. With the sharp decline in the number of policy debaters, the pool from which coaches can be drawn shrinks. Even programs, such as one run by the Minnesota Debate Teachers Association to train coaches or one run by the National Debate Coaches Association to provide scholarships for teachers to attend debate institutes, have met with only mixed success. Without an influx of adults to organize programs, the future is in doubt.

The Costs of Intellectual Success

While some contend that debate has never been stonger intellectually, this increased sophistication in argumentation and research paradoxically comes at a cost. The activity, at its highest levels, is more complex than it has ever been and demands more effort by students. As a result, debate has seemed more esoteric, and the divergence between strong and weak schools has never been greater. The development of a national circuit, owing much to collegiate forensic theory, helped produce these changes.

The development of Lincoln-Douglas debate was in part a result of these changes, but simultaneously it has made policy debate seem more specialized, draining energy that might have prevented specialization. Some of the problems that policy debate faces were unintentionally of its own making.

Many have commented on the growing complexity of arguments. Unlike high school sports, debate has become an activity that cannot be enjoyed by most parents and fellow students. Only experts are moved by the flows of competitors. Without an appreciative and knowledgeable audience, public support is difficult. Debate has become increasingly specialized, separated from the lives of most potential supporters:

> A cost/benefit analysis is useful here. The benefits to debate have remained relatively fixed. . . . However, the costs to participating in debate have gone up. Rather than needing to know the 3–4 "stock issues," and those only how they were applied to your speeches, we now expect debaters to fully understand innumerable positions and paradigms. These "costs" of learning debate have not gone up overnight, just as participation in debate has not sharply fallen overnight.[29]

> Debate culture becomes hermetically sealed off from the rest of the world. It becomes a monolith that produces all its own values, language and customs, even its own vision of social reality: one in which the general welfare is maximized by weighing alternative scenarios with mechanical links and apocalyptic impacts that sound very foolish to anyone who gives serious thought to actual policy issues. . . . Closed cultures—whatever their individual merits—almost always atrophy over time. . . . Once the population of [policy] debaters and coaches falls below a certain threshold it is unlikely to sustain itself.[30]

Coaches at smaller schools, those with less background, and those with time constraints feel that they are unable to compete on the same level as others. Their students routinely lose the rounds in which they participate. While it might be suggested that these adolescents should work harder, when they do work diligently, given other constraints, and get beaten each week, frustration results. In the long run, the successful teams harm themselves by decreasing competition. As one coach of a school with a weak program put it:

> The big schools that want to beat everybody up, they do it. . . . How long is anybody going to get beat up? . . . I mean nobody in their right mind is going to stay around . . . where you can't win. (interview)

A coach at one of the larger, more powerful schools notes the same thing, emphasizing their access to libraries, large enrollment, and affluent families: "How many times do [debaters from a small school] have to come to the Twin Cities, and [our team] crush them, crush them, crush them, before they just say why are we doing this?" (interview). In an important sense it is these students—those from rural communities and inner-city areas—for whom debate is particularly useful, but the activity has changed to discourage their participation. One coach commented:

> I think that policy debate as we're doing it is going to have a hard time main-taining itself, and the reason is that we've gotten so good at it. Our kids, the kids that do well, work so hard at it, dedicate so much time to it that really only a handful of kids can do that. First of all, if you take average kids and they want to put in an average amount of time on it, they're gonna get killed. We've got kids who are in the top of their class, kids who are National Merit Scholarship finalists and are spending thirty hours a week on debate, and so that it's become so academically strong that there really isn't too much of a place for it for the kid who just wants to learn how to speak or who wants to think on his feet. (interview)

If debate is a competitive sport, such a model might matter less. After all, benefits go to those who work the hardest. But as an educational activity, such pressure discourages participation. Until the world of debate gets large enough that different divisions can be established, the problems will continue.

The Money Train and the Doughnut Effect

If one mapped debate programs in most states, one would find that schools form a doughnut around the large cities.[31] That certainly is the case within Minnesota, where before the 1970s city and rural schools had frequently been debate champions. During the period of my research, only one public high school in the Twin Cities participated in debate. Few rural high schools had debate programs. The financial commitment is too great, given other pressures. The schools outside the Twin Cities that had debate programs were localized in mid-sized cities, like Grand Rapids, Duluth, Mankato, or Moorhead. Most high schools with debate pro-grams were located in suburban communities. Given economic realities and pressures on students to succeed academically such a doughnut effect is surely not surprising.

The development of any leisure activity involves the provisioning of resources.[32] Alternative activities, such as Model UN programs, even if less intensive, can involve more students at lower cost. Those activities that survive are those that are able to gain access to a stable source of income. As cutbacks and tight budgets affected high schools in the 1980s and 1990s, debate programs without an independent source of funding or a dependable base of support proved to be vulnerable to economic pressures. Even if principals supported debate, other programs with more pull proved irresistible. With the growth of English as a Second Language (ESL) programs, women's athletics, and programs for the disabled, such programs as debate were pressured. Nowhere was this more evident than in city schools, formerly debate powerhouses, but now required to serve a variety of social service needs. Budget cuts are made where there is the least resistance. Although as I noted in chapter 7, some programs succeed in fund-raising or obtaining corporate support, many do not. In fact, some school districts prohibit fund-raising by individual extracurricular activities, being afraid that they will cannibalize backing for other school projects.

The financial struggles of competitive debate might seem odd in that the ranks of former debaters include some of the wealthiest, most power-ful, and most accomplished Americans. I was surprised to learn that nei-ther the National Forensic League nor individual state groups keep track of former debaters—a group that might provide political pressure or eco-nomic support. Under a rule of the National Association of Secondary School Principals' Contest and Activity Committee, student organiza-tions are not permitted to collect student names and addresses. This rule, devised to prevent organizations from selling their lists to vendors and political parties, makes the creation of a support group for educational programs impossible.[33] Ironically, such a rule has the unintended conse-quence of preventing additional financial support for education. With appropriate limits on the privacy of information, such a rule should be overturned. Limited by organizational resources and privacy laws, the National Forensic League has been unable to be a special-interest group. The possibility of establishing an endowment or trust fund for debate has never been implemented. This absence of active fund-raising, coupled with complaints about insufficient publicity, has led to some criticism among coaches of the National Forensic League. An activist who com-piled a list of former debaters in Congress, and then attempted to coordi-nate federal support, would provide a real service.

Some suggest that the activity could be separated from schools and be privately funded to decrease pressure on schools from less wealthy areas.[34] Such a proposal would eliminate the institutional stability, infor-mal support structure, and convenience that debate in schools provides. Whether such ameliorative programs would succeed—given the prob-lems of retaining teachers, a context in which competitive debate success is problematic, and the lack of funding—is unclear.

Predicting the survival of high school debate is risky. A cautious pessi-mism is surely warranted. Yet, at the same time, activities can become faddish, suddenly being recognized as a panacea for the problems that face us. A U.S. President—a former debater perhaps—who decides to make policy debate the linchpin of her national education program, could change funding priorities, could recruit teachers, and could expand student participation. A popular feature film about competitive debate could also alter the image of the activity.[35] Without these political and cultural quakes, and with the graying of the teaching profession, the increasing complexity of debate, and the lack of secure school funding, substantial growth seems less likely than continued decline.

Debating Education

American education struggles to achieve a sense of purpose, a belief that teachers and schoolwork can effectively shape the lives of children who are entrusted to the charge of these uncertain institutions. Statistics and parents agree that all is not well with how we train our progeny.

In contrast, we find that competitive high school debate is paradoxically in decline. Yet, all evidence suggests that debate benefits participants. Even if many of these claims are anecdotal or from participants, I know of no study—have spoken to no participant, listened to no outsider—that suggests that debate does harm, unless an overabundance of attorneys is a plague! While there are calls for altering debate, diminishing some of its flights of argumentative fancy, all agree that the activity provides a real intellectual challenge.

Some suggest that every school should offer a debate program, permitting gifted and other interested students to find a supportive community and an opportunity to learn critical thinking, research skills, organization, communication, and self-confidence. Others go further, suggesting that just as we require English, history, foreign language, physical education, mathematics, and sex education, we should require forensics.[36] Does not a participatory democratic society require skilled communicators and those able to judge this communication? Are not there clearer public policy justifications for debate as a requirement than for chemistry or European history? Should not schools train every student to be able to participate in public discourse?

I am unable to argue against those who would push debate education as necessary for every student, although we must be cautious about the desire to demand to make every benefit a school requirement. Still, as this chapter should have made evident, the benefits are plausible and compelling. The aim of having students write poetry, paint canvases, do trigonometry, and run laps is not to produce legions of experts, but to provide a map of the skills that society considers essential. A society filled with argument and noise can easily justify the demand for skills in the name of expanding policy evaluation and empowerment.

Nine

Debate and the Adolescent Toolkit

LIKE THE debaters with whom I have traveled, I wish to emphasize a few points in closing. While much evidence has been presented, some salient arguments must be underlined: policy debate is a domain of youth, talk, evidence, competition, attachment, and schooling. In the terminology of debaters, I present an overview of my themes and their implications, setting aside the details of field notes and interview abstracts. My fundamental claim is that high school debate is a social world that, like any community, establishes its own moral order, addresses its divisions, and shares boundaries with related social worlds. Although for those outside its boundaries, high school debate seems an amusingly esoteric activity, under some measure of institutional pressure, the activity has a vibrant culture and provides a welcoming home for participants.

In this conclusion, I present an array of concepts that reflect the importance of high school policy debate and related social scenes. Specifically, I address six fundamental concepts that animate the analysis: adolescence, discourse, proof, game, community, and education.

Adolescence

Competitive debate is an adolescent activity, localized to high school and college, with participants ranging in age from fourteen to twenty-two. Competitive debate is not found in elementary school and only rarely in middle school.[1] Although debate is said to be a *life skill*, once a young adult graduates from college, opportunities for competitive debate vanish, even though activities such as litigating and legislating have some of the thrill of debate. Unlike golf, swimming, chess, or poker, debate per se is not a lifetime activity, although debate skills serve well in many careers.

Debate is situated within the life course. It is a transitional activity, located between childhood and adulthood. Because of its powerful social, emotional, and cognitive satisfactions, debaters often find disengagement difficult. To disengage is explicitly to leave one life stage for another. That participants are adolescents shapes all that occurs.

Because of their class backgrounds, their educational success and commitment, and often their lack of opportunities, debaters seem less directly involved with deviant behaviors than other teens, but these temptations and the knowledge of them are still real. Given that debaters travel to tournaments, the opportunity and decision to engage in these vices may be heavily moderated by the fact that they represent their institutions and that adults from these institutions are required to monitor their actions.

Ultimately, teenage interests shape the substance of debate: the audacious playing with "ideas" that characterizes the most obscure and bizarre debate arguments and cases follows directly from the adolescent desire to test limits and cross boundaries—to determine how far they can trespass intellectually. This may explain why one often finds extreme idealism among teenage activists, whether they are radical leftists, libertarians, conservatives, or racist skinheads. Debate represents a taming of this extremism, but not its elimination, and as a result it is not surprising that teens enjoy making arguments that *anything*, no matter how mild, can lead to nuclear war or ecological extinction, or that prison overcrowding can be alleviated by establishing penal colonies, blasting prisoners into space, or other aberrant plans. Similarly, the desire to spew information as rapidly as possible reflects this desire to test the limits of one's mastery. The fashions that emerge in preferred debate arguments likewise can be interpreted as a means by which cohorts of adolescents draw boundaries, emphasizing their unique capacities.

Fundamental to this analysis is the claim that high school debate is characterized by an oscillation between a seriousness of purpose and an indulgent immaturity, and that this characterizes other adolescent arenas. Adolescents have incorporated the behavioral and social skills of adults into their "cultural toolkit," but they have not discarded the skills of childhood. Within any given circumstance, adolescents draw upon a wide range of behaviors. This willingness to select from behaviors characterizing adults and children makes this life stage distinctive, as opposed to being characterized by the existence of a unique set of behaviors. While adolescence surely is a period in which boys and girls test models of conduct, as they shape and define their public and personal identities, this conduct is drawn both from exposure to adult culture—exposure that intensifies over the teenage years—and from comforting experiences of childhood.

For this reason, adolescence of all of the recognized life stages most dramatically demonstrates the power of the metaphor of a cultural toolkit. Again and again we find much behavior drawn from adult worlds, leavened by acts of childish innocence and what adults call poor judgment—meaning that teens alternatively rely on behavior previously tolerated as appropriate for younger children or, in contrast, on behavior for which teenagers are not considered ready. Passing through adoles-

cence, the balance between acts that adults define as mature and immature shifts, as authorities define appropriate behavior. They reward some
choices and sanction others that teens newly define as appropriate. Adults
are startled by how much these adolescents have learned about adult concerns. For instance, adults are impressed by how much teens understand
about policy and how poised they seem in their suits and dresses. In other
cases, adults are dismayed by how skilled teens are in the domains of
crime and sexuality. Simultaneously, adults may be equally startled that
this maturity is not evident in all situations: drug dealers who retreat to
childhood, mothers who seem as young as their daughters, or debaters
whose giggly arguments are those of preteens and who treat their hotel
rooms with the giddy destruction of one who believes that someone will
come to clean up the mess. The contrast between the skills of the adult
and the skills of the child, as it coalesces into the realm of adolescent
culture, is dramatic. This contrast reflects divergent standards of self-
presentation, suggesting that the image of adolescence as a separate psychological or behavioral stage, easily delimited from what came before
and what is yet to come, is misleading.

Teenagers are persons who, in creating their own authentic culture,
feel comfortable drawing on both adult and child behaviors—what they
have recently acquired and what they have yet to discard. They are exposed to the gamut of adult behaviors, but often perform these acts in
ways that harken back to previous standards of acceptable behavior.
These youngsters may participate in the spectrum of deviant activities
(sex, drugs, violence, crime), and do so knowingly, but these activities are
often seen as lacking consequences by those who trust that they will be
protected from the repercussions of their actions

In sum, competitive debate, as currently structured, could hardly be
other than an adolescent activity; its outlandish qualities make it well
designed for teen needs: the desire to perform the unacceptable under the
guise of the normal, the need to adopt adult trappings with the satisfactions of childhood irresponsibility. Debate constitutes one of the teenage
subcultures that dot our cultural landscape.[2] These adolescents, embracing an esoteric cultural domain, a transformation of adult society, are not
all that different from mods and rockers, skinheads, hip-hoppers, hack-
ers, and punks.

Discourse

Debate is a world of talk: rhetorical, if only in its specialized fashion.
Even if much analysis is written on the flowpads that debaters and judges
hold close and dear, what is said is the basis of the competition. Some

adults express dismay at the fact that so much activity in a debate round is not persuasive in the sense that we imagine good oratory should be. These debaters do not engage in "bloviating." Flowery language in debate, although not necessarily in other speech events, is unfashionable, even in traditional venues such as Minnesota.

One of the more impressive subcultural skills is the ability to talk fast—very, very fast—up to 400 words per minute, twice as rapid as normal discourse. This ability is a status marker within this social world. Talk is not merely talk, but a mark of the self. For those less able, this spewing is accompanied by shuddering and stuttering, gulping for air, and other forms of hyperventilation. A debate round is not always pretty. The intellectual justification for this odd, compulsive yapping is that debate is a form of information processing. To evaluate the outcome requires an honest broker, sitting in the back of the room with the responsibility to judge. As a consequence, debate remains a *persuasive* activity, even if the grounds on which persuasion is measured are singular. The relics of a more rhetorical style can be discerned in the opening and closing of arguments, but throughout the speeches recognition of the need to convince another is evident.

As with other forms of rhetoric, debate depends on claims and warrants: what is and what ought to be. Debaters cobble together strings of arguments and transform these arguments to suggest a perspective on the topic or resolution. Such presentations rely on the assumptions that society takes for granted, even if, supposedly, anything goes. In policy debate, the affirmative is obliged to present a case that supports or affirms the resolution and a plan that can put that case into effect; the negative must demonstrate that the case and plan are inadequate, either in not solving the problem or in causing additional problems through unintended consequences of the change. Both in the original presentations and in the final rebuttals, speakers present narratives that serve, in discursive form, to justify action or inaction. Debaters are called on, at least briefly, to provide a global account in the face of a wealth of specific arguments, assertions, and facts.

Over the years a body of knowledge—debate theory—has developed that suggests how to present these contentions. The divergences in debate theory and the continual changes in fashion suggest that the model for what constitutes appropriate discourse is intellectually contentious. The existence of forms of talk and argument—and the evaluation of these as connected to status—emphasizes that discourse is not merely technical or instrumental, but is a social matter. The ability to judge talk by community standards is at the heart of debate, but, of course, also applies to all talk beyond the corners of this esoteric world.

Proof

How will we know truth when we hear it? Debaters search for the "perfect card," like knights on a quest for the Holy Grail. The fantasy is that by announcing this magical piece of evidence, debate will cease; triumph will be undeniable. Of course, participants know this is an illusion; no claim is ever such that a counterclaim is impossible. No truth is fully transparent.

Still, this image has considerable motivational power. Debaters cannot rely on their own wits alone, but must depend on discovering the claims of others. A tacit phalanx of allies stands behind each talker. The diversity and pluralism of opinion in American society, and the institutional fragmentation that permits these opinions to reach print and cyberspace, makes debate possible. One cannot imagine the existence of competitive debate in George Orwell's 1984, if for no other reason than the paucity of evidence. In America, liberals, conservatives, libertarians, socialists, fascists, anarchists, fundamentalists, and atheists all have their say. Publications present their claims, and institutions archive these publications. With the rise of evidence from the Internet, the range of sources and the ease of access are expanding exponentially. "Any idiot" can now be cited. Each side must marshal evidence, creating through their briefs a team of partisans.

But what to use and how to use it? The demand for perfect cards—in which experts present the debater's perspective unambiguously and vigorously without qualification, and, ideally, with a concise explanation— is such that debaters are pressured to misuse evidence. The temptations are great, and because typically debaters do not indict the evidence of others, the risks are small. Debaters rarely create evidence; more often they massage or overclaim evidence, jerking it from its context, erasing authorial intent. Because of the demand for experts to make claims that debaters wish to make themselves,[3] issues of the proper use of evidence are endemic. Since many pieces of evidence are little more than opinion, they might be thought to have little more standing than the analysis or logic of the participants. Yet, because these beliefs were published, they have a life of their own and gain legitimacy. Given that evidence may come from anyone, opponents do not see indicting sources as an effective strategy, and judges feel they should not insert their evaluations. Scientists, journalists, activists, and crackpots have equal standing. Results of empirical studies are occasionally cited, although because of time pressures in the round, these are rarely described in detail or assessed as to competence. As a result, their value as "proof" is uncertain, although they can be potent within a round. In practice, any study often serves as well as any other.

Debaters speak of cards, standing for evidence. Evidence is the truth statements of those who have the authority to know by virtue of being published, while cards are the selections that debaters make from these expert texts. Cards, not evidence, are the coin of the debate round, and debaters are known for the number of cards to which they have access. In the last two decades, debaters have moved from collecting information to put into card files to placing the information on the cards onto sheets of paper, cementing shards of evidence and bits of argumentation, creating proofs termed briefs. Briefs create an extended argument from cards; in the process, given that the briefs are written texts, they decrease the flexibility of debaters in constructing arguments. Since briefs have a material reality, shifting the order of cards or skipping parts of the argument is more challenging. While briefs are not always read in their entirety, especially by the best debaters, their existence structures arguments in advance, reifying them.

As with discourse, the judge must evaluate the evidence, which because of the rapidity of debaters' speech is a challenge. At the end of the contest, the judge needs to decide whether the evidence presented answers the evidence of opponents. Even judges who prefer not to intervene in a round, hoping to analyze claims only in light of other claims, cannot escape their obligation to weigh the significance of evidence within the argumentative flow. This active involvement of the judge emphasizes that the role of evidence in debate rounds is not so different from that in families or in workplaces—strategic assertions that stand for truth until undercut. As Michael Billig emphasizes,[4] we strive to select those forms of proof that accord with the way our audience makes judgments. Although we imagine that we are information processors, embracing the metaphor of the computer, we present and accept information that fits our images and goals. The processing of information is forever social. The acquisition of the ability to shape and display arguments by teenagers, so necessary an ability for professionals of all stripes, provides debate with its educational power.

Game

Much of social life can be conceptualized as a game, as the dramaturgical model of social interaction emphasizes. Debate in its explicitly gamelike features parallels other activity. As competitive activity, debate rounds and tournaments generate winners and losers, and teams must cope with the significance of their record for their self-esteem and evaluation of ability. While this ethos of intense competition might seem unusual for an educational domain, it is often the case—particularly in upper-middle-class domains—that competition is an objective marker of learning and ability.[5] Yet, this assumes that all will subscribe to the same level of intensity, a belief that is routinely disproved. The fact that policy debate occurs between two-person teams means that debate outcomes sometimes produce tension between team partners, who have different levels of ability or commitment.

Debate games are situated within a context of understanding social problems. Homelessness, retirement security, the Middle East, juvenile justice, and national security are among the bases of cases and counterplans. Debaters are moral entrepreneurs who justify social action. Deploying expert claims, compelling statistics, and dramatic horror stories, debaters create a social problem in the mind of an receptive judge. Unlike much evaluation of policy in natural discourse ("the real world"), the judge should be open to all assertions. Most judges limit their willingness to intervene or interject themselves in the round, waiting for the negative team to provide arguments that they can weigh against the need for action or to choose between a plan and a counterplan. Even if this openness is never absolute, as some arguments fall easily, the assumption is that anything goes. In theory, a debate round should represent a scene open to all strategies and contentions.

While much of the game occurs within the boundaries of the activity itself, outside forces affect outcomes, as they do in courts, legislatures, and classrooms. Herein lies the realm of debate politics. In some measure, these are hard to escape. The idea that a judge comes into a room as a blank slate—tabula rasa—is an illusion: judges have expectations based on the reputation of the teams, the amount of evidence they lug, their dress, and the ties of the judge with the coach or other members of the squad. I do not claim that debate rounds are fixed or that judges are unfair, but that expectations and desires do affect outcomes. It is just as it is in court, where juries will often decide to convict or acquit based on the race of the defendant, the skill or clothing of the lawyer, or perceived threats from one side or another. In politics, the public expects that legislators will vote not only on what they (or their constituents) feel is right, but also on who has pressured them.

Competitive policy debate is a particularly American activity and is mirrored in our institutions of law and politics. For good or ill, Americans see law and politics as games in which two opposing sides attempt to win at all costs. This implies the danger that beliefs do not matter and that winning becomes the measure of success, rather than discovering truth, solving the problem, or reaching consensus. Yet, simultaneously seeing an institution as a game drains passion from the battles. Seeing law or politics as *only* a game contributes to the stability of these social systems: tomorrow is another contest. When opponents are assessed by external evaluators (judges, juries, voters), the fact that the participants are not fully committed to their ideologies or claims matters less, since one can rely on the good sense of the evaluators. Debate in this sense, while a game, provides excellent training for participating in those central institutions that organize American society.

Community

Participants in all activities surround themselves with like-minded others. We do not just act, but we act in concert with others about whom we care—perhaps admire, perhaps resent, perhaps envy—but rarely is emotion lacking. The debate community operates on several levels. The partner relationship is a cornerstone of community. Long-term partnerships are as complicated as marriages.

Beyond the partner relationship is the debate squad, a small group of adolescents who share a common focus, typically directed by an adult teacher or coach. Like the partnership, the team is both instrumental and expressive, with teenagers attempting to acquire skills of speaking, thinking, and researching that will permit them to triumph at debate tournaments, and simultaneously to have fun doing so. If debaters did not have fun—as a consequence of the competitive and social elements—education or résumé building would be insufficient to maintain impassioned involvement.

Finally, the debate community consists of a network that spreads across metropolitan areas, states, or, in the case of national circuit debate, the nation. The networks that develop among cohorts of debaters are duplicated in the networks of coaches. One does not simply compete, but one competes against friends, acquaintances, and rivals.

Each level of community constitutes a status system in which esteem is distributed according to group standards. Individuals are located in social worlds as a result of how they are evaluated on criteria that participants deem to matter. Thus, partners judge each other, sometimes leading to breaches when there is sharp disagreement over relative status or over the proper level of commitment. Similarly, teams are characterized by high- and low-status members, evaluations that change over time, particularly as the more experienced participants graduate, letting younger cohorts "move up." Within networks, reputations exist as well, and are shaped at each tournament. Some debaters are well known and highly esteemed by their peers and the adults associated with the activity, producing an "economy of esteem." This esteem can translate into privileges, even to advantages in the round, based on credit and reputation.

Part of the interest in debate as a subculture is that schools and teams are not interchangeable. Teams have reputations in the debate community, and within the network some teams are close, while others are socially distant. Further, the world of debate changes each academic year as a new cohort of seniors become the central players. Only through the establishment of an institutional history—made possible by coaches and those who continue to be involved at the margins—does a meaningful culture continue over several years. For coaches, the alliances and occasional enmity are much more solidified than they are for adolescents.

The presence of linkages is by no means unique to debate, but is found in many reticulated venues in which numerous teams or groups participate, where a subculture is composed of a network of groups. The networks of debate are mirrored among chess teams and basketball squads. Even activities such as mushroom collecting, not grounded on competition, reveal the existence of networking through national and regional forays. To the extent that groups and institutional settings permit participants to know and care about each other, voluntary leisure worlds can become locations of extended relationships. As a result, a social world is not entirely defined by the activity or interests of participants, but equally by their relationships. In this, debate is a model for other activities.

Education

It is fitting that debate is embedded in educational institutions. Perhaps the competitive nature of American society makes it appropriate that debate belongs to schooling; in other nations, there is no close equivalent to our country's high school policy debate (adolescent debate in Canada, Great Britain, and Australia is much more rhetorical—more like values debate or parliamentary debate, mirroring, perhaps, their parliamentary systems). Policy debate is another instance of "American exceptionalism."

I have emphasized the skills learned by adolescents in their debate activity. Perhaps as a former debater, my allegiance is to be expected, and proponents of educational alternatives—sometimes less expensive, less intense, incorporating more students—have their own case to make. However, I believe a strong case can be made that debate is educational and should be widely available. How many other activities involve adolescents voluntarily engaging in hours of research, learning how to argument strategically, developing critical thinking, presenting a public persona, and discussing how to solve obdurate social problems? While a selection factor is evident and debate is, by any criteria, elitist, participants represent the best and brightest. Although debaters reveal a range of educational achievement, a large number could by any definition be defined as "gifted." For instance, if it wished, Princeton could fill its entering class with debaters, and find no significant diminution of intellectual ability, although perhaps the group would be both less diverse and more contentious than usual.

While there have been fads and fashions in educational theory over "gifted education" and in "tracking" in general, most school districts maintain something equivalent to gifted education. Parents—often with cultural capital and political influence—demand such training, and elected school boards accept these programs, either from ideological commitment or community pressure. Policy debate could be an important element of these programs. Since debate does not appeal to all gifted students, using it as the sole method of gifted education would not be justifiable, but debate could enrich all forms of gifted education.

However, one might go further and suggest that policy debate could enhance all education—if not for every student, for many. One of the realities that debate professionals confront is the "doughnut effect," in which many schools located in suburban communities maintain active programs (as do some private schools), but in which inner-city and rural schools lack the resources for these programs. Debate has been a haven for the children of elites, who can learn those skills and develop networks that serve them well. To the extent that society is concerned with equalizing the educational opportunities for minority and disadvantaged students, the absence of debate programs is particularly unfortunate. Debate produces lawyers and policymakers, and with its competitive ethos would seem to be a boon for inner-city schools. The verbal fluency of minorities has never been doubted, as evident in the ministerial and musical traditions in African-American communities; when this skill is coupled with skills in research and argumentation, motivated by competition, one would expect that a portion of the student body would participate, particularly given the availability of college scholarships and career opportunities. Students enrolled in these schools have gifted potential, even if they have lack opportunities and homes with cultural capital. In urban communities that are home to universities with strong debate programs (for instance, Atlanta, Chicago, and Los Angeles), coaches should be readily available, even if skilled mentors are not on the faculty of high schools. A modest commitment of resources—federally, locally, or through businesses or colleges—is essential. School districts could hire speech teachers. Local urban leagues are beginning to emerge in which these students compete, but such leagues are only in their early stages and need to be expanded. Given the sterling public image of debate, corporate sponsors should be available. These local leagues can operate alongside the state and national tournaments, providing a multitiered system, as is found in football and basketball programs. This system could be sufficiently open and flexible that the strongest inner-city and rural teams could compete at a higher level.

Debate should be part of American education. That every student should be exposed to speech education is both reasonable and practical, and would likely contribute to greater political involvement in electoral politics and policy discourse. Scholars who argue that schools should be "teaching the conflicts" as a means of engaging students and transcending the culture wars can find in the various formats of high school debate models that exemplify the strengths of that claim. Should not every citizen be able to participate in the public arena? Should not every citizen be able to appreciate the claims on both sides of an argument? Mastering techniques of speech communication and debate is crucial in this regard. Yet, while we insist that adolescents learn chemistry and European history, public speaking is ignored, if not seen as laughable. Yet, which would make more difference in the lives of an informed and prepared citizenry? While universities could not produce speech professionals in sufficient numbers overnight, bodies follow job opportunities. The fact that a few high schools require that every student have a course on communication prior to graduation, and that many high schools *once* had that requirement, suggests that the proposal is worthy of consideration. It would be naive to suggest that debate and rhetorical training could save the American Republic, although some debaters would make that claim passionately. They might be right.[6] The naive may be visionary. To be a good citizen is to be able to contend with those who hold different images of social order. Americans need not only personal morality, but gifted tongues as well.

Appendix

Communities of Debate

THINK of leisure world participation as a market. New activities are publicized that have the potential for recruiting participants from ongoing activities; economic conditions change that alter participation; and culture and ideology evolve. Thus, leaders and even participants in an activity must to some degree be moral entrepreneurs, patrolling the boundaries and securing new recruits. Change is always threatening, and those who control the activity must decide which innovations to incorporate.

In several senses, there is no correct way to debate. Standards, and even rules, differ between—and sometimes within—communities. Imagine if basketball referees or baseball umpires had radically different ways of calling games. Suppose that these were not merely idiosyncratic variations, but that officials were open about their preferences. Referees in one state or region could hold radically different standards, arguing vociferously for their choices. To the extent that judges within a region accept these standards, little chaos would result, but when regions overlapped, or in a national event, participants would be confused or angry. Such is the case with high school debate. From a sociological perspective, competing standards speak to the problems of organizing a subculture in the face of distinct ideologies and tight-knit communities.

On the college level, divisions are even more extreme, mediated by the fact that different organizations serve the interests of different programs. As college debate depends on national tournaments, regional differences, while present in terms of the type of debate preferred, typically do not affect standards within a particular style of debate. There are at least eight distinct college debate organizations with their own rules and styles of debate.[1] The first split in college debate resulted from the belief among many coaches that the collegiate style of debate involved too rapid speech and the presentation of too much evidence, making the activity both insufficiently persuasive (speeches lacked oratorical effectiveness) and simultaneously too time-consuming. These concerns remain at both the college and the high school levels. Indeed, to outsiders such complaints seem reasonable: acquiring the skills of public speaking might seem to be a building block of debate, at least as the public understands it, but the necessity to spend over forty hours a week on research would seem contrary to the nature of the college experience. If football players spent eight hours a day practicing, the public would recognize that something was deeply amiss. As a result of this critique, a splinter group, the Cross-Examination Debate Association (CEDA), centered in southern California, broke away from the National Debate Tournament (NDT) in 1971, in response to criticism of speed and overuse of evidence, and from a desire to incorporate cross-examination into the debate round. At first the CEDA group spread rapidly. One college coach estimated that by the late 1980s CEDA was four times as large as its NDT rivals. By 1990, in Minnesota there was only one NDT school, and only four in the five states of the Upper Midwest. CEDA's explicit goal was to create a style of debate in which speakers would not be rewarded for spewing, and in which debate evidence did not have the prominence that it had in NDT debate. Originally, CEDA debate topics emphasized values over explicit policy, a decision that prevented debaters from relying on evidence. However, over time, CEDA debate became more like NDT debate in part because there is a competitive value to speaking rapidly and using large amounts of evidence, which allows the speaker to make more arguments for an opponent to rebut. The divisions have become so minor that the two groups are in the process of merging (partly a function of the decline of collegiate debate) and now use the same topic for their annual resolution. Both groups represent the elite of college debate. Two other college organizations, the National Parliamentary Debate Association and the American Parliamentary Debate Association, focus on parliamentary-style debate, with an emphasis on oratory. Students are given topics minutes before the round, eliminating the possibility of relying on evidence. The former group relies on faculty coaches, the latter group depends on student-run groups. Several other splinter groups exist, each serving a constituency, dividing the activity further.

In contrast, in high school debate a single organization, the National Forensic League, is dominant. This umbrella group, founded in 1925, runs the national tournament each June, publishes a monthly magazine, *The Rostrum*, and keeps track of the number of "points" participants in forensics activities have won,[2] awarding pins and certificates. The National Forensic League not only organizes debate, but other speech events as well, including extemporaneous speaking, original oratory, dramatic interpretation, and student congress. The National Forensic League sets the rules for its own tournament, and its magazine serves as a bully pulpit for those who wish to change the rules of debate.[3]

In practice, the National Forensic League has only limited authority. The topic for each year for policy debate is selected by the National Federation of State High School Associations, the organization that oversees high school sports and other extracurricular activities. Further, debate as a high school activity (or sport) is controlled by an organization in each state, linked directly or indirectly to the state Department of Education. Each state, in effect, makes its own rules for the structure of the activity: the number of tournaments permitted, the length of the tournaments, the rules of eligibility, and the determination of the state championship. In Minnesota, the Minnesota State High School League has authority to regulate debate as a high school activity, which it does in association with the Minnesota Debate Teachers Association. The National Federation of State High School Associations coordinates the governing bodies for high school activities in each state, publishes material (e.g., *The Forensic Educator*), and sponsors conferences. Further, local school boards (or, in the case of private schools, trustees) can limit the activity of debaters (e.g., the number of tournaments that can be attended, the number of school days that can be missed). Despite the prominence of the National Forensic League, it does not have the authority to determine the structure of debate, other than in limited domains.

During the 1970s strains emerged in high school debate, linked to a decline in the number of high schools with teams, finances, a shortage of qualified teachers, and changes in debate styles. Some schools—a handful of private schools and elite public schools (notably those for gifted students and those in wealthy suburbs or college communities)[4]—became influenced by the rapid-fire collegiate style of debate, often because these schools hired college debaters as assistant coaches, who were committed to this style and enthusiastically taught their impressionable young charges. Eventually these schools developed a national circuit with its own distinctive style, developing tournaments and a pool of sympathetic judges. These teams traveled around the country each weekend, perfecting a style of debate that rewarded speed and generic arguments. What the National Tournament of the National Forensic League is to the debate world generally, the Tournament of Champions, held six weeks earlier at the University of Kentucky, is to national circuit teams. James Copeland, the executive director of the National Forensic League, compared the two tournaments to golf's National Open and the Masters. The approximately two dozen wealthy, visible, successful schools in this group had great impact on the high school debate community. These coaches formed their own organization, the National Debate Coaches Association, which, while it is open to any debate coach, is primarily for coaches whose teams participate on the national circuit. While other communities (particularly in the Midwest, such as Minnesota) remained strong, and resistant to the charms of national circuit debate, resentment toward these schools runs high. Their style of debate and their success have underlined the dissatisfaction with two-person policy debate, which each year increasingly seemed to mimic the national circuit style.

As on the collegiate scene, pressure was exerted to provide other opportunities for debaters in light of the criticism of policy debate as being too time-consuming, insufficiently oriented to persuasion and rhetorical skills, too linked to generic arguments, and emphasizing too heavily the presentation of evidence. This was tied to resentment, by coaches at underfunded programs, aimed at those elite schools that had the funding to hire assistant coaches, maintain a flush copying budget, and provide money for travel. For instance, my son's first high school, Woodward Academy, a national circuit school located in Atlanta, had three debate/speech teachers on staff, and did not charge parents for trips to North Carolina, Tennessee, Texas, Louisiana, Kentucky, Massachusetts, and Illinois.

The criticisms of policy debate had the effect in 1979 of encouraging the creation of a second form of high school debate, Lincoln-Douglas or values debate. Values-oriented topics (e.g., Resolved: That communities in the United States ought to have the right to suppress pornography), which changed every two months, required less commitment, less reliance on evidence, and a greater emphasis on persuasion. Lincoln-Douglas debate also does not involve teams of two debaters. Students debate individually, allowing small schools to participate more easily (although increasing the number of judges needed).[5] In some regions (e.g., California, New York), Lincoln-Douglas has become dominant, much to the frustration of policy debaters, who feel that their style of debate is more sophisticated and more intellectually rigorous.

My research focused on Minnesota policy debaters. The individuals with whom I had the most contact were committed to the "traditional" style that Minnesotans cherished. My discussion of Lincoln-Douglas and national circuit policy debate,[6] and the politics of regional debate, is colored by this ethnographic site. After my observations ended, I joined an e-mail policy debate list, and I learned from colleagues on the speech team at the University of Georgia (notably their coach, Professor Ed Pennetta, and Doyle Srader, currently at Arizona State University) and from my son and his coaches and colleagues as he debated on the national circuit for both Woodward Academy in Georgia and for Glenbrook South High School in Illinois. However, partisans of both Lincoln-Douglas and national circuit style debate may find my Minnesota evidence stacked against them. Compared to other regions of the country, neither Lincoln-Douglas (LD) nor national circuit style debate was particular strong in Minnesota during my research. From a sociological perspective this is not necessarily harmful, as my concern is with the social construction of boundaries and the development of stigma and cultural deviance.

The World of LD Debate

Our collective memory of political discourse in the 1850s has a rosy glow, despite physical violence, threats, and charges of treason.[7] The 1858 Lincoln-Douglas debates, which were influential in sending Stephen Douglas to the United States Senate, represent our contemporary vision of political rhetoric, even if that image is only loosely connected to the rough reality of antebellum oration: two men standing before an interested, impassioned audience, debating the issues of the day with wit, thoughtfulness, passion, and brio. The establishment of Lincoln-Douglas debate as a high school activity was an attempt to teach these rhetorical skills to adolescents and to capitalize on this romantic image. This was to be real competitive *speech*, avoiding the pitfalls of artificial policy debate. According to one proponent of Lincoln-Douglas debate:

> Lincoln-Douglas debate was started in 1979, largely as an adverse reaction to what policy debate had become, which is illustrated by . . . "tons of evidence," "sheer speed," "200 ideas a minute." The policy debater, to read his tons of evidence, speaks like a machine gun, racing through his evidence, gasping for breath, hoping to overwhelm his opponents with some obscure argument. Lincoln-Douglas debaters must use reason and logic as primary debating tools, occasionally citing an authority to buttress a point. They must study philosophical and political theories, adapting them to modern society. . . . We often say that debating is fine preparation for becoming a lawyer. Policy debaters would lose every case—the jury could not understand them. The whole purpose of communication is to be understood and exchange ideas. Lincoln-Douglas debaters do it better![8]

A Minnesota coach, who taught both LD and policy debate, felt that Lincoln-Douglas was more challenging to teach in that it was difficult to train adolescents to work "with theories, not concrete evidence." One debater who preferred LD to policy debate, explained: "You can win a policy debate on facts and information on cards. You can't do that in Lincoln-Douglas. You have to think. . . . Not everybody is creative" (interview).

Observers at a Lincoln-Douglas round will more likely find themselves at home with the style. Lincoln-Douglas debate was instituted because in the late 1970s executives at Phillips Petroleum, a generous supporter of the NFL since 1976, attended the final round of the 1979 national tournament, and were dismayed and embarrassed by what they heard, reminding us of the dilemmas entailed in accepting even noble corporate sponsorship.[9] As James Copeland noted, "Rumor had it that the executives left in the middle of the debate and that one made the comment, 'If this is what our money is being used for we need to rethink our grant.'"[10] These oil executives were not alone in their confusion; many others saw debate drifting from communication, persuasion, and the expertise of the common man. The executives attended a NFL executive council, explaining their concerns. After much discussion and consideration of various options, such as banning note-taking during a round or penalizing too many arguments, the council decided to adopt an innovation pioneered in Colorado—Lincoln-Douglas debate—including it in the national tournament the following year. Policy debate continued on its merry way, but those dismayed by its trends had another option. Phillips Petroleum continued to support the NFL, and Lincoln National Life Insurance Company now sponsors the Lincoln-Douglas portion of the tournament.

At the rounds I observed, the better Lincoln-Douglas debaters start with a clear and cogent introduction, present definitions relevant to the topic, describe their core values, and proceed to connect these values to the topic. Core values on the topic about communities regulating pornography included "social good," "freedom," "moral commitment," and "democracy." Sources cited included Jean-Jacques Rousseau and Immanuel Kant. Lincoln-Douglas debaters talk to and look directly at the judge, rare in policy debate, where debaters are looking at their briefs and cards. Because Lincoln-Douglas is still relatively young, several coaches told me that they felt that the theory of LD debate needed to be expanded, and there was a sense that (as with collegiate CEDA debate) Lincoln-Douglas debate was beginning to be faster and more linked to evidence; there was even talk about having an LD topic for a full year, rather than for two months, to allow for "more research." As judges often are former policy debaters, this transition might be rewarded. One coach, seeing this, worries that LD debate could be "polluted by the strategies that are in policy."

Lincoln-Douglas proved to be quite successful, so that even in Minnesota in 1990, part of the heartland of policy debate, Lincoln-Douglas held almost the same number of tournament rounds as policy debate (although with fewer debaters, since LD involves single-person teams). Minnesota coaches did not consider LD debate as significant as policy debate, but its impact was growing, and within a few years Minnesota teams had become well known nationally in LD debate, with a Minnesotan winning the national tournament in 1996. Because it did not require as much research, and because it required less specialized knowledge, LD appeared to be an answer for smaller and less prosperous schools. One coach re-marked:

> I think it is really going to be the thing that comes in the future. Especially for
> inner-city schools . . . because we're not going to have to do all that research.
> When you can just pick a value, I think you could easily have our kids do that.
> (interview)

With the decline of debate programs, LD might be a way of keeping the activity alive, retaining positions for speech teachers. The fear among some policy coaches is that school districts may see LD as a cheaper way of running a program, even if the students do not learn the research skills taught by policy debate.

The success of this innovation has posed a status threat to policy de-baters and coaches, and, as a result, moral lines have been drawn. Some policy debaters ("real" debaters) consider LDers to be "speech people" (field notes). Even the National Forensic League at their 1990 National Tournament distinguished between "Debate" (i.e., Policy Debate) and "Lincoln-Douglas Debate," a distinction that was not lost on Lincoln-Douglas debaters. As with any group that perceives itself under attack, boundaries tighten,[11] and the remarks of policy debaters can be nasty. Thus, it is said that LD stands for Logically Deprived, Loser Debate, Lack of Documentation, Learning Disabled,[12] Lesser Debate, Lame Debate, or Lite Debate. Policy debaters describe LD as "wimp debate" or "nothing debate." In Lincoln-Douglas debate, evidence and the range of arguments are missing; it appears to lack "substance." Many committed policy de-baters consider that LD is designed "for people who couldn't cut policy" (interview). In fact, at Randall Park, Lincoln-Douglas debate is used in that way. Mrs. Miller urges those class members who are not enthusiastic about policy debate, or do not want to spend the time, to try LD. In the words of one policy debater: "People tend to think that Lincoln-Douglas people are lazy because, especially at Randall Park, Lincoln-Douglas peo-ple are failed policy people" (interview).[13]

One debater congratulated a fellow policy (CX or cross-examination) debater who came in second at an LD tournament in a way that some LD participants would find offensive: "Congrats to Vicki Olson—the Queen of LD—a fellow CXer, on recently kicking some LD ass at a tourna-ment. . . . She showed the superiority of CXers, even mentioning a disad and nonuniqueness in the final round"[14] (presumably the round that she lost). Likewise, a Minnesota coach told her assistant that he should watch their policy debaters, "But if you get desperate, you can hear the LDers" (field notes). Three Minnesota policy judges were sitting in the judges' lounge at the Randall Park tournament, joking about having to judge LD rounds. These men joke about using the paradigms they use in judging policy debate, translating them to LD: tabula values (tabula rasa), value maker (policy maker), and value tester (hypothesis tester). They assume the legitimacy of policy debate, and try to force LD debaters into their mold (field notes).

This boiled down to a standard view among coaches who prefer policy debate that it would be relatively easy to transform a successful policy debater into a successful LDer (as in the note about the "Queen of LD"), but that the opposite transformation would be more challenging. One coach was explicit about this, wanting her LDers to have a year of policy debate to train them "in logical thinking." She expanded:

> I think a year of policy debate at the beginning is fundamental to anything. I think to be a good Lincoln-Douglas debater you should have a background in policy debate. . . . In Lincoln-Douglas debate, if students get into the philo-sophical thinking before they have the fundamentals of structure and language and vocabulary and these other things, they don't know what to hang all this philosophy on. (interview)

Another coach dismissed LD debate:

> Any policy debater could go into an LD tournament, and just slow down and talk persuasively and do well. You can always as a policy debater easily shift to LD, but you can't pick up policy the other way as fast because there's more to it. . . . In its own way it's valuable, although I think it's at the expense of pol-icy. . . . It doesn't take as long to prepare. You can do it on your own . . . if you want to be in swimming, you don't hurt a partner by being in swimming and then doing LD later. (interview)

It is notable that the praise of LD debate by this policy coach is precisely along the lines of criticism: it is "Lite Debate." Yet, the fact that the growth of one often is at the expense of the other makes the politics of debate styles consequential. Will "watering down" the activity, as many policy coaches fear, bring more involvement or destroy the activity?

One policy coach, focusing on the attacks of LD coaches on policy debate, recognized the dilemma:

> I felt at one time that the Lincoln-Douglas debate coaches had set about attack-ing policy debate and were trying to strengthen the Lincoln-Douglas debate community by attracting coaches away from policy debate. . . . I mean we were really at war with each other. . . . If Lincoln-Douglas was going to thrive be-cause they had found lots of disgruntled policy coaches, I didn't think that was a very healthy basis for Lincoln-Douglas, and obviously we didn't need to lose any programs in policy debate. (interview)

At this point the coach explains in detail what he objects to about LD debate, but the underlying point is that there is a fear that debate operates in a zero-sum world; a novel debate activity has the potential to cannibalize other debate activities (here, policy debate) whose footing is none too sure. Policy debaters must define their rivals in such a way as to provide legitimacy for their style of debate as a preferred means of capturing the market.

Riding the National Circuit

For those who are unfamiliar with the world of debate, it must be startling to learn of the existence of a national circuit of debate: to learn that each weekend a group of sixteen- and seventeen-year-olds head to the airport with suitcases and boxes of evidence in tow to fly across the United States, sometimes missing two or three days of school in the process. If one had suggested that a high school basketball squad should maintain that punishing schedule, critics would immediately holler that the school was taking sport too seriously, professionalizing it, noting that, after all, these are just teenagers. Yet, this is how some one hundred schoolchildren spend their year. Most coaches, even those who are highly critical of the style of debate that the national circuit has come to represent, are envious of the opportunities of these students.

The national circuit, despite its geographic spread, represents a community. Coaches know each other, seeing each other weekends over the years, and have participated in the same political battles. Even their students know each other. Most of my son's friends were debaters from other schools from around the nation, making it easier to move a teenager from Georgia to Illinois. Further, the nature of the job market contributes to the sense of community. Top coaches move from one national circuit team to another. Alex Pritchard coached for Creighton Prep in Omaha, Nebraska, before he moved to Greenhill in Dallas, Texas; Matt Whipple coached for San Antonio–Churchill before being hired by Glenbrook South in Glenview, Illinois. This stands in stark contrast to Minnesota, where movement is within the state. Some national circuit coaches have been pushing (as yet unsuccessfully) for a national ranking of debate teams, a proposal that would make little sense without the national sense of community that the national circuit provides.

Criticism of the national circuit may not be devoid of feelings of envy, and this is clearly tied to the perception among some debaters and coaches that these elite national circuit students have an advantage because of their social background and cultural capital. While some national circuit coaches contend that their programs do not represent "elitist" debate, it is surely true that fund-raising is easier in some school districts than in others. Some school districts can raise money for coaches, travel, copying, and the other associated expenses of high-level debate, while others cannot. If there are not walls to participation in debate, there certainly are doors that some can unlock more readily than others. Social class matters here as elsewhere.

While no school is turned away from national circuit tournaments, unless the school's debate coach is trained in that style of debate the experience of participation is likely to be negative. The two Minnesota teams that attended the Tournament of Champions, the most prestigious national circuit tournament, left with records of 2 wins, 5 losses, and 1 win, 6 losses. More significantly, they departed with their prejudices intact. Why should an underpaid and overworked teacher spend so much time and money simply to have the team leave depressed. Both did much better at the NFL tournament. The point is not that these Minnesotans were treated unfairly or were "cheated" by members of the club, but the styles of debate were so different that it was nearly like participating in two different activities.[15] In turn, the team that won the Tournament of Champions in 1989, St. Marks of Dallas, Texas, scored only 1 win, 3 losses, at the NFL tournament that year. A similar result occurred in 1998 when my son and his partner at Glenbrook South High School won the Tournament of Champions, and then did not clear after the first six rounds at the national tournament held in Missouri, a state whose teams were known for their conservative style of debate.[16] Debate is so diverse that the NFL publishes a reference sheet at that tournament that details the preferences of judges on divisive issues of debate theory.

The hostility between traditional and national circuit debate, while not applying to every participant, is palpable. Respect for differences is often hard to find. The criticism of the national circuit is phrased as an intellectual issue. Just as many Minnesota coaches are harsh toward Lincoln-Douglas as lesser debate, they are equally harsh toward national circuit debate because of its speaking style, its arguments, its informality, its game playing, and the desire to win at all costs. Ironically, just as Minnesota policy debaters refer to Lincoln-Douglas debate as wimp debate, debaters on the national circuit refer to the traditional style of debate, of which Minnesota debate is an exemplar, as wimp debate. A school that practices this style of debate is referred to as East Bumblefuck High School, capturing the backwater quality of their debate, according to these "more sophisticated" practitioners. Traditional debaters may be seen as not bright, preferring oratory ("cheap rhetoric") to issues. One assistant coach placed the blame for the criticism squarely on traditional coaches:

> There are coaches out there that don't want their own squads to travel the national circuit or to go to national tournaments at all. Unfortunately, they

also tend to impose their beliefs on neighboring schools. They try to prevent other squads from traveling, screaming asymmetry, or some other bullshit. I know why—and this is bound to offend someone. It's because they are NOT SUCCESSFUL COACHES, AND ARE INSECURE WITH THEIR LACK OF SUCCESS. When their own debaters always lose to the "elite" national circuit teams, they tend to lash out with . . . rules rather than learning successful coaching strategies.[17]

This ad hominem attack is surely wrong in its vehemence, but it under-lines the mistrust between the proponents of different debate ideologies. Significantly, both groups believe that research, teamwork, competition, evidence, arguments, logic, and even communication with judges are im-portant; yet, how these values get played out differs. As any Lincoln-Douglas debater can attest, revering the same set of values does not lead to the same set of conclusions.

Minnesota coaches feel that national circuit debate is not as educa-tional as stock-issues debate. One coach explained:

National circuit [debate] is primarily a handful of perhaps a dozen schools that are sort of inbred. . . . I know you're going to Kentucky [for the Tournament of Champions], and I will bet you dollars to doughnuts, if you sit in on a few rounds . . . you're going to hear identical first negative arguments that are all planned attacks and disadvantages of, maybe, nuclear war [on the prison over-crowding topic]. They're going to be almost identical arguments that have ab-solutely no relationship to what you heard in that first affirmative speech. . . . And to me, that's specious and that defeats the purpose of debate. [Question: Why?] Because it then becomes gamesmanship. . . . That defeats the purpose of what debate is there for, for education. . . . You're not thinking. (interview)

Some national circuit debaters agree that the round is a game, but that the learning comes in preparing for that game, conducting research, and put-ting together the massive number of briefs necessary. In contrast, debate in Minnesota focuses on the advantages and disadvantages of the specific affirmative case. The affirmative must present a case that demonstrates that the status quo needs to change in accord with the resolution: demon-strating a *need* for change, *harms* under the current system, that the harms are *significant*, that the problem is *inherent* within the current sys-tem, and that the particular plan that the affirmative team presents will *solve* the harms and may have other advantages as well, related to the topic (the "stock issues" of debate). The negative attacks these claims, focusing on the specific disadvantages of the plan. These stock issues are at the heart of traditional debate.

In contrast, national circuit debate often ignores the stock issues of the affirmative case, leading Minnesota coaches to complain that there is no clash in the round and that debaters talk past each other.[18] These debaters connect the topic to larger advantages or disadvantages (tyranny, nuclear war, racism) in ways that Minnesota debaters consider far-fetched—such as that prison riots are good—claiming that the unintended consequences outweigh the immediate disadvantages. Minnesota debaters joke that national circuit teams (and national circuit wannabes) always place "nuclear war on the flow." Minnesota coaches typify national circuit debate by suggesting that all they want to talk about is nuclear war:

> It seems to me that on the debate circuit it's really gotten to the point where it's rather absurd and illogical that many of the teams do not seem to think you need a link anymore. You just sort of scream a disadvantage, and it's like your disadvantage is worse than their advantage. . . . I mean, the prime example was when I took my kids to [a tournament] one year, and we essentially had to listen to a debate about which team had the most nuclear war scenarios. . . . I'm sitting back there as a rational person, saying, "One good nuclear war and I'm dead!" (interview)

> I think it would be very easy to go coach a national circuit team and . . . the arguments are so intuitively ridiculous. . . . I can sit around and think of a lot of really intuitively ridiculous arguments, and probably find some guy to support them, but I don't see any point in doing that. (interview)

It must be pointed out that, as with any style of debate, there are good teams and poor teams, and perhaps these teams were unable to adapt to the style of the judge. Further, neither coach had much experience with the range of national circuit teams. Still, their typifications fit the responses of many listeners, if they could make sense of the spewing in the round.[19]

In national circuit debate, the negative team will typically not focus on the harms or inherency of the problems within status quo, but will focus on the larger—and indirect—effects. Thus, for example, the argument may be that any policy that increases the President's popularity will increase the likelihood that the President will engage in military adventurism. The negative team will have evidence saying that the policy will increase the President's popularity; they will have evidence suggesting that if the President is more popular, he may engage in some particular act; and they will then have evidence suggesting that this act increases the likelihood of nuclear war or global destruction. As a matter of logic, they ask whether the affirmative policy—say, building more prisons—is worth *any* increased risk of nuclear war. The negative can do this for every plan that might increase the President's popularity. Negative arguments can also be made for plans that decrease the President's popularity, or do the same for Congress, plans that strengthen or weaken the economy, or plans that increase or decrease federalism. These arguments, not connected to the substance of any particular plan, are labeled *generic disadvantages*. The negative often presents counterplans, which may have little to do with the affirmative case. A telling example occurred when a Minnesota assistant coach judged a round between an affirmative Minnesota team and a negative national circuit team that ran a disadvantage, claiming that the plan of the affirmative team would lead to an Orwellian nightmare, instead of running lack of an inherent need on which the affirmative plan was vulnerable. When the coach asked the losing negative team why they had not used inherency as an argument, one of the negative debaters commented: "That's a wimpy way to win a round." This coach responded with emphasis: "That's the Minnesota way to win a round." Later, he commented to me: "In Minnesota, if you run a counterplan in the final round, you say, 'Oh, God, why did you do that?' National judges say, if you run inherency, 'Why did you do that?' " (field notes).

Minnesota coaches observe that these arguments have little to do with the affirmative case, and seemingly little to do with the resolution. Critics look at the resolution and the final conclusion—for example, that reducing prison overcrowding might lead to global destruction or nuclear war—and suggest that national circuit style is "loony" and that these arguments could "poison" debate, making it "tough to justify this as an activity when an administrator walks in there and sees what's going on." This critic concludes, "If an administrator were to ever see one of these national circuit rounds, he would have a heart attack and say, 'What in the world? This isn't worth a penny!' " (interview). The links, when taken together, seem preposterous. Proponents of this type of argument emphasize each individual link and suggest that this represents logical thinking, recognizing the importance of being able to address the possibility of unintended and unexpected consequences. Some suggest that the difference between traditional debate and national circuit debate is between persuasion and argumentation.

Further, these arguments can be justified as playing with ideas. My son's team, Woodward Academy, the 1997 Georgia State Debate Champions, ran an affirmative case that advocated legalizing cannabis, cocaine, and heroin to decrease juvenile crime. The delicious and potent irony was that they represented a private school with a severe "no tolerance" drug policy, a school that had expelled twenty-one eighth graders that same year for involvement with drugs. One wonders whether administrators were aware that their remarkable forensic success—a success of which the school was justifiably proud—was grounded in a rejection of a policy that was at the heart of their school's educational philosophy.[20] These students were not necessarily arguing for drug use as citizens, but they recognized that a powerful argument could be made that a radical change in America's drug policy was justified. Proponents of a national circuit style see intellectual game playing as itself a virtue.

Decorum and the National Circuit

Teenagers do not have the reputation of being sensitive to politesse; yet, decorum and respect, as it is defined by participants, matters. One element that sets traditional debate apart from national circuit debate is the heightened informality of the latter. Les Phillips, a distinguished national circuit coach at Lexington (Massachusetts) High School, speaks of a "clash of tournament cultures." He notes that national circuit debate is criticized because it "doesn't have any rules." By this, he refers not only to the well-defined stock-issues paradigm, but also to a laxness at tournaments, noting in regard to controversy over the disqualification of a top national team for being late to a round at a state tournament:

> The national high school circuit conditions students to the notion that—regardless of what's written in the packet or said at the opening—there's no real forfeit deadline or rule, that judges will be as late or later than the contestants will ever be, that the tab room will understand and tolerate. . . . We . . . noticed that [when] we traveled to the Blake tournament in Minneapolis . . . that Minnesota debate culture takes round start times very seriously; kids are conditioned to move promptly from round to round. . . . And it is very clear that the tab room *means it.*[21]

At local tournaments, debaters and coaches want to leave as quickly as possible after the tournament is over, whereas at three-day national circuit tournaments, as long as the tournament is over by the time of the plane reservations, no one will complain.

However, the issue is more than the timing of the tournaments. It involves behavior within the round. National circuit teams behave in ways that Minnesota teams consider rude. When Greenhaven attended the Tournament of Champions, they were appalled at what they considered inappropriate behavior:

> In one round, the negative team talks to each other during the Greenhaven first affirmative. In another round, their opponents talk to each other and to the judge during Greenhaven's preparation time, even briefly sarcastically interrupting Greenhaven's speeches. These actions are unacceptable in Minnesota. One of Greenhaven's opponents gives the judge a slinky, which he plays with

during the round. Vic commented that he almost refused to shake hands after one round: "It was respect for debate at its lowest.... We didn't learn anything." His partner, Laurie, added bitterly: "I learned that he was an idiot and she was a 'ho.'" (field notes)

On other occasions, teams question each other during prep time, judges will leave the room during cross-examination, and onlookers listen to the debate while lounging on the floor. National circuit debates seem more collegiate in atmosphere than do Minnesota debates, which have more high school discipline.

In the end, while these two groups are doing "the same thing," they are operating from very different cultures. As long as national circuit debate has resources and publicity within the subculture, the strains evidenced in the attacks of Minnesota debaters will continue. Minnesota debate has changed, becoming more like what national circuit debate had been, but national circuit debate has changed as well, becoming even more radical, outlandish, sophisticated, or wise.

Regional Worlds of Debate

In fact, the situation is more complex than a simple rivalry between two groups: the traditionalists and the national circuit. Multiple cultures exist within the world of debate, as fifty states have fifty distinct debate cultures, with the national circuit being both separate and occasionally linked. That there is a belief that there should be one set of values and rules (a belief bolstered by the existence of the NFL tournament and other multistate tournaments) leads proponents to see their claims as representing standards that are right and proper. The strain to create a single, national world of debate is powerful, although over the years some have suggested that the world of high school debate needs to be fragmented further—either by dividing slow debate and fast debate, or limiting the amount of evidence that can be presented in any speech.

It is surely true that within the world of debate there are strong and weak regions. The South and the Midwest are generally seen as the heartlands of competitive debate. James Copeland, the Executive Secretary of the National Forensic League, told me, "It is said at [the NFL] tournament, you could take a paint roller down the middle of the United States, and you'd get two-thirds of the teams that would break" (field notes). These strong states—oriented to both traditional and national circuit debate, include Minnesota, Wisconsin, South Dakota, Iowa, Illinois, Nebraska, Kansas, Missouri, Louisiana, and Texas. In the thirty-four years from 1966 to 1999, the NFL tournament was won by southern and midwestern schools twenty-eight times. Five of the other winners were from

Los Angeles and Pennsylvania. Only once (in 1952) was the tournament held in the Northeast, and, as of 1997, no member of the NFL Hall of Fame was from New England. While these are each different measures with somewhat different causes, each points to the importance of region. Other states have limited activity in debate or maintain rules that make success outside the state difficult by prohibiting out-of-state travel or limiting the number of tournaments students can attend. Styles differ further within region. Iowa debate is "radical," linked to a national circuit style.[22] Georgia schools were very heavily influenced by the collegiate NDT debate culture, perhaps because of the influence of Emory University in Atlanta. In contrast, South Dakota, Missouri, and Kansas, all strong debate states, are even more conservative than Minnesota. Kansas does not permit debaters to travel out of state, except for the National Tournament;[23] debaters can attend only eight tournaments, and they cannot attend summer debate institutes. These state debate cultures are typified, so that the team from Eau Clare Memorial explained to me that they "were not a real Wisconsin team," being "less liberal," but closer to Minnesota in style. Further, state debate cultures change at different rates. Debate styles in Minnesota and Iowa were similar in the 1970s, but diverged in the 1980s.

Minnesota Exceptionalism

In some areas, debate is flourishing, Minnesota among them. Even though debate has declined in Minnesota as elsewhere from the 1960s and 1970s, the debate community is vigorous, and major local tournaments have some sixty teams in attendance. As one out-of-state debater noted: "Minnesota is a scary state to debate in. People take it seriously" (field notes). The pride in Minnesota debate is real, and, thus, when a coach moved to Minnesota as a student, she felt it was necessary to attend a summer institute in the state "to learn how to debate Minnesota style" (interview). Another wrote on her ballot, giving a win to a Minnesota team over a fast team from Wisconsin, recognizing regional differences: "When in Rome, do as the Romans do" (field notes). A third noted to her students, defending Minnesota debate: "Whether we're behind or whether we're sensible depends on who you talk to. Some people consider that we're in the dark ages" (field notes).

This strength and pride is one reason that Minnesota debate has been relatively resistant to change, in contrast to debate in Iowa or Texas:

> We had a lot of schools, and so there was really no reason to travel elsewhere and to deal with other schools, and so we were able to stay in the same mold,

because we were able to get enough competition from within our own borders. . . . We were able to stay pure. (interview)

I think as a group [Minnesota coaches are] pretty professional. . . . We are, oh maybe, a bit stodgy [laughs], a bit prudish in our pride. I think Minnesota coaches have more of a [view] on the total system, the total education program of the students. (interview)

Minnesota debate constitutes, for better or worse, an insulated scene in which teachers are socialized by other teachers, and in which participation has been sufficiently strong that there was no need to go outside the community for additional input.

THE ROLE OF COLLEGES

From where might this additional input come? One major impetus for change in the debate world has been collegiate debate programs. In communities in which there has been active involvement of college students, it is evident that high school students model themselves on their slightly older peers, as well as gain access to their mounds of evidence and generic arguments. These collegiate debaters often serve as coaches or assistant coaches. A "trickle-down" effect exists from college to high school debate. As college debate became faster and more jargon-laden in the early 1970s,[24] it affected high school students. To demonstrate one was a "real debater," one attempted to flow as fast as one could talk. Some critics of the national circuit style allege, "We've handed the sport over to college kids" (field notes); a Minnesota coach claimed that at the Tournament of Champions, "I didn't see too many people that looked like they were mainstream, regular, old high school teachers. It looked like a lot of people who were ex-college people." While some national circuit coaches are mainstream, regular, old teachers, he is pointing to the fact that these coaches are younger, tied to college debate, and perhaps are less devoted to formal schooling. During my research I was not aware of any Minnesota coach who had been a NDT college debater in the previous decade. In contrast, high schools in Iowa were coached by former NDT debaters well versed in the faster collegiate style of debate. Some Minnesota coaches worry that college debaters may enter the state to be "caretakers" for high school debate programs, "contaminating" the programs (interview).

Summer institutes play an important role in imparting the collegiate style, particularly influential national circuit institutes of the 1980s at Georgetown, Northwestern, and Baylor. At one tournament, I spoke with Professor Walter Ulrich of the University of Northern Iowa who explained to me that the reason that debate in Iowa was so fast was because of the influence of the University of Iowa summer institute, which many Iowa high school students attended. The University of Iowa was a strong NDT school. In contrast, the main Minnesota debate institute was at Macalester College, a CEDA school during a period in which a significant stylistic difference existed between NDT and CEDA debate. By the time of my research, that institute had closed, and the main institute in the state was staffed by high school teachers.

Ironically, Minnesota benefited from an odd organizational reality: the decline of collegiate debate. In 1990, only one team in Minnesota was an NDT school. Indeed, during this period the University of Minnesota did not have a debate team. The institutional decision of the University of Minnesota to eliminate debate reverberated with other institutional arenas in ways that were not considered when the decision was made. While some college students served as assistant coaches, for the most part these were former high school debaters from Minnesota who had not been "polluted" by the ideology of collegiate debate. The primary debate teachers in Minnesota were middle-aged educators, who saw their role as teachers, rather than as coaches.[25] As one Minnesotan put it, contrasting Iowa with Minnesota: "You go to Iowa and much of the . . . actual coaching is done by college debaters from the Iowa colleges. In Minnesota, college debate programs have largely died" (interview).

Minnesota exceptionalism is not simply a function of ideology, but a series of structural realities that served to isolate Minnesota from other states—notably Wisconsin and Iowa—that were changing more rapidly. The demise of the University of Minnesota debate program probably did what a conscious decision could not have done: keep the state free of the influence of collegiate debate. Thus, the development of a subculture is not necessarily conscious, but a result of obstacles that make broader cultural transmission more problematic.

Communities of Debate

This appendix speaks to the existence of real divisions within the world of debate. Given the limited size of this activity, an outsider might be surprised by such divisions, but the issue is, as it always is, the control of resources and status. While one should not push these divisions too far—after all these are not enemies—often enough the divisions are connected to moral issues as to how the activity is to be performed and organized. Lincoln-Douglas debaters, traditional policy debaters, and national circuit debaters each believe that their chosen style has benefits that the others lack. Further, states with local traditions look at other states with considerable smugness or suspicion. Without a national organization in

charge of the procedures of debate, an improbable change as states jeal-
ously guard their rights to make educational policy, it does not seem
likely that a single debate culture will emerge.

The world of high school debate, as I noted in chapter 6, is a subculture, and like most subcultures it seems more unified from the outside
than from within. These communities within the world of debate are real,
and participants believe in the moral order that is implicated by their
perspective. Whatever our desire to wish away these differences, they
seem an unshakable part of the world as it has been formulated.

Notes

Introduction

1. Erving Goffman, *Presentation of Self in Everyday Life* (New York: Anchor, 1959).

2. Douglas W. Maynard and Marilyn R. Whalen, "Language, Action and Social Interaction," in Karen S. Cook, Gary Alan Fine, and James S. House, *Sociological Perspectives on Social Psychology* (Boston: Allyn and Bacon, 1995), 149–75.

3. Florian Znaniecki, *Cultural Sciences* (Urbana: University of Illinois Press, 1952), 269.

4. Tom Shachtman, *The Inarticulate Society* (New York: Free Press, 1995), 1–2.

5. Deborah Tannen, *The Argument Culture: Moving from Debate to Dialogue* (New York: Random House, 1998), 3–6.

6. A related example from Tibetan philosophical arguments can be found in Kenneth Liberman, "'Universal Reason' as a Local Organizational Method." *Human Studies* 19 (1996): 289–301.

7. While most debaters are high school students, competitive policy debate also occurs on the collegiate level, involving a somewhat older population. The younger college students are, of course, teens as well.

8. Ann Swidler, "Culture in Action: Symbols and Strategies," *American Sociological Review* 51 (1986): 273–86.

9. Gerald Graff, *Beyond the Culture Wars: How Teaching the Conflicts Can Revitalize American Education* (New York: W. W. Norton, 1992).

10. Donna Eder, *School Talk: Gender and Adolescent Culture* (New Brunswick, N.J.: Rutgers University Press, 1995); Philip A. Cusick, *Inside High School: The Student's World* (New York: Holt, Rinehart, and Winston, 1973); James S. Coleman, *The Adolescent Society* (New York: Free Press, 1961).

11. Michael Billig, *Arguing and Thinking* (Cambridge: Cambridge University Press, 1987); Charles Antaki, *Explaining and Arguing: The Social Organization of Accounts* (London: Sage, 1994); Deanna Kuhn, *Skills of Argument* (New York: Cambridge University Press, 1991); Adrian Furnham, *Lay Theories: Everyday Understanding of Problems in the Social Sciences* (New York: Pergamon Press, 1988).

12. With the exception of quotations from the debate rounds themselves, in which the specific verbal infelicities are important, I tidy up some of the more obvious errors in speech made in interviews and participant observations. I want these talkers to sound as clear as they wish to, unless it is their errors and missteps that are at issue.

13. Egbert Ray Nichols, "A Historical Sketch of Inter-Collegiate Debating: I," *Quarterly Journal of Speech* 22 (1936): 214.

14. Kathleen Hall Jamieson and David S. Birdsell, *Presidential Debates: The Challenge of Creating an Informed Electorate* (New York: Oxford University Press, 1988), 6.

15. Thomas C. Trueblood, "A Chapter on the Organization of College Courses in Public Speaking," *Quarterly Journal of Speech* 12 (1926): 5.

16. Nichols, "Historical Sketch," 213.

17. Shachtman, *The Inarticulate Society*, 249.

18. This material was previously published in Patrick Schmidt and Gary Alan Fine, "Debaters: Who are They?" *Rostrum* 65, no. 3 (November 1990): 8.

19. Approximately 30 percent of the schools responded to the survey, with differing numbers of debaters filling out questionnaires. Given that this was sent during the spring, after debate season, we felt that the response was adequate, if imperfect. Surely the sample is more heavily weighted to the varsity debaters and those most committed to the activity. Given that coaches may have selected their best and most conscientious students, the data must be treated with some caution. It is reasonable to assume that the average debater was not as successful academically or not from as privileged a background as those others. The data are meant to be suggestive, rather than definitive.

20. These data were collected prior to the recentering of the SAT. As a result, current scores may well be higher.

21. David Snow, Louis A. Zurcher Jr., and Sheldon Ekland-Olson, "Social Networks and Social Movements: A Microstructural Approach to Differential Recruitment," *American Sociological Review* 45 (1980): 787–801.

22. This coach refers to a particular student as an example of a student that he "couldn't reach." The coach, referring to this now prominent attorney, claimed that he debated for "egotistical reasons . . . as a way of demonstrating his superiority to others. . . . I don't think he ever learned cooperation or sensitivity to others" (interview).

23. A new form of debate, parliamentary debate, is beginning to emerge to capture the interest of those students (mostly college students at this point) who like to argue, but are less interested in collecting evidence or speaking in the rapid-fire style that has come to characterize policy debate.

24. The research did not permit an answer to the question of why some recruits stick with the activity and thrive, others remain marginal, and many others drop out.

Chapter One
Learning to Talk

1. Jay Heinrichs, "How Harvard Destroyed Rhetoric," *Harvard Magazine* (July–August 1995): 37–42.

2. Other elements, such as content, can also threaten the debater's self-image. This same speaker comments that in one round he was embarrassed when he claimed that the *Christian Science Monitor* was a fanatical religious publication with no journalistic standards.

3. Gregory Hayken, "The Value and Role of Accelerating Speech in Academic Debate." Unpublished manuscript, 1996; one account suggests that the average

speaking rate in college debate was 270 words per minute (Michael McGough, "Pull It Across Your Flow," *New Republic*, October 10, 1988, 19).

4. Herbert Blumer, "Fashion: From Class Differentiation to Collective Selection." *Sociological Quarterly* 10 (1969): 275–91.

5. Fast debaters sometimes equate speed with intelligence, and must be warned that slower speakers are not stupid. In a similar way, southern drawls are sometimes taken by those outside the region as an indication of intellectual backwardness. Speed, of course, is relative, and just as national circuit debate is to Minnesota, Minnesota debate is to Missouri (personal communication, Patrick Schmidt, 1999).

6. E-mail from Tom Preston (scprest@umslvma.umsl.edu) to cx-l@debate.net; no date.

7. E-mail from Michael Korcok to CEDA-L@cornell.edu, December 11, 1995.

8. Michael Billig, *Arguing and Thinking* (Cambridge: Cambridge University Press, 1987), 156–89.

9. E-mail from Leslie E. Phillips (Leslie.E.Phillips@Dartmouth.EDU) to cx-l@debate.net, 1996.

10. E-mail from Michael Dugaw to CEDA-L@cornell.edu, December 11, 1995.

11. Conversation analysts have this problem, of course, but in those transcripts a buzz of activity swirls around the speakers.

12. Hayken, "The Value and Role of Accelerating Speech."

13. E-mail from Sean Upton (socrates@confusion.net) to cx-l@debate.net, 1996.

14. E-mail from Lucas Penick (lpenick@blue.weeg.uiowa.edu) to cx-l@debate.net, 1996.

15. E-mail from Bob Lechtreck (db8coach@lightspeed.net) to cx-l@debate.net, June 28, 1996.

16. E-mail from Ben Coonfield (ben.coonfield@bfi.com) to cx-l@debate.net, 1996.

17. I was told of such cases, although they might have been apocryphal.

18. E-mail from Arnie Madsen (madsen@vms.cis.pit.edu) to unknown recipient, "Speaking Drills," June 2, 1994.

19. No author, "Speaking Drills: A Practicum," collected 1998, Glenbrook South High School.

20. Don Davis tells Sean that he should attempt to memorize the first paragraph of his first constructive, adding: "After that you can put your head in there [your papers]. Pop your head up every once in awhile" (field notes).

21. Erving Goffman, *Frame Analysis* (Cambridge: Harvard University Press, 1974).

22. Albert Lord, *The Singer of Tales* (Cambridge: Harvard University Press, 1960); Bruce Rosenberg, *The Art of the American Folk Preacher* (New York: Oxford University Press, 1970); John Miles Foley, *The Theory of Oral Composition* (Bloomington: Indiana University Press, 1988).

23. "Curing" annoying gestures is as difficult, although not always as commented upon. On one occasion Mrs. Miller told Phil not to make so many little hand gestures as he was speaking. Brian placed Phil's hand in a plastic cup, "so

he'll be too embarrassed to move it." The team laughed when I suggested that we put his hand in a cast (field notes).

Chapter Two
Rites of Arguments

1. William Corsaro and Thomas A. Rizzo, "*Discussione* and Friendship: Socialization Processes in the Peer Culture of Italian Nursery School Students," *American Sociological Review* 53 (1988): 879–93; Douglas Maynard, "How Children Start Arguments," *Language in Society* 14 (1985): 1–29.

2. Marjorie H. Goodwin, *He Said, She Said: Talk as Soical Organization among Black Children* (Bloomington: Indiana University Press, 1990), 143–89; Laura Lein and Donald Brenneis, "Children's Disputes in Three Speech Communities," *Language in Society* 7 (1978): 299–323.

3. Michael Billig, *Arguing and Thinking* (Cambridge: Cambridge University Press, 1987); Charles Antaki, *Explaining and Arguing* (London: Sage, 1994), 139–62.

4. Kenneth Burke, *A Rhetoric of Motives* (Berkeley: University of California Press, 1969), 55–56.

5. George Herbert Mead, *Mind, Self, and Society* (Chicago: University of Chicago Press, 1934), 152–64.

6. Norton Long, "The Local Community as an Ecology of Games," *American Journal of Sociology* 64 (1958): 252.

7. Erving Goffman, *The Presentation of Self in Everyday Life* (New York: Anchor, 1959); Erving Goffman, *Strategic Interaction* (Philadelphia: University of Pennsylvania Press, 1969).

8. Erving Goffman, *Frame Analysis* (Cambridge: Harvard University Press, 1974).

9. Deborah Tannen, *The Argument Culture: Moving from Debate to Dialogue* (New York: Random House, 1998), 3.

10. Peter V. MacDonald, "The Best Trial Lawyers Are Great Salesmen," *Sunday Toronto Star*, October 8, 1989, D5.

11. Cited in Jeffrey Toobin, *The Run of His Life: The People v. O. J. Simpson*. (New York: Random House, 1996), 235.

12. Although I emphasize the institutions of law and politics, the classroom itself has some of the features of a "game," as grades are distributed for suitable performances of knowledge, and in which a "curve" ensures that classroom activity generates "winners" and "losers."

13. Lawrence Kohlberg, "The Study of Moral Development," in David Goslin, ed., *Handbook of Socialization Theory and Research* (Chicago: Rand-McNally, 1969).

14. Robert C. Rowland, "The Debate Judge as Debate Judge: A Functional Paradigm for Evaluating Debates." *Journal of the American Forensic Association* 20 (spring 1984): 183–93; Alfred C. Snider, "Games without Frontiers: A Design for Communication Scholars and Forensic Educators." *Journal of the American Forensic Association* 20 (winter 1984): 162–70.

15. David Nyberg, *The Varnished Truth: Truth Telling and Deceiving in Or-*

dinary Life. (Chicago: University of Chicago Press, 1993), 50; C. Hardin and E. Tory Higgins, "Shared Reality: How Social Verification Makes the Subjective Objective," in R. M. Sorrentino and E.T. Higgins, eds., *Handbook of Motivation and Cognition: Foundations of Social Behavior* (New York: Guilford, 1995).

16. E-mail from Nick Henson (nhenson@mail.coin.missouri.edu) to cx-l@uga.cc.uga.edu, 1995.

17. Stuart Walker, *Winning: The Psychology of Competition* (New York: W. W. Norton, 1980). One might speculate that there are significant gender differences in approaches to competition that give an edge to boys, who have been socialized to think of sports competition as central to their identity.

18. Snider, "Games without Frontiers."

19. E-mail from Alan Teo (Kafkaesk@aol.com) to cx-l@uga.cc.uga.edu, November 24, 1995.

20. Erving Goffman, *Frame Analysis*, 21–28.

21. Jim Hanson, *NTC's Dictionary of Debate* (Lincolnwood, Ill.: National Textbook Company, 1990), 67.

22. E-mail from Daniel Yeager (dany@dmi.net) to cx-l@uga.cc.uga.edu, 1995.

23. E-mail from Chris Ryan (qqpk50a@prodigy.com) to cx-l@uga.cc.uga.edu, November 4, 1995.

24. Teams do change their cases when they find that these cases are unsuccessful and/or they don't believe in them. As one debater noted about a community service case: "I don't think we ever thought of the Constitution when we came up with it." (field notes).

25. E-mail from Les Phillips (l_phillips@sch.ci.lexington.ma.us) to cx-l@debate.net, 1996.

26. Deborah Tannen, *The Argument Culture*, 10–11, raises the question of "two sides" to every issue in light of the historical validity of the Holocaust (and, somewhat more problematically, about evolutionary theory).

27. E-mail from Jason Lantz (jlantz@onramp.net) to cx-l@debate.net, March 29, 1996.

28. Personal communication, Patrick Schmidt, 1999.

29. Joel Best, *Threatened Children* (Chicago: University of Chicago Press, 1990); Donileen Loseke, *Thinking about Social Problems* (Hawthorne, N.Y.: Aldine de Gruyter, 1999).

30. Different topics have their own styles of argumentation, and quantification is not always so central. The challenge of "decreasing overcrowding" calls out for statistical analysis.

31. Inspectors for the Occupational Safety and Health Administration (OSHA) speak of situations in which there is "blood on the floor"—actual deaths or severe injuries that legitimize their action. Such blood provides a presumption that the employer has done something wrong and must be punished (Patrick Schmidt, personal communication, 1999). In debate lingo, the "flow pad" is where arguments are recorded.

32. E-mail from Sean Upton (socrates@confusion.net) to cx-l@debate.net, May 13, 1996.

33. One described a particular disadvantage, with some awe, as "the ultimate college student disad" (field notes).

34. A kritik suggests that one's opponents have a flawed assumption in their debating, perhaps based on value objections to the resolution itself, as opposed to the specifics of the case per se. A kritik is, thus, a critique of the activity as it relates to the world of debate, rather than to the "world out there." The negative implications of accepting this kind of argument in the debate round itself outweigh the impacts of the plan. Kritiks involve debate about the ground rules of debate, and constitute "meta-arguments," potentially undermining the activity itself. Popular kritiks include poststructuralism, statism, critical race theory, and normativity. The novel spelling of critique is part of the status-enhancing use of the argument.

35. E-mail from Aaron Wesley Timmons Jr. (aaront@tenet.edu) to cx-l@debate.net, 1996–1997.

36. This argument is similar to "counterwarrants," which were popular in the late 1970s on the college circuit, and have since fallen out of fashion (David Zarefsky, personal communication, 1998).

37. E-mail from Casey Stevens (ccsteven@AiS.highland.nmhs.edu) to cx-l@debate.net, March 7, 1997.

38. The fantasy of physical violence is not unknown in debate, although its practice is. One Randall Park debater suggested, "I know a really cheap way to answer extratopicality." His partner interrupted, "Hit them," adding, "Should we burn their evidence, throw it out the window? . . . I'll go get a bat" (field notes).

39. Richard H. Gaskins, *Burdens of Proof in Moden Discourse* (New Haven: Yale University Press, 1992).

40. E-mail from Doyle Srader (dsrader@uga.cc.uga.edu) to cx-l@debate.net, May 28, 1996.

41. E-mail from B. J. Hoffpauir (nshof4838@alpha.nsula.edu), quoting John Grace, to cx-l@debate.net, July 6, 1996.

42. E-mail from Kevin Miles (george@UNICOM.NET), quoting unnamed source, to cx-l@uga.cc.uga.edu, January 27, 1996.

43. E-mail from Chris Casey (csc2sd@Seedsnet.stark.k12.oh.us) to cx-l@debate.net, November 1996.

44. E-mail from Les Phillips (Leslie.E.Phillips@Dartmouth.EDU) to cx-l@debate.net, July 6, 1996.

45. E-mail from John T. Kane (jkane@pen.k12.va.us) to cx-l@debate.net, July 6, 1996.

46. In contrast, in one round the negative team decided to focus on the funding mechanism of the affirmative team, which was to take money from the space program, arguing that, if the affirmative plan to decrease prison overcrowding was put into effect, "the space station will fall apart," leading through a series of tortured links to the end of life on Earth. In a debate on prison overcrowding, the negative team kept emphasizing the space program in a round lacking substantial clash.

47. Joanne Martin and Melanie Powers, "Organizational Stories: More Vivid and Persuasive than Quantitative Data," in Barry Staw, ed., *Psychological Foundations of Organizational Behavior* (Glenview, Ill.: Scott, Foresman 1983), 161–68.

48. One rule is that no new arguments are allowed in final rebuttals, since no time exists to answer them. Some debaters find ways of inserting these new arguments, suggesting that they are old arguments in disguise.

49. Thus, one coach suggests, "Instead of saying 'pull D,' say 'community service will solve.' Just in terms of persuasion, it's much better" (field notes). Tags and points should be meaningful.

50. E-mail from Adam Cureton (adam@csranet.com) to cx-l@debate.net, February 20, 1997.

Chapter Three
Evidence and the Creation of Truth

1. Michael Billig, *Thinking and Arguing* (Cambridge: Cambridge University Press. 1987).

2. Michael Billig, *Talking of the Royal Family* (London: Routledge, 1992), 41.

3. Lynn Goodnight, *Getting Started in Debate* (Lincolnwood, Ill.: National Textbook Company, 1989), 44–69.

4. As one of the claims that debaters make is about public opinion, it is significant that, in contrast to the view of policy makers, journalists, and activists, opinion surveys are seen as particularly persuasive, as opposed to indicators of public opinion though dramatic examples, interest-group claims, or newspaper content (see Susan Herbst, *Reading Public Opinion* [Chicago: University of Chicago Press, 1998]).

5. E-mail from Jennifer Catherine Chiang (jayci@ix.netcom.com) to cx-l@debate.net, November 28, 1996.

6. E-mail from Brett Clark (hackerbc@initco.net) to cx-l@debate.net, November 28, 1996.

7. See Gary Alan Fine, *Morel Tales: The Culture of Mushrooming* (Cambridge: Harvard University Press, 1998), chap. 5.

8. One coach noted sarcastically, "This is a money-making thing. A bunch of college kids get together on a college debate team [and they say] 'How are we going to make some money so we can drink beer this summer? Let's write a handbook'" (interview). Some handbook organizers would take umbrage at the inaccuracy of this estimation, but this view is not uncommon among users.

9. One coach claimed that he could tell handbook evidence "from a mile away . . . a lot of it is just crap. A lot of it is really long and wordy cards that don't say anything" (interview).

10. Anne Matthews, "For Some Elite Students Debate's the Thing." *New York Times*, June 28, 1989, 17.

11. E-mail from Gary Leff (gleff@gmu.edu) to cx-l@debate.net, November 20, 1996. Mr. Leff explains that he does not know the context of the card, or whether the remark was made in jest, but it *is* a card.

12. Some social psychological research, referred to as the Sleeper Effect, suggests that under certain circumstances the credibility of the source tends to be forgotten over time. See T. D. Cook, C. L. Gruder, K. M. Hennigan, and B. R. Flay, "History of the Sleeper Effect: Some Logical Pitfalls in Accepting the Null Hypothesis," *Psychological Bulletin* 86 (1979): 662–79.

13. E-mail from Aaron Klemz (Aaron.R.Klemz-1@tc.umn.edu) to cx-l@ uga.cc.uga.edu, December 23, 1995.

14. E-mail from Jason Morrow (jmorrow@pcis.net) to cx-l@debate.net, quoting anonymous source, February 20, 1997.

15. Personal communication, James Copeland, 1998.

16. On one occasion Don tells Brian, "You don't want to run two cards on systemwide effects" (field notes). One card will suffice. Additional evidence on the same subject is saved for "extensions" of one's argument in later speeches.

17. Personal communication, James Copeland, 1998. It is not clear if this anecdote is apocryphal.

18. In one novice round, a debater provided evidence without a proper citation. Frank, a novice debater at Randall Park, noted: "This girl gives this strange evidence. Barry [his partner] says, 'Who said this?' She said, 'A reliable source.' Barry said, 'Who is this reliable source?' She said, 'Me.' Barry said, 'Thank you' " (field notes).

19. E-mail from Les Phillips (l_phillips@sch.ci.lexington.ma.us) to cx-l@ debate.net, May 21, 1996.

20. E-mail from Robert Frost (frost@nyc.pipeline.com) to cx-l@debate.net, May 21, 1996.

21. E-mail from Alfred C. Snider (asnider@zoo.uvm.edu) to cx-l@debate.net, March 14, 1997.

22. The judge in the round intervened, dropped the team, and had them disqualified from the tournament. E-mail from Gary Alperson (ALPERSON@ turing.law.nyu.edu) to cx-l@debate.net, May 22, 1996.

23. There are now references to a debate technique referred to as "cross-reading," in which debaters will read only selected words in a card, perhaps one or two per line—fully destroying the idea of debate as communication. Currently the practice, though it has a name, is not accepted.

24. The 1990–1991 topic was space exploration; the 1991–1992 topic was the homeless; the 1992–1993 topic was the environment; the 1993–1994 topic was health care; the 1994–1995 topic was immigration; the 1995–1996 topic was U.S.-China relations; the 1996–1997 topic was juvenile crime; the 1997–1998 topic was renewable energy; the 1998–1999 topic was U.S.-Russia relations; the 1999–2000 topic was educational reform.

25. I was told that on the national circuit, the year was slanted to the affirmative.

26. Personal communication, Susan Herbst, 1998. My son had this experience, when, after having been a debater for four years, he spent a summer as an intern at the Center for Strategic and International Studies in Washington, D.C. He was dismayed by the fact that the "best" ideas were routinely ignored because they were not politically feasible.

27. On occasion, this vagueness or ambiguity is a deliberate strategy to prevent the negative from attacking problematic aspects of the plan. Indeed, most cases, not surprisingly, attempt to gloss over their weakest aspects. Further, some cases are "slimy" as a strategy, in which opponents are led to believe that some points are important, while in practice others are.

28. Some cases are hot at various times of the season. Simple and straight-forward cases (such as drug legalization) predominate at the beginning of the season. In time, those cases that succeed best or that have the most compelling evidence are most frequently used. Few teams will use a single case the entire season.

29. E-mail from Eric Truett (etruett@worldweb.net) to cx-l@uga.cc.uga.edu, October 3, 1995.

30. E-mail from Alan Coverstone (Alancov@aol.com) to cx-l@uga.cc.uga.edu, October 3, 1995.

31. E-mail from Richard Sodikow (sodikowr@voyager.bxscience.edu) to cx-l@uga.cc.uga.edu, October 3, 1995.

32. E-mail from Gregg Fishbein (fishbgm_+la+radmin_server%Schatz_Paquin@mcimail.com) to cx-l@uga.cc.uga.edu. October 3, 1995.

33. Regional differences exist on which cases are considered "squirrels." These cases are defined by community practice. The definition of a squirrel case may also change throughout the season. New cases that appeared late in the season were more likely to be considered "squirrelly" than if they had been run all along (personal communication, Patrick Schmidt, 1999).

Chapter Four
In the Round

1. E-mail from John Nickle (Cnfuzzd@aol.com) to cx-l@debate.net, April 15, 1997.

2. An example of this occurred at the 1997 Louisiana state tournament when a top squad was disqualified for being late to the start of a round. The formal rules were followed in the face of what, for many, were community practices.

3. Informal after-school round robins also occur, at least in Minnesota, in which each team debates two or three rounds.

4. These hidden break rounds eliminate the possibility of "scouting" one's future opponents to scope their case. Public break rounds at major tournaments are well attended by coaches and by debaters who have been eliminated.

5. This appears to be a regional difference. In Minnesota, the award ceremony is typically right before or after the final round, while in Georgia it is after the preliminary rounds (allowing schools that did not "break" to leave early, but also making finding judges for final rounds difficult).

6. This does not always happen, as at the 1997 Catholic Forensic League tournament in Baltimore. According to one disappointed participant:

Baltimore City College didn't even open until an hour after people got there. There was no breakfast provided, like there was in Chicago. The food was not there until 2. . . . I walked to get food at a McDonalds and returned an hour later. . . . There wasn't water anywhere except for two water bottles, which ran out some times. The bathrooms were the only place with water half the times, but I wasn't about to take a straw to the water on the floor. Lunch sucked, especially for those who hate Pepsi and ate vegetarian. The breaks were over an hour long because [the tab room] couldn't use a computer. (E-mail from Jon [MableLover@aol.com] to cx-l@debate.net, May 27, 1997)

7. Although in the later rounds of the tournament, many of the judges are less conservative and more in tune with the "national circuit" style of debate.

8. The political aspect of which tournament to attend is real. One of the assistant coaches told me that she was disappointed that so few schools attended the Randall Park tournament, going to a tournament at Concordia College in Moorhead (near Fargo) instead, and that many that did show up sent their second varsity teams (such as Greenhaven). This coach commented about Greenhaven, "I'm really shocked that Janice [Nyberg, Greenhaven's coach] doesn't respect us enough to come," meaning that she [Janice] didn't respect her good friend, Annette Miller. This coach noted that Randall Park went to Greenhaven's tournament when it was new.

9. This unenforced "dress code" tends to make underprivileged students feel subtly out of place. As one coach noted, "It's a real problem when you have some kids from some less affluent families." This is an activity for those whose fathers wear suits to work and whose mothers wear designer dresses or tailored outfits.

10. Robert Caro, "LBJ: Debate Coach." *Rostrum* 66, no. 3 (November 1991): 4, taken from Robert Caro, *The Years of Lyndon Johnson: The Path to Power* (New York: Knopf, 1982).

11. Behavior in the round is not always as formal as clothing suggests, as boys sometimes shed their jackets and girls their heels. Debaters sometimes slouched or, as was common in Minnesota debate, or stood with a foot on a chair, using their leg to balance their notes.

12. See Mihalyi Csikszentmihalyi, Kevin Rathunde, and Samuel Whalen, *Talented Teenagers: The Roots of Success and Failure* (New York: Cambridge University Press, 1993), 14.

13. See Erving Goffman, "Radio Talk," in *Forms of Talk* (Philadelphia: University of Pennsylvania Press, 1981), 197–327.

14. E-mail from Ron Cousins (rcousins@netcom.com) to cx-l@debate.net, 1996.

15. Material quoted from another debater in e-mail from Chris Roddy (chris.roddy@mustang.com) to cx-l@debate.net, 1996.

16. Arlie Hochschild, *The Managed Heart* (Berkeley: University of California Press, 1983).

17. Marjorie H. Goodwin, *He Said, She Said: Talk as Social Organization among Black Children* (Bloomington: Indiana University Press, 1990), 229–38.

18. This poses a problem when debaters are involved in "boring" rounds, like slow days at work, when there is not enough to think about (Gary Alan Fine, *Kitchens: The Culture of Restaurant Work* [Berkeley: University of California Press, 1996], chap. 2). One debater told me he has literally fallen asleep in a few rounds—a problem not unknown to judges, who must keep up with a gush of words after a short night's sleep.

19. E-mail from Chris Smith (cdsmith@brain.uccs.edu) to cx-l@debate.net; no date.

20. See Gary Alan Fine, *With the Boys: Little League Baseball and Preadolescent Culture* (Chicago: University of Chicago Press, 1987), 73–77.

21. Erving Goffman, *Frame Analysis* (Cambridge: Harvard University, 1974); Gregory Bateson, *Steps To an Ecology of Mind* (New York: Ballantine, 1972).

22. Arlie Russell Hochschild, *The Managed Heart* (Berkeley: University of California Press, 1983).

23. E-mail from Chris Diamant (csd2sd@seedsnet.stark.k12.oh.us) to cx-l@debate.net, June 13, 1996.

24. E-mail from lame-o (poser@lenin.dabney.caltech.edu) to cx-l@debate.net, 1996. Because of the nature of the signature, one should be cautious about accepting this as representing anything more than an adolescent fantasy, but it is significant as a fantasy.

25. During my research, the team that was frequently mentioned was this varsity team of two girls (with a male coach). These two young women were frequently referred to as "bitches" by debaters and coaches of both genders. However, they were not the only girls so labeled; one female varsity debater referred to another by saying "that cross-examination made her look like the utmost bitch" (field notes).

26. E-mail from Lucas Penick (lpenick@blue.weeg.uiowa.edu) to cx-l@debate.net, November 1996.

27. This coach told me that, first, it wasn't a conscious decision on her part, and, second, she warns against acting in similar ways. However, it is not hard to imagine that this little episode fires up teenage angst and fantasies.

28. There are regional differences in this regard, as cross-examination debate was already well established in Minnesota in the early 1960s.

29. One coach said to a debater after he had ended his cross-examination early in a practice debate: "Never have 45 seconds left. Your partner is dying over them [preparing for his speech]. Ask what his phone number is. Don't [end early] again" (field notes).

30. One supporter of tag-team cross-examination sees it as reflecting part of the change in debate:

> I'm pretty sick of anal rules like "don't do tag-team" and "don't prompt your partner." These "rules," enforced by debate judges and coaches who haven't caught up from the 70's, and are not willing to let the round be "fun." (After all, who needs "fun" anyway?) (E-mail from Sean Upton [socrates@CONFUSION.NET] to cx-l@uga.cc.uga.edu, November 25, 1995)

It is not entirely clear what the difference is between a rule and an anal rule, other than the opinion of the evaluator. Proponents of one-on-one debate suggest that just as one shouldn't have one debater do all the speaking, that person shouldn't answer all the questions.

31. I thank Susan Herbst for this insight (personal communication, 1998).

32. As this is not a book on debate theory, I do not discuss the allocation of time with regard to particular types of arguments. In terms of rebuttals in Minnesota, the assumption was that half the time would be spent on case and half on plan.

33. One difference between national circuit and Minnesota debate is in the use of prep time. Minnesota teams tend to use a lot of prep time before the first negative constructive speech, getting material to attack the particular case. National circuit teams often run generic arguments in this speech and use their prep time later in the round.

34. Gary Alan Fine, *Kitchens: The Culture of Restaurant Work* (Berkeley: University of California Press, 1996), 74.

35. What constitutes the proper number of points is a matter of dispute. Most judges award a very narrow range of points, typically from 24 to 30. While a debater who received 20 points would typically have done a very poor job, not all judges hold to these standards. This can affect a team's pairings in subsequent rounds and determine whether they get into "break rounds" and whether a debater receives a speaker award. The relationship between number and quality has been redefined. As in the case of grade inflation, we find point inflation, with higher point totals becoming increasingly meaningless.

36. Walter Ulrich, *Judging Academic Debate* (Lincolnwood, Ill.: National Textbook Company, 1986), 4–9.

37. Kathleen H. Jamieson and David S. Birdsell, *Presidential Debates: The Challenge of Creating an Informed Electorate* (New York: Oxford University Press, 1988).

38. Ulrich, *Judging Academic Debate*, 58–62.

39. Erving Goffman, *Presentation of Self in Everyday Life* (New York: Anchor, 1959), 70–76.

40. Taking field notes while judging a round proved to be a major challenge, even though that was my purpose for being present.

41. Daryl J. Fisher, "A Survey of Judging Philosophies at the N.F.L. National Tournament," *Rostrum* (1989): 21.

42. E-mail from Joshua Gonzalez (gonzales@ENGIN.UMICH.EDU) to cx-l@uga.cc.uga.edu, November 27, 1995.

43. E-mail from Michelin Massey (Michelin.Massey@Colorado.EDU) to cx-l@debate.net, May 1, 1997.

44. Michael McGough, "Pull It Across Your Flow." *New Republic*, October 10, 1988, 19.

45. E-mail from Brett of Antioch (hackerbc@initco.net) to cx-l@debate.net, May 15, 1997.

46. E-mail from Roxanna Manoochehri (xslbkm@flash.net) to cx-l@debate.net, May 7, 1997.

47. E-mail from Brian Gleeson (gleesonb@BVSD.K12.CO.US) to cx-l@uga.cc.uga.edu, January 6, 1996.

48. I was told that one former student of Mrs. Miller's gave Randall Park teams only one victory in the thirty times she judged them (field notes).

49. While most discussions of debate politics involve judging, politics may also be claimed in the decisions of tournament directors to have teams face each other or to assign particular judges to rounds for political purposes. As one coach noted: "A year ago at the state tournament, the politics was so bad that I was ready to go home and say I never want to get in this mess again. The in-group of

old boys who just were so involved in this—not coaching anymore, but deciding who should do what and who should win what. And it became blatant" (interview).

50. E-mail from Ari Meltzer (ameltzer@juno.com) to cx-l@debate.net, April 5, 1997.

Chapter Five
Our Team

1. Gary Alan Fine, *Morel Tales: The Culture of Mushrooming* (Cambridge: Harvard University Press, 1998), chap. 5.

2. For purposes of this chapter, I will use the term "debate team," although some schools prefer the label "debate club," as it downplays the competitive aspect of debate. In my experience, most debaters speak of themselves as being on teams. In many schools those who participate in public-speaking events (such as original oratory, dramatic interpretation, or extemporaneous speaking) are also members of the team, which sometimes is called a "speech team" or a "forensics team."

3. The Glenbrook South High School team had sixty members in the years my son debated. This included policy debaters and participants in "Congress."

4. Robert Bellah, Richard Madsen, William M. Sullivan, Ann Swidler, and Steven M. Tipton, *Habits of the Heart: Individualism and Commitment in American Life* (Berkeley: University of California Press, 1985).

5. This is often a function of being unable to gain an adult supervisor for a particular tournament or violating school district rules about travel or excused absences.

6. Robert Stebbins, "On Misunderstanding the Concept of Commitment," *Social Forces* 48 (1970): 526–29.

7. This is more intense on national circuit teams, where the tournament may be across the country, and often lasts for three days. Some school boards place limits on student (or teacher) absences, such as the school district in the Glenbrook School district of Illinois, which determined that debaters can miss no more than sixteen days of school each year for out-of-state debate tournaments. The fact that they would need to make this rule indicates the intensity of high-level debate; one can hardly imagine such a rule being necessary for a high school football squad or chess team.

8. In the year before I moved from the University of Georgia to Northwestern University, we discussed the possibility that my son would spend his final two years of high school living with friends, so that he could continue to debate. Fortunately, the suburbs surrounding Northwestern have an outstanding debate tradition; however, had I moved to Princeton or Purdue, communities that lacked such a tradition, the possibility would have been more appealing.

9. Bill Davis, "Squad Spirit or a Christmas Quarrel," *Rostrum* 64 (December 1989): 5.

10. Erving Goffman, *Encounters* (Indianapolis: Bobbs-Merrill, 1961), 105–10.

11. For example, students at schools that award a high school letter for debate must decide whether to wear that letter in public. Do they see themselves as "real" athletes?

12. Richard Young, "Why Not a Fanatic?" *Rostrum* 64 (December 1984): 9.

13. Coaches have the same struggles. They speak of their children as having "debate birthdays" (January through June), meaning that the child was conceived outside of debate season (field notes).

14. Later in this interview this coach informed me that the resentment of his daughter had a history, in which he was involved:

> [My daughter] had been sick for about ten days prior to [the national qualifying] tournament, and I probably should have pulled her out, but here's where ex-wife and father coach . . . had a major confrontation. And I gave in to the ex, and allowed [my daughter] to debate, and I probably shouldn't have. [Her team lost in the semifinal round.] They [the team] firmly believe that coach is not making the decision; father is making the decisions to try and get his daughter to nationals. And as long as those kids thought that, I had a problem. (interview)

While this candid coach denies that it was father making the decision, he admits that it was ex-husband making the decision, a role of which his charges may have been unaware.

15. Cecelia Ridgeway and Henry A. Walker, "Status Structures," in Karen S. Cook, Gary Alan Fine, and James S. House, eds., *Sociological Perspectives on Social Psychology* (Boston: Allyn and Bacon, 1995), 281–310.

16. Don Davis, Randall Park's assistant coach, was in the top lab at the University of Michigan high school debate institute in the summer before his senior year. He told me, "At Michigan, when you're in the top lab, you're top dog." He told me that a girl from that lab was caught on the boy's floor. Normally, she would have been asked to leave the institute, but as she was one of the best debaters she was allowed to stay, although she had to stay in her room all night.

17. Although I don't discuss this explicitly, parents are also involved in the search for status, hoping to provide a better experience for their offspring, or to increase their child's marketability for college, or simply over jealousy toward parents with more esteemed adolescents. This was not a problem in my observations, but in subsequent years Mrs. Miller had to cope with some parental dissatisfaction over her debate pairings.

18. Danny did quite well in Congress (a competitive simulation of the U.S. Congress), and represented Randall Park at the National Forensic League tournament.

19. Gary Alan Fine, "Small Groups and Culture Creation," *American Sociological Review* 44 (1979): 733–45.

20. Robert Freed Bales, "Task Roles and Social Roles in Problem Solving Groups," in E. E. Maccoby, T. M. Newcomb, and E. L. Hartley, eds., *Readings in Social Psychology*, 3d ed. (New York: Holt, 1958), 437–47.

21. David A. Thomas, "Squad Spirit," in David A. Thomas, ed., *Advanced Debate* (Lincolnwood, Ill.: National Textbook Company, 1979), 28–31.

22. A form of "emotion work," as described by Arlie Hochschild, *The Managed Heart* (Berkeley: University of California Press, 1983).

23. E-mail from "The Man" (adam@csra.net) to cx-l@debate.net, December 2, 1996.

24. E-mail from Robert Frost (frost@pipeline.com) to cx-l@debate.net, December 2, 1996.

25. I will discuss only heterosexual linkages here. I have no doubt that a similar, if more complex, argument could be made about homosexual linkages. Yet, I was not aware of any in the course of my research.

26. E-mail from Bob Jordan (rwj850t@vma.smsu.edu) to cx-l@uga.cc.uga. edu, October 30, 1995.

27. John W. Thibault and Harold H. Kelley, *The Social Psychology of Groups* (New York: Wiley, 1959).

28. E-mail from Kate Berenson (TravelerOn@aol.com) to cx-l@debate.net, April 1, 1996.

29. E-mail from Josh Bau (lthsjdb@northstar.k12.ak.us) to cx-l@debate.net, April 1, 1996.

30. A similar relationship occurred between Barry and Frank, good friends at the beginning of the year. At first, neither was particularly committed to debate, wanting primarily to have fun. Barry noted: "Toward the end of the year I started getting really competitive and Frank wanted to go back to have more fun, and I really personally enjoyed the competitiveness more than having fun" (interview). For his part, Frank wanted to gain Barry's approval and "work up to his level, because I really wanted to be his partner next year, and I feel I had to work so hard" (interview).

31. Although it was traditional that one speaker would give the first constructive and first rebuttal speeches, this is not always the case. Some debaters give the first constructive and second rebuttals ("outsides") or second constructive and first rebuttals ("insides"). This is particularly common when one is debating the affirmative. Typically, the stronger debater will debate "inside."

32. Strategies change, and what might be typical in one time or place may not apply at others. Further, some 1As debate as 2Ns, as 1Ns may debate as 2As.

Chapter Six
Debate Culture

1. See, for instance, Erik Erikson, *Childhood and Society*, 2d ed. (New York: W. W. Norton, 1963); Roberta G. Simmons and Dale A. Blyth, *Moving into Adolescence: The Impact of Pubertal Change and Social Context* (New York: Aldine de Gruyter, 1987).

2. Eviatar Zerubavel, *The Fine Line* (New York: Free Press, 1991), 2–4; Michele Lamont and Marcel Fournier, "Introduction," in Michele Lamont and Marcel Fournier, eds., *Cultivating Differences: Symbolic Boundaries and the Making of Inequality* (Chicago: University of Chicago Press, 1992), 1–17.

3. This sheltering is surely a matter of degree, and observers note changes in American childhood as a function of greater exposure to the mass media and other forms of adult life. See Gary Alan Fine and Jay Mechling, "Minor

Difficulties: Changing Children in the Late Twentieth Century," in Alan Wolfe, ed., *America at Century's End* (Berkeley: University of California Press, 1991), 58–78; Neil Postman, *The Disappearance of Childhood* (New York: Delacourt, 1982); Joshua Meyrowitz, *No Sense of Place: The Impact of Electronic Media on Social Behavior* (New York: Oxford University Press, 1985). Each of these approaches suggests a blurring of lines that separate what are labeled developmental "stages."

4. Ann Swidler, "Culture in Action: Symbols and Strategies," *American Sociological Review* 51 (1986): 273–86.

5. Thirteen-year-olds are quite different from eighteen-year-olds, not just biologically, but in terms of their cultural tools.

6. Jennifer Egan, "James Is a Girl," *New York Times Magazine*, February 4, 1996, 29.

7. It is a central insight of Freudian psychoanalytic theory that adults can "regress": that is, engage in those behaviors that served them well as children. Freudians are prone to assert that the child is father to the man—one continues to rely on dear old Dad throughout one's life.

8. Because of the possibility of forged messages, something not unknown on the list, I shall not cite the "author" or "address." The message was directed to cx-l@debate.net, in 1997.

9. Name and address (withheld) to cx-l@debate.net, 1997.

10. The enthusiasm with which drug legalization cases were run is a testament to the scorn with which these laws are regarded—even by nonusers.

11. Howard Becker, "Social-Class Variations in the Teacher-Pupil Relationship," *Journal of Educational Sociology* 25 (1952): 459.

12. E-mail from Joshua A. Gonzalez (gonzalez@engin.umich.edu) to cx-l@uga.cc.uga.edu, October 3, 1995.

13. It is not unknown for sexual relationships to develop between coaches (typically male) and students (typically female). This also occurs outside the world of debate, of course. Staying in hotels away from home provides an opportunity that might not otherwise be present. When we are discussing middle-aged teachers and students, moral condemnation is clear; however, often assistant coaches are only a year or two older than their varsity debaters, and many relationships are mutual, if morally ambiguous.

14. E-mail from Robert Frost (frost@pipeline.com) to cx-l@debate.net, January 21, 1997.

15. Vernon Allen and David B. Greenberger, "An Aesthetic Theory of Vandalism," *Crime and Delinquency* 24 (1978): 309–21.

16. E-mail from Michael P. Kraabel (mpkraabel@tiny.computing.cbsbju) to cx-l@uga.cc.uga.edu, 1996.

17. William Chambliss, "The Saints and the Roughnecks," *Society* 8 (December 1973): 124–31.

18. E-mail from John L. Niedfeldt-Thomas (jthomas@essential.org), forwarding a message from Monte R. Johnson (Monte.R.Johnson@Dartmouth.edu) to cx-l@uga.cc.uga.edu; no date.

19. I thank Patrick Schmidt (personal communication, 1999) for this insight. See Roy B. Flemming, Peter F. Nardulli, and James Eisenstein, *The Craft of Jus-*

tice: Politics and Work in Criminal Court Communities (Philadelphia: University of Pennsylvania Press, 1992). It may be that men and women respond differently to the rough and tumble of competition, with men having been socialized to see personal attacks as more of a game (Jay Mechling, personal communication, 2000), although my data are not such as to support or refute this point.

20. The issue of cost is a serious issue for those interested in the social-class position of debate. Some attempts have been made to provide full or partial scholarships, although even these gestures do not replace the money lost by the lack of summer employment. Institutes remain, for the most part, a haven for middle-class debaters. For many of the Minnesota debaters, the comparative cost of camps was an important issue in making a selection.

21. E-mail from Jeremy Liebman (liebman@fastlane.net) to cx-l@debate.net, August 8, 1996.

22. Institute roommates may become even closer, but, like partners, the intensity of the relationship can create problems.

23. E-mail from Peter A. Barta (pab1355@is2.nyu.edu) to cx-l@debate.net, 1996.

24. E-mail from Philip Butler (butlerpg@ix.netcom.com) to cx-l@uga.cc.uga.edu, December 26, 1996.

25. The coach of this team, which primarily debates on the novice and junior-varsity levels, while not opposing the trading of evidence, admits that he is "a little envious and a little angry" (interview). He also notes that trading between large, successful teams hurts his students.

26. E-mail from Gregg Fishbein (fishbgm_+la+radmin_server%Schatz_Paquin @mcimail.com) to cx-l@uga.cc.uga.edu, December 7, 1995.

27. E-mail from Les Phillips (l_phillips@sch.ci.lexington.ma.us) to cx-l@uga.cc.uga.edu, December 7, 1995.

28. Michael McGough, "Pull It Across Your Flow." *New Republic*, October 10, 1988, 19.

29. Gary Alan Fine and Sherryl Kleinman, "Rethinking Subculture," *American Journal of Sociology* 85 (1979): 1–20.

30. The "rumor" that Michael Stipe, the lead singer of R.E.M. was a high school and college debater (at the University of Georgia), and that his song "End of the World" is about debate has something of this quality of creating a shared history for debate. I am assured by a friend on the UGA squad that the story is accurate.

31. E-mail from Ken R. Johnson (mainline@micron.net) to cx-l@uga.cc.uga.edu, 1995.

32. Fine, *Morel Tales*, chap. 4.

33. E-mail from Tyler Alsen (alsen@groupz.net) to cx-l@debate.net; no date. As a public service for those wishing to fake debate status, I present an account of how to flip a pen backwards:

> 1. Spin it with your fourth finger instead of your third. . . . 2. When you catch it, don't let it fall into the cleft between your index finger and thumb. Instead, actually grab it with the tips of those two fingers. . . . 3. Make an "OK" sign with your finger and thumb, and hold your pen between those two fingers.

Now, attempt to flip your pen backwards by making a movement somewhat like scratching the pen. 4. Once you've mastered 1–3, put them together. Spin the pen with your fourth finger, catch it with your index fingertip and thumb, and "scratch" the pen backward. (E-mail from Doyle Srader [dsrader@ uga.cc.uga.edu] to cx-l@ uga.cc.uga.edu, no date)

One needn't dwell on the Freudian interpretations of "twirling one's pen."

34. See Eric Partridge, *Slang* (Oxford: Clarendon Press, 1940); David W. Maurer, *Language of the Underworld* (Lexington: University Press of Kentucky, 1981).

35. For a discussion of the more formal instrumental terms of competitive debate, see Jim Hanson, *NTC's Dictionary of Debate* (Lincolnwood, Ill.: National Textbook Company, 1990).

36. See Macolm Cowley, "Sociological Habit Patterns in Transmogrification," *Reporter* 20 (September 1956): 41ff.

37. See Robert Freed Bales, *Personality and Interpersonal Behavior* (New York: Holt, Rinehart, and Winston, 1970), 148; Gary Alan Fine, "The Manson Family: The Folklore Traditions of a Small Group," *Journal of the Folklore Institute* 19 (1982): 47–60.

38. Patricia A. Adler and Peter Adler, *Backboards and Blackboards: College Athletes and Role Engulfment* (New York: Columbia University Press, 1990).

39. Gary Alan Fine and Lori Holyfield, "Secrecy, Trust, and Dangerous Leisure: Generating Group Cohesion in Voluntary Organizations," *Social Psychology Quarterly* 59 (1996): 22–38.

Chapter Seven
Teachers and Coaches

1. E-mail from Michael D. Kobeski (mikeski@eskimo.com) to cx-l@ debate.net, 1996.

2. E-mail from Les Phillips, cited by Jacob D. Lewis (jdlewis@brain.uccs.edu) to cx-l@debate.net, July 22, 1996.

3. Nationally, almost 70 percent of all coaches receive compensation within this range.

4. One Minnesota coach estimated that his school could have a national circuit team with a budget of $10,000–$15,000; given current standards, that would be a low-visibility national circuit team.

5. E-mail from Jane G. Boyd (jgboyd@tenet.edu) to cx-l@debate.net, December 6, 1996.

6. E-mail from J. Alan Trivett (trivetfj@wfu.edu) to cx-l@debate.net, June 2, 1996.

7. E-mail from Michael Roston (ending@ripco.com) to cx-l@debate.net, July 18, 1997.

8. The issue of "talent" is tricky. Excluding the unprovable and racial claim that members of some groups are born with more of the relevant talents necessary for debate than others, it is clear that by adolescence a lifetime of advantages and disadvantages has already taken its toll. Knowledge of politics, how to conduct

research, and how to succeed at school are well differentiated by high school, and thus, some high schools and some students are easier to recruit for debate. The question of whether the "wall" is money alone ignores the structural issues that produce varied adolescent abilities.

9. Robert Merton, *The Sociology of Science: An Episodic Memoir* (Carbondale: Southern Illinois University Press, 1979), 120–21.

10. Urban high schools set up as gifted and talented programs (such as the Bronx Academy of Science) are the exceptions that prove the rule.

11. It is this last task that many directors find particularly onerous. There was even some joking talk that Mrs. Miller might quit had she not received some help with her piles of administrative paperwork.

12. Donald Klopf and Stanley Rives, "Characteristics of High School and Collegiate Forensic Directors," *Journal of the American Forensic Association* 2 (January 1965): 35.

13. Klopf and Rives, "Characteristics," 35.

14. Much of this material comes from Patrick Schmidt and Gary Alan Fine, "Coaching." *Forensic Educator* 6, no. 2 (summer 1992): 7–9.

15. In this section I refer to debate coaches, discussing the choice of label—coach or teacher—later in this chapter.

16. We received a combined return rate for these samples of approximately 30 percent, not counting surveys that were returned without reaching their targets, for a total of 81 respondents from thirty-four states. We have no reason to believe that the return rate was systematically biased on any major variable, except that teacher/coaches were probably oversampled as opposed to part-time hired coaches, although we do not have proof for this assumption. However, this may make the sample older and more secure than the full population.

17. For similar results, see Wayne E. Hensley, "A Profile of the N.F.L. High School Forensic Director." *Journal of the American Forensic Association* 9 (summer 1972): 283–84.

18. In terms of the 1989–1990 topic (Resolved: The Federal Government Should Adopt a Nationwide Program to Decrease Overcrowding in Prisons and Jails in the United States), the sample of coaches was more liberal than the general public. Only 49 percent of the coaches supported the death penalty, compared to 79 percent of the general public in Gallup Polls taken in 1989–1990. Further, 85 percent of the coaches sample, compared to 66 percent of the general public, felt that the best way to deal with criminals was to "attack social problems" as opposed to "improve law enforcement." When asked whether the courts' treatment of criminals was too harsh, about right, or not harsh enough, 41 percent of the coaches said that the courts were not harsh enough, compared to 83 percent of the public.

19. Another debate coach was active in Democratic politics in his suburb.

20. The previous year, one of her assistant coaches was an outspoken conservative, but although he helped the first few weeks of the season, other commitments prevented his active involvement during my research.

21. E-mail from Les Phillips (Leslie.E.Phillips@Dartmouth.EDU) to cx-l@debate.net, 1996.

22. Gary Alan Fine, "Justifying Work: Occupational Rhetorics as Resources

in Restaurant Kitchens," *Administrative Science Quarterly* 41 (1996): 90–115.

23. E-mail from Kim Hutchens (khutchen@scs.unr.edu) to cx-l@debate.net, July 1996.

24. E-mail from Dale Reed (ndrc@shadow.net) to cx-l@debate.net, July 30, 1996.

25. E-mail from Michael "Bear" Bryant (mbryant@central.weber.edu) to cx-l@debate.net, July 1996.

26. A related issue concerns the legitimacy of preround coaching at tournaments. Again, the issue is between seeing debate as a sport (in which coaches are expected to be directing the team in detail) or as an educational exercise (in which the student's personal ability is to be judged). Imagine a football game without coach involvement as opposed to a spelling bee with a teacher holding a dictionary behind the curtain.

27. Lewis Coser, *Greedy Institutions: Patterns of Undivided Commitment* (New York: Free Press, 1974).

28. Richard Young, "Why Not a Fanatic?" *Rostrum* 64, no. 4 (December 1984): 9.

29. E-mail from Kim Hutchens (khutchen@scs.unr.edu) to cx-l@debate.net, 1996.

30. E-mail from Kim Hutchens (khutchen@scs.unr.edu) to cx-l@debate.net, 1996.

31. E-mail from Nick J. Alexiou (nickalexiou@juno.com) to cx-l@debate.net, October 31, 1996.

32. E-mail from John Grace IV (jgrace@ix.netcom.com) to cx-l@debate.net, 1996.

33. E-mail from Les Phillips (l_phillips@sch.ci.lexington.ma.us) to cx-l@debate.net, 1996.

34. Young, "Why Not a Fanatic?"

35. E-mail from Steven Hunt (hunt@lclark.edu) to cx-l@debate.net, 1996.

Chapter Eight
Gifted Leisure and the Politics of Debate

1. Michael McGough, "Pull It Across Your Flow," *New Republic*, October 10, 1988, 17.

2. Ibid., 18.

3. Some states still use lay judges, but this is becoming increasingly uncommon, and many debaters object to these "ignorant" outsiders evaluating their efforts.

4. E-mail from Jed Link (link@sisna.com) to cx-l@debate.net, 1997.

5. Randall Park distributes a weekly bulletin listing sports events; debate tournaments are not included.

6. E-mail from James Talley (JTalley4n6@aol.com) to cx-l@debate.net, October 12, 1996.

7. James Coleman, *The Adolescent Society* (Glencoe, Ill.: Free Press, 1961); C. Wayne Gordon, *The Social System of the High School* (Glencoe, Ill.: Free

Press, 1957); Philip A. Cusick, *Inside High School: The Student's World* (New York: Holt, Rinehart, and Winston, 1973).

8. Gary Alan Fine, "Justifying Fun, or, Why We Do Not Teach 'Exotic Dance' in High School," *Play and Culture* 4 (1991): 87–99.

9. E-mail from Michael P. Kraabel (kpkraabel@tiny.computing.csbsju.edu) to cx-l@uga.cc.uga.edu, 1995–1996.

10. Anne Matthews, "For Some Elite Students, the Debate's the Thing." *New York Times*, June 28, 1989.

11. Maridell Fryar, David A. Thomas, and Lynn Goodnight, *Basic Debate*, 3d ed. (Lincolnwood, Ill.: National Textbook Company, 1989), 5.

12. One wonders again about how selection bias explains the behavior of the debate team.

13. "Thomas D. Stolen, 51, Dies; Was Speech and Debate Coach." *Star/Tribune*, October 9, 1989.

14. Because many of these students have done so well, even a substantial decline in grades lets them get by.

15. I know of no study that attempts to link SAT scores with high school debate, although one could easily imagine a strong argument that verbal scores would increase, because of the exposure to new vocabulary and analytic skills. Such a study, like all research on the effects of debate, would have to control for selection bias.

16. One coach told me in this vein:

When I was in Iowa, the state of Iowa gave a $12,000 grant to gifted education. . . . I was on the debate advisory committee for the state of Iowa at the time, and we contacted the talented and gifted state agency, and asked them if they had any money for debate. And they said, "Well, we've got about $1100 left." I said, "Well, where did the rest of it go?" They said, "Well, here and there, but we wrote a check for $1000 to the junior rodeo, because there's nothing like watching a 14-year-old ride a 2,000-pound bull." And that's a true story, and I just threw up my hands. (interview)

This "true story" sounds too pungent to be narrowly true, but it points to different definitions of what gifted education consists.

17. See Ellen Winner, *Gifted Children: Myths and Realities* (New York: Basic Books, 1996).

18. As an indicator of cultural capital, I was impressed by the fact that debaters at Randall Park would on occasion listen to classical music; as one said, "It's nice music to debate to. It doesn't get you violent" (field notes). Preferring classical music does not, of course, necessarily indicate giftedness, but it does suggest that one is linked to culturally elite forms of expression, in a way that self-consciously differentiates these students from most other adolescents.

19. Joan T. Smith, "Old-fashioned Debates Help Hone Students' Thinking Skills," *American School Board Journal* 173 (May 1986): 43.

20. Mihalyi Csikszentmihalyi, Kevin Ratunde, and Samuel Whalen, *Talented Teenagers: The Roots of Success and Failure* (New York: Cambridge University Press, 1993), 35.

21. Ibid., 14.

22. Ibid., 188. He even suggests the value of the master-apprentice relationship.

23. Donald Klopf and Stanley Rives, "Characteristics of High School and College Forensics Directors," *Journal of the American Forensic Association* 2 (January 1965): 35.

24. To learn about the decline of once-great debate programs is depressing. During the year I conducted research, Dentin High School had one of the top programs in the state; six years later it was nearly moribund.

25. Two e-mails from Dick Ramey (rramey@surf-ici.com) to cx-l@debate.net, 1996.

26. E-mail from Les Phillips (l_phillips@sch.ci.lexington.ma.us) to cx-l@debate.net, 1996.

27. E-mail from Aaron Timmons Jr. (aaront@tenet.edu) to cx-l@debate.net, June 12, 1996.

28. To be fair, when teacher-coaches "retire," they often remain on the teaching staff, unlike the case with some football coaches. It is hard to imagine a school with five former football coaches on staff.

29. E-mail from Jacob Lewis (jdlewis@brain.uccs.edu) to cx-l@debate.net, April 5, 1996.

30. E-mail from David Beers (Cervezas@aol.com) to cx-l@debate.net, 1996.

31. Around Houston, this circle of suburban schools is referred to as "the ring of fire" (E-mail from Ken Ogden [thepig@flex.net] to cx-l@debate.net, August 13, 1996).

32. Gary Alan Fine, "Mobilizing Fun: Provisioning Resources in Leisure Worlds," *Sport Sociology Journal* 6 (1989): 319–34.

33. Personal communication, James Copeland, 1998.

34. E-mail from Ede Warner Jr. (e0warn01@homer.louisville.edu) to cx-l@debate.net, December 16, 1996.

35. The 1989 film, *Listen to Me*, about college debate, was only mildly successful, but who knows about a film called *Mouth Wide Shut*, with Cruse and Kidman?

36. Smith, "Old-fashioned Debates."

Chapter Nine
Debate and the Adolescent Toolkit

1. There are now increasing attempts to establish debate in middle schools, epitomized by the formation of the National Junior Forensic League in the early 1990s. The number of schools that participate at this level is still relatively small.

2. See Dick Hebdige, *Subculture: The Meaning of Style* (London: Methuen, 1979).

3. This is a problem for journalists, who search for experts who will say what the journalist would have said if given the option.

4. Michael Billig, *Arguing and Thinking*, (Cambridge: Cambridge University Press, 1987).

5. Patricia A. Adler and Peter Adler, "Social Reproduction and the Corporate Other: The Institutionalization of Afterschool Activities," *Sociological Quarterly* 35 (1994): 309–28.

6. See Tom Shachtman, *The Inarticulate Society*, (New York: Free Press, 1995), 235–60.

Appendix

1. For this section, I draw upon a detailed e-mail from Tom Preston (scprest@umslvma.umsl.edu) to cx-l@debate.net, June 28, 1997.

2. Debaters gain 6 points for each victory; 3 points for each loss. With 25 points, a student becomes a "member" and then gains certificates or pins at various plateaus.

3. A National Catholic Forensic League also exists, which holds its own national tournament, but in most areas of the country it is less visible and less influential than the National Forensic League. Public and private schools often qualify for (and win) this tournament.

4. Among the more prominent of these elite private schools are Westminster School, Woodward Academy (Atlanta, Georgia), St. Marks, Greenhill (Dallas, Texas), Georgetown Day School (Washington, D.C.), Montgomery Bell (Nashville, Tennessee), and Newburgh Free Academy (Newburgh, New York). Among the elite and wealthy public schools are the Bronx High School of Science (in New York), Glenbrook South and North, New Trier High School (in Glenview, Northbrook, and Winnetka, Illinois), and Lexington High School (Lexington, Massachusetts). While other national circuit schools do not fit as easily into these categories, the categories generally hold. Geographically, these schools are generally located along a crescent from the Chicago area, through Ohio to New York, down the Eastern Seaboard to Georgia, and then to Louisiana and Texas.

5. Because Lincoln-Douglas debates are shorter than policy debates, some tournaments attempt to solve the problem of the number of judges by having judges evaluate two LD debates in rapid succession in the same round.

6. It should be noted that there exists a "national circuit" for Lincoln-Douglas debate, but I don't discuss that social realm here.

7. Michael Schudson, *The Good Citizen* (New York: Free Press, 1998), 133–43; David Zarefsky, *Lincoln, Douglas, and Slavery: In the Crucible of Public Debate* (Chicago: University of Chicago Press, 1990).

8. James W. Corey, "Two Styles of Debate Also Stir a Debate," *New York Times*, July 24, 1989.

9. A somewhat similar situation occurred with regard to Little League baseball, in which the United States Rubber Company supported the fledgling Little League Baseball organization and then became involved in shaping how the organization would be run, insuring their investment would be well used (see Gary Alan Fine, *With the Boys: Little League Baseball and Preadolescent Culture* [Chicago: University of Chicago Press, 1987], 5–7). In the world of debate, it is perhaps significant that during the early years of competitive debate, Oklahoma debate was particularly powerful (Oklahoma teams won eleven of the first twenty-

one national debate championships), while today Texas and Louisiana are centers of debate activity. I was told that Pepsi-Cola once offered a large amount of money for sponsorship, but this was turned down because the National Forensic League did not want the level of corporate involvement that the arrangement would have entailed.

10. James M. Copeland, "Present at the Beginning," in William Bennett, ed., *The C.D.E. Book of Advanced CEDA and Lincoln Douglas Debate* (Taos, N. Mex.: CDA, n.d.; bennett@laplaza.org), 277–81.

11. Kai Erikson, *Wayward Puritans* (New York: Wiley, 1966); Nachman Ben-Yahuda, *Deviance and Moral Boundaries: Witchcraft, the Occult, Science Fiction, Deviant Sciences, and Scientists* (Chicago: University of Chicago, 1985).

12. E-mail from Arnold Hayden (hayden@icsi.net) to cx-l@uga.cc.uga.edu, February 8, 1996.

13. This debater notes that the rivalry is mutual:

With Lincoln-Douglas [debators], they think that policy people are just people who talk really fast and have all of this evidence, and they're really not saying anything. They think more on the terms of analysis. I knew someone who was in Lincoln-Douglas debate, and he was so against policy [debate]. He just thought we were so dumb. Like, "You guys don't even think about it. All you want to do is read as many evidence cards as you possibly can." (interview)

14. E-mail from Michael Tubman (tubman@alaska.net) to cx-l@debate.net, April 19, 1997.

15. One Minnesota coach told me that national circuit tournaments don't like Minnesota teams to attend because their judges view rounds differently from national circuit judges: "We're sort of a drag on it. We have conservative judges" (field notes).

16. How national circuit teams do at the NFL tournament is a function of its location and, thus, its judging pool. At tournaments held in very traditional areas, national circuit teams are likely to find unsympathetic judges, and will not do well unless they can adapt.

17. E-mail from Sean Upton (socrates@confusion.net) to cx-l@debate.net, 1996.

18. Don Davis told me about one national circuit round on the Latin American topic in which a Cuban subsidy case was met by a Japanese rearmament counterplan. He described the teams as "like ships passing each other in the night" (field notes).

19. One national circuit debater, who a Minnesota coach couldn't understand, came up after a round, claiming that he slowed down just for her, and that he was "the sixth fastest speaker in the United States," a claim she found incredibly amusing and somewhat sad (field notes).

20. Similar concerns revolve around whether students from Catholic schools can legitimately advocate abortion as a debate case, particularly if parents are likely to judge. In a world in which tough choices must be made, how do we weigh the freedom of the individual against the future of the community?

21. E-mail from Les Phillips (l_phillips@sch.ci.lexington.ma.us) to cx-l@debate.net, April 16, 1997.

22. Some suggest that Iowa debate is imperfectly split by Interstate 80, with schools near and south of that route more "radical" than those north of it. I have been told that there are three different debate styles within Illinois.

23. Committed debaters from states with this policy, such as Kansas or Idaho, will occasion travel out of state as "independent" or "maverick" teams without the knowledge or approval of their school boards, occasionally using false names.

24. This change, particularly the inclusion of a large number of arguments and evidence ("spreading one's opponent"), is often attributed to Lawrence Tribe, now a prominent professor of law at Harvard, but in the early 1970s a star debater at Harvard and instructor at the summer debate workshop at Georgetown. See Michael McGough, "Pull It Across Your Flow," *New Republic*, October 10, 1988, 18.

25. I mention in chapter 7 that the debate organization in Minnesota was very consciously called the Minnesota Debate *Teachers* Association, not the Minnesota Debate *Coaches* Association.

Glossary of Debate Terms _____

Break Rounds — The elimination rounds after the preliminary rounds in which the teams with the best records will face each other until a champion is declared.

Briefs — Arguments, typically placed on sheets of paper, that link pieces of evidence together into a seamless analysis.

Brink — The point at which a disadvantage will take effect.

Case Limits — Limiting the potential cases that can be run, often used in novice debate tournaments at the beginning of a season.

CBA (Cost Benefit Analysis) — The argument that compares the cost (or disadvantages) of a plan with its benefits (or advantages).

Counterplan — A policy proposal presented by the negative team that must be better than the plan that the affirmative team proposes.

Cross-Examination (Cross-X) — The three-minute period in which one debater is able to question a debater on the opposing team.

DA (Disad, Disadvantage) — An adverse outcome of the plan that the affirmative presents that is not directly related to the goal of the plan.

D-Rule (Decision Rule) — The rule, proposed by a debate team, by which the judge should evaluate the arguments in the round.

Fiat — The ability to assume that the plan can be put into effect without having to debate its implementation. This prevents discussion of whether the plan could actually be enacted under current circumstances.

Flow — A means by which debaters and judges note or keep track of arguments, typically on legal-sized pads.

Generic Disadvantage — A disadvantage that applies to a number of different cases or by the topic area itself. Often found in national circuit debate.

Hasty Generalization — Generalizing an argument on the basis of insufficient evidence.

Hypo Testing (Hypothesis Testing) — A debate paradigm that believes that the purpose of debate is to test the merits of the resolution. It treats the resolution as a hypothesis to be judged.

Inherency — One of the stock issue that demonstrates that the plan has not been implemented, and there is a barrier to its implementation.

Judge Adaptation — Adjusting one's arguments or style of speech to the preferences of the judge.

Kritik — A philosophical argument that questions a metaphysical assumption of the plan; often it involves the nature and effects of debate itself.

Lincoln-Douglas Debate — Debate in which individual students debate values issues, topics that change every two months. This style of debate was founded in 1979 (see Appendix).

Maverick — An independent debate team, not associated with any school.

National Circuit — Those high schools that travel around the country debating in a series of tournaments (see Appendix).

NFL (National Forensic League) — The national organization, headquartered in Ripon, Wisconsin, that keeps track of the standings of high school debaters, determines debate policy, and runs the national debate tournament in June.

PMA (Plan Meets Advantages) — The affirmative argument that claims that the plan has the benefits that the debaters claim for it.

Prelims — Preliminary rounds that determine which teams will advance to the final or break rounds.

Prep Time — The time that each team has to prepare its arguments in a debate round (usually five or ten minutes).

Round Robin — A format of a small debate tournament in which every team debates every other team.

Solvency — The stock issue that tests whether the plan would be successful in alleviating the harm or problem that it was designed to fix.

Spread — A colloquial term for speaking rapidly, often involving presenting more arguments than the opposing team will have time to answer.

Squirrel Case — A narrow, bizarre, or trivial affirmative case.

Stock Issues — The fundamental burdens of proof that an affirmative policy must meet to prove the resolutions. They include inherency, harms, significance, solvency, and topicality.

Tabula Rasa — The debate philosophy that believes that the round should be judged based only on what the debaters say and that the judge should not intervene in making a decision based on any outside information or personal beliefs.

TOC (Tournament of Champions) — The major national tournament for national circuit debate teams, held each year in late April or early May at the University of Kentucky.

Topical Counterplan — A plan presented by the negative team that is within the bounds of the resolution, but is different from the affirmative plan. Dispute exists as to whether topical counterplans are legitimate in high school debate.

T (Topicality) — The affirmative burden to prove that the specific plan presented is an example of the resolution. To prove topicality, debaters often define words in the resolution.

Compiled with the assistance of Todd David Fine

Index